A

BOOK

The Philip E. Lilienthal imprint
honors special books
in commemoration of a man whose work
at the University of California Press from 1954 to 1979
was marked by dedication to young authors
and to high standards in the field of Asian Studies.
Friends, family, authors, and foundations have together
endowed the Lilienthal Fund, which enables the Press
to publish under this imprint selected books
in a way that reflects the taste and judgment
of a great and beloved editor.

The publisher gratefully acknowledges the generous contribution to this book provided by the Philip E. Lilienthal Asian Studies Endowment Fund of the University of California Press Foundation, which is supported by a major gift from Sally Lilienthal.

CINDERELLA'S SISTERS

CINDERELLA'S SISTERS

A REVISIONIST HISTORY OF FOOTBINDING

DOROTHY KO

UNIVERSITY OF CALIFORNIA PRESS
BERKELEY
LOS ANGELES
LONDON

University of California Press
Berkeley and Los Angeles, California

University of California Press, Ltd.
London, England

Library of Congress Cataloging-in-Publication Data

Ko, Dorothy.
    Cinderella's sisters : a revisionist history
of footbinding / Dorothy Ko.
        p.   cm.
    "Philip E. Lilienthal Asian Studies imprint"
    Includes bibliographical references and index.
    ISBN 0-520-21884-1 (alk. paper).
    1. Footbinding—China. I. Title:
Revisionist history of footbinding.   II. Title.

    GT498.F66K55   2005
    391.4'13'0951—dc22   2005002626

Manufactured in the United States of America
14   13   12   11   10   09   08   07   06   05
10   9   8   7   6   5   4   3   2   1

The paper used in this publication meets the
minimum requirements of ANSI/NISO z39.48–
1992 (R 1997) (Permanence of Paper).

TO SUSAN MANN,

WHO BLAZES INTELLECTUAL TRAILS,

OPENS INSTITUTIONAL DOORS,

AND BUILDS EMOTIONAL SHELTERS

CONTENTS

ILLUSTRATIONS

ACKNOWLEDGMENTS

There are no compelling reasons why this book, as incomplete and fragmentary as it may still remain, could have taken so long. I can only take comfort in the fact that the process—like any good adventure—has been riveting, humbling, and life-changing.

Always the visionary, Hal Kahn was there in the front row during the first public presentation of my revisionist views on footbinding on May 20, 1994. If he had not tapped me on my shoulder with excitement in his eyes as I returned to my hot seat, I might not have gone ahead.

I have not been alone. Susan Mann has always been there with me, for me, and ahead of me with her musings on sentiments and texts. Charlotte Furth has thought about the tricky business of knowing the history of bodies from language frontally, backward, and upside down. Suzanne Cahill brings poetics to the phenomenological bodies of Tang Daoist women; nobody else I know has pondered gravity with more grace. Judith Zeitlin, in evoking the ephemeral beauty of haunting and hankerings, brings us closer to the truth. Bonnie Smith indulges us in fantastic and brilliant obsessions, the stuff that history is made of. If they had not cleared the path, I would still be in the bushes.

Footbinding is nowhere but everywhere. Every historian and, in particular, every anthropologist seems to have a hidden foot buried in her archives or field notes. So when word got out that I was interested in the subject, friends and strangers began to send bundles of materials. They include Ina Asim, Mary Buck, Michael Chang, Ding Yizhuang, Madeleine Yue Dong, Mark Elliott, Susan Fernsebner, Joshua Fogel, Po-shek Fu, Joshua Goldstein, Marta Hansen, Clara Ho Wing-chung, Jackie Armijo-Huessin, Rebecca Karl, Man-Bun Kwan, Nhi Lieu, Tobie Meyer-Fong, Qian Nanxiu, Evelyn Rawski, Ruth Rogaski, Matthew Sommer, Reiko Suetsugu, Ann Waltner, Wang Zheng, Xu Xueqing, Setsuko Yanagida, Judy Yung, and Zhang Enhua. Chiu-min Lin and Sakamoto Hiroko, fellow-travelers in the history of footbinding, generously shared their own publications.

I have had many opportunities to discuss my work with engaged and engaging audiences. I am grateful to my colleagues who invited me to workshops, conferences, and talks at Yale University; the Institute of Modern History at the Academia Sinica, National Taiwan University; the American Museum of Natural History; Washington University, St. Louis; Haverford College; the University of Pittsburgh; the Arthur M. Sackler Gallery; Princeton University; the University of Chicago; the University of Washington; the University of California, Los Angeles; the University of Michigan; the Institute for Advanced Study, Princeton; the Metropolitan Museum, New York; the University of California, Davis; the University of Toronto; Franklin & Marshall College; the Pembroke Center at Brown University; The China Institute; Würzburg University; Peking University; Nanjing University; and others.

At each of these occasions I have met colleagues who are generous with their time and insights. I have also met men and women who were visibly offended and distressed by my suggestion that condemnation of footbinding need not be our only response. I was always challenged but never attacked; for the forbearance and indulgence of my audiences I am most thankful. They have pushed me to clarify my arguments and sometimes even changed my mind. I hope that this book is better because of it. Students in my seminars at the University of California, San Diego, Rutgers, and Barnard have taught me a great deal about the body as a concrete but elusive subject of history. Among others, Sean Hoffman, Stephen Sanger, and Samantha Pinto have changed the way I look at the subject.

Generous fellowships from the President's Office of the University of California, the John Simon Guggenheim Memorial Foundation, the Institute for Advanced Study at Princeton, and the National Endowment for the Humanities allowed me to take sustained time off during the initial and concluding stages of this project. Executive Dean Richard Foley and Dean Barry Qualls at Rutgers, as well as Provost Elizabeth Boylan at Barnard, have been supportive of my work in numerous ways.

Appreciation is due to my respected colleagues and friends Rey Chow, Hsiung Ping-chen, Benjamin Elman, Susan Naquin, Francesca Bray, and Louisa Schein for their timely advice and unfailing support. Charlotte Furth and William Rowe, first and last readers of the complete book manuscript, have been incisive, honest, and kind. Their responses were invaluable to my process of revision. I am grateful to Veronica Jerng, Nancy Norton Tomasko, Zhao Feng, Gao Jianzhong, Régine Thiriez, and Lewis Stein for providing some of the artwork and artifacts reproduced in this book, and again to Dr. Thiriez for her expert help in dating photographs. It is also a pleasure to ac-knowledge Ye Wa, Valerie Steele, Angela Leung, Ellen Widmer, Kang-i Sun Chang, Hua Wei, Lin Wei-hung, Li Hsiao-t'i, Liu Ching-cheng, Lee Jender, Hu Siao-chen, Kishimoto Mio, Oki Yasushi, Dieter Kuhn, Du Fangqin, Deng Xiaonan, Zhang Hongsheng, He Yun'ao, and Xu Yiyi for gifts of inspiring books and pleasurable company in disparate parts of the world.

My journey into the world of shoes and other objects was guided by the exquisite tastes and fabulous collections of Dr. Chi-sheng Ko, Mrs. Sonja Bata of the Bata Shoe Museum, Yang Shaorong, Glenn Roberts, Xie Yanfang, Don J. Cohn, and Jonathan Hay. During the most productive periods of writ-ing, I benefited from the research assistance of Lai Ying-yu in Taipei and Mei Mei in Nanjing. Sheila Levine at the University of California Press has sup-ported this project from its inception and guided it to the finish line.

Although my mother did not live to see this book, the unconditional sup-port that she and my father have provided makes all the difference. To my friends Lauren Lazin, Syou-ling Fu, and Cynthia Perry—powerful women all, with a firm grip on reality—thank you for not letting go.

An abridged version of chapter 3 appeared in Chinese as "Dang'an, chan-zushi, yuwang: youxi *Caifeilu*" (The archive; history of footbinding; desires: playing with *Picking Radishes*), in *Qingyu Ming-Qing*, ed. Hsiung Ping-chen and Yu An-bang (Taipei: Maitian chuban, 2004). An earlier and shorter version of chapter 4 was published as "The Presence of Antiquity: Ming Discourses on Footbinding's Origins," in *Die Gegenwart des Altertums,* ed. Dieter Kuhn and Helga Stahl (Heidelberg: Edition Forum, 2001).

NOTES ON CONVENTIONS

1. All ages are given in Chinese rendering, which assumes a person to be one year old *(sui)* when born.

2. In China, as elsewhere, units of measurement were not consistent. One Chinese inch *(cun)*, for instance, may vary in length from dynasty to dynasty or from one region to another during the same period. Different scales could also coexist in one locale simultaneously. Therefore, linear measurements referred to in Chinese texts are simply translated without conversion. Hence, 1 *chi* (Chinese foot) is rendered 1 foot; 3 *cun*, 3 inches. The subunit *fen* is rendered 0.1 inch. An exception is made for *li*, which appears in romanized form instead of "mile." The span designated by one *li* varies considerably with time and locale; in 1929 it was standardized to 500 meters.

3. To avoid confusion, the contemporary measurement of, say, a shoe from the Song dynasty is given first in the metric system, followed by conversion to the American inch in parentheses: 21 cm (8.4 inches).

4. Units of weight measurement are translated without conversion. Hence, 2 *liang* is rendered 2 ounces. Since there are 10 *qian* to 1 *liang*, 3 *qian* is rendered 0.3 ounces.

DYNASTIES AND PERIODS

Xia	21c.–16c. BCE
Shang	16c.–ca. 1045 BCE
Zhou	ca. 1045–256 BCE
Spring and Autumn period	721–481 BCE
Warring States period	403–221 BCE
Qin	221–206 BCE
Former (Western) Han	206 BCE–8 CE
Later (Eastern) Han	25–220
Three Kingdoms period	220–80
Six Dynasties period	222–589
Northern and Southern Dynasties period	317–589
Sui	581–618
Tang	618–907
Five Dynasties period	907–60
Northern Song	960–1127
Southern Song	1127–1279
Yuan	1279–1368
Ming	1368–1644
Qing	1644–1911
Republic of China	1912–1949

The following abbreviations are used in the text and the notes:

CFJHL   Yao Lingxi, comp. *Caifei jinghualu, shangjuan.* Tianjin: Tianjin shuju, 1941.

CFL   Yao Lingxi, comp. *Caifeilu [chubian].* Tianjin: Shidai gongsi, 1934.

CFL II Yao Lingxi, comp. *Caifeilu xubian.* Tianjin: Shidai gongsi, 1936.

CFL III Yao Lingxi, comp. *Caifeilu sanbian.* Tianjin: Tianjin shuju, 1936.

CFL IV Yao Lingxi, comp. *Caifeilu sibian.* Tianjin: Tianjin shuju, 1938.

CFXB   Yao Lingxi, comp. *Caifei xinbian.* Tianjin: Tianjin shuju, 1941.

Of footbinding, my colleague Stephen West has this to say, in his characteristic deadpan manner: "It was."[1] On a subject that has engendered lengthy treatises, strong emotions, and endless fascination, I wish to emulate Professor West's lack of sentimentality in this book even though his economy is beyond my reach.

I started with a simple goal: to write a history of footbinding, which has never been attempted except in derision. All of the erudite books and articles that bear titles to that effect, I maintain, are histories of *anti*-footbinding. They begin with the premise that footbinding is despicable and generally end with the same conclusion.[2] Many of these works focus on the heroic achievements of the anti-footbinding movement, or they extrapolate from the anti-footbinding polemics the pitiful ordeal premodern women suffered. Condemnation seems the goal of writing history.

But "it was." My premise is that footbinding was an embodied experience, a reality to a select group of women from the twelfth to twentieth centuries. Instead of denouncing it, I seek to understand the powerful forces that made binding feet a conventional practice for them. The reality of the practice lies not only in the screams and tears ("they were") on a girl's first day of binding, but also in the assiduous maintenance and care she had to lavish on her feet every day for the rest of her life.[3] I seek to locate the woman's agency and subjectivity not only in the world that the pain destroyed, but also in the subsequent unfolding and creation of meanings: for each woman, footbinding was an ongoing process, just as each body was located in a specific time and place. Therein lies the possibility of a history.

The thesis of this book is that there is not one footbinding but many. In the nineteenth to twentieth centuries, each region and often each village featured its own way of binding, rituals, and shoe styles. Unfortunately we do not have the data to document the development of this spatial diversity. We will see, however, that people in successive historical periods from the twelfth to the nineteenth centuries wrote about footbinding in vastly different ways, even as they remained faithful to a rich repertoire of classical allusions and generic conventions. These textual fractures and developments, not to mention the myriad ways to name the practice in Chinese, are suggestive of the multiple and contested meanings of footbinding in each period. Also evident is the extent to which the practice, its rationale, and its reception changed over time during its almost millennium-long spread across class and geographical boundaries.

Powerful minds have applied themselves to the explanation of footbinding. Most influential is perhaps Freud's psychological-sexual explanation. Fetishism, Freud wrote in his 1927 essay, involves a man's projection of his castration anxieties onto the body of the woman. In searching futilely for the mother's penis, the boy invests substitute body parts—the foot, the shoe, hair—with eroticized meanings. Footbinding is thus a symbol of the castration of woman.[4]

Equally notable is the sociologist Thorstein Veblen's theory of so-called "conspicuous consumption," which traces the development of the American leisure class on an evolutionary scheme. The feminine ideal at the stage of conspicuous leisure demanded that women of the leisure class be made delicate, with "diminutive hands and feet and a slender waist." As such "she is useless and expensive, and she is consequently valuable as evidence of pecuniary strength." The practice of "constricted waist" in Western culture and "the deformed foot of the Chinese" are salient examples. The appeal of family wealth, which the wasted woman personified, was so powerful that it inverted the aesthetic judgment of men, turning mutilation into beauty.[5]

More recently, the anthropologists Hill Gates and Laurel Bossen have furnished a third explanation of footbinding, from a Marxist-feminist perspective, which I term "mystification of female labor." Having conducted extensive fieldwork in Sichuan and Fujian, Gates has developed the argument that in China's "petty capitalist" mode of production, a woman made important but unacknowledged contributions to the household economy. The binding of feet, which made the women *appear* wasted, allowed the patriarchs to mask the value of female labor. Peasant women with bound feet routinely performed such tasks as spinning and weaving, oyster shucking, and tea picking, which required strength and skills in her hands but not her feet. Footbinding lost its raison d'être when factory-based textile production replaced home-based spinning and weaving.[6]

Following this line of inquiry that seeks to restore value and visibility to female domestic labor, Bossen has provided a fascinating account of economic change in a remote Yunnan village, where virtually every woman had bound feet at the turn of the century. "If homemade cloth was no longer economically competitive, the underlying reason for footbinding disappeared." Hence the practice went into decline around 1925–35, when even the last form of domestic textile production, specialized weaving, ceased to be profitable, and women were drafted to perform such heavy labor as porterage, mining, road construction, and rice farming. Both Gates and Bossen have argued that the decision to start and stop binding was made on economic calculations alone; Gates has gone as far as to suggest that footbinding in Sichuan was a "cultureless custom."[7]

Less theorized but perhaps most influential is a powerful ethnographic voice derived from interviews with women with bound feet in the recent past. Call it the "marrying-up" thesis. One of the earlier voices heard in this regard is that of Ning Lao-t'ai-t'ai (b. 1867), the daughter of a cake-peddler in Shandong, who told interviewer Ida Pruitt that "Match-makers were not asked 'Is she beautiful?' but 'How small are her feet?' A plain face is given by heaven but poorly bound feet are a sign of laziness."[8] Also couched in terms of "only servants have big feet," this explanation is built on the recognition that marriage constituted the best if not the only avenue for female self-advancement. Bound feet, a ticket to a brighter future for the bride and her family, translated into "good destiny" or social prestige.

As illuminating as these economic, social, symbolic, and psychological explanations are, in the end they fall short because they assume that footbinding is a uniform and timeless practice motivated by a single cause. But footbinding is too enduring and widespread to be subsumed under one descriptive or explanatory framework. Fetishism may explain how some Chinese men—and many modern Western men and women—have lodged their sexual fantasies in the erotic paintings or small shoes they collect.[9] But it distorts the cosmology wrought of place, things, and flowery words that structured elite male desires during footbinding's heyday.

Veblen's theory of conspicuous leisure, in turn, makes such intuitive sense that few readers have questioned the validity of placing medieval China in the same industrial developmental stage as Victorian England or America. Nonetheless, it has explanatory power for the early history of footbinding, when small feet remained a privilege reserved for entertainers and wives who served the same class of elite men. In contrast, the mystification of labor and marrying-up theses are applicable primarily for the modern period— after footbinding had undergone a sea change in its social composition— when the majority of practitioners were peasant women.[10]

The manufacturing of footbinding as a uniform subject by dismissing contending points of view as "feudal" is the most enduring legacy of the modern anti-footbinding movement. The difficulties involved in writing a bona fide history of footbinding stem in part from this modern bias: we are accustomed to viewing footbinding only from an anti-footbinding perspective. If my quest for the submerged voices and an alternative history is to succeed, it can only do so by resisting the totalizing impulse, the oversimplification, and the moralistic tones that structure our present knowledge of footbinding.

Joan Scott has cautioned that a historian needs "analytic distance" from her subject, because "a feminist history that takes for granted the inevitability of progress, [and] the autonomy of individual agents . . . reproduces without interrogation the terms of the ideological discourse within which feminism has operated."[11] Situating myself outside the anti-footbinding enlightenment discourse, I offer in this book neither grand theories, comprehensive coverage, nor a linear progressive history. Instead, I have cobbled together a history from partial perspectives, incongruous words, people who were left out or left behind, and stories that often do not add up.

The working title of this book—"Footbinding Is History"—carries a double meaning, each evoking a constellation of emotions. "Footbinding is *history*" conveys a sense of relief. The last reported case of girls' binding came to a halt in 1957. Although not all women with bound feet are dead, footbinding as a customary practice is; there is no possibility for its revival. To a large extent this book is written to explain this unequivocal death, which has created a space for an academic exercise such as this by affording an analytic distance.[12] In other words, the finality frees me from the political imperative of championing its demise, hence enabling me to approach the subject as a historical instead of a polemical issue.[13]

"Footbinding *is* history," in turn, speaks to the thrill and trepidation I have felt in contemplating the possibilities of an alternative history and methods of writing history. A practice so central to the mechanisms of Chinese society and gender relations requires a history, and the women who endured the pain and inconvenience deserve it. However fragmentary and incomplete, here it is.

This book begins with the end of footbinding as a social practice and moves backward in time, ending with the height of its cultural prestige and erotic appeal. My reason for this inverted chronology is that our present knowledge about footbinding is derived almost entirely from the perspectives and literature of the anti-footbinding movement, as outlined in Part I. Beginning with the end may help clear the ground for alternative ways of seeing and knowing.

Chapter 1 focuses on the birth of the category of "natural feet" *(tianzu)*. Not only did it introduce a view of the body as a machine, it also facilitated the visualization of a new global reality in the late nineteenth century. As part of an enlightenment discourse, *tianzu* was instrumental to the imagining of a nascent Chinese nation. Chapter 2 turns to examine the implementation of the *tianzu* message in local schools and village homes in the Letting-feet-out *(fangzu)* campaigns in the 1900s–1930s, where the abstract doctrine encountered the resistance of stubborn bodies. Chapter 3 analyzes the new knowledge and desires generated in an encyclopedic compilation, *Picking Radishes (Caifeilu)*, popular in the treaty ports in the 1930s. The untimely obsession of its editors and readers signaled the extinguishing of footbinding's aura in modern China.

If Part I could not have been written without the explosion of textual and visual documentation of footbinding in the nineteenth and twentieth centuries, Part II examines the various strategies of concealment that constituted and perpetuated its aura and mystique from the twelfth to early nineteenth centuries.

Chapter 4 seeks to map the discursive limits of a debate on the origins of footbinding waged by philologists in the seventeenth to nineteenth centuries.

Although couched in an objective, empiricist tone, these treatises are often thinly veiled attacks on the prevalent practice of binding feet. The anecdotes and poetic allusions the philologists cited and recycled, however, contributed inadvertently to the perpetuation of footbinding's aura. Instead of fetish, Chapter 5 paints an alternative picture of male desires for small feet, which were bound up with an imaginary geography of the northwest. Attaching ephemeral pleasures to a place, I argue, allowed male travelers and readers to concretize them, a function also served by writing about their fantasies and experiences.

In contrast, female desires were concrete, lodged in a cosmology of quotidian things that they made and that made them. Chapter 6 focuses on a key item in women's material culture—shoes—as craft, extensions of the body-self, focal point of fashion regimes, and integuments of illusion. This chapter concludes the main body of the book with a study of the rise and fall of the cult of the golden lotus by way of the history of footwear fashion and shoemaking.

THE BODY EXPOSED

PART ONE

GIGANTIC HISTORIES OF
THE NATION IN THE GLOBE

The Rhetoric of *Tianzu,* 1880s–1910s

The last assembly line of the last factory producing shoes for bound feet ground to a halt in November 1999. Using eight pairs of wooden lasts, old craftsmen in the Zhiqiang Shoe Factory in Harbin had been making three hundred pairs of "lotus shoes" annually since 1991, but lately over half of the inventory had languished in the warehouse. The customers were all more than eighty years old and dwindling fast. In a solemn ceremony, the factory donated the lasts to the Heilongjiang Museum of Ethnography. A curator voiced a widely shared sentiment: "The 'three-inch golden lotus' is a historical testament to the bodily and psychological damage that women suffered in feudal society. The sad songs of small feet would never be sung again; so much pain and tears are etched on the wooden lasts." A reporter echoed: "Something as tiny as the lasts stands as a testament to the progress of Chinese women from *being* oppressed to *being* given a new life" (emphases mine).[1]

Both the tone and terminology of the article are familiar; condemnation and pity are the only acceptable ways of discoursing on small feet in modern China. The sense of relief is palpable and heartfelt—as a remnant of a feudal past, footbinding can finally be relegated to the museum. Yet underneath the disavowal there lurks a wistfulness, as evinced by the repeated use of historical "testament." The wooden lasts bear a contradictory witness, to past oppression and present liberation. Let bygones be bygones, but we cannot and should not forget. Footbinding as a haunting has been useful to the project of envisioning a modern China. It had to be present, displayed, and reiterated as modernity's Other.

This disquiet continues to ignite the potency and relevance of the subject. The "Culture Fever" in the mid- to late-1980s that ensued from Deng Xiaoping's reforms prompted renewed interest in traditional culture, resulting in a glut of books and articles on footbinding in the 1990s that are cut from the same cloth. In these works, the bound foot remains a shorthand for all that was wrong with traditional China: oppression of women, insularity, despotism, and disregard for human rights.[2] Such reflections on the past are grounded in the present, affording a progressive view of history: things are getting better; our lives are freer than theirs. One troubling aspect of this view of history is encapsulated in the passive voice used by the reporter: women were so oppressed that they could not save themselves. Liberation depended on a bestowal of new life from a reformist state or the educated elite.

This degrading view of women with bound feet, a hallmark of the modern nationalist discourse, has seldom been challenged by feminist or Marxist scholars who share many of the nationalist's modernist assumptions about freedom and agency. Curiously, a subject as incendiary as footbinding has thus been the most *un*controversial issue in and out of China. In troubling this consensus, it is essential to first examine the extent to which the imaginations of a modern Chinese nation were rooted in the rhetoric of "natural feet" and the social campaigns of the anti-footbinding movement in the last quarter of the nineteenth century. We begin, therefore, with the end.

THE END: TWO KINDS OF HISTORY;
THREE KINDS OF TIME; SECONDHAND VOICES

At first glance, identifying the end of footbinding as a social practice in modern China seems an uncomplicated task. Successive regimes have issued prohibition edicts with titles and dates; official and unofficial campaigns to eradicate footbinding have also left a long and visible paper trail. Tracing their incomplete and contested implementation, however, is a different matter. The magnitude of local variations also defies a generalized chronology of national patterns.[3]

Even more vexing is the problem of ontological ambiguity: in any given locale, did footbinding end when the majority of young girls ceased to bind or when adult women had to let their feet out? What do we make of the women who hid themselves from government inspection teams or reapplied the binders as soon as the inspectors left? Consider the tale of a defiant woman who handed a donut twist to the foot inspector dispatched by the state. She would let her feet out, she promised, if he could undo the frying and untwist the pastry back into a piece of pliable dough. Unlike the cutting of men's queues, footbinding is an irrevocable bodily process once the bones are bent and new muscular habits formed. "Liberated feet," as they were called, were harder to walk on and more deformed than bound feet.[4]

The end of a phenomenon as widespread and varied as footbinding is a drawn-out process. The decades from the 1880s to the 1930s witnessed the disintegration of the previously coherent subject of "footbinding" into three components, or three kinds of time: on the level of cosmology or episteme, the cultural prestige or justification of footbinding; on the level of customs and conventions, footbinding as a social practice; and on the level of personal experience, footbinding as individual embodiment. The end did not come in the form of a linear progression from bondage to liberation, in which the old gave way to the new overnight. Instead, the end meant linguistic and emotional confusion as the three kinds of time grew out of sync: in one locale the old raison d'être became dated but mothers kept binding their daughters' feet; in another locale the age-old practice was outlawed, but people clung to the customary thinking of small feet as desirable.

The end of footbinding is thus characterized not by a clean break or a sense of finality but by its opposite: a lingering in-between-ness, a seesawing motion of time, sentiments, and fashion. By focusing on a cast of previously ignored characters—Chinese women reformers, unrepentant connoisseurs, girl students, women who struggled to let their feet out, foot inspectors, tabloid writers, and shopkeepers who collected picture postcards as a hobby, for example—this and the next two chapters seek to present an alternative picture of this transitional period. On the local if not visceral and bodily level, the demise of footbinding appeared to be more problematic than the story told from a linear enlightenment perspective penned by the leading male thinkers in the twentieth century.

The stubbornness of women's bodies stands out as the most visible yet perplexing aspect of this alternative history. Time's arrow traveled its course steadily on the level of individual lives as national time and global time, histories external to the women's bodies, hurried ahead by leaps and bounds. This simple fact dictates that no state decree or social movement can truly end footbinding until the individual lives have expired one by one. The "voice" of these women—not articulated voices but murmurs from within their bodies—arose from an ambiguous space between individual and national histories. How do we hear them, in multiple tones and pitches, when the language they speak is often a language not of words but of the body, and is thus alien to us?

Anti-footbinding legislation and campaigns belong to the realm of "gigantic history." Since they are traceable through public documents and amenable to the methods of political and social history, it is not surprising that they have been widely analyzed. But Susan Stewart has reminded us that there are two kinds of history: "We find the miniature at the origin of private, individual history, but we find the gigantic at the origin of public and natural history." We know the miniature only as the contained, "a spatial whole or temporal parts," whereas the gigantic is the container.[5] Likewise, there are two rhythms of women's history in China, one private-individual and the other public-national. We have mistaken the latter as the only narrative because the voices in it are familiar to us and require little translation, contained as they are by narratives of the nation with which we can identify.

We have heard the voice of the modern woman in Qiu Jin (1875–1907), the knight-errant who denounced footbinding, left her marriage, traveled to Japan, cross-dressed as Charlie Chaplin for the camera, and became a martyr for the republican revolution. We have also celebrated the career of Ding Ling (1904–86), who took lovers, traveled to Yanan, and became the resident feminist writer of the communist revolution.[6] Theirs were journeys of the romantic hero in quest of personal and national salvation. In their pathos of political activism, self-realization, and sexual yearnings, we have found images of our cherished selves. We have thus succumbed to the seduction of their rhetoric: they speak the language of individual freedom and self-determination, but this individualism is in fact a reflected ideal that has no life outside the nationalist discourse. Their female voices were contained by, and were speaking in the *terms* of, the gigantic history of the nation.[7]

There are many other female speaking selves on the margins of or outside gigantic history. Those of the illiterate footbound women constitute one example.[8] Their voices, however, are not immediately audible to us. Two kinds of translation are necessary before these "miniaturized" or "contained" histories are brought to light. The first involves a translation from the silent presence of the footbound woman's body to her hidden inner world. The second involves a translation from others' writings quoting her utterances. In this and the next two chapters, we will strain to hear these secondhand voices, be they bodily murmurs, reasoned articulation, or screams of anguish. These are refracted instead of "authentic" voices, contained as they are by male narratives, gigantic histories, and other exterior concerns. But they are no less "real" because of that.

Even when we have, on occasion, transcripts of interviews with village women describing their experience of binding feet, the linguistic terms they used and political awareness they exhibited were acquired after the fact. For example, when the filmmakers Carma Hinton and Richard Gordon interviewed three footbound grannies from Long Bow Village for their acclaimed documentary *Small Happiness*, one spoke of learning the word *fengjian* (feudal) from the communists, who invented it. The word enabled her to name the roots of her oppression (another invented word) in old China, but does not convey her actual feelings when she had her feet bound as a young girl.[9] Because of this inevitable intervention of time and the intrusion of new linguistic categories that reorganize one's memories, even female voices as seemingly unmediated as in face-to-face interviews are in fact secondhand voices that require translation. There is no "authentic" female voice.

Ironically, only by way of translation can we hope to be faithful to the multiple tonalities of a confusing time. The period from the 1880s to the 1930s comprised a transitional stage when the rhythms beneath the woman's skin seem out of sync with the body politic at large. New visions of female and social bodies had taken shape, but old values, embodied by women with bound feet, remained concrete and visible. The footbound woman in modern China is thus a remnant; her presence demands attention and analysis, not condemnation. For it is in the corporeality of her presence that we seek her "agency," in conjunction with what she purportedly wrote or said. In focusing on the cerebral voices of women writers and activists, our current picture of the range of experiences and subjectivities of women in modern China is woefully incomplete and disembodied.

If efforts to end footbinding were complicated by the stubbornness of individual bodies, the "end" should be seen not as an unequivocal moment but a confusing period of bind-unbind-bind-unbind. Somehow during the tug-of-war footbinding shrank in stature. It was not so much outlawed as outmoded; footbinding came to a virtual death when its cultural prestige extinguished. To put it another way, the end came when the practice exhausted all justifications within the existing repertoire of cultural symbols and values, even as myriad women continued to tighten their binding cloths every day. The lingering presence of footbound women as they were seen hobbling on the streets of treaty ports or pulling a plough in a Shandong village elicited pity and curiosity because they appeared dated and out of place. (See fig. 1.) They were not even supposed to walk or venture outdoors! These incongruities bring to the fore the contradictions that a woman had to embody as remnant of the old order and bearer of the new.

THE MISSIONARY CATEGORY OF *TIANZU*

The invention of the term "natural feet" or "heavenly feet" *(tianzu)*—as the antithesis of "bound feet" *(chanzu, guozu)*—marked the point of no return in the cultural and social demise of footbinding. The public use of the English term can be traced to one morning in 1875 in the southern treaty port of Amoy (Xiamen), when Rev. John MacGowan presided over a meeting that led to the formation of the Heavenly Foot Society. MacGowan (d. 1922), of the London Missionary Society, first arrived in Amoy on the heels of the Second Opium War, which opened up five treaty ports to foreign commerce and the interior to missionary penetration in 1860. Almost immediately, he and his wife learned firsthand the evils of footbinding when the shrieks of a neighbor's daughter pierced the walls. Mrs. MacGowan hurried over to intervene, only to be greeted by a lecture from the girl's mother: "But you are an Englishwoman, and you do not understand the burden that is laid upon us women of China. This footbinding is the evil fortune that we inherit from the past, that our fathers have handed down to us, and no one in all this wide Empire of ours can bring us deliverance." If the daughter did not have her feet bound, "she would be laughed at and despised and treated as a slave-girl."[10]

The Reverend did not forget. Fifteen years later, prompted by a divine revelation, he called a meeting of all the women who attended Christian churches in Amoy. Amidst warnings of a riot in the city—so threatening was the idea of a female assembly—sixty to seventy showed up, all uneducated women of the working class according to MacGowan. After the Reverend spoke, a "tall, handsome-looking" mother of seven daughters rose from her seat: "Your efforts to arouse a conscience on the subject has made me think very seriously upon the wrong that we Christians have been doing in consenting to carry on a custom that is inflicting such sorrows upon ourselves and on the women of this city." She vowed to leave her daughters' feet unbound even if it meant they would not find husbands. Reverend Mac-Gowan recalled fondly that "here her beautiful face was lighted up with a smile that came from her very soul. 'Then I shall keep them at home with me, and they shall cook my rice for me.'" Other women also spoke up. At the end of the meeting, nine women "signed" a pledge to eradicate the heathen practice in their homes and beyond by drawing a cross against their names written out by a Chinese pastor.[11]

If the Reverend had not called the meeting—or written about it almost three decades later—these illiterate women would not have had a chance to speak up in a public assembly, let alone to have their words preserved for posterity. Although thoroughly contained by MacGowan's gospel narrative with a gigantic title, *How England Saved China,* the mother of seven daughters impresses us as having a mind of her own that eluded the Reverend. What MacGowan interpreted as the determination of a heroic Christian soul can be construed as a veiled display of family status: my daughters would stay home and serve me because we can afford to feed them. It is perhaps no accident that she dared to speak first. As was customary in a Chinese social gathering, the senior members of a group tend to be the first and last to speak. Hence the woman who spoke at the end of the assembly was a seventy-year-old elder from a respected Christian family, whom MacGowan called "the mother of the Church."

The tall mother's pragmatic concern for her daughters' future, couched in terms of "cooking rice," echoed that of the Reverend's neighbor fifteen years earlier. MacGowan's theological perspectives on footbinding appear more abstract: "It had completely destroyed the grace and symmetry with which Nature had endowed the women. We are apt to forget that within the feet lies the secret of the exquisite poise and beautiful carriage that embody within them the very poetry of motion, and that add so much to the charm that women by a divine right seem naturally to possess."[12] Footbinding is anti-Christian because Nature—the Creator—endowed women with integral, natural bodies. The doctrine of Heavenly feet is thus predicated on the construction of a God-given natural body.

In christening his anti-footbinding society "Heavenly Foot," MacGowan foregrounded Christian doctrines while appealing to native belief and ter-minology. Although the concept of a personal God is unknown to Chinese, he wrote, their Heaven is a mysterious force that is "analogous to God" in some aspects. "The sages in ancient times had declared that men were the offspring of Heaven. . . . If so, then women also were the product of the same great Power, and consequently the feet of the little girls when they were born had been designed with their exquisite beauty by It."[13] The doctrine of Heavenly feet is thus co-extensive with gender equality.

MacGowan's hybrid appeal to Christian and Chinese reference systems is typical. In Chinese he was known by the moniker of Guangzhao (Shin-ing light), a Buddhist-monk-sounding name.[14] The Chinese name of the anti-footbinding society, too, adopted the indigenous rubric of "Jie chanzu hui" (Quit binding-feet society), an allusion to the "quit opium-smoking" societies. Yet all these efforts of linguistic indigenization only served to high-light the alienness of *tianzu* (heavenly or natural feet) in the mid-1870s. Al-though the concept of natural feet had been expounded as a Christian doc-trine and hence was familiar to churchgoers, the translated term *tianzu* did not enter the Chinese lexicon until 1895, with the founding of the Tianzu hui (Natural Feet Society) by Mrs. Alicia Little in Shanghai.[15]

Neither the concept of a natural, integral body nor attacks on footbind-ing were new to Chinese discourses.[16] The significance of the category *tianzu* lies in the transnational context of its birth and its overt Christian justification. In 1878, a participant at one of the biannual meetings of the Heavenly Feet Society transcribed a long essay by a Reverend Ye entitled "Discourse on Quitting Footbinding" ("Jie chanzu lun"). The Chinese pas-tor displayed a malaise at being scrutinized by the world that was absent in MacGowan: "Looking around the world today, no women other than those in China bind their feet. This shows that when God made men, there was no divergence in the shape of male and female feet. This [lack of gender disparity] is a principle applicable to the past as to the present." China was thus uniquely barbaric in world time and geography. Reverend Ye's argu-ment then turned to the body's utility: "When God created human beings, He intended the four limbs and five senses to be put to their appropriate uses. This is true for both males and females." Footbinding is a manmade contrivance, analogous to the tower of Babel, that paraded human wisdom as superior to that of God. It is thus a sinful act.[17]

Whereas MacGowan was sympathetic to the plight of mothers, Reverend Ye placed the blame squarely on them. "The [Christian] principle of loving others begins with loving one's own children. How can you inflict pain onto your daughter's feet at age five or six, binding them as tightly as a branding iron, blocking the *qi* from circulating like putting a cangue on the ankle? . . . I see that during binding, the daughter often cries in pain, but the mother would strike her and make the pain even more unbearable." If Reverend Ye had nothing but contempt for the mother, he harbored even less sympathy toward the daughter, a "seductress" *(yaoji)* who "beautifies her looks to promote licentiousness." She has sinned in "drawing others' gaze to her." There is no mention of men's responsibility or complicity.[18]

This formulation of footbinding as sinful on three accounts—as cultural contrivance, as a violation of parental love, and as a sexual threat to the God-loving man—is Christian in logic and rhetoric. This early apology for natural feet set the tone for subsequent polemics by secular Chinese officials, reformers, and revolutionaries at the height of the anti-footbinding agitation in 1895–98.[19] All the essential elements of that agitation were rehearsed in Reverend Ye's essays two decades earlier: a transnational awareness of China's parochialism, a utilitarian view of the natural body as a machine, and the assertion of parity between males and females.[20] Most importantly, the status of women became a yardstick for the civility of an entire country. The parity between China and the West depended on gender equality, which stood the Confucian principle of gender hierarchy on its head. For all of these progressive elements, however, the discourse of *tianzu* betrayed a male bias in perpetuating the view of women as femmes fatales and blaming mothers and daughters for their own misery. These less salutary elements, too, became more pronounced in subsequent Chinese nationalistic writings.[21]

Who brought footbinding to an end—was it missionaries and foreigners or indigenous reformers? This question has been a matter of historical contention because Chinese agency and sovereignty remain cherished goals among nationalistic historians today.[22] My limited argument here has been that *tianzu* is a linguistic category born of a new transnational traffic in the last quarter of the nineteenth century. It was absent in the native vocabulary and became imaginable only by standing the familiar category of *chanzu* on its head. In time this logic of dichotomizing and negation spread, and *tianzu* became the antithesis of a host of larger deficiencies in traditional culture: gender inequality, parental authority, and, as we will see, class discrimination. Whatever its origins, *tianzu* (natural unbound feet) has thus remained the most poignant symbol of national self-determination, from its inception through the early years of the republic and unto today.

In the early years of the Republic, Chinese writers made various attempts to "nationalize" the origins and history of the anti-footbinding movement. Among them, the man of letters Xu Ke (1869–1928) offered a China-centered narrative of the birth of *tianzu* as a category and a social movement. Xu, author of "A Survey of Natural Feet" ("Tianzu kaolüe") and its sequel, "Words of Knowing Feet" ("Zhizu yu"; *zhizu* is a pun meaning contentment and knowing feet) opened with the familiar global gaze: "Women of our country are known throughout the world for their bound feet, which has long been criticized by the people in Europe and America. In the year *wushu* of the Qing Guangxu reign [1898], scholar-officials in Shanghai established the Natural Feet Society [Tianzu hui] and the Anti-Footbinding Society [Bu chanzu hui]. They issued books and gave lectures, spreading words of admonition afar. Women in the entire country were to preserve their naturalness *[zhen]* if they had not yet bound, or receive relief from their stricture if they had already bound. The development of their physique will be promoted, and the shame of the national citizens will be shed."[23] In coupling the establishment of anti-footbinding societies with the Hundred Days Reform of 1898 and in attributing the founding of anti-footbinding organizations to Chinese scholar-officials in Shanghai, Xu recast the motive force of this movement from one of missionary salvation or foreign innovation to that of Chinese elite male agency.

In Xu's eyes, the eradication of footbinding is prerequisite to China's parity with Europe and America, hence it is an urgent nationalist project. Although Xu used the traditional rendition of time in terms of dynastic reign years, he showed an acute awareness of the forward march of global time against which China was to be measured. Yet an equally strong impulse was to rescue some progressive elements from tradition and native categories. Xu continued: "The *tianzu* [in 'Tianzu hui'] means 'natural foot' *[tianran zhi zu]*. Only then did the two words 'tian-zu' become a noun, a name. Little did we know that in the ancient times, we had [the practice of] natural feet, and it is in fact quite common in the recent past." Later, in 1928, Xu Ke found a classical name to this practice: "Today if we say 'natural foot' *[tianzu]*, everyone in the metropolis and urban areas would know what you mean. In ancient times there was no such term as *tianzu;* they called it 'plain or unadorned feet' *[suzu]*."[24]

Mention of unadorned feet, however, was too vulgar to be preserved in the chronicles of old, controlled as they were by the literate elite. "But our common people *[renmin]* have long been accustomed to authoritarianism; the class distinctions between the rich and poor are deeply ingrained in their hearts. The scholar-officials *[shidafu]* did not see what was practiced in the fields because it was different from their own custom, or even when they saw it, they chose to ignore it. Moreover, since the elite considered themselves 'civilized,' they regarded lands with natural feet as barbaric. . . . I am enraged by them, by the extreme inequality that separated the rich and powerful from the poor and mean."[25] In this innovative formulation, natural feet stand for the wholesome but submerged culture of the plebeians, whereas bound feet signal the corruption and domination of the patrician class. The rhetoric of tianzu is thus harnessed as an apology for democracy.

Xu's project of documenting the neglected practices of natural feet in Chinese history is nationalist in goal and intention. Further, his nationalism involves the leveling of hierarchies and distances on global, national, and local levels: parity of China with Europe and America as well as equality between the classes and status groups within China. "A Survey of Natural Feet" is thus an unabashed piece of revolutionary writing. Instead of discarding traditional culture altogether, however, Xu resuscitated a usable past, represented by the "unadorned feet" of the common people.

In his global awareness, political egalitarianism, and Chinese pride, Xu Ke shared the outlook of his more famous reformist contemporaries such as Kang Youwei (1858–1927), who helped found the Do Not Bind Feet Society (Bu guozu hui) in 1883.[26] Xu, a native of Hangzhou and holder of a licentiate *(juren)* degree, had one foot in the world of the civil service examination and another foot in the world of treaty port culture. In 1899, he left his minor bureaucratic post in Beijing and eventually settled in Shanghai, where his wife, He Mojun, worked as a school teacher, and his son and daughter were enrolled in new schools. His son was later sent to England and Paris for an advanced degree. Xu made a living as a writer and editor and was widely known as the compiler of *A Classified Collection of Anec-*

dotes on the Qing Dynasty (Qingbai leichao), a monumental collection of unique notations about the last dynasty.

Like the literati of old, Xu frequented wine shops and restaurants, building networks over drinking games and poetry contests. He later published his contributions, poems that document elegant gatherings in which men of letters in the Yangzi delta viewed antique ceramics and manuscripts, saw friends off on journeys, or inscribed each other's paintings. Yet even as they sought to re-create the tranquil world of the imperial literati, the violence of the times showed through: a poem was crafted for a friend who was felled by assassins; they mourned the loss of a drawing of an ancient rock in a Suzhou garden during the 1911 revolution (or "military disturbance").[27]

One of the friends who exchanged poetry with Xu was a fellow sojourner Tang Yisuo (fl. 1904), a native of Suzhou. In his preface to Xu's pamphlet on beautiful Suzhou women with natural feet, Tang recounted his early exposure to Christian advocacy of natural feet in the 1880s. Like Xu Ke, Tang received the tianzu rhetoric with a Chinese nationalist frame of mind. Stricken with a severe illness, he once sought treatment from an American doctor, Bai Lewen [Brockman?]. As follow-up, his tiny-footed wife Shi Jingkai frequented the doctor's residence to renew prescriptions. One day Shi brought along a thirteen-year-old maid named Yilan. Mrs. Bai, the doctor's wife, looked Shi in the eyes and said, "Footbinding and waistbinding are both bad customs. Look how charming is Yilan, with her two feet in their natural state *[tianran],* free from the sufferings of pretension. She must be a native of Suzhou, isn't she? In my extended travels, I have discovered that within the area of several hundred *li* in Suzhou prefecture, not only do maids and peasant women have natural feet, but also those fishing, gathering firewood, selling vegetables and flowers, and porting. They mingle in the company of men and perform laborious chores requiring physical strength. Occasionally I see men resting and waiting to be fed, while their women toil away without complaint. Of course they are blessed with an obliging temperament, but who can deny that they also enjoy the convenience of having natural hands and feet?" Shi Jingkai felt these words deeply and conveyed them to Tang upon returning home.[28]

Mrs. Bai's valuation of female labor anticipated a national concern with women's livelihood at the turn of the twentieth century. Cast in positive terms, women's self-reliance *(zili)* or economic independence became the condition of their liberation and hence the strongest justification for their education. Often, however, the issue was cast in a damning light: women were parasites. In a seminal essay written in 1896–97, "On Women's Education," a leading reformist thinker, Liang Qichao (1873–1929), denigrated the female half of the population as "those with round heads but pointy feet." Referring to a saying by Mencius that "those who dwell in leisure without an education are close to beasts," Liang stated that since every woman "from the ancient times to the present day" has been unschooled, they have fared no better than beasts. Although the majority of men are also uneducated, he conceded, these men are at least ashamed of themselves, but the women are so ignorant that they do not even feel the shame. This is the root of China's weakness. "All two hundred million of our women are consumers [*fenli,* partakers of profit]; not a single one has produced anything of profit. . . . No wonder men keep them as dogs, horses, and slaves."[29]

Liang Qichao, the most powerful polemist in modern China, used strong language to incite his readers to action. But in so doing, he perpetuated an insulting and erroneous image of women, erasing their traditional learning and domestic labor from the history of the nation. Unfortunately, so influential was Liang that the image of women with bound feet as parasites, beasts, and slaves remained the standard view. Shortly after the publication of Liang's treatise on cultural reform, a New Year's print from Yangliuqing, "Women's Self-Strengthening" ("Nüzi ziqiang"), drives the same message home. The print shows a father sitting on one side of a square table while his dainty wife, a son, and a daughter beckon from the other side. The caption, written in a vernacular popular after the aborted 1898 reform movement, reads: "In China, most married men with a family to support are being weighed down. Do you know where the problem lies? It is not that men cannot make money, but that one man has to feed many mouths. A woman on a pair of tiny bound feet cannot exert herself in many lines of work. She has to depend on men for what she eats and what she wears. How can the men not be burdened?" The caption concludes, "China is weak; this is the most serious sickness."[30]

When these messages became commonplace in the 1900s, Tang Yisuo and Shi Jingkai had moved to Shanghai, Yilan had died, and the anti-footbinding movement was widespread in cities and towns. Tang regretted that Yilan did not live to see natural feet becoming fashionable. "If she had lived a little longer, I could have remonstrated in front of our relatives and friends that in my house we have a maid who was ahead of the times." But Tang reported that his wife, by then fifty years old, decided to "unwrap her band-age to relax her toes." Shi told her husband, "In the past, I intuited that what Mrs. Bai said about the convenience of hands and feet was right, but now I can experience the reason behind her words."[31] As recorded by her husband, Shi's voice was calm and matter-of-fact. We do not know how "re-laxed" her toes became. Although the subject of her speech was the chang-ing consciousness of a footbound woman, no interiority was disclosed. The experience of her conversion is credible, but Tang Yisuo has framed the bod-ily process as a rational and linear one. Shi's voice is true but incomplete.

To Shi, the natural body is an abstract concept, but its functionalist corol-lary, the convenience and use of a productive body, made a deep impres-sion. She fantasized with her husband about an idyllic life spent in physi-cal exertion after they retired: "If you have a plot of land to plough, I would bring lunch to you; if you have a mountain in which to gather firewood, I would bundle them up for you. If you only have a pond or a brook, I would pick lotus root and trap fishes and shrimps, take them to the market in the morning and return with wine in the evening. Forgetting the world, we can while the rest of our years away." Against the stark reality of women and children slaving away in the Shanghai cotton mills during the early stage of China's industrialization, Shi conjured up a pastoral and utopian picture of conjugal companionship built on shared labor in a primitive economy.[32]

Tang's essay reveals the subtle changes in concepts of bodies and the dim-ming of the cultural prestige of footbinding in the pivotal era of the 1880s to the 1900s. It also reveals how the value of natural feet was entangled with family pride and the pride of locale. He ended by recounting a conversa-tion with Xu Ke, who declared: "The beauty of Suzhou women is famous. Yet people only know of the arched foot in the city, and are ignorant of the fact that the natural foot of rural women is even more beautiful. This ig-norance is similar to that of the officials in an autocratic country, who only recognize pedigree but not real talent." This is a thinly veiled attack on the dynastic order. Also palpable is Xu's awareness of China in a global world: "The Westerners have a saying, that the women of Spain are the most beau-tiful in Europe, and the women of Suzhou are the most beautiful in Asia. It is clear from this coupling of Spanish and Suzhou women that natural feet are desirable. The beauty of Suzhou natural feet is recognized by the entire world. Better still, it has existed from our distant past, before the pro-motion of the 'new learning' [xinxue] reformers today" (23b).

The coupling of Spain and Suzhou may strike us as odd, but these words encapsulate the commingling of global, national, and local awareness around the turn of the century. Xu has accepted without question the authority of the "West" (in the form of Spain) as the arbiter of taste and value. The natural-footed rural working woman, unsullied by habits of the city, was made the embodiment of a modern standard of Chinese beauty, a standard also espoused by Mrs. Bai. Furthermore, Xu's and Tang's endorsement of the tianzu doctrine involves a splitting of local history into the good and the bad, the latter being the imperial examination system, which sanctioned a hierarchical order. With this split, the new ideals of equality, freedom, and democracy can be pursued without discarding tradition altogether.

Xu Ke and Tang Yisuo were transitional figures. Chronologically they straddled the end of one millennium and the beginning of the next; politically and culturally they witnessed the collapse of the dynastic order and the shaky beginnings of the Republic in 1912. It is remarkable that they narrated these momentous transitions without a sense of rupture or struggle. Although schooled in the classics, they had little political or economic stake in the imperial system. The calmness with which they nationalized the rhetoric of tianzu, its attendant episteme of the functionalist body, and an egalitarian body politic bespeaks the extent to which the foundation of old literati culture had eroded. The aura of footbinding was dimmed and eventually extinguished in the process.

WOMAN AS EGG YOLK: A NEW GLOBAL EPISTEME

The lack of struggle—for both Xu Ke and his wife—about the liberation of feet in his personal memoirs recurred in Tang Yisuo's *Huang Xiuqiu,* a long novel named after its heroine. Its first twenty-six chapters were serialized in *New Fiction (Xin xiaoshuo)* in 1904 or 1905; the final four chapters were added when it was issued under separate cover in 1906 or 1907. *New Fiction,* a monthly founded in 1902 by Liang Qichao in Yokohama, was the earliest and one of the most influential of the literary journals. As a result, *Huang Xiuqiu* ranks as one of the better known examples of progressive late-Qing fiction. In its linking of the liberation of feet to national salvation and its focus on a speaking female protagonist, the novel presents a prototype of the modern Chinese womanhood scripted by the history of the nation.[33]

Huang Xiuqiu is set in Freedom Village, situated in the temperate zone

in the eastern half of Asia and home of the Huang (Yellow) clan. The male
protagonist is a man in his thirties, Huang Tongli (enlightened principle,
or one who understands reason), who sought to overhaul village custom and
politics in a gradual manner. His wife, Huang Xiuqiu, unwrapped her binding cloths and then convinced Tongli that the best place to start his campaign was to set up a private girls' school. Together, they battled the superstition of nuns, the corruption of Manchu officials, and the conspiracy of
a clansman Huang Huo (yellow peril). In the end, they managed to export
the successful girls' school model to a neighboring village, champion local
self-government in a village meeting, and organize male and female mili-
tias. Although not much is known about Tang Yisuo apart from his friendship with Xu Ke, it is clear that *Huang Xiuqiu* is a straightforward statement
of the progressive beliefs of its author.

In its global awareness, glorification of the female will, and valorization
of unimpeded circulation *(jiaotong)*, both within individual bodies and between trading nations, the novel places the liberated woman at the center
of a new episteme. Tang's global awareness takes the form of a fascination
with the earth as a ball-shaped object. The gigantic and abstract concept of
"the globe" is miniaturized, assuming concrete shapes and vivid colors: desk-
top globe; watermelon; egg. The earth is inhabited by five races, Huang
Tongli told his wife, but only the yellows and whites matter.[34] Whereas
Tongli referred to geography *(dili)* to describe the struggle of the two main
races, Xiuqiu referred to astronomy *(tianwen)* to describe her doctrine of
the equality of the sexes. Revising traditional Chinese cosmology, which construes heaven *(tian)* as a dome-shaped sphere covering the square earth *(di)*
like a lid, Huang Xiuqiu said: "We now know from astronomy that heaven
is egg-shaped instead of dome-shaped. Earth is encased by heaven, like an
egg yolk, not a detached piece of square. Heaven and earth are intercon-
nected; it is impossible to deem heaven higher or superior" (177). Between
them, they are describing a new cosmology and global politics marked by
the ideals of equality and the reality of struggling for survival. In struggle
or in parity, China can be defined and located only in relation to other countries and races.

The cosmology of the egg also teaches the lesson of gender equality.
"Woman is egg yolk. Although she is inside, surrounded by egg white and
shell, without the yolk there would be no white nor shell. . . . All the heroes among men, even emperors, are born of women. So women should be

valued higher than men. Why are they being oppressed instead? These days one hears the words of equal rights and equal status *[pingquan pingdeng]* between males and females. . . . Since the two sexes are united, there should be no distinctions of . . . high or low, big or small . . . between them" (177). This argument for gender equality, however, is built on a paradox: although woman is superior to man in function and equal in status and rights, her location remains "inside" and is in fact enveloped by the egg white that stands for man. Furthermore, the value of woman is realized in the act of giving birth.[35] The Confucian gendered division of space, which construed the ideal woman as the inner person, thus found a new expression in the doctrine of gender equality. This incongruity bespeaks the confusion about a woman's proper place and roles in late-Qing society.

In *Huang Xiuqiu,* the egg is thus at once a metaphor for different-but-equal gender relations, global social-Darwinian politics, and Copernican cosmology. The conjoining of these three realms is in itself nothing new; Confucian cosmology has long held the correlative links between individual, social, political, and heavenly bodies. The egg-as-globe, however, teaches a new episteme because it requires a new perspective, looking from the outside in. China can be viewed in its entirety, not in parts, only after it is brought down in size and placed within a global community of nations; similarly the earth appears as a globular object only when the viewer is suspended in space. In other words, the totality of the nation and sphericity of the globe are products of miniaturization. Miniaturization, in turn, is possible only with the viewing subject's detachment: stepping back from the object of vision and looking from a distance.

Astronomy (*tianwen,* phenomena of the sky) and geography (*dili,* principles of the earth), subjects born of this new way of seeing, became popular in school curriculum around the turn of the century. In Sichuan province, a local son whose father ran a private school *(shishu)* for boys, Zhang Xiushu (b. 1895), recalled his love of history, geography, and astronomy. Seventy years later, he could still recite the bulk of several primers on these subjects taught to him between ages three and thirteen. Particularly eye-opening and memorable was a geography primer, *The Globe in Rhymes (Diqiu yunyan).* Although the volume was no longer in Zhang's possession, he remembered details about its author, Huang Zhi, a *juren* scholar who studied in Japan and who was the principal of a local upper primary school *(gaodeng xiaoxue)* in 1903. Fascinated by the primer, Zhang Xiushu sought

Huang out to audit his geography course, only to discover that the subject Huang was teaching was the Confucian classic *Book of Songs*.[36]

Published between 1898 and 1903, *The Globe in Rhymes* consists of songs in five-word and seven-word lines. Each song takes up a lesson in physical and human geography. The perils of colonialism and the lure of democracy were themes in several songs still etched in Zhang's mind: Sichuan province, inner and outer Mongolia, Africa, and America. Opening with a song on the imperial capital, the primer leads the student through lessons on the five continents, China's eighteen provinces, inner and outer Mongolia, capital cities of global nations, and concludes with China's treaty ports. The ordering of songs taught the nascent national consciousness by beginning with the political center of China and ending with its devolution and loss of sovereignty.[37] The new global episteme, which taught that the globe was populated by sovereign nation-states represented by their capitals, had a distinctly nationalistic hue. Consciousness of the nation is thus wrought of two opposite processes: that of distancing, or viewing China in a global community of nation-states, and of centering, or an obsession with the dissipation and loss of Chinese territories and sovereignty.

The boy student was also fascinated by astronomy. Besides *The Globe in Rhymes,* Zhang's other favorite primer was *Songs of Phenomena in Heaven and Earth (Tianwen diyu gekuo),* which offered lessons in the evolution of the stars, the planetary system, the orbiting of the moon, the longitudes, prime meridian, and latitudes, thunder, snow, and rainbows. The earth, visualized on different scales, appears as a slightly flattened round object, one of the planets evolving in oval orbits, a ball whose surface was marked by navigators into grids, and surrounded by an atmosphere governed by thermodynamics.[38] Although Zhang did not recall seeing a globe in his father's classroom—his father-teacher was probably too poor to afford props—he effectively visualized the spherical globe in its miniaturized form by way of rhymes and songs.

Pictures of the globe were quite popular in the first decades of the twentieth century. In a pioneering effort in 1898, China's first women's journal, *Chinese Girls' Progress (Nü xuebao),* published an illustration of a classroom in a girls' school showing six students huddled in front of a model of the globe on the teacher's desk. On the wall behind the lady teacher hangs a huge map of Asia.[39] The cover of *The Continent* magazine *(Dalu)* published in Shanghai in 1902 features a globe in the clasp of a flying dragon. In the

Republican era, the globe remained a fetishized object signifying a modern way of seeing and a national awareness. In Beiping Women's Normal College (Beiping nüzhi shifan xueyuan), the training ground for many Republican women writers, professional women, and feminist activists, students organized a Globe Society (Diqiu she) and published a monthly entitled *The Globe (Diqiu)* in 1929.[40]

The correlation between the orbiting globe in perpetual motion and unhampered circulation in individual bodies was not lost on observers. A loathing for the stagnant female body, so out of sync with the times and the new cosmology, contributed to the appeal of tianzu as a linguistic category and a social program. The word *tian* conjures up a modern sensibility, not only because *tian*-as-naturalness promises deliverance from the contrivance of Chinese culture, but also because *tian*-as-heaven suggests the orbiting of heavenly bodies in a clockwork universe. If the pursuit of science and the global episteme cast the footbound woman as out of step and out of place— the traditional other of China's modern self—the fate of the Confucian classic in which all male reformers were schooled was more ambivalent. Huang Zhi taught *The Book of Songs* in his primary school instead of geography. We do not know his rationale, but his composition of songs as pedagogical tools bespeaks his interest in orality. As literature of the common people, the *Songs* are compatible with the populist sentiment in modern nationalism, already expressed in Xu Ke's discourse of *suzu,* unadorned feet.

Another Confucian classic, *The Book of Changes,* supplies the language of a generative universe in which the modern anti-footbinding arguments were couched. Thus opens a 1917 essay entitled "Discourse on tianzu": "*The Book of Changes* says that in the beginning there was heaven and earth, and the myriad things followed. From the myriad things there emerged the man, from the man there emerged husband and wife. . . . The Han Confucianists came up with the theory that husband is the bond *[gang]* of the wife, and that the woman's proper role is to follow others in docility." This Han degeneration from a natural universe resulted in "an artificial contrivance" and a "loss of natural genuineness" *(tianzhen)* which, the author implied, accounted for the eventual rise of footbinding.[41]

The anti-footbinding movement was an effort to return from culture to nature as described in *The Book of Changes.* "The women's world is under a different sky. We tremble at the self-generating power of the evolving *tian [tianxing zhi ziqiang]*; we are pained by the [footbound women's] difficulty in taking natural strides *[tianbu]*. This is the reason for the growth of the Tianzu hui."[42] The substitution of *tianbu* for *tianzu* underscored the value placed on movement, footsteps, and traffic in the early years of the republic. This valorization of speed, in turn, was part and parcel of a larger picture of a universe in perpetual motion with its evolving globe. This equation of *tianxing* and *tianbu,* of evolving universe and walking bodies, however, fostered a view of the body as an abstract entity or a metaphorical site. This erasure of the physicality of the female body, so prevalent in the anti-footbinding discourse, rendered any realistic description of pain difficult. There is no better illustration of this than the novelist's treatment of Huang Xiuqiu's footbinding experience and its undoing.

<h2>FEMALE AGENCY: WILL OVER BODY</h2>

This erasure of the physical body is central to Tang Yisuo's portrayal of Huang Xiuqiu's agency, which was almost entirely wrought of her self-awareness and volition. An orphan, she suffered indignities and neglect in the hands of the maternal aunt who raised her. Concerned that Xiuqiu would not be able to marry, the aunt took great care in binding her feet despite the girl's screams and tears. These early pains formed a sediment of determination, which one day propelled Xiuqiu to make something of her life by working side-by-side with men (8–12). Tang Yisuo was careful to ascribe Huang Xiuqiu's awakening to a latent strength inside her, not to foreign inspiration or her husband, who was supportive but at first incredulous. It is significant that Madame Roland, a heroine of the French Revolution, came to her in a dream the night *after* Xiuqiu liberated her own feet (16–19). However, it is equally significant that Huang Tongli and Madame Roland supplied the "theory" that guided Xiuqiu's subsequent actions, the latter by transmitting three books and the former by explaining them.[43]

Huang Xiuqiu's agency is established by her changing her name, from Xiuqiu (elegant autumn) to Xiuqiu (embroidering Earth). Brushing aside her husband's warning that if she unwraps her binding cloth she may not be able to walk and that she will be laughed at, she declares: "As a person I stand on the surface of the earth. If I fail to do something, I fail to become a person; that would be truly laughable. Now I am letting out my feet; it is nobody else's business. If anyone laughs at me, not only am I not afraid, I will persuade all the women in our village to let theirs out. . . . I may feel uncomfortable in the first couple of days, but in ten days or so, I will be able to fly and run. Just watch" (13–14). What a statement of the ideal of the volitional agent! Ironically, the logic of Huang Xiuqiu's ambition is that of the male Confucian gentleman as presented in the classic *Great Learning:* rouse one's will, improve and brighten up ("embroider") the village, then the neighboring village; then the whole country can be transformed.

Having let her feet out, Huang Xiuqiu is present and active throughout the story. She is poised, courageous, and wise, a fitting heroine for new China. The change from bound to unbound is a point of departure for Huang Xiuqiu and the novel. She is thrown into jail for seditious gender-bending. Binding and unbinding are construed as social and political problems, not personal or bodily ones (145–46). After her release, however, there is scarcely any mention of her feet. As a symbol footbinding is vital to the story, but as an embodied practice or firsthand experience it is marginal if not irrelevant. Footbinding is a symbol of her early humiliation, and unbinding, a sign of her will to be a public agent. The unbound foot does recur, however, as a sign of the new culture: Dr. Bi, a well-traveled woman doctor from the south, is big-footed (*dajiao*, 58; *tianzu* is not used in the novel).[44] And later, Huang Xiuqiu insists that her school will not admit footbound girls (213–14). Above all, the bound foot is a metonymy of the congested body, a symbol of the Chinese interior which was choking to death on its own phlegm (81). It is not surprising that the novelist—a stickler for robust circulation in the body—would name as his heroes explorers and colonialists who circumnavigated and civilized the globe: Columbus, Magellan, and Livingston (131–32, 224).

To the novelist, the bound foot is an external sign useful in its symbolism, not an embodied reality. Xiuqiu's feet cease to be an issue after she "liberates" them: she travels, reasons, and acts, willfully ignoring the pile of bent bones, the donut twist that could not be straightened or uncooked. The body of the footbound woman appears as though feet were a change of clothes that could be refashioned at will. Huang Xiuqiu's agency is built on her will at the expense of her absent body. Despite great attention paid to her words, motives, and reasoning, she has no interiority. Herein lies the male perspective of the novel. Contained by this male reformist perspective, the female voice in *Huang Xiuqiu* is an inflected voice that arises not from the depth of her body but from the ephemeral realm of her will.

When the body does appear in the novel, it has the same instrumental and symbolic quality as Huang Xiuqiu's feet. Hence Huang Tongli pontifi-cates: "A person has a body like a tree has branches. No matter how sorry a shape the trunk is in, the branches would still grow. No matter how un-worthy is the person, if he or she can eat bitterness and toughen his or her will, no one can fail to be a useful vessel" (132). This is the functionalist body described above by Tang's wife, Shi Jingkai. The feeling and sensuous body is erased. The body-as-machine makes for a convenient signpost whose use is advertised on its surface. A signpost has no use for interiority.

Specifically, the body in *Huang Xiuqiu* is a signpost for displaying one's cultural allegiance. Shanghai girl students decked out in fashionable dress, bobbed hair, and leather shoes are renegades who prostitute themselves to fashionable causes and Westernized playboys (73–74, 76–77). The New Party reformers, too, incurred Tang Yisuo's wrath. Chanting slogans of "Love my country; save my race," they plotted to murder their parents. These hyp-ocrites are always clad in Japanese-style hats or straw hats and leather shoes (80, 119). "These people should be put on display at the Chinese Exposi-tion, ridiculed by people from countries east and west" (80). Fully-clothed, embodied people, male and female, have taken on the symbolic poignancy of China's national shame usually imputed onto one female body part, the bound foot.

GU HONGMING:
THE HUMILIATION OF BEING LOOKED AT

Tang Yisuo's suggested punishment of public display bespeaks an awareness not only of the global context that China found itself in, but also of the heightened importance of visuality in transactions between nations. To be the object of eyesight is an unequal exchange that often confers humilia-tion. In particular, educated Chinese men's awareness of being in the transnational world took the form of an awareness of being-looked-at. Men's queues and women's bound feet became eyesores only after they came un-der the scrutiny of people in advanced nations. It is thus not surprising that the first generation of native reformers who rallied against footbinding had traveled outside China or had extensive dealings with foreigners. We have already seen the embarrassment expressed by Reverend Ye, MacGowan's col-league in Amoy. Other salient examples include Wang Tao (1828–97) and Zheng Guanying (1842–1922).[45]

The vantage point of reformers' anti-footbinding discourse is thus situated outside China; it is one of a Chinese man looking at China from the outside in, and in so doing, he also looks back at the Westerner or Japanese who looks down on him. This politics of seeing is inter-national, and eyesight—physical and metaphorical—is instrumental to the imagining of a new Chinese identity or ethnicity in a global context. Like the free-floating globe that cannot be espied in full until one travels to space, modern Chinese national consciousness is by definition transnational in reference; it originated from the gaze from the outside in.[46] The narratives that then sprouted are "gigantic" in their abilities to invent a point of view that lies outside the boundaries of the national body.

If the anti-footbinding rhetoric was born of an offshore vantage point, the passion of the most famous "defender" of footbinding, Gu Hongming (Ku Hung-ming, 1857–1928), is explicable only in the same transnational context. Gu became an icon—the lotus lover—because no other educated person in the modern world had such ridiculous taste. Gu's love of small feet, which he allegedly called China's national essence, stems from the peculiar nature of his nationalism, which was underscored by his even more peculiar appearance. One of Gu's students at Peking University, where he was a professor of English literature, thus remembered him: "When we looked at Gu Hongming after the establishment of the Republic [1912], on the surface he did appear to be a stubborn conservative: a thinning queue dangled at his back, a gown and a riding jacket from sometime in the Qianlong-Jiaqing-Daoguang reigns [1736–1874] covered his body, an old and worn-out hat sat on his head, and cloth booties on his feet. All were shabby and dirty. His desolate appearance invited derision and laughter."[47] He looked the part of his self-chosen identity after the fall of the imperium, that of the leftover elder. His nationalism took the form of nostalgia for the last emperor.

Ignored or maligned by generations of Chinese scholars, Gu's antiquarian tastes are seldom seen as what they really are: badges of authenticity for an outsider. Critics and admirers alike overlook that Gu was an overseas "Chinese"—a colonial subject no less—whose Chineseness had to be acquired, tested, and worn on his sleeve. Gu was born in Penang, Malaya, to a Chinese father who descended from a long line of professional elite in the service of British colonizers. Gu remained resolutely silent about his mother, about whom nothing is known, prompting widespread rumors that she was

European.[48] Educated in Europe (primarily Edinburgh and Leipzig) from the age of thirteen to twenty-two, Gu had no home nation or culture to call his own until he embraced Chinese culture and the Chinese patriotic viewpoint with ferocity around 1879–81. Gu likened this turning point to a religious conversion, after which he was made to "become again a Chinaman."[49]

Gu's use of "again," implying that he had a secure Chinese identity before his European education, was misleading. Gu grew up with only rudimentary knowledge of Chinese language and cultural practices. Although as a child he learned the Amoy dialect spoken by the "Babas" of Malaya, he did not read a word of Chinese. A maverick proficient in Malay (his first language), English, German, French, Japanese, Greek, and Latin, Gu formally learned classical Chinese when he became a secretary and foreign affairs advisor to Zhang Zhidong, governor-general of Hunan and Hubei, at age thirty.[50] Some legends describe how Zhang hired tutors to teach him a text as rudimentary as the *Analects;* others relay how he sought to master the language by reciting the arcane *Kangxi Dictionary.* Decades later, his students reported that the characters he scribbled on the blackboard often had missing or extra strokes. So accustomed was the public to thinking of him as a Chinese scholar that when admirers asked for his calligraphy, a customary flattery, they were shocked by the awkward proportion and spacing of his scrawl.[51]

In fact, Gu was schooled in a different learned tradition: a disciple of Thomas Carlyle, his prose was said to rival that of Matthew Arnold. Most heartening to Chinese readers were his correspondence with Tolstoy, his meeting with Somerset Maugham, and his being the subject of philosopher fan clubs in Germany. In gossip and bantering, the Chinese loved to relate his ability to beat the Westerner at his own game and to stand the latter on his head. For example, Gu, who introduced Goethe to China, was said to read German newspapers upside down on a train because otherwise it would be too boring; his genius in English involved the recitation of *Paradise Lost* backward fifty times. Invariably, the unsuspecting foreigner who set out to ridicule him was shamed.[52] Gu's Western learning, then, was a matter of nationalistic pride in the eyes of his compatriots. His valorization of classical Chinese, couched in terms of his infamous opposition to the introduction of vernacular literature, was the homage of a hybrid prodigal son. A tribute to him that circulated in Beijing expressed the sentiment: "After the Boxer indemnities, if there weren't a Gu Hongming propping up the face of our country, those Westerners wouldn't even think that the Chinese [are advanced enough to] have noses on our faces!"[53]

From personal experience, Gu was acutely aware of the linkage of visuality with national pride in the global world. His liberal colleague at Peking University, Hu Shi, related a story Gu told of his early days in Scotland: "Everyday I stepped outside, children on the streets followed me and shouted, 'Look! A Chinaman's pigtail.'" Another story relates that when Gu disembarked at Southampton, a hotel maid mistook him for a girl because of his queue and tried to stop him from entering the men's bathroom. Later in life, as if to spite the Europeans, Gu wore his queue as "a badge and insignia—almost a religious symbol—the flag of Chinese nationality."[54] The fact that Chineseness was an identity that Gu self-consciously embraced, as a response to being ridiculed, is often lost on his critics who condemned his support for the monarchy, concubinage, and footbinding. While we will return to Gu's ultraconservatism below, here it is important to recognize the distinction that Gu made between "to observe others" and "to be observed by others."

Gu once was turned off by the smirk on the face of a finely-attired late-Qing official whose photograph appeared in a newspaper. He recounted (or perhaps invented) a lesson about appearance and class he learned in England as a teenager. One day he chanced upon an aristocrat wearing a coat embroidered in gold and a hat adorned with bouquets sitting in a handsome horse-drawn carriage. Before he could finish feasting his eyes, a servant emerged from the market and drove the carriage away. When Gu mentioned the scene to his landlord, the latter told him that the gentleman in finery was in fact the servant and the shabby servant, the master. "It is because an exalted person only wants to observe others, not to seek to please others." Gu concluded with a story closer to home: "Actors have always been despised according to our Chinese custom; it is exactly because their daily exercise consists of 'seeking the other's gaze.'"[55] Politicians who publicized their photographs—who offered themselves visually to the public—were thus inverting the hierarchy between high and low. So sensitive was Gu to the power inequalities between the seeing and the seen that he couched them in terms of the starkness of class distinctions.

Gu's valorization of concealment or self-effacement should not be taken too literally, for after all he acquired global fame by flaunting a queue in Republican Beijing. Observers have noted that Gu was a born contrarian who delighted in scandalous provocation. Perhaps the same spirit accounts in part for Gu's love of the bound foot. There is also a deeper nationalistic logic underneath Gu's defense of traditional Chinese culture, as embodied in a superior Chinese femininity. In two crucial aspects Gu shared the premises of his progressive colleagues who championed tianzu and new culture: a belief in women's status as the marker of a civilization and a profound understanding of the humiliation implied in being the subject of unilateral gaze.

RESISTING THE GAZE: IDEAL WOMANHOOD

The "society women" of the West, Gu wrote in 1904, "exemplified the decline and degeneration of European civilization in the present age" in their robust, gender-bending masculinity. "In China, these busybodies have tried to reform our wonderful women with small feet" so that the latter would turn into the same type of manlike women. In a rare written defense of footbinding, Gu explained that he saw it as female self-protection: life in China was so impoverished that women were forced to bind their feet, thus excusing themselves from the most exhausting forms of labor.[56] In contrast to the chaotic gender relations in Europe, a gender harmony built on male-female distinctions signals the superiority of Chinese civilization.

The feminine ideal in China, Gu argued, consists of a selfless devotion to others. The perfect woman is at once cheerful ("debonair") and bashful.[57] Although he did not articulate it, following this logic, footbinding can be understood as the bodily expression of the most admirable quality of Chinese women: passivity and serenity. Just as the shabbily clad English servant who was the true master, the demure Chinese woman was exalted in status in refusing to draw attention to herself. Gu's love of footbinding thus rests on an idealized womanhood that is saintlike and sovereign, a sphere of inviolability in a turbulent age.

That the two "defenses" he furnished for footbinding—as self-protection from hard labor and as an expression of passive virtue—are contradictory does not matter. Nor does it matter that his views are at odds with the sociological reality of his times. The historian Hui-min Lo, the most authoritative and clear-eyed biographer of Gu, has observed that the colonial plantation in which Gu grew up was "in the backwoods of the island [Penang]"; he was "surrounded by people, including his parents, who knew next to nothing about China or Chinese culture beyond fanciful hearsay and dubious versions of occasional rituals performed by hired Tamils." Therefore, as an adult Gu suffered the need—and enjoyed the freedom—to invent a picture of a pristine, timeless China to suit his politics. "With his literary gifts and exceptional imagination, Ku Hung-ming [Gu Hongming] created for himself a picture of his people and their civilisation which could only 'exist' in wishful thinking."[58]

What kind of a lotus lover was Gu Hongming in everyday life? In their remembrances published in the early 1930s, not long after Gu's death in 1928, colleagues Hu Shi and Zhou Zuoren as well as his student Luo Jialun, all famous intellectuals associated with new culture, did not mention Gu's predilection. Accounts that appeared in Taiwan in the 1970s were more graphic. These stories talked of his two daily medicines: his wife, allegedly a footbound Hunanese beauty, was his stimulant whereas his natural-footed Japanese concubine was his sedative. Whenever Gu suffered from writer's block, he would summon his wife to his side and squeeze her "lamb's trotter." Gu was also said to have muttered a seven-word mantra that summarized the mysterious beauty of bound feet: "slender, small, pointy, arched, fragrant, soft, and straight." One anecdote had him equating the delight of bound feet to eating fried fermented beancurd and rotten eggs, native delicacies that no foreigner would touch.[59]

Given how famous or infamous Gu Hongming was as a lotus lover, it is surprising that he did not discuss it at length in his writings, that none of his contemporaries described it in writing, and that when it was reported later, the limited number of anecdotes were reiterated and embellished in subsequent accounts. Instead of trying to separate Gu Hongming's person from legend, it is more fruitful to focus on the two interlocking processes of mythmaking surrounding Gu: his own idealization of "traditional China" and the public's fascination with his idealization. His love of footbinding was always recited as part and parcel of his alleged apologies of concubinage, caning, infanticide, eight-legged essays, opium smoking, spitting in public—all signs of Chinese backwardness perpetuated by a century of missionary writings.[60] Although few Chinese readers had stomach for these vices, they relished the ridiculous attempt of someone talking back in a quixotic gesture of defiance: What you take as national shame, we take as national pride.

Such is the irony of Gu Hongming, born a British colonial subject and a descendent of compradors who devoted his entire life to ranting about imperialism. So radical was his critique that he had to manufacture and idolize a perfect China before the violence of colonial contact. The radical implications of this posture lie in his tactic of exaggerating the distance between China and the rest of the world: China is to be judged not by Enlightenment standards, but by its own definitions of womanhood, justice, and human value. This deliberate distancing stems from the same nationalistic impulse as the reformers' eagerness to seek parity by the "catching up" rhetoric embedded in their linear history of the nation as we have seen in Xu Ke and Tang Yisuo.

Gu was clearly not a feminist who championed women's liberation; but in being a defender of Chinese culture he was a nationalist, even a patriot. His idealized Chinese woman, in fact, was a metaphor of the sovereign Chinese nation who could resist not only the foreigner's gaze but also his way of seeing. Indeed, Gu Hongming was an even more fervent nationalist than such reformers as Zheng Guanying or Liang Qichao because he refused to take Western standards of progress and civilization as Chinese yardsticks. He alone could talk back in German, French, or English and declare them parochial tongues. When footbinding found its sole defender in such an odd character, we can only conclude that it had ceased to be a prestigious or even relevant practice during the first two decades of the twentieth century. Therein lies the success of the tianzu movement that Reverend Mac-Gowan had called into being over a quarter-century earlier in Gu Hongming's ancestral home of Amoy.

In sum, the linguistic category of tianzu gained currency in a key transitional period in modern history: the 1890s–1900s. Under the watchful eyes of foreign powers, the Qing multiethnic empire sought to reinvent itself as a modern nation-state; Chinese culture lost its footing and became an open question. In this era of uncertainties, the discourse of tianzu offered moral and ontological certainty. It did so in part by way of its logic of assertion-negation: the new "natural feet" became imaginable only by standing the native practice of chanzu on its head. As such, the rhetorical power of tianzu is both destructive and constructive.

The constructive power of tianzu manifested itself most strongly in the progressive view of history it facilitated: modernity as negation of tradition. The discourse of tianzu engendered not only a new valuation of the body, but also a new way of looking at the world, hence of being in the world. In specific terms, the tianzu movement promulgated an enlightenment epis-teme: one founded on faith in circulation within the individual body, in the social body, and on the surface of the earth. As such it ushered in a global awareness of heightened visuality, a nationalism built on strong bodies, and a social vision of gender equality.

The establishment of the new, however, required the denigration or dis-missal of the old. So overwhelming was the destructive power of tianzu that we seldom take stock of the detritus littering its path: the stubborn body of Huang Xiuqiu, the pastoral yearnings of Shi Jingkai, the anticolonial conser-vatism of Gu Hongming. They are out of sync and out of place. Nor have we paused and analyzed the two mechanisms of the rhetorical power of the tianzu discourse, containment and visual exposé. The strategy of containment works by minimizing perspectives or voices that do not fit, as we have seen in this chapter. In its power to miniaturize other views of the body and the world, tianzu is integral to gigantic histories of the nation in the globe.

The strategy of visual exposé, in turn, works by shaming the other by sub-jecting her to one's unilateral gaze. In this chapter, we have seen how this visual logic was rooted in the humiliation that China and the Chinese suf-fered under the patronizing eyes of missionaries and foreigners, which Gu Hongming keenly felt. By the beginning of the Republican era, chanzu had been thoroughly photographed and dissected, hence exposed and discred-ited as China's national shame. (In chapter 2 we will examine how the Chi-nese reformers relied on the same strategy of exposé in anti-footbinding ral-lies, as if the women could be humiliated into submission.)

The thesis of this chapter is that the rhetoric and discourse of tianzu con-tributed to the extinction of the *aura* of footbinding. The unquestioned ac-ceptance of the tianzu episteme by such a range of writers as Liang Qichao, Xu Ke, Tang Yisuo, and even to a significant extent Gu Hongming signals that footbinding had lost all its cultural prestige or justification by the 1910s. On the levels of social practice and individual reception, however, the order-liness of the enlightenment episteme broke down. As people listened to speeches in stadium rallies or glanced at a poster on a lamppost, they took from them only those partial truths that fit their lives and outlooks, essen-tially miniaturizing the gigantic narratives by cutting them down to size. A fuller assessment of the anti-footbinding movement, therefore, must also include an examination of the local conditions of its implementation from the 1900s to the 1930s, to which we move in the next chapter.

2

THE BODY INSIDE OUT

The Practice of *Fangzu*, 1900s–1930s

The tianzu movement acquired national urgency in 1898, when the reformer Kang Youwei submitted a passionate memorial to the Guangxu emperor, urging him to ban footbinding because it put China at a disadvantage in global competition.[1] Encouraged by the furor, a Madame Shen spoke up about her suffering in a letter to Xue Shaohui (1855–1911), editor-in-chief of the journal *Chinese Girls' Progress (Nü xuebao)*. Xue, a classically educated gentrywoman, was one of eight founders of the Chinese Girls' School (Nü xuetang), which was masterminded by none other than Liang Qichao, author of "On Women's Education," and Jing Yuanshan, head of the Shanghai Telegraph Bureau. Other founders included Zheng Guanying and Kang Youwei's brother Guangren, all early agitators against footbinding. Xue's husband and his brother, Chen Jitong, both graduates of the Naval Academy in Fuzhou, as well as Jitong's French wife, were also part of the pioneering group.[2] Considering Xue's own activism and the Western-learning background of her family and colleagues, Madame Shen had probably expected her to chime in with a powerful condemnation of footbinding.

XUE SHAOHUI: "NEITHER A HORSE NOR AN ASS"

Yet Xue Shaohui had a mind of her own. In her response to Shen's complaints, Xue expressed opinions about footbinding that are so far removed from the enlightenment perspective that they were as singular in her times as they are today. "Your intentions are admirable, but your words seem excessive," she began. She then proceeded to stand two prevalent arguments of the anti-footbinding discourse on their heads: that it was not sanctioned by tradition and that women with bound feet are femmes fatales. Citing a spate of standard allusions to small feet in classical texts, Xue adopted the method of philologists to argue that footbinding did enjoy precedent in ancient times. (As it happens, she was wrong.)[3]

In disputing the tianzu polemics Xue's goal was not to defend footbinding, as Gu Hongming had done, but to introduce a vantage point that had been missing in the gigantic histories: a subjective view from inside the woman's body. She began by rebutting one of Kang Youwei's objections, that footbinding detracted from parental love: "[A parent's] compassion is not harmed by ear piercing; how can we say that parents are unkind? In the bed chambers [the joy of footbinding] exceeds having your husband paint your eyebrows; it is not that men are disrespectful [of women]." With indirection and tact Xue voiced a rare woman's perspective that had not been heard before on how footbinding was conducive to conjugal pleasures.

Furthermore, the contributions that a woman can make to her family and country depend on "her ten fingers pushing a needle and thread year after year; the companionship she shares with her spouse, and the diligence with which she manages the household and the kitchen." If this seems a traditional view of female virtues, Xue added that a woman's self-strengthening (ziqiang) is rooted in her education, her way with "poetry and books."[4] Her point is that footbinding is a trivial, private matter; bound or unbound, a woman's foot is simply irrelevant to her mission in life and her contributions to the nation.

"Those who think that footbinding is heresy or perverse, what would they say about the current fad of small waists in Western countries, which has not resulted in mass starvation, or that the practice of blackening teeth has survived in Japan, without being detrimental to health?" Although the global comparative viewpoint was common, Xue's logic was not. Her intention was not to make the usual relativist argument that "we have our vice but so do they," but to call attention to the power of culture—what Pierre Bourdieu would call "habitus"—in sustaining a meaningful everyday life. The sediment of conventions makes a practice that appears outrageous to an outsider seem entirely natural to the insider.

Xue Shaohui did not find bound feet admirable. They constituted a form of cultural contrivance, and "no matter how dainty and pitiful the 'twin hooks' *[shuanggou]* and 'lotus petals' *[lianban]* may look, the 'curved arch' *[gongwan]* barely inches long makes for clumsy and hesitant steps." In the transitional period she witnessed, "the rise and fall of tastes are as whimsical as switching from salty to sour, the demure and the trendy each follows her own fashion of decoration. Therefore, why shouldn't it be that it is all right to have bound feet, just as it is all right not to bind?" Xue's tolerance stems from her appreciation of the stubbornness of bodies: "Now they suggest that those who have already bound should all let their feet out at once. But no magical pill can grow a new set of bones; a severed head cannot be reattached. If you insist on bending crooked into straight by force, you create something that is neither a horse nor an ass. How would that improve customs and reform society?"[5]

Xue's views, which construe the body as both marginal and essential to a woman, seem contradictory at first glance. The shape of a woman's body is irrelevant to her ability to read books and study mathematics; her value as a person and a citizen depends in large part on her education, her mind, and her will. At the same time, Xue shows a rare appreciation for the unidirectional nature of time's arrow, an irrevocability of processes that defines the body's physical limits. It is this understanding, seldom voiced by the male anti-footbinding advocates, that defines Xue's female sensitivity. This sensitivity allows her to transcend the moral certainty embedded in the "*tianzu*-good: *chanzu*-bad" formulation. Instead of adopting a judgmental attitude about what other people should do with their bodies, Xue counseled: leave the women alone. In so doing she anticipated the promises and problems of *fangzu* (letting feet out) as a political and social movement.

FROM *TIANZU* TO *FANGZU*

It is unfortunate that Xue Shaohui's appreciation for the staying power of culture or an embodied way of life was out of step with the quickening revolutionary clamor around her. Caught up in a sense of urgency in the 1900s as the dynasty was breathing its last, reformers and revolutionaries sought to overhaul old customs overnight, making the "liberation" of feet a matter of life and death for the nation.[6] If tianzu was an abstract, disembodied discourse, the social agenda of fangzu was pragmatic and locally situated. For it to succeed, it would have to confront and defuse the resistance not only of women's habits of thinking but also of the stubbornness of their bodies. In this confrontation, new views of and knowledge about female bodies were created, as we will see, as were new female subjectivities.

The activities and targets of anti-footbinding societies that flourished in the late 1890s and 1900s fall under two rubrics. The first involves a covenant of patriarchs, with members vowing that they would not bind their daughters' feet, nor would they bring in a tiny-footed daughter-in-law. As family heads and community leaders, they took it upon themselves to transform social customs. The focus expanded to other-directed education and propaganda efforts as time went on, and old women as well as young girls became the targets of intense propaganda work. The fangzu message was imparted to the public first and foremost by the traditional medium of literature. Hence government notices were plastered on street corners and city walls in railroad towns in the north; the Tianzu hui reported that it distributed a hundred thousand pamphlets and tracts in Shanghai, Chengtu, and Xi'an by 1904; and numerous essay contests were sponsored by the anti-binding societies.[7] These, together with the newsletters and annual reports of the organizations, inundated the market with a wealth of information about footbinding, much of which had never been committed to writing before.

Following a long-standing Confucian association of visuality with woman—pictures were supposed to appeal to illiterates and females—many of the tracts are illustrated. Perhaps more than the proliferation of words, it is in the circulation of visual images that the anti-binding societies became an agent of perceptual change. Visual representation of the bound foot, even fully shod, was provocative to Chinese eyes; the exposure of bare feet was taboo even in the ars erotica before the nineteenth century. The introduction of Western imaging techniques, photography and later X-ray radiography, undermined this visual taboo almost overnight. In the 1860s, commercial photographers in Shanghai paid or coerced poor women to unwrap their binding cloth, producing the first images of the bare bound foot. Régine Thiriez, a historian of early photography in China and Europe, has noted that both the transaction and the images were considered risqué. In spite of it, or perhaps because of it, by 1865 it was customary to include at least one image of Chinese vice—opium smoking, footbinding, or execution—in photo albums that tourists would buy in Shanghai, Yokohama, or Paris. Presented as part of timeless "Chinese customs," a small number of images of naked feet were recycled into the 1910s and 1920s.[8]

Missionary doctors circulated virtually identical images of the bare foot in scientific treatises published in medical journals. Having studied amputated feet and live specimens, general practitioners and surgeons illustrated their findings with drawings and later also with regular and X-ray photographs (see fig. 3).[9] Both the commercial photographs and the medical reports had a restricted, primarily Western circulation. But images have a social life that reverberates into unlikely corners even without direct contact. Chinese scholars might not have souvenir albums in their living rooms, but they could feel the humiliation in their bones. Kang Youwei revealed in his 1898 memorial that "foreigners have long taken photographs of [our vices] and laughed at us, calling us barbaric. And the most laughable matter that brings us the most humiliation is footbinding. Your humble servant is deeply ashamed of it."[10]

Most ironically, the anti-binding crusaders were the first to utilize these shameful images and promulgate them to a massive Chinese audience at the turn of the century.[11] In due time, the parameters of what was permissible to look at expanded for Chinese viewers. The unseen and the indecent became an everyday sight; the female body was turned inside out. Thiriez has discerned a momentum of exposé in photographic portraits of Chinese women: "[S]ettings and postures generally became more daring as the century drew to an end and a new one dawned."[12] When formerly provocative postures became familiar, the envelope was pushed, resulting in even more revealing images. In this way, too, the anti-footbinding societies circulated new visual knowledge about feet and renewed the provocation by more blatant displays from the 1900s to the 1920s.

In heralding a public ritual—the rally—the anti-footbinding movement became an especially effective venue for the transmission of new, visceral knowledge about footbinding. These rallies, held in churches, schools, government offices, and athletic grounds, were highly theatrical performances. They worked by putting the female body on display, sometimes with props and sometimes without. Since natural, unbound feet are not particularly interesting to look at, they have no shock value. To provoke people to action, the fangzu movement resorted to a spectatorship of its opposite—chanzu, now presented with a live specimen or with models ranging from realistic to grotesque. The Shanghai Tianzu hui, founded in 1895, heralded public meetings with props and visual aids such as wooden or plaster models of a truncated foot with the four digits neatly folded down, toenails painted white (see fig. 4).[13] The more familiar the previously taboo sight of the bare foot

became, the organizers seem to imply, the easier it would be to imagine female pain, and the more natural or desirable tianzu would appear.

SCHOOL-BOUND:

THE GLORIOUS RECOVERY OF CAI AIHUA

In the first decade of the twentieth century, tianzu became domesticated as
part of the daily lexicon as local schools began to stage fangzu rallies. In December 1904, one such meeting was held at the Germinating Enlightenment
School (Fameng xuetang) in Daixi, a prosperous town in Wuxi county, Zhejiang, to commemorate the liberation of a girl's feet. Two reports in the *Tocsin
Daily (Jingzhong ribao)* offer a fascinating glimpse into the novelty of such
public rituals and the recruitment of females as both the passive exhibit and
the speaking subject, not to mention the gap in the strategies and concerns
of female and male anti-binding crusaders.

As described by the unnamed reporter:

> Girl student Cai Aihua was enrolled in the Germinating Enlightenment School
> in spring. Having been educated for less than a year, she has already acquired
> "civilized thoughts" *[wenming sixiang]*. On the fifth day of this month, [her
> teachers] Xu Zehua, Lin Menghuan, and Cai Lünong gave speeches vehemently
> denouncing *[tengchen]* the harm of footbinding during their ninth children's
> assembly. Then on the fifteenth, the president of the Anti-Footbinding Society
> in Lili [a town in the neighboring Wujiang county, Jiangsu province], Mrs. Ni
> Mu'ou, mailed her a gift of patterns for new shoes and booties, as well as
> instructions *[chenshe]* for letting feet out. The student thus came to see and
> feel much, and resolved to let her feet out. She decided to start that very day,
> which coincidentally was another day off [days ending with five were off-days].
> Therefore, after the tenth children's assembly that afternoon, a commemora-
> tive meeting was called in the same venue. Cai Lünong gave her a gift of four
> words: "Gloriously recovering a lost object" *[guangfu guwu]*.[14]

We surmise that these words were written on a banner or a scroll.

These are curious words, in Chinese as well as in English, and we will
elaborate on their implications on the making of the female speaking subject below. Suffice it here to note the primacy of words in male-initiated
anti-binding efforts. Reformist teachers and reporters lectured on the harm
of footbinding, composed lyrics, and wrote articles, all integral parts of their
enlightenment project. The word for "vehemently denounce" (*tengchen,* lit-

THE BODY EXPOSED   44

erally, painstaking-disclose) conveys a sense of urgency that propels one to speak up. In contrast, Mrs. Ni of the Lili Anti-Footbinding Society displayed a female insider's perspective in her sensitivity to the practical nuisance of unbinding that is reminiscent of Xue Shaohui's. The explanation *(chenshe)* she provided was in the form of practical instructions, together with patterns for making shoes. In other words, disclosing, speaking, and instructing *(chen)* comprised the operative mode of male and female crusaders alike. But women like Mrs. Ni showed concern for the material needs of the girl, for she understood that the care and maintenance of the feet would not end with their "liberation." This perspective contrasts with the male crusaders' view of the female body as an external object that can be lost and recovered, as in the eyes of Cai Lünong, or manipulated like a machine, as in the eyes of Tang Yisou. Mrs. Ni, also known by her maiden name Wang Shouzhi, was one of several Chinese female founders of anti-footbinding societies.[15]

Adopting a structured format as precise as a laboratory report, the second version of this story, dated December 31, 1904, is subdivided into three headings: (1) Rationale [of Cai's decision to unbind]; (2) Making Speeches; (3) Singing. Before turning to Cai's motives, we may take note of the exaggerated tone of the meeting:

> (2) Making Speeches: First, the "huizhu" [the protagonist of the assembly] Cai Aihua vehemently denounced *[tengchen]* the suffering and harm of footbinding. [She said words like] starting today the binders will be unwrapped. Second, teacher Xu Zehua ascended the podium *[dengtan]* and made a speech; so overjoyed was he that he looked crazed. He first congratulated the "huizhu" and admonished other girls to follow, so that they can compete with each other in gloriously recovering the lost body *[guangfu guti]*. He also admonished the "huizhu" not to pride herself on her tianzu, but to show pity on her community *[tongqun]*, persuade them, so as to deliver the myriad beings to the other shore *[pudu zhongsheng]*. Together they may jump from the fire pit and ascend the world of supreme happiness. Third, the head teacher Cai Lünong ascended the podium and offered congratulations. He deliberately praised the "huizhu" profusely, so as to make those who have yet to unbind jealous. He also admonished the boy students not to marry footbound women. After the speech, he was so pleased that his glee was palpable. (882–83)

Teacher Xu and Teacher Cai both looked possessed. Such exaggerated emotions befit a Christian baptism or revival meeting, although here, in the secular setting of a school, instead of sermons there were speeches and in the place of hymns, a song on the joy of letting feet out. Cai Aihua did not confess her sins but did speak of a crime being inflicted on her. Against the Christian tenor and the conversion narrative that structures the meeting, the reporter's persistent use of Buddhist terms appears incongruous. The rituals of "ascending the podium" and "making speeches" (yanshuo) are borrowed from Buddhist liturgy; Cai Aihua's missions of "deliver[ing] the myriad beings to the other shore" and "ascend[ing] the world of supreme happiness" are compassionate acts of the Boddhisattva.

Indeed, so alien is the spectacle of a public assembly organized around the bodily state of a young girl that the imported Christian liturgy, which provided some of the ritual forms, did not suffice. Buddhist words and concepts were inserted to lend familiarity. The meeting ended with a third inspirational ritual, this time borrowed from modern political rallies with imperial overtones: "(3) Singing: Teacher Xu Zehua led the entire class of scores of boys and girls, together with guests and head teachers, through a chorus of 'The Joy of Letting Feet Out' three times. At the end of the refrain, Xu exclaimed: 'Cai Aihua wansui [ten thousand years]! Daixi womanhood [nüjie] wansui! The future of Chinese women [nüzi] wansui! Wansui! Wanwansui!' Meeting dismissed" (883). Earlier Cai Aihua was being compared to a Boddhisattva, now she was being saluted as the goddess of the new republic.

One longs to know more about Cai Aihua, who was said to have "barbaric" parents but a "civilized" brother, none other than the head teacher Cai Lünong. The reporter described her struggles leading up to the crucial moment of unbinding in a long passage entitled "(1) Rationale," but it rings hollow. Under the influence of her brother, for years she had harbored "natural feet thoughts" (tianzu sixiang), but she hesitated because her resolution was weak and she did not want to be a vanguard. Then she was moved upon hearing the speeches at the children's assembly, where Xu called footbinding a shameful, self-degrading act of "shaping your body after prostitutes and actors" (changyou qi shen). Then her brother and Xu lobbied her intensely for days. Finally Mrs. Ni's gift sealed the deal, and Cai was ushered onto the podium to broadcast the pain and harm of binding to her classmates (882).

The narrative of budding awareness and hesitation giving way to resolution and action recalls that of a Christian testimony detailing a believer's journey from ignorance to salvation. Cai's conversion to the gospel of tianzu was construed as the result of personal resolution and external guidance, albeit without divine intervention. Yet the reader does not really know her inner struggles, her feelings of pain and jubilation. She was said to have spoken, but she did not say much and her actual words were not quoted. She was construed as a speaking subject with an agency of her own, but she appeared more as a spectacle on the podium, even an Exhibit A for Daixi womanhood.

Earlier Cai was said to have recovered a "lost object" and a "lost body." In a third variation of the "gloriously recovering" formulation, the reporter praised her as "a Columbus who gloriously recovers tianzu" in Daixi ("guang-fu tianzu zhi Gelunbo"; 882). As a navigator of uncharted oceans and "discoverer" of new lands, Columbus was a hero to late-Qing reformers, as we have seen in *Huang Xiuqiu*. A Columbus who *re*covers something is either a mixed metaphor or a contradiction; this curious expression thus betrays an ontological ambiguity of tianzu as a new creation and as an improvement on a previous state. These three variants of "glorious recovery" are premised on two opposite views of the female body. To call Cai Aihua the Columbus of Daixi who "recovers tianzu" is to evoke an image of the female body as a piece of pliant dough. Tianzu refers to a primordial state of not-binding. The personal history of the embodied self—whether a girl's feet were once bound and let out or never bound—becomes irrelevant. This view of tianzu as Columbus's exploit thus operates on an erasure of time and history.

The other two formulations, tianzu as the recovery of a lost body or a lost object, locate the female body in history but insist that despite having been broken or lost, the "natural" body can be recovered by female will. All three formulations, therefore, privilege female will over the physicality of her body. Moreover, in framing the problem of unbinding as that of "gloriously recovering," the male reformers used a nationalistic term that equates female bodies with lost territories or sovereignty. In this way, female bodies were made central to the project of national salvation, but only as a metaphor outside the realm of a woman's embodied experience.

If the conversion narrative erases the physicality of the body, it dramatizes the conflict felt by girls who found a new authority structure in male (and occasionally female) teachers and activists while being beholden to the old mores of mothers and grandmothers. What happened to Cai Aihua when she returned home after the rally? Did her mother scold her and apply the binders even tighter? Did she guard her recovered body with heightened resolution, having been emboldened by her public speaking experience (and what exactly *did* she say)? Did she put the binding cloths on and off in a seesawing battle of parental and brotherly will? As we leave Daixi to meet other females whose bodies have become templates for national histories and whose privacy was put on display, we long to hear the words she was supposed to have uttered that fateful day.

THE JOY OF LETTING FEET OUT

The song that Xu Zehua led the students in singing was composed by Cai Aihua's brother, Lünong. Perhaps taking clues from his sister, the song instructs on the practical procedures of letting feet out instead of celebrating tianzu as an unproblematic natural state:

> *The joy of letting feet out, what joy!*
> *Please listen to my letting-feet-out song.*
> *Stuff cotton wool between toes,*
> *Walk steadily on flat ground.*
> *Wash feet with vinegar and water,*
> *Stop using a long binding cloth.*
> *Shorten the cloth by one foot every seven days,*
> *Take special care for one month.*
> *Go to sleep without the binders,*
> *So that the blood can circulate.*
> *Once you let your feet out,*
> *Don't be afraid of troubles that others make.*
> *The joy of letting feet out, what joy!*
> *Let's all sing the letting-feet-out song. (883)*

Although we are not told of Cai Aihua's age, since she was enrolled in school for less than a year, she was unlikely to be older than ten, hence her feet must have been in their initial stage of binding. These simple instructions, based on the principle of gradually reducing pressure on the bent foot and enhancing blood circulation, would probably suffice.[16] Fangzu for young girls like Cai was merely a step-by-step procedure; once they resolved to unbind, they were likely to "recover" the function of their feet if not their entire shape.

Older women, however, had to battle bodies more resistant. For them, fangzu was not a one-time procedure but an ongoing bodily state that is not inherently different from chanzu: never completely successful; always a work in progress. A leaflet published by the Letting Feet Out Society (Fangzu hui) in Suzhou and addressed to adult and old women presents a realistic picture of the hurdles involved in letting feet out. Written in the first-person by twenty named ladies "who all had been binding our feet since young, and only recently began to let them out," the tract details five methods that they had tested on themselves: (1) making looser stockings and shoes; (2) gradually getting rid of the binding cloth; (3) straightening the toes and the ball of the foot; (4) applying cures for the broken skin and corns that would accompany the letting out ordeal; (5) getting rid of the habit of wearing inner high heels.[17]

The twenty ladies gave methodical and practical instructions that only a woman with bound feet could fathom. For example, they suggested making a series of shoes and stockings, each half an inch longer and two-to-three-tenths of an inch wider than the last; making the soles of the shoes one-to-two-tenths of an inch wider than the feet could improve stability (72). This was never done for shoes for bound feet, as it would make the feet appear bigger. The instructions for doing away with the binding cloth, likewise, are based on a gradual inversion of the familiar ways of binding. Do not discard the binding cloth overnight, as the sudden surge in circulation would cause the feet to swell. Keep the four digits loosely bent by wrapping them once or twice with a short length of cloth, two to three feet long, tucking the remainder under the heels. Originally, to achieve a small pair of feet, the proper way of wrapping the toes was from top to bottom, or clockwise from the outside in *(shunrao)* for the left foot but the opposite *(fanrao)* for the right foot. Now since the goal was to reverse the binding, the loose wrappers should be applied backwards: clockwise for the right foot and counter-clockwise for the left. After six months, there would be no need for the binding cloth (72–73).

The method of dispensing with inner high heels *(li gaodi)* also reveals (to us) the hidden mechanics of binding feet as it instructs the practitioner to unbind. Inner high heels are triangular wooden lifts that women slipped onto the heel area of their shoes. Not only did they make the bound feet appear smaller by elevating the heel, but in helping to distribute the body weight more evenly they also provided support and comfort. The Suzhou ladies counseled substituting pieces of cardboard or cattail bags stacked to a similar height. Since these materials are soft, the lift would flatten upon prolong wearing, when it would be replaced. As the arch of the foot gradually flattens, the paper or cattail lift would eventually be rendered unnecessary (74–75).[18] Such detailed instructions were never committed to writing when footbinding was a viable practice because they were transmitted orally and demonstrated corporeally. The availability of written instructions to unbind feet (and to bind, by inference) in itself signaled the creation of new knowledge about women's bodies and new venues of its national circulation.

The meticulous concern of the Suzhou ladies is manifested in their recommendation of a foreign oil, "yellow Vaseline" *(huang huashiling),* as the best relief for corns and calluses that would ensue from the torturous reversals inflicted on one's feet. But if a woman did not have access to a foreign pharmacy, the oil from the bones of a freshly killed goat would suffice (74). Finally, they invited all women who desired further instructions or suffered discomfort to drop by during their consultation hours, held on the fifteenth day of every month after three o'clock at Wang's residence, Five Dragon Hall Lane, Ten Spring Street, inside the Feng Gate in the city of Suzhou. Those who lived elsewhere were welcome to write (76). While inviting other "comrades" *(tongzhi)* to share their methods, the Suzhou ladies vouched that old and young had let their feet out successfully using their method, including an old lady in her seventies or eighties. "The comfort and convenience of letting feet out are comparable to a blind man regaining his sight—they are beyond words. Nor can a person who has not let her feet out imagine [the joy]" (75).

The comparison of letting feet out to the miraculous healing of the blind contradicts the carefully constructed message in the rest of the tract.[19] In their meticulous attention paid to the physicality of flesh and bones, the Suzhou ladies have made a persuasive argument about the reversibility of footbinding. With details of each of the five methods laid out, they drove home the impression that with patience, determination, and the ability to endure more pain, any woman could successfully let her feet out in due time. Yet they knew better than to present the body as a piece of molding clay or a lost object (or eyesight) that can be recovered. Perhaps for this reason they did not describe the wobbly and misshapen let-out feet that were the best that women who had bound feet for a long time could hope to achieve. The hope of a miraculous rebirth that they slipped into their instructions underscores how difficult, painful, and incomplete the process of letting feet out was for older women.

YAN XISHAN'S
ANTI-FOOTBINDING CAMPAIGNS IN SHANXI

This fact was lost on a new generation of bureaucrats charged with fangzu in their districts. The drive to end footbinding received a boost after the establishment of the Republic in 1912, when a fragmented state brought itself to bear on the bodies of its citizens. But, in fact, Sun Yat-sen's Republic was short-lived, and its 1912 proclamation to ban footbinding was never implemented.[20] In many provinces, which were virtually independent states, however, civilizing regimes sought to reform customs as the foundation of a modern body politic. Not only did the anti-footbinding movement become entangled with local politics, it also served as the vehicle through which people contested the encroachment of state power, and in the process they articulated their parameters of privacy.

These developments unfolded in Shanxi under the warlord Yan Xishan (1883–1960), the first to engineer and sustain province-wide campaigns to eradicate footbinding, from 1917 to 1922.[21] Not content with education and persuasion, he brought the power of the state to bear on legislation, police enforcement, and the dispatch of feet inspectors into people's homes. Yan's rhetoric was akin to that of the natural feet societies in the coastal areas. But the will and ability to use state power, however fragmented and circumscribed, changed the nature of the anti-footbinding movement from voluntary social action to state mandate and surveillance. This, together with the availability of a sizable number of edicts, circulars, and notices compiled by the legacy-conscious Yan, makes an examination of the Shanxi case especially revealing.

As a prototype for the entire province, in 1912–14 Yan organized a militia group, the Peace-Keeping Association (Baoan she), in his home county of Wutai. The militia was charged with the somewhat contradictory tasks of maintaining public order and instigating social reform. The village headmen and local leaders were empowered to conduct household inspections; families whose women refused to let their feet out were fined. They brought along one female chaperone on their inspection tour, going as far as peeling off the socks of footbound women. Villages north of the Hutuo river complied, but those south of the river rose up in arms and had to be pacified.[22]

Yan Xishan, the military governor *(dujun)* of Shanxi who also assumed civil responsibilities in 1917, was undeterred. The eradication of footbinding became a province-wide target under his "Six Policies" campaign,

1917–22. Stated in positive terms, the six priorities are water control, sericulture, tree planting, ending opium smoking, tianzu, and queue cutting. In 1918 "Three Matters" of livelihood were added: cotton cultivation, forestation, and animal husbandry. In his declaration, Yan followed the national script prevalent since the 1898 reform period that construed women with bound feet as a terrible financial burden: "The people of Shanxi live in abject poverty. The cause of poverty is that those who produce are few and those who eat are many. . . . Among our population of about 10 million, half are women and most of them are not engaged in production." Ostensibly, footbinding was opposed for economic reasons; later it was grouped with opium smoking and gambling as the "Three Ills."[23]

Male haircutting, in turn, was mandated because of its obvious political symbolism. Although the 1645 Qing order for all Han men to conform to Manchu hairstyle was met with violent resistance, almost three centuries later the habit had been naturalized to the extent that many men kept their queue after the collapse of the Qing imperium. In 1919 Yan rebuked a county teacher "whose queue was dangling like a rope. What a horrid sight!" Yan ordered not only the clipping of queues but also a close cropping or clean shaving of the head; even hair two to three inches long was suspect because so ingrained was the identification of queues with the old order that any unkempt hair—a queue in the making—signaled an incipient restoration movement. The order, first intended for officials, students, and merchants, was declared a success in May 1918 and was extended to "ordinary people" *(putong renmin)*.[24]

The symbolic import of tianzu was as unmistakable as the queue. Although the binding of feet posed no political threat, it was the sign of national shame. Yan, a graduate of the Tokyo Military Academy in Japan, had internalized the global episteme that produced the category of tianzu in the late Qing. "The harm of footbinding is great. It hinders the movement of females and maims their bodies. Not only is it absent in the five continents and ten thousand countries of the world, even the imperial family and Banner people of the former Qing dynasty had tianzu," he wrote in a 1918 notice to all people *(renmin)*, warning of an imminent fine. "Moreover, nowhere is the Han custom of footbinding more severe than in Shanxi. This is why our population is dwindling, our bodies are becoming frail, and our people are sinking into deeper poverty." Over one hundred thousand copies of the notice were printed and distributed to county authorities for posting.[25]

In a speech to middle school students the following year, Yan described a different temporal relationship between the world, China, and Shanxi. "The scores of countries in the world are like China: they do not have the custom of footbinding. Bringing upon China the ridicule of the world, footbinding had become China's greatest shame. China occupies a part of the world, and Shanxi occupies a small part of China. Now, the habit of footbinding has been eradicated in all of China's other provinces. If Shanxi does not pull itself up, how can we stand tall on the surface of the earth?"[26] Although empirically untrue, Yan's belief that Shanxi alone was backward conveyed his determination to catch up. In applying the national narrative of civilization and progress to Shanxi, Yan's rhetoric is nationalistic even as he highlighted the division of the country between the progressive coastal cities marked by tianzu and a backward interior marked by chanzu.

Yan Xishan's approach to social change was top-down. Administratively, he dispatched edicts and supervisors from the provincial capital; at the local level, he relied on enlightened bureaucrats, students, and teachers to provide personal examples and to implement prohibition measures. Since the literacy rate was low, Yan saw speech making as the best method for mass education and mobilization. "Lecturers" *(xuanjiang yuan)* were dispatched periodically from the capital to explain policies and directives. In addition, when thirty thousand students from the upper primary schools and above were preparing to return home for the new year holidays in 1919, Yan "commissioned" them to give speeches on tianzu and other matters outlined in a primer, *What the People Should Know*. He admonished them to form itinerant lecturing teams with former imperial students and graduates of modern schools in their home villages, and ordered the local authorities to assist in the organizing efforts.[27]

Yan's grassroots mobilization promulgated the global episteme to the most remote villages in the interior northwestern province. These efforts established tianzu and male haircutting as urgent matters of public concern. The political import of personal appearance is built on a concept of the body that bifurcates it into outward form and inner spirit, but places the personal and social bodies on a continuum. As Yan put it in a speech to newly elected lawmakers: "Although haircutting is an outward matter that pertains to the individual body, who are we to say that the thinking *[guannian]* of the people wouldn't change because of it?"[28]

By May 1918, eight months after the initial directive, one Tianzu hui had been established in each of the 105 counties, boasting a total membership of over twenty thousand. The remarkable speed was due to the fact that all civil servants in county offices and all village heads were made compulsory members, the former at the threat of dismissal. Among commoners, all males twenty and older were eligible to join. The members' main duties were to make donations to the association and to admonish nonmembers to change their thinking. They were also to serve as models by enforcing fangzu and tianzu in their own houses.[29] The pervasiveness of Tianzu hui could only mean one thing: that footbinding was still practiced in every county of the province.

CRIMINALIZATION OF CHANZU

Even before his "Six Policies" campaign, in late 1916, Yan recruited local leaders and male students to help enforce his decree titled "Regulations for the Strict Prohibition of Footbinding." In conception and terms this decree shows an engagement with the messy realm of local practice absent in national proclamations. From the day it took effect, which was the day that it was posted in public, young girls were forbidden to start binding, girls under the age of fifteen who had already started to bind were to let their feet out (*jiefang*, to unwrap and release), and those over fifteen were not allowed to wear shoes with arched wooden soles (*mudi*; see figs. 5, 7e). After a grace period of one month, the parents of newly bound girls would be fined, as would the makers and vendors of wooden heels (3–30 yuan). After three months, fines would be levied on those who refused to let their feet out or those who held on to their soles (2–20 yuan). After six months, anyone who served as a matchmaker for footbound ladies or brides caught wearing arched soles would be fined (3–30 yuan). The magistrate in counties and the head of police bureaus in municipalities were charged with the implementation.[30] Chanzu, in its various sartorial guises, was thus criminalized.

Two years after the decree, Yan Xishan received reports that in over fifty counties, or half of the total in the province, the feet of all girls under fifteen were let out. Buoyed by the instantaneous result, in his 1918 notice (cited above) he extended the fangzu order to girls under ten. Staking the prestige of his office, which was also his personal prestige, on the success of the implementation, Yan vowed to dispatch state inspectors in July to impose punishments on parents, parents-in-law, village headmen, and magistrates who were lax.[31]

The terms of the stipulations and the structure of penalties bespeak Yan's astute understanding of the personal and cultural forces that contributed to the popularity of footbinding. He understood that female bodies were not slabs of pliant dough. Hence older women were spared the pain of unbinding, but they were no longer permitted to perpetuate the cultural prestige of small feet and its attendant standards of beauty by wearing shoes with arched soles or, as stipulated in a later notice, decorating their ankles with copper bracelets. Arched soles, a notable feature of Shanxi-style shoes, accentuated the curve of the bent metatarsals and made the foot look dainty. In the coastal cities, as early as the 1900s a new style of shoes with a far gentler wooden sole became fashionable as women gradually relaxed the regimen of arching without necessarily giving up the binding of feet. Called Kun-shoes *(kunxie)*, some examples of this store-bought footwear featured downright flat soles made of fabric or leather (see figs. 6, 7). Some observers considered them a sign of the beginning of the end.[32] We may recall the difficulties in completely straightening out the bent toes and the arch in the fangzu instructions given by the Suzhou ladies. With their flatter arch, Kun-shoes made sensible footwear for let-out feet or "half-bound" feet *(ban chanjiao)*.

But in Shanxi the high arch and the attendant crevice underneath were still prized in the early years of the Republic. When women started to make Kun-shoes in Yuwu township, they were hailed as a sign of reform in 1918. To remake cultural norms, Yan went as far as ordering all operatic troupes in the province to stop performing with stilts that mimic the sway of bound feet.[33] In paying attention to the artifices of illusion-making on stage and in everyday life, he showed an uncanny understanding of the cultural aura and sexual appeal of footbinding. In singling out matchmakers for penalty, he also acknowledged the importance of marriage as the institution that reproduced female customs.[34]

One unintended outcome of the criminalization of footbinding was the establishment of an adult female legal agency. When a footbound woman was older than fifteen and wore heels, she herself *(benren)* or her "household head" *(jiazhang,* either parent or in-law) would have to pay up. It is not clear how many women did pay, nor is it specified by whom and on what basis the decision would be made. But this female agency was circumscribed by the very conditions of its production. The prohibition was enforceable only by social surveillance, as evinced by Yan's curious wording: "when others inform against her, or when [the authorities] discern that the offense is true." The "or" makes it difficult to ascertain whether a girl's neighbors or state agents were primarily responsible for reporting the offense. In either case, what agency she had came in tandem with heightened scrutiny of two often contending authorities.

A second unintended consequence of the prohibition edicts was that they served to define discursively the boundaries of chanzu. Although the policy goal was articulated as tianzu, unlike the earlier missionaries Yan was not interested in the ontological status of the natural foot. The main concern of the result-oriented administrator was in fact fangzu. Yan's pragmatism may account for a convoluted and self-contradictory usage: "to alter and let out natural feet" *(gaifang tianzu)*.[35] Many women caught in between fashion regimes experienced fangzu as a perpetual transitional state: neither tianzu nor chanzu. In the eyes of the state, however, fangzu involved differentiating between degrees of bondage according to age and ornamentation. For girls fifteen (or ten) and under, wrapping one's feet with a binding cloth constituted footbinding. For those older, footbinding was signified not by a piece of cloth but by wooden soles. The meting out of punishment required unambiguous material signs. What mattered was not the size or physiological state of each individual's feet, but standardized reckoning of surface accoutrements that were readily visible, hence countable and accountable by the efficiency-minded bureaucrats.

THE STATE AGAINST THE PATRIARCHS

The enforcement of these decrees hinged on the state's ability to inspect women's feet, hence literally subjecting women to its gaze. The heads of the newly installed districts and county authorities were to "scrutinize and look" *(chajian)* and tabulate the number of footbound females in each locale; their auditors were to verify the data and to ascertain the percentage of footbound women "on the basis of what met their eyes" *(yi yanjian wei zhun)*.[36] The abuses and complaints that resulted were so ferocious that Yan had to issue restraining orders. In March 1918, Yan ordered that all inspections had to be conducted "after sunrise and before sunset." The village wardens had to notify the women by calling their names from the outside and asking them to step into the courtyard or go out to the front gate. Only the county mag-istrate had the authority to impose fines.[37] One can imagine the potential threat of state agents entering people's living quarters in the dark, harassing the men, molesting the women, and extorting money. Yet measures devised to ensure a certain communal accountability by conducting the inspection outside had the ironic effect of making the women's humiliation more pub-lic. Despite the restraining orders, rumors persisted that feet inspection was an excuse for fondling women.[38]

In March 1919, Yan pled with the counties to hire female inspectors and authorized the channeling of fines to finance the operation. After all, he mused, having the male police force and bureaucrats interfering in matters that concerned the bodies of women was inappropriate for the body politic (*zhengti*).[39] Later that year, regulations for the dispatch of female inspectors into villages were announced. The ideal inspector was a middle-school grad-uate over twenty years old, but given the scarcity of educated women, any hardworking woman of good repute would do as long as she had unbound or let-out feet. She would receive a salary and travel expenses from the county. Her job was to report offenses to the county authorities, but she had no power to impose or collect fines.[40]

The bureaucratization of feet inspection became an arena in which people contested or negotiated with the state the boundaries of their pri-vacy. Successive regulations outlining the conduct and jurisdiction of feet inspectors give an indication of the violence of this encounter and the pre-carious position of the inspector. Yan stipulated that a female inspector could bring a patrolman to the villages with the explicit task of "protecting" her, but he had to wait outside the front gate and was not to extort bribes. At the same time, the villagers needed protection from the inspector. Hence rules stated that she could not linger in the house, nor should she make "ir-relevant remarks" on the styles of other articles of clothing and jewelry on the women's bodies. Before inspection could commence, she had to notify the headman or ward warden of each village, who would accompany her.[41]

Changing the gender identity of the inspectors did not alleviate opposi-tion and may even have exacerbated the patriarchs' resentment. People saw anti-footbinding, enforced by humiliating inspections and onerous fines, as a frivolous project of an overreaching state. Yan related an instinctive reac-tion on the streets: "What does this trivial matter have to do with politics, so that the government should interfere in all seriousness?" Implied in the term "trivial matter" *(suoshi)* is a concept of the bodily-private that people assumed should be immune from state micromanagement. The people drew a clear line between the personal and the governmental. The same rhetorical opposition between official power and privacy was evident two years later when, after the high tide of fangzu subsided, rumors raged that "The government *[guanting]* has given up meddling *[guan]* in women's bound feet."[42]

Yan's logic, that unless women unwrapped their binding cloths, Shanxi would be a laughing stock in the rest of China and China would lose face in the world, must have seemed opaque to many. The national and global connections were simply too distant to be relevant to their daily lives. Unable to see from Yan's gigantic perspective, people sought the "real" reason for the government's intrusion from whirls of rumor. Once the women stopped binding, according to one rumor, Yan Xishan would draft them into the army and dispatch them into battle. Other rumors betrayed fears that were more immediate: old scholar-gentry feared that the end of binding would destroy morality and female docility, making women unmarriageable. In a pair of adjacent counties in the south, families vied to marry off girls as young as thirteen or fourteen upon hearing a rumor that the authorities would force their will only on daughters but not on brides.[43]

That rumor probably started when the female inspectors in one of the counties, Lucheng, inspected daughters but left brides alone. That so many parents found the rumor believable may suggest a malaise about the ambivalent status of daughters in their natal families. Once ensconced in the authority of her in-laws *(pojia)*, people expected her body to be off limits to the state. Coupled with the widespread anxiety that a tianzu woman would be unmarriageable, this rumor accentuated the precarious position of unmarried daughters in a "no-man's" land. Enforced unbinding was thus an assault on the patriarch's jurisdiction over his daughter-in-law. Teenage marriage, already a common practice that Yan sought to end, became an expression of people's resistance to the government's intrusion into their private lives.[44]

Although we do not have the account books for each county, circumstantial evidence suggests that many patriarchs simply paid the fines to get the state off their back. After all, this was merely one of the many levies they had already swallowed, as Yan himself so succinctly described: "The three duties of the people are: serving as a soldier, paying taxes, and getting an education. Don't forget!" By July 1918, the fines were pouring in. In theory, the Tianzu hui in each county was entitled to 30 percent of the income, whereas the remainder would finance the county girls' school (or, if there was none, the boys' school).[45] Yan complained that although the amount of deposits was logged, the cash was often unaccounted for. He ordered all counties to designate a separate set of books for the fines, listing activities in four columns: opening balance, deposit, withdrawal (with receipts), and ending balance. New books were to be submitted every two months.[46] The political business of fangzu thus created, at least on paper, a self-sufficient economy administered by the county authorities.

From the patriarch's perspective, the fine was a squeeze by an overzealous governor aligned with a corrupt local gentry. The extractions provided for more inspections and further penalties, lining the pockets of the officials and local gentry who controlled the Tianzu hui and the schools. The abuses were so severe that in June 1920 Yan ordered county authorities to allocate all Tianzu hui expenditures for the salaries of female inspectors, which in effect meant the disbanding of the Tianzu hui. He admitted: "Upon recent inspection, the majority of the county Tianzu hui's are empty shells." In Pinglu county, the penalties were so excessive that Yan cautioned "administrative fines, meant to teach a lesson, are different from criminal penalties." Referring to the large number of people being caught, he suggested that not all should be fined to the maximum amount stipulated. In Shouyang county, Yan discovered that county authorities descended upon the villages, arbitrarily appointed village women as inspectors, and pocketed 40 percent of the fines thus collected.[47] The abuses foreseen in a satirical short story, "Excising Small Feet," discussed in the next chapter, had become a reality.

GENDER AND CLASS: BIFURCATED WOMANHOOD

Even with the employment of female inspectors, by design Yan Xishan's anti-footbinding campaign was a male-to-male operation. The leaders and primary constituency of the anti-binding movement remained male, as evinced by the proposed establishment of a Refusing to Marry Footbound Brides association in every county, which automatically enlisted all male students as members.[48] The constitution of the Tianzu hui, in turn, was written explicitly for the male subject, as we have seen. Yan's strategy was to mobilize male students, teachers, bureaucrats, and local gentry to change female behavior by making their patriarchs accountable. All of the former were people from the upper echelon *(shangdeng renjia)* who should take the initiative in reforming social customs.[49] Yan's was thus an "elitist" vision that rested on a utopian alliance between the old male elite and the new.

In practice, the conservative gentry often provided the most steadfast resistance, spreading rumors and arousing fears about women's marriageability. Officialdom fared only slightly better. In 1918, Yan warned that he could see through local officials covering up their lack of action with charades of "empty words." In his annual review of the tianzu work of county magistrates the following year, Yan singled out twenty-four for formal praise and reprimand. Fifteen were deemed praiseworthy, two of whom were rated particularly commendable, whereas nine were reprimanded, one seriously.[50] Contrary to Yan's vision, the campaign became a battleground between reform-minded men, often urban and younger, and the entrenched conservative forces that the village gentry and recalcitrant bureaucrat personified.

A handful of women did join the Tianzu hui; in Xiangling county five were commended, along with six men, for their extraordinary dedication. The men received a horizontal plaque inscribed with an auspicious saying whereas the women's prize was a standing trophy. In Fanshi county, the magistrate's wife and daughter traveled from village to village inspecting and persuading women to unbind. They also received a trophy from Yan.[51] Although the prizes are differentiated by gender, these women occupied the same privileged social position as the elite men. The anti-binding movement thus created two diametrically opposed female subject positions. This is perhaps not by intention, since the recruitment of female helpers was not in Yan's original plan. But with the participation of female inspectors and the magistrate's female kin, womanhood in Shanxi was divided into the educated and privileged who served as agents of the state on one side, and village illiterate women who resisted their encroachment on the other.

Given the extensive nature of the campaign and the voluminous documentation it generated, it is remarkable how little of women's feelings or experience, on both sides of the divide, they reveal. Pain as a subjective bodily experience was curiously absent in Yan's anti-footbinding rhetoric, which is predominantly a discourse of shame. On the rare occasion of addressing all women older than sixteen in a December 1919 directive, he adopted the paternalistic tone of a patriarch lecturing his subjects. Referring to himself as "this governor," he called upon "you women and girls, old or young, to hurry up and loosen your binding cloth." Yan sounded like a stern father:

"I hear that many girls around ten are not binding, or have let their feet out. But those older than sixteen, although they are not wearing high heel shoes on the outside, inside their feet are still wrapped in strips of cloth. Look at you! Don't you have any self-respect? What are you doing this for, harming your own body and causing others to look down upon you?"[52]

The discourse of shame is predicated on pairs of "social eyes" judging the woman, but it also recognized her individual volition. Yan sounded almost naïve in his eagerness to assign miraculous power to women's will to unbind. He told older women, for example, to simply "take the binders off and in several days, your tendons and bones would stretch out, the blood and *qi* would circulate freely. How much more convenient it is!"[53] He had in fact shown more appreciation of the stubbornness of old women's bodies in his legislation.

Yan concluded with a personal warning: "Today I send this notice, going to such length to persuade you, because in truth I pity you so, you ignorant women. Hurry up and get rid of your old bad habits, don't let my concern for you be in vain. From now on, if you still bind and swaddle, the female inspector will find out and you'll be severely punished. By then your regrets would be too late!"[54] In his words, the girls who embraced tianzu appeared to be adults, whereas the old women who resisted were children. The infantilizing of footbound women is also evinced in the rewards that Yan designed for them. At the inception of the campaign, Yan printed over one hundred thousand copies of "a colored drawing" to be handed out as prizes. Later in 1918, he ordered each village to identify the first woman who let her feet out, promising her an "artistic trophy."[55] The association of the female with visuality, contrasted here with the award of plaques with inscribed words to men, betrayed an ingrained gender hierarchy. Females, and children, were deemed especially receptive to sounds and sights. As the state sought to remake them into modern citizens, they were locked all the more tightly in an inferior female place.

Ostensible partners in the civilizing project, female inspectors were no match for the male leaders in authority and power. Occasionally these women were educated and could stand on their own. For example, in Yan-shi county, female primary school teachers were hired in 1918 to "supervise and urge" *(duze)* the provincial lecturers and village heads and to help persuade the footbound women. In the provincial capital, in early 1919, female students from the Normal, Gongli, and Shangzhi schools were mobilized

to take turns to inspect feet on Sundays.[56] For the most part, however, inspectors were local women who may or may not have been literate. We do
not know the extent to which each identified with the tianzu episteme. In
any case, her success depended less on her ability to persuade other women
and more on the resolve of the magistrate to impose fines and on the patriarch's ability to pay. Caught between male authority and complacency,
she was a pawn in a duel between state and local society.

The unprecedented invasion of state power into people's bedrooms was
all the more transgressive because it was conducted primarily by women and
on women. The recruitment of educated women as representatives of the
state, although limited in number, precluded the possibilities of female alliance or sisterhood across class lines. Even as they were standing in the same
courtyard staring at each other, women who personified the enlightenment
project could not be coeval with the old women stuck in their shameful ways.
The unequal power dynamics of missionaries civilizing a pagan nation were
now being played out by one group of Chinese women to another. No wonder that the latter resisted and held on to their customary ways, now cherished all the more as their own.

The antagonism between the educated women and the illiterate women
they tried to "liberate" was dramatized in an anecdote recorded by Zhou
Songyao, a male reformist writer, in an anti-footbinding pamphlet published
around 1929. One Madame Liu Guofang, a teacher at the Wushi Girls'
School in Gao'an, Jiangxi province, went down to the villages with several
colleagues from the Women's Association to persuade peasant women to let
their feet out. They were greeted by a barrage of curses: "What business do
you have meddling with *my* feet! I'm old and don't need to eat from my
looks *[niang laole, you buxiang mai yangzi]*. Why on earth do you girlie students care about the long and short of others' feet?"[57] The footbound
woman's robust ego is evinced by her term of self-address, *niang*. Literally
"mother" but more appropriately "*your* mother," it conveys her sense of superiority over both the hoity-toity teachers and lowly prostitutes by virtue
of her seniority in the family system. Unlike prostitutes and actors who had
fallen through the kinship safety net and had to eke out a living by drawing the gaze of others to themselves *(mai yangzi)*, she had won her security
and power in the time-honored way—giving birth to sons and serving her
in-laws. And the teacher from the city had nothing over her. The gulf between the subject positions of the educated woman and the footbound

woman is thus rooted in the conflict between two authority structures and channels of success for women: the new school and the old family.

THE RECKONING

Between 1918 and 1920, Yan issued numerous decrees and orders to goad individual counties to take anti-binding seriously. Indeed, no one can doubt his sincerity and vigilance upon examining the mountain of legislation, directives, and primers he produced, only a fraction of which was discussed here. In 1920, Yan received reports that almost all of the girls under fifteen had ceased to bind and felt optimistic enough to begin enforcing fangzu among older women, who were understandably the most resistant. Some agents imposed fines on the older women, but few bothered trying to persuade them to change their habit. Other than harassment, the campaign had made no impact on the lives of older women.[58] Even the victory with girls was mostly illusionary. In 1921, rumors spread that the government had ceased to be concerned with women's feet, and girls promptly began binding in many counties. A desperate Yan repeatedly goaded his officials to keep up the momentum; giving up midway would mean a complete waste of earlier efforts.

Yet the administrative will to dispatch inspectors and impose fines could not be, and indeed was not intended to be, sustained forever. Once the pressure receded, county reports that girls had resumed binding did in fact begin to trickle in.[59] Like the mass movements that Mao Zedong would conduct decades later, Yan Xishan's fangzu campaign was launched with fanfare but tapered off in the early 1920s, even as weathered signs and posters still hung from lamp posts and brick walls in towns and villages. Yan held onto his anti-footbinding platform in successive village administrative reforms in the late 1920s and even after 1932, but any reformist fervor rings hollow at its second sounding, a reminder of the promised transformation that the first attempt had failed to deliver.

Census reports suggested that modest gains were made: in 1928 the proportion of footbound women among the female population of the province was 17.8 percent. In 1934 it was reduced to 8.63 percent, or 435,497 females. A 1932–33 census, however, counted almost one million women aged thirty and under who had bound feet (under 15 *sui*, over 323,000; from 16 to 30 *sui*, over 625,000), although the definitions of "bound feet" used are not specified.[60] Furthermore, without village-by-village statistics through a period of time, it is hard to ascertain the reliability of these figures and the meaning of such arbitrary comparisons across a span of years. Nonetheless, Yan's campaigns had likely reduced the number of young girls who bound, especially in the urban areas, and the subsequent unrest with the Japanese invasion of China in 1937 provided a more compelling deterrent. The need to run away from marauding soldiers persuaded many mothers that they could no longer afford to bind their daughters' feet.

In Shanxi as elsewhere, however, the tianzu rhetoric was irrelevant to the older women whose bodies were accustomed to decades of binding. For them, chanzu was a "natural" state in terms of their everyday, embodied reality. They could be intimidated into unwrapping the binders momentarily in front of the foot inspectors, but no amount of administrative order or criminalization could return their feet to the "natural" state of tianzu. To the older women, the state-imposed fangzu movement was no more than a make-believe: a performance of compliance if not a charade.

THEATER OF THE ABSURD

From a logical point of view, the surest way to eradicate footbinding would be to dissuade young girls from starting. Given the stubbornness of older women's bodies and their resistance to the harassment, it would make sense to leave them alone. In a matter of decades, footbinding would come to a natural end.[61] The fangzu movement in the twentieth century, however, did not have the leisure to pursue this option because of two conditions of its birth. The sense of national urgency and the personal humiliation that the male reformers felt under the global gaze compelled them to seek immediate and visible results, no matter how symbolic. The tactic of visual display that the movement adopted, in turn, goaded the reformers to find more and more shocking props and new slogans for their rallies that were held in athletic grounds or party headquarters throughout the provinces after the establishment of the Nationalist government in Nanjing in 1927.[62] The cessation of binding by girls, like tianzu, lacks drama, hence is not interesting to look at. In contrast, fangzu—literally the unwrapping of older women's binding cloths—is full of blood, sweat, and tears, promising endless entertainment.

Indeed, symbolic victory became the substance of the fangzu movement as it became routine in the late 1920s and 1930s; performance was an end in itself. The fluxes inside a woman's body, the contractions and swellings that render chanzu and fangzu more gradations on a spectrum than its two poles, are not amenable to representation. Objects exterior to the body—the material implements needed for binding feet—came to symbolize both footbinding and its enemy. In Yan Xishan's Shanxi, arched wooden soles served that function. Elsewhere, strips of binding cloth, the fabric most intimate to a woman's skin, fluttered in public spaces to announce the end of the footbinding era.[63]

The exhibition of the binding cloth was attributed to Deng Changyao, the head of the Office of Civil Affairs (Minzhengting chang) in Shaanxi, a province west of Shanxi. Charged with the letting out of feet, Deng drafted a three-stage program in 1928 that mimicked Sun Yat-sen's tutelage program toward developing parliamentary democracy: admonition; enforcement; penalty.[64] In the first stage of admonition, a Tianzu hui was to be established in the provincial capital with branches in the county seats. They would send educators to primary schools in the villages who would see to it that every schoolboy would wear a cloth banner declaring: "I refuse to marry a boundfoot woman." In the next stage, enforcement, inspectors were dispatched with a gong to each household. Having forced the women to unbind, the old binding cloths were to be collected and shipped to the county office. Those under thirty who still refused to unbind would be fined and their parents detained.

The image of thousands upon thousands of used binding cloths piling up in the magistrate's august office was amusing, if not hilarious, and soon Deng became nationally famous. An article in the newspaper *Shenbao* told of Deng and his runners scouting the neighborhoods to snatch away every cloth binder in sight and stockpiling them in his office. Soon his collection in fact reached several thousand. When he invited officials and "the people" *(renmin)* to a binding cloth exhibition, everyone covered their noses and chuckled. Deng also led a pageant of "bare-legs-tiny-feet" into the villages, entertaining with songs and speeches. It is not clear who bared their legs. Having offered a reward of five dollars *(dayang)* for each hundred confiscated binding cloths, in one month he was said to have collected over 25,400 trophy strips. Similar slogans and exhibitions sprang up across the country; in Jiangxi province a mountain of confiscated shoelaces was erected, with a tombstone, as public monument.[65]

The bureaucratization of anti-footbinding campaigns brought two formerly incongruous elements into the same discursive space: male bureaucratic order and female bodily odor. This incongruity prompted parodies of overreaching state power, creating sympathy for the footbound woman as the subject of harassment. Hence popular accounts of these exhibitions depict them as farces and exercises in excess. The *Shenbao* article presented Deng's fangzu rally as a vanity fair: "A large-scale 'cherishing the people' meeting was held in mid-November 1927 at the Office of Civil Affairs. The decoration was most unusual: the two corridors behind the front entrance displayed binding cloths of all sizes: long, short, wide, narrow. Strip after strip they draped, like the scarves on display in department stores. Some were stained with blood and had yet to be washed. Several hundred pairs of red embroidered slippers were hoisted above the middle entrance. They were all pointy like horn and corn, what a treat for the eyes!" In the hall, sheets of "fangzu songs" were on display, and behind the hall a straw canopy was set up with a stage, ready for a "carnivalesque talk show *[huazhuang jiang-yan]*."[66] In an age of visual overkill, even bloody binders failed to elicit outrage. Instead, they reminded the reporter of merchandise artfully displayed in department stores to tug at the buyer's purse strings.

Nor was Deng Changyao's performance interpreted as intended. "That day, Deng ascended the stage and performed a talk show that was funny and absurd *[huaji tuti]*. When he talked, he sniffed the binders and shoes held in his hands and acted as if he were going to vomit. The audience laughed so hard that they could not sit up. It happened that several ladies with three-inch golden lotuses wandered into the hall. Deng ushered them on stage and, having lectured the masses *[qunzhong]* on the benefits of fang-zu, unwrapped the ladies' binders personally. The masses applauded like thunder. After his speech, the masses requested Mrs. Deng on stage so that they could examine if she had big feet. Mrs. Deng boldly went on stage and held up her two feet for all to scrutinize. The audience broke out in cheers that pierced the sky."[67] Deng's performance was evidently enjoyed by all. But it is less clear how the unwrapping of the ladies' binders and Mrs. Deng's self-exhibition were supposed to persuade more women to unbind their feet. Some among the masses had probably thought that they were watching a show at the temple fair.

By the 1930s, there prevailed a sense of exhaustion as the anti-footbinding campaign went from a spontaneous missionary movement to a local reformist effort to a routine national bureaucratic operation. The strategy of exposing female suffering and shame had also come full-circle, as exposure now brought ridicule and laughter directed at the male bureaucrat. It was said that as county magistrates had to fulfill monthly quotas, many proceeded to purchase new fabric on the market to entice women to give up their used and putrid ones.[68] What began as an effort to end footbinding ended up refurbishing the one material implement that had come to symbolize the custom in the 1930s. What would the women do with an endless supply of fresh, clean binding cloth, gratis from the county magistrate? Could the anti-binding movement have actually prolonged and facilitated the binding of feet?

One of the stories that encapsulates this curious reversal and shiftiness of meanings during the last stage of the fangzu movement concerns an over-seas-born young man known as Overseas-Chinese-Lotus-Lover (Ailian Qiaosheng). As recounted in a 1938 anthology, the story tells of how he was so enamored by the bound foot that he sailed to China to locate a dream wife. Yet the pickings were slim in an age when footbinding had lost its prestige. Young women with bound feet were scarce, and the handful who resisted the tide were so traditional that they refused to be looked at. He could not even locate photographs of their lovely slippers. In a last-ditch effort, he enlisted as a foot inspector for the fangzu movement in an unnamed province, keeping a secret roster of all the beauties with chanzu. He then revisited the eligible candidates, ostensibly to ascertain if they had started to unbind, and inspected the smoothness of the skin on their bare feet. Thus he secured his bride. When others criticized him for contradiction between words and deeds and confusing the public with private interests, he retorted: "I'm only liberating her!" He made a model of her foot and special-ordered a pair of shoes, with the moniker "liberation." Both the structure and the shape were old-fashioned arch shoes, but the vamp was made of golden kidskin with cut-off relief; the inside was lined with red felt. He asked his bride to unwrap her binding cloth and slip them on her bare skin.[69]

This curious story of a foot fetishist derives its comical appeal from excesses and instabilities. Not only do deeds stand words on their head, the words also double up on themselves. To the overseas Chinese man, "liberating" the woman means saving her from the fangzu regime (which claims to liberate her), only to deliver her to the bondage of his golden kid arched slippers. Less than a century after the deprecating eyes of the Euro-Americans stared the Chinese scholar out of his complacency, the reading public in the 1930s treaty ports had turned the West into an imaginary place: home of the last lotus lover who would put Gu Hongming to shame. The paradox of a connoisseur of chanzu camouflaged as a fangzu inspector bespeaks a fracture between the outside and the inside, or between appearance and the real. The next chapter argues that in this very fracture and instability of meaning lies the end of footbinding's history.

The anti-footbinding movement, with its rhetoric of tianzu and practice of organized fangzu, enjoyed considerable success in achieving its stated enlightenment goals. In circulating new images of and knowledge about footbinding, it helped extinguish the appeal of a custom whose mystique had already suffered from its diffusion throughout all social classes. The premises of modern Chinese nationalism and feminism—the inevitability of progress and the autonomy of individual agents—were crystallized in the intellectual and social efforts to end footbinding during the last decades of the Qing dynasty. In the Republican period and especially in the 1920s, the fangzu campaigns were among the first organized reform efforts that spread an enlightenment episteme to the countryside and in such interior provinces as Shanxi.

Previous scholarship has uniformly celebrated the anti-footbinding movement as a milestone in the liberation of Chinese women, but my conclusions are somewhat less sanguine.[70] My first reservation concerns the inherent difficulty in defining and tabulating the success of the letting-feet-out movement. The rhetoric of tianzu and its attendant narratives of miraculous conversion connote moral and ontological certainty. Behind the artificial precision of statistical figures, however, there are in fact no objective, universal criteria that measure fangzu as a successful, permanent state. On the aggregate level that confounded the bureaucrat, did success mean a certain percentage of girls unwrapping the binding cloth the day the foot inspector came by? Or did it mean older women had stopped binding tightly over an extended period of time? The ambiguity was more pronounced if the matter is considered on an individual level. What if a woman loosened her binding cloths for months and then tightened them again because of discomfort or a change of mind? Do four folded digits but a flatter arch mean chanzu or fangzu?

More than merely semantic problems, these ambiguities reveal the power inequalities that plagued the anti-footbinding movement from the start. Tianzu and fangzu are "gigantic" categories formulated from a vantage point outside the concerns and rhythms of the women's embodied lives. Tianzu, defined as an original state they had already lost, condemns them to reliance on a miracle whereas fangzu places them in the position of the acted-upon. No wonder that the women with bound feet—young or old—did not think in such terms. After the movement had raged and tapered off, they continued to purchase or make Kun-shoes with flattened soles, decorated in traditional floral motifs but in fashionable hues of bright pink, magenta, and lapis blue that only imported chemical dyes could produce.

The most glaring deficiency of the anti-footbinding movement is the misogynist attitude expressed toward women with bound feet. Whereas the leading male thinkers called them parasites and femmes fatales harmful to the nation, the campaigns either infantilized or humiliated them by exposing their bodies to ridicule or inspection in public. The humiliation did not stem from abuses or imperfect execution, but was embedded in the culture of national shame that produced the urgency to unbind feet in the first place. Furthermore, the tactic of the campaigns is inherently paradoxical: the spectacle of female suffering, which provoked people to change their thinking and behavior, accentuated the association of femaleness with passivity and victimhood. Narratives of female suffering conferred power onto those who publicized them, be they male nationalist reformers or urban educated women, who occupied a male subject position. One woman's pride and freedom was predicated on another woman's shame and bondage.

3

THE BOUND FOOT AS ANTIQUE:

Connoisseurship in an Age of Disavowal, 1930s–1941

From hindsight, the most significant achievement of the anti-footbinding movement lies in the new visual and textual knowledge about feet that it created and circulated. The luxury of hindsight, which makes a complete history of footbinding possible, is afforded by an encyclopedic compilation, *Picking Radishes (Caifeilu)*, which contains all that there is to know about binding feet. The project was the labor of love of Yao Lingxi (1899–ca. 1961), a man of letters from Dantu, Jiangsu province, who wound up in the British Settlement of the northern treaty port of Tianjin after a string of minor bureaucratic posts.[1] First serialized in 1933–34 in *Heavenly Wind (Tianfeng bao)*, a tabloid published in Tianjin, these columns on feet include citations from earlier works and new submissions by Yao, his friends, and readers.

The writings were later anthologized in five volumes and issued under the editorship of Yao between 1934 and 1941. A sixth volume, a selection of the choicest entries from the earlier books, also appeared in 1941.[2] The more popular of these stories thus traversed multiple loops: from whatever the source to tabloid; from tabloid to book; from book to "the best of . . ."; from printed word to hearsay; and back to the printed word. The result of this roundabout quotation is a monument of redundancy, more than a million words that spread across some two thousand pages. If the project had not been interrupted by war, it might well have ended from sheer exhaustion. There is nothing more to be said and known about footbinding.

Whereas the tone of the entries ranges from scholarly, scientific, autobiographical, or erotic to comical, the nature of *Picking Radishes* is pornographic: men exposing women's bodies for male pleasure and commercial gain. Yao Lingxi was unabashed about his profit-making motives, and, as we will see, equally unabashed was the sexual explicitness of some of the accounts. Yet the gesture of this pornography is serious, as is its purpose of exhaustive documentation and comprehensive knowledge. This exhaustion provided closure, allowing these disparate fragments to constitute a complete field of knowledge.

YAO LINGXI AND HIS FRIENDS:
COLLECTORS OF THE RECENTLY DATED

Picking Radishes is a gold mine. Every scholar who has read it—Howard Levy is a prime example—has cited individual entries from it as documentation of certain aspects of the historical truth about footbinding, be it regional distribution, gradual decline, or female experience. But a text with pretensions of total representation cannot be read so randomly. The truth or message carried by *Picking Radishes* is embedded in its very encyclopedic and serial form, which took shape as a result of textual imitation, recycling, and invention.[3]

In its serialized origins, fragmentary form, and open appeal for manuscript submissions toward future sequels, *Picking Radishes* resembles a traditional collectanea or encyclopedia. The social locations of the editors and contributors, their nostalgic backward-glancing posture, and the nature of the knowledge produced, however, are meaningful only in the thoroughly modern context of treaty port urban culture. The world of *Picking Radishes* is thus rife with contradictions, although that did not seem to bother Yao and his friends.

They were, however, extremely defensive about the object of their desire. It was, to say the least, embarrassing to be a connoisseur of the bound foot and its paraphernalia in an age of disavowal. Over three decades after the proliferation of anti-footbinding societies in the 1890s, by the 1930s condemnation of footbinding had become the norm among the educated sector in the coastal cities. Yao Lingxi and his colleagues were all too aware of the absurdity of their obsession and the impossibility of self-defense. They tried anyway.

The punch line was delivered by Tao Baopi, a scholar and fiction writer who was said to have been shocked to death in 1927 when the Communists occupied his hometown of Changsha, Hunan province, and ordered the liberation of feet. Tao, an unrepentant lotus lover, left behind these memorable lines: "The bound foot is an antique. We won't think of making a piece of antique to order, but what's wrong with admiring what is already here?" (CFL: 356). In denying that appreciation leads to promotion, Tao underscored the finality with which the cultural prestige of footbinding had expired.[4] One of Tao's admirers, Zhou Ying, explained: "People ridiculed us for wanting to promote footbinding. But even if we had wanted to, we wouldn't have been able to. . . . No woman is so stupid that she would suffer pain for something that is no longer à la mode *[modeng]*. In due time, the extinction of footbinding will come as a natural trend of history" (CFL: 355; CFL II: 289).

Zhou Ying, a resident of Shanghai who became Yao Lingxi's associate editor, claimed to be a modern observer of the progressive march of history who recognized the futility of turning back the tide.[5] There is no reason to doubt his sincerity. In the 1930s, readers in the treaty ports firmly associated footbinding with backwardness and regarded it with disdain. Zhou's and Tao Baopi's gesture of disavowing footbinding was echoed by Yao Lingxi in his choice of the anthologies' title. "Picking radishes" (*caifei*) is a clever play on words that allows at least two readings, both hinging on an unflattering assessment of bound feet. A song from the classic *Book of Songs* provided the allusion:

> *Caifeng caifei (picking—wild greens—picking—radishes),*
> *Wuyi xiati (not—to—lower—body).*

The conventional reading can be translated as: "Do not discard the leaves just because the roots ('lower body') are bitter or defective." In other words, even an unworthy body has partial virtues. Yao thus offered this interpretation: although admittedly footbinding is a defect, we should not discredit the female body, nor should we shun the subject matter (CFL II: iii–iv). Could Yao be sending a more provocative message at the same time? The second line can also be read: "Do not disdain the female private parts." The "lower body" is euphemism for genitals.[6]

The connoisseurs depicted footbinding as a remnant—not a phantom but a concrete presence—caught in the process of vanishing. An expression, so vivid in conveying the pathos of living in transitional time, recurred in *Radishes:* "[In the split second it takes to] turn your body, it has become a relic" (*fuyang zhijian, yicheng chenji*), and "The future will look upon us as we now look upon the past" (CFL IV: 161; CFL II: 370). Their alleged intention was not to revive a dying practice or to arrest the tide of history, but merely to capture the fleeting traces in words and pictures for posterity. Moreover, the lotus lovers suggested that these traces should be seen through a historicist lens; the customs of each epoch should be judged in the context of prevailing values at the time.

Even more insistent was the connoisseurs' pose as ethnographers, using the language of the ethnography *(minsu xue)* movement popular in the 1930s. "Yao Lingxi wants to do a history of customs *[fengsu shi]* while we still can, before the tiny-footed women become extinct," quipped a friend. "If you say *Picking Radishes* promotes footbinding, do you also suppose that those who study ancient history want to be emperors, or that vendors of chamber pots love to drink urine?" (CFL: 7). Emperors had vanished; the bound foot was dated and disappearing. As relics from the imperial past, they were coupled as objects of nostalgic longing. Chamber pots? That was a non sequitur.

THE PRODUCTION OF NEW ETHNOGRAPHIC KNOWLEDGE

In the name of preserving customs, the *Radishes* editorial team appealed for submission of memoirs, interviews, surveys, photographs, drawings, and stowed-away shoes from readers throughout the country. The knowledge they sought was empirical and their preferred inscription machine was the camera. Yao and Zhou repeatedly admonished their readers to take clear photographs, send postcards, and, when all else failed, make drawings (CFL IV: 200). One reader considered this impulse a Western trait: "I have read monographs written by Westerners on Chinese customs. They always attach the *true image* of our women's slender toes in the form of *bare-all [chi luoluo]* camera shots or diagrams. They show frontal and side views; they pry open the bent toes and heels to take pictures. The reader has a complete glimpse" (CFL: 354–55; emphasis mine). Photographs or diagrams were taken to be more thorough methods of inscription than words because, like the X-ray machines, they revealed the inner truth in a more realistic manner.

Not only are all the visual angles covered, but also the full temporal sequence is revealed: "Some shots are taken when the binders are being tightened; some are taken after binding is completed and the shoes are being slipped on; some when the anklet and embroidered shoes are in place. There are even photographs of an array of binders and shoes, all classified and categorized. . . . Westerners are high on curiosity [that we Chinese should not imitate], but we cannot be second to their venturesome spirit of scrutinizing every matter and every object" (CFL: 354–55). What distinguished the Westerners, then, was not their imaging machines but their inquisitive spirit and all-seeing eyes.

Heeding this call, Yao opened *The Best of Picking Radishes* (*Caifei jinghualu*, 1941) with forty new photographs (presumably taken by Chinese). Some are composite studies showing variations of regional or period styles in the soles, heels, and shape of shoes. But the majority of connoisseurs seemed ill at ease with the scientific discourse that had won intellectual high ground by the late 1920s.[7] Some "scientific" treatises on, for example, the aesthetics of feet or the physics of lilt smack of mimicry if not parody (CFL IV: 54–63; CFL II: 103). Clearly the reader did not have to adore science to find the photograph of a tiny-footed courtesan pleasurable.

A handful of connoisseurs appeared to be practitioners of positivist scientism. Hu Yanxian, a frequent contributor and supplier of the composite photographic studies, showed an impressive propensity for measuring and tabulating with frightening accuracy. A native of Beijing, he documented the twenty steps involved in the making of Banner shoes fashioned by the Manchus and Chinese martial (Hanjun) women, who did not bind their feet, as well as their sartorial rituals (CFL: 206–9; 229–30). Unveiled in even more minute detail are the lengths of each part of the foot (unbound and bound compared), presented in a table with thirty-two columns and five rows; the anatomy of fourteen parts of a shoe, described with a drawing, legend, and notes (see fig. 6); the six stages of evolution of the shape of soles in the recent century, explained with two sets of drawings, one sectional and the other aerial (see fig. 5); and designs and patterns of socks (see fig. 8; CFL: 221–29). If Hu Yanxian had meant the excessive documentation to be a satire of positivism, his strategy misfired. His measurements are so exacting that his sincerity seems overwhelming.

It is evident by now that even as these lotus lovers claimed to be mere recorders of a vanishing custom, they were generating new knowledge on the pages of *Picking Radishes*. The bound foot had never been photographed and measured in such detail before the age of its vanishing. Scientific realism supplanted literary imagination as the entree to footbinding's truth. Not only the epistemology of these connoisseurs but also their inscription machines and medium were modern. With or without visual aids, the printed word seemed a lot more contagious, a lot more likely to get entangled with life, when it circulated on the pages of tabloids and mass-produced books in an age of modern transportation.

In a transitional age when personal knowledge of footbinding was increasingly scant, the anthologies became practical textbooks and guidebooks. Several years into the serialization, readers began to submit impressions of their travels to cities or districts described in *Picking Radishes,* some carrying a copy of the book like a *Lonely Planet* tour guide. One reader professed to have learned everything he knew about bound feet from Yao Lingxi's columns. He later traveled to Tianjin, Yao's hometown, surveyed the brothel district and reported the sightings of two footbound prostitutes. He wrote to Yao at the tabloid; Yao visited the two shortly, composed poems to commemorate the encounter, and published the entire sequence of texts in a later anthology (CFL IV: 313–16).[8]

To facilitate text-to-life-to-text encounters, Yao launched a "Lotus-Seeking Club" in 1938 and drafted a covenant. All who read *Picking Radishes* and had their interest piqued, especially those skilled in drawing, photography, and sculpture (note the emphasis on the visual), were welcomed to join. If they discovered writings about feet or were inspired to craft their own (classical Chinese please), Yao would consider publishing them. Viewpoints, research, or reports of "contacts with lotus feet" were of value. Yao was also interested in any article of clothing that covered the tiny foot, in material form or in photograph. He would pay cash for the use of the objects or negotiate a price for purchase. Photographs would be shared with other members willing to bear the expenses of reproduction. Good photos of both the arched *and* never-bound foot were also welcomed. Attached were detailed instructions for submission as well as the addresses of Yao Lingxi in Tianjin and Zhou Ying in Shanghai. The two were to circulate mimeographed address updates of new members every month (CFL IV: 201–3).

Club members were also encouraged to collect other kinds of information: If you find a footbound woman willing to unwrap her binding cloths, introduce her to us. If you know a tiny-footed prostitute, send her name, rank in brothel, age, native place, name of troupe, and address to the club "to facilitate investigation" (CFL IV: 202). It is self-evident that the unspecified gender of Yao's and Zhou's intended readers is male. We do not know how many joined, but the covenant is an apt summary of the editorial preferences that produced the *Picking Radishes* anthologies.[9]

With this fan club trading in information and objects, it became difficult to sustain Yao's earlier disclaimer that appreciation of footbinding can be divorced from its promotion. He might not have succeeded in enticing modern girls to take up binding, but in keeping the knowledge alive and information current, he promoted the connoisseurship of feet.[10] This connoisseurship, even as it speaks the modern language of investigative science and ethnography, is deeply nostalgic by nature and in rhetoric. Yao Lingxi's identification lies not with the forward-looking modernizers but with the vanished literati. It is no accident that he announced the launching of the Lotus-Seeking Club in the form of a covenant *(sheyue)*, a genre popular in the late-Ming when gatherings of moon-gazing poets or romantic politicians abounded.

Such connoisseurs as Yao Lingxi, Tao Baopi, Zhou Ying, and Hu Yanxian were schooled enough in the old world of the literati to pull off a studied imitation. Yao Lingxi is acclaimed today not as a tabloid writer but as a credible authority on the Ming novel *Plum in the Golden Vase* (also known as *Golden Lotus*). There is no mistake, however, about their location as cultural producers in a new world of heightened circulation of news and information. Hence Tao, the unrepentant lotus lover, styled himself Baopi, "addicted to newspapers." Surely they were "transitional figures," but the overused label does not do these people justice. What distinguishes the connoisseurs from such transitional writers as Tang Yisuo and Xu Ke decades earlier is the former's posture: they want to seize the present moment by looking back, not forward. Their goal is not to resuscitate the past but merely to savor whatever is left of it.

Indeed, their lack of self-consciousness and agony set them apart from serious intellectuals in early twentieth-century China. They embraced such opposites as appreciation and disapproval of the bound foot or scientific measurements and literary imageries without a trace of incongruity but with barrels of laughter. Their world has no paradoxes, only fragmentary knowledge and body parts that generate infinite amusement. They shouldered no "gate of darkness," only gaieties. Nor did they suffer crises of identity, only hangovers and a lack of sleep. On the surface, these purveyors of knowledge about women's feet appear to be the happiest and most well-adjusted writers in modern China.

The connoisseurs' playfulness should not be mistaken for a lack of purpose. Playing *(youxi)* was a prevalent way of life and mode of writing for a distinct group of male scholars after the abolishment of the civil service examination in 1905. The significance of this seminal event in the changing fortunes of Confucian culture *(wen)* cannot be overemphasized. The formal severance of political power from the written word and knowledge of the classics created a vacuum but also new possibilities, one of which was writing as and for entertainment. Playing or whiling leisure away *(xiaoxian)* became serious business.[11] Previous scholars have focused on the anxieties generated after the ground rules that had scripted imperial Chinese life were swept away. The productive purpose of reconstituting new rules through playing has gone unnoticed.

All the recognized major events of modern Chinese history are political: from the 1898 Reforms to the 1911 Revolution; from the May Fourth Patriotic Movement to the Northern Expedition. The private, the sentimental, and the sensual have been thoroughly erased. If we pause long enough from the public world inhabited by nationalistic reformers and revolutionaries, we may notice a striking unfamiliarity in the *tempo* and *rhythm* of the world of Yao Lingxi and his friends. It is a forgotten world of private male pleasures, of fragments that do not add up to overarching theories, of indulgences that matter little, and passions that do not save the nation or anybody. Male connoisseurs of the foot and its paraphernalia did not so much resist national history as ignore it. But in playing with feet they were also playing with time, and, in so doing, they carved out a space of repose outside the purposeful march of the nation.[12]

Two kinds of regression in time—of nostalgia—are involved in the connoisseurship of feet: reclamation of personal childhood, discussed below, and playful imitation of the literati, the paragon of male privilege that ceased to be reproduced after the end of the examination system. Worse still, after the fall of the dynasty in 1911, the literati became an appendage to a hollowed center: the emperor they were supposed to serve and the dynastic or-

der to which they pledged loyalty had ceased to exist. The ontological ambiguity of this leftover man is similar to that of the footbound woman, which
helps explain his identification with her. Both his and her presences were
concrete and visible; they were spotted in the marketplace and on the pages
of newspapers. But slowly the individual bodies expired, one by one, bringing an entire institution to a close. Meanwhile, their phantom bodies elicited
laughter, ridicule, and pity from the modernizers.

Even as they shared a disdain for grand narratives and a fascination with
body parts, the lotus lovers who appeared in *Picking Radishes* were not a
uniform group. Their generation can be measured by the distance between
them and the receding literati world. Tao Baopi, among the older generation, provided a crucial link between the world of "new fiction" in the late
nineteenth century and the world of treaty port pictorials in the 1930s. From
the literary careers of Tao and his contemporaries we can see how "small-
talk" *(xiaoshuo)* was the common denominator of disparate genres of traditional fiction, late-Qing fiction, and modern newspapers.[13]

Tao Baopi was at once an author and a critic of a new genre—fiction published in periodicals, often in serialized form—that inherited the cultural
prestige invested in the old genre of eight-legged examination essays. In his
short story "Excising Small Feet," Tao heralded the connoisseurship of
footbinding-as-antique which was later embraced by the Picking Radishes
group. Set in 1904, one year before the examination system was abolished,
the story was first published in 1907 in *Stories Every Month (Yueyue xiaoshuo)*,
a magazine specializing in original short stories and detective stories in translation. Written in a classical prose laden with bureaucratic jargon, Tao's story
tells of a certain sixty-something official-in-waiting *(xunjian)*, a pathetic
figure who purchased a degree which made him eligible for an appointment
but for years had failed to land a formal post. He had the look of the ailing
imperial China: "His bones are saturated with suffering; his face yellow and
emaciated. His strides are hesitant and his spirits decrepit. If you regard him
closely he has the look of an opium addict, or maybe he is suffering from
oversex."[14]

To ingratiate himself to his boss *(daoyuan)*, who complained of an empty
coffer depleted by the Boxer indemnities and the training of a modern army,
the old scholar racked his brain for a moneymaking venture. He stumbled
into the bedchamber and eyed his concubine, who was sitting by the bed-
side, head lowered and absorbed in something. "Is she worrying about

monthly expenses? Is she sewing diligently? No, no. She is tending to her tiny golden lotus like a silkworm bound by her own cocoon. She wants to ingratiate herself to the old goat and avail herself as his plaything" (179–80). Echoing the slogan of the anti-footbinding movement, that footbinding turns potentially productive citizens into men's sex objects, Tao did not show any sympathy for the lotus lover throughout the story.

His concubine's feet excited the official-in-waiting. He summoned two butlers to grind ink and drafted a memorial in proper format. He hit upon a perfect plan: "Everybody knows about the vice of footbinding. But being a custom that is handed down for generations, it cannot be eradicated all of a sudden. Why not excise the small feet so that the state can be richer and the women can gradually be free? . . . All females whose feet measure two-and-some inches have to pay a daily tax of fifty coppers [wen]. Knock off ten coppers if they measure an inch longer, and those at least six inches would be exempted."[15] The daoyuan, thinking it an excellent idea, forwarded the memorial to the regional inspectors.

The inspectors rejected the proposal as laughable, unenforceable, and dangerous. Who would go around taking measurements? What if the people, already weary of missionary encroachments, interpreted it as another assault on their way of life? The old scholar tried to garner support from his colleagues: "Excising small feet would change a bad custom and open up new opportunities. Both the country and the people will benefit. What's wrong with it?" One responded, "Are you looking for a job under the skirt? But first of all, are you willing to let out the lovely tiny feet of your concubine? If not, you will have to pay through your nose even if you manage to land the tax-collecting job to grease your pockets!" (183–85).[16]

The lotus lover, corrupt and spent, is a laughable figure. The object of his desire also appears dated and ridiculous, a relic from a decrepit world. Tao Baopi, a connoisseur of footbinding, did not promote its virtues in this story but merely sent the message: leave the women alone. As antique, footbinding is dated and will in due time pass away. The overreaching state and its greedy officials bear the brunt of his satire.[17]

When the dynastic order was breathing its last in the first decade of the twentieth century, it became transparent that the prestige of footbinding and the civil service examination were intrinsically linked. The premise of "Excising Small Feet" and Huang Xiuqiu, discussed in chapter 1, is that bound feet, like eight-legged essays, are remnants of an ossified order, su-

perfluous in their exquisite details. A profusion of form masked the empti-
ness inside, devoid of content and utility.[18] After the fall of the Qing dynasty, this identification of the two leftover objects became explicit. *Picking Radishes* reports banter popular at the time: What do the woman who
liked to bind her feet and a candidate who fussed with his examination essays have in common? They both wanted to show off (CFL II: 240). A couplet, supposedly crafted during the 1860 decade of restoration, thus described
the ultimate male privileges in the old imperium: "Watching a concubine
bind [or wash] her feet; / Being chosen as the Presented Scholar" (CFL II:
79, 311). So firm was the identification of word and foot that one relict of
the literati, Ye Dehui, was said to have loved to hold a tiny foot in his hand
while he read and wrote (CFL IV: 294).

    After the fall of the imperium, the scholar-official, who used to enjoy un-
matched public glory and private pleasures, had become an object of nostalgic longing or contempt, depending on one's political stance. In either
case, the lost art of footbinding and its literati admirers were conjoined as
symbols of male privilege. Hence despite Tao's ridicule of the official-in-
waiting, his own favorite pastime took the form of a literati gathering: a
group of drinking friends composing poems to a set theme (shoelaces, for
example) or to each other's rhyme (CFL: 100–118). Such gaming recalls the
world of Xu Ke and Tang Yisuo in Shanghai. As advocates of tianzu, Xu and
Tang may seem Tao's polar opposites at first glance. Yet curiously "Excising Small Feet" resonates with *Huang Xiuqiu* in language and intent, for
both use women's feet to tell an anti-bureaucratic reformist story. Moreover,
Tao and Tang displayed a similar familiarity with the vainglories of bureaucratic culture and the hollowness of official essays. These writers of *xiaoshuo* in fact hail from a similar cultural and textual world, one that was
mimetic of the traditional literati. This gesture of deliberate imitation
marked them as irreducibly modern.

THE CONFLATION OF *TIANZU* AND *CHANZU*

That Tang Yisuo and Tao Baopi could appear so similar is more than a function of their shared cultural milieu. It is also rooted in a dynamic of textual
citation and anthologizing itself. At the moment of its birth, the novel category *tianzu* was construed as the opposite of *chanzu*. Yet in the pamphlets
and treatises that the anti-footbinding movement produced, the simple

phrase had to be expanded into wordy polemics. In so doing, proponents of tianzu used legends and expressions from the pre-existing discourse of chanzu. They simply lifted verbatim, for example, the origins myths of Consort Pan, Consort Yang, or Yaoniang. As such, the discourse of tianzu often appears to be curiously identical to that of chanzu.

In his search for incipient practices of natural feet in Chinese history, Xu Ke recycled lengthy sections from old texts—philological treatises and connoisseurship literature—often without adding commentary of his own. If the polemical prefaces and afterword of "A Survey of Natural Feet" and "Words of Knowing Feet" are deleted, the reader would not be able to glean the compilation date or intention from the bulk of the main texts. The only exception is a section entitled "Modern Tianzu" in the former. In fact, appended to "A Survey" is a study of footbinding that is equal in length to the survey of natural feet.[19]

This curious conflation is also evident on the pages of *Picking Radishes,* where Xu's treatises were anthologized in a slightly abridged form (CFL: 43–52) right before the manifestos of the classic lotus lovers Li Yu and Fang Xuan. Not only did they appear under the same heading, "Evidential studies" ("Kaozheng"), they even drew from the same repertoire of legends and poetic allusions. Without the vocabulary developed for connoisseurship, much of it gathered by the evidential scholars in the previous centuries, tianzu would not have had a linguistic leg to stand on. Whether one claims to be for, against, or indifferent to footbinding, the knowledge that one transmits in writing—in the form of fragments of poems or anecdotes from the classics and histories—is in fact the same.[20]

There is no better illustration of this indeterminacy than the oeuvre of the poet Lotus Addict (Lianchi), a prolific author of poems in praise of natural feet *and* a profusion of elegies for bound feet and their assorted paraphernalia: shoes, bedslippers, soles, shoe patterns, heels, shoelaces, and others (CFL II: 73–91). In one breath he declared:

> *Stubbornly and obsessively I adore the lotus.*
> *Since infancy I have fixed my eyes on hems of skirts.*
> *In old age my addiction is now worse than ever,*
> *Without pausing I seek to reveal all mysteries of the lotus. (CFL II: 80)*

In another breath, he adopted a female voice in a classic anti-footbinding song that could have been featured on a tract:

Afraid of boarding a train, I think it is a tumbling tower.
Getting on and off an ocean liner brings even more peril.
Having traversed rivers and oceans to afar,
I now know that big-feet are better than golden hooks. (CFL II: 91)

Is he a lotus lover or a hater? The poems in themselves provide no definite answer. Lotus Addict, fully aware of this, was having fun playing with the inventive possibilities.

Don't say that Lotus Addict is fickle,
Now repudiating his old love for the lotus.

Are they sincere, these new lyrics of mine?
Writing a history of the lotus [lianshi],
I await a new era and chronicle [jiyuan]. *(CFL II: 90–91)*

Yao Lingxi remarked astutely that Lotus Addict was an innovator whose lyrics and posture are irreducibly modern. "Poems praising tianzu have no previous allusions to rely on *[qiangwu gushi]*. Hence unless they are accompanied by lyrics on chanzu, one would not know where to begin." Lotus Addict's set of six tianzu lyrics, of which the trains and ocean liner poem quoted above is one, shun all received footbinding allusions. Evoking a brave new world of high-rise buildings and globe trotting, the poet invented not only new expressions but also a new system of reference. Thus his lyrics comprise an original modern text (CFL II: 91–92; cf.73 and CFL III: 34–40).

The polemical message of an anti-footbinding song is embedded in its context, such as the venue of a Tianzu hui rally, and its tone of delivery. Taken out of context, anti-footbinding polemics may serve other purposes, or none at all. As we have already noted, the proliferation of anti-footbinding literature of the 1890s to 1920s made knowledge of binding feet more accessible and may have thus ironically prolonged its life as a social practice even as it helped diminish its cultural aura. Yet by the time all of these texts were incorporated into *Picking Radishes* in the 1930s, words seem to have lost their social moorings altogether. In this sense, the *Radishes* volumes constituted a disembodied textual universe, an empty vessel that served as a receptacle of conflicting desires and an incubator of new meanings. It is ironic then that an encyclopedia formed in no small part by recycling old texts and suffused with nostalgia turns out to be not only modern but also extremely inventive.[21]

THE INVENTION OF FANG XUAN

This paradox of invention from recycling is key to understanding the discourse of connoisseurship in *Picking Radishes.* Connoisseurship is a form of identification. Since the ninth century, with the invention of the category of "antique," connoisseurship has been associated with collecting.[22] Obsession for all kinds of objects reached new heights in the commercialized urban culture of the late Ming. Judith Zeitlin has analyzed the idealization of obsession (*pi)* itself in the sixteenth century and its association with the cult of genuine love *(qing).* True love for an object melts the distance between self and object, rendering connoisseurship what the late-Ming aesthete Yuan Hongdao called an act of "self loving the self." In its extreme, connoisseurship is a form of self-expression.[23] Modern lovers of feet, however, fashion playful, exaggerated, and contrived selves that are far cries from the connoisseurs of Yuan Hongdao.

Two types of bound-foot connoisseurs appeared in *Picking Radishes:* those who wrote and those who were written about by others. Fang Xuan was one of the two foremost representatives of the former (the other being Li Yu, to be discussed in chapter 5). Nothing is known about this author of five short treatises on footbinding but his profusion of sobriquets. Although he has been identified variously as a writer from the Qianlong, Kangxi, or "ancient" periods, Fang's earliest appearance was in 1914, when the treatises were anthologized in two collectanea that appeared in the same year.[24]

Fang Xuan was a master of playing games with words. All five of his treatises are exercises in imitating the literati in their preferred genres and brothel drinking games. One popular treatise is "Miscellaneous Sayings from Jinyuan" ("Jinyuan zazuan"), a collection of banters. One example: "Likeness: The small foot is like the silver dollar; everybody loves it. Big foot clad in a tiny platform shoe is like the squeaking of toads." Or, "No lasting harshness: A kind mother binding her dear daughter's feet."[25] Imitative of the genre *zazuan* initiated by the Tang poet Li Shangyin, these are games of association that embody no deep meanings, only the diction and wit of rhetoric. One imagines them to be drinking games or musings of bored travelers.

Another treatise, "Aesthetics of the Fragrant Lotus" ("Xianglian pinzao"), was cast as a *xiaopin*-essay, a popular genre among late-Ming literati. Modeled after the "Aesthetics of Plum Blossoms," a treatise on refined taste in everyday life, "Fragrant Lotus" features short lists such as "the nine ranks of fragrant lotus" or "four taboos of fragrant lotus." The presumed reader was the not-so-refined voyeur, who was supposed to derive pleasures from such recommendations as the "four unspeakable delights of binding and washing feet: secret espying from behind a screen; smelling their fragrance in the dark; watching their shadow on water; viewing their image in the mirror."[26]

The perspective of viewing and the angle of the gaze are crucial, as evinced by Fang's comments on the "three best sites for lotus sightings." "The slender spring arch only touches the floor; the narrow new moon descends not from the sky. In my travels I found three scenic spots where the moon traces and arch shadows can be espied from below by lifting one's head, and not confined to an aerial examination. The famous mountains and auspicious sites under heaven are full of gatherings of skirts, hence there must be other scenic spots [for such viewing]. In the years to come, as my waxed traveling clogs hit the trail, I will select other spots." The three sites are, coincidentally, "In front of the Three Mountains Gate, Tiger Hill, Suzhou; behind the temple of Wang Tianjun, Maoshan, Jintan; under the osmanthus tree in Pingshan Hall, Yangzhou."[27]

This is voyeurism at its worst; the woman is literally turned into a piece of art, an object scrutinized from all angles. Given its explicitness, "Aesthetics of the Fragrant Lotus" was quoted in virtually every subsequent work on footbinding as a document of the lure of the bound foot (CFL: 155ff). Many of the connoisseurs in *Picking Radishes* showed a taken-for-granted familiarity with his words (CFL: 4, 102; CFL II: 5, 17; 264, 267; CFL IV: 54; CFXB: 253). Yao Lingxi and Zhou Ying considered Fang Xuan and Li Yu connoisseurs par excellence, praising their skills in writing about the aesthetics of feet but stopping short of discussing sex in the open (CFL II: 284; CFL IV: 340). One contributor to *Radishes,* who called himself "A Faithful of Lotusism" (Lianjiao xinshi), wrote that his love for "Aesthetics of the Fragrant Lotus" was so deep that when he first came upon it twenty years ago he could not bear to let it out of his fingers (CFL II: 99–103).

Could not bear to let it out of his fingers? Was he serious or exaggerating? How literally should we take these voyeuristic connoisseurs who appear more and more like sexual perverts or morons? With readers and admirers like these, Fang Xuan's "Aesthetics"—forty fragments jotted in jest—attained canonical status as the manifesto of connoisseurship of footbinding in "traditional" China. How much weight can Fang's flimsy text and, for that matter, women's bound feet bear? The sheer absurdity of contrast between tone and purported meaning cautions us not to read Fang's treatises and other words of feet appreciation in *Radishes* too literally.

The truth is that Fang Xuan is a curious author, and his treatises are enigmatic by design. What the unsuspecting modern reader may not know is that "Aesthetics" is the only text of its kind in the history of Chinese literature. Everybody quotes it because it is singular in its obsessive details and explicit longing. Yao Lingxi made a perceptive comment: "Talking about the lotus began with Fang Lichang [Xuan]. But other than ranking and commenting, most of his are empty words" (CFL IV: iii). New words on feet in an old bottle of imitative genres, the treatises are literally an invention. Yao presented Fang as an "ancient" *(guren)* along with the seventeenth-century connoisseur Li Yu (CFL IV: 340), but I am not convinced. None of his works contain reliable internal references to the time and place of their production, nor can I find any textual traces or mentions of them before their first publication in 1914.[28]

If indeterminacy in time characterizes the texts produced by Fang Xuan, every known fact about the author is a gesture of imitation and offers multiple interpretive possibilities. The name Fang Xuan itself is imitative of a Song poet. Internal references suggest that he sojourned in Guangping, a common place name which could be in Zhili, Henan, Jiangsu, or Anhui. He gave the impression that he was a scholar-official who frequented courtesan parties, went sightseeing at scenic spots, and was conversant with literati genres associated with leisure. Above all, he established his authorial identity on his imitation of literati genres and their games. Was he one of them? In his afterword to "Miscellaneous Sayings from Jinyuan," he feigned fear of revenge by an army of women who, angry for his teasing the lotus, would kick and knock his writing brush *(guancheng)* out of his hand: "I finished writing and broke down in laughter."[29] Perhaps Fang Xuan—whoever he was— was also laughing at the readers who took him too seriously or literally.

Almost every scholar who studies footbinding has quoted Fang Xuan as evidence of foot fetish in China. Until we know more about the date and circumstances of the production of these treatises, however, we should not take his words in such a straightforward manner. Fang's import lies in that he figured as "the original" literati connoisseur for others to imitate. Writ-

ing commentaries or sequels is a prevalent way of paying tribute by imitation. A Faithful of Lotus-ism who could not bear to let "Aesthetics" leave
his hands lamented that Fang's coverage was confined to feet from China
proper (Zhongyuan) and proceeded to supplement it with his knowledge
of Guangdong. Quotation and anthologizing constitute another means of
textual imitation, and Fang's originality was evinced by the frequency with
which he was being cited in entirety or fragments.[30] Identification with an
"ancient" connoisseur led to the production of more texts. The result is the
insufferable wordiness of the connoisseurship literature.

For all its superficial fascination with voyeurism, the literature of connoisseurship crafted by Fang Xuan and the Radishes crowd is not interested
in looking at the female body, which got lost in a mountain of superfluous
words. The voyeurs were less seduced by the bound foot than by the word
as a vehicle of representation. The connoisseur who writes is obsessed with
his own verbosity. Once again, connoisseurship is the ultimate expression
of self loving the self.

SECONDHAND SEX:
THE CONNOISSEUR AS BOY, IMPOSTOR, AND COLLECTOR

To be more precise, the Radishes connoisseurs' obsession is a form of self-
as-modern-men-of-letters loving the self-as-traditional-literati. By definition
it is backward-looking and nostalgic. In its excessive sentimentalism, this
obsession exhausts and exceeds the aesthete's *xiaopin*-essay genre and requires
new modes of narration. Hence the most emotionally and sexually explicit
passages in *Picking Radishes* are also the most innovative and modern. There
is no textual precedent for such revealing psychological descriptions of the
eroticism of foot.[31] The same is true for narratives of pain from within the
women's bodies.

A small number of lotus lovers wrote about their direct erotic contacts
with the bound foot. These accounts are always framed by deliberate distancing between the time-space of the encounter and that of storytelling:
couching the story as childhood memory, shrouding the encounter in a haze
of smoke and intoxicating liquor (CFL II: 136), or presenting the sexual
memoir as a posthumous work (CFL IV: 305). Therein lies the boundary
between decent and indecent exposure in a 1930s treaty port tabloid. In particular, the most frequently used distancing device is the all-seeing eye of

the boy. The innocence of prepubescence allows the voyeur to gain entrance into the female quarters, play all he wants with an adult woman with bound feet, and narrate the sensuous excitement of kissing the foot or sniffing the toe without social or moral sanction (CFL IV: 305–6; cf. CFL: 293).[32]

Ironically, when erotic games with feet are presented as those of the prepubescent boy, they of course appear as indulgences of the presexual stage. The sexuality of the male is thus denied. This bifurcation of eroticism and sex finds a forceful statement in one of the most blatantly sensuous stories about the sex of footbinding, when the narrator solemnly declares that playing with a foot is qualitatively different from sexual intercourse (CFL IV: 211–25). The story details an eighteen-month affair between a twenty-something maid and her master half her age, Yu Aitong (Same love as mine). It was authored secondhand by one Jinling Aitesheng (The scholar from Nanjing who loves peculiar things), who claimed to be Yu's friend. Yet the entire thirteen-page narrative is put in the first person: a long quotation without quotation marks.

The maid Plum Girl (Mei'er) and her master devised many games in their mutual seduction. She once retrieved a tiny paper bag of minced water chestnut (*lingjiao,* one of the metaphors for the bound foot because of its triangular arched shape) from the crevice at the bottom of her foot—the erotogenic zone—and fed it to him. His fondling her foot could "make her brook flow" and he would ejaculate as she collapsed into his arms (CFL IV: 218). Yet Plum Girl is the first to articulate the difference between these games and sexual intercourse. The master asked: "When you let me fondle you, are you suffering or are you happy?" Plum Girl answered: "Who would let others fondle her at will? Especially the body of a woman is inviolable, but things are different when the fondler is someone you love. . . . But there is a difference in feelings of pleasure *[kuaigan]:* the arousal of sexual desire *[qingyu]* brings happiness that lasts only that one tensed moment; afterward one feels all the more tired and lethargic."

If intercourse exhausts, loving tenderness restores. "But after a hard day's work, when I get a good caressing and kneading from you, my body would be soothed all over and my spirits rekindled. Moreover, your thousand kinds of tenderness and ten thousand ways of cherishing me make my joy overflow" (CFL IV: 222). Later, he added that she refused to have intercourse because she was afraid of getting pregnant (CFL IV: 223).[33] This seemingly straightforward statement of female desire, however, is not what it seems, because it is told by a man, and in quotation for that matter. No matter how realistic and believable Plum Girl may sound, she is more a provocateur of male desire than an informant on female desire.

Sexually explicit narratives like this are rare in *Radishes*. This is in part due to the fact that footbinding was dead in the 1930s treaty ports—hence the amazing confessions of many connoisseurs that they have, in fact, never laid eyes on a bound foot, let alone fondled one. They are impostors. One may dismiss such disclaimers as those of perverted men letting themselves off the hook, but I choose to believe them, for it explains the curious insistence on authenticity in their narratives and their empiricist tone. Without much personal experience to rely on, they had to smother the reader with emotions or to narrate in exquisite detail their sexual encounters in order to make their accounts believable.

Zhou Ying, Yao Lingxi's associate editor, confessed that "since childhood I have worshipped the tiny foot," a lifelong love kindled by reading a novel about a connoisseur, Hu Xueyan (CFL IV: 144, 157–58). The problem for "crazed foot-worshippers like us is that although we are devoted, we have scant opportunities to play with the lotus. We speak [about footbinding] as if flowers are falling from the sky; in fact, we are doing no better than going to bed hugging a stiff board." The fact that modern connoisseurs are impostors means that they are first and foremost collectors. "Since we cannot find any real targets, we turn to collecting materials about feet. This is like painting a loaf of bread when you are hungry" (CFL II: 288–89).

Words, images, and things are traces of a lost world and disappearing bodies. "What we collect is, first of all, words about the lotus. All fellow connoisseurs have a large miscellaneous collection of these, regardless of whether they are words praising or trashing the lotus. For words trashing the lotus often reflect its beauty. Secondly, we collect photographs of beautiful women's lotus feet. Those of naked feet are the hardest to come by, hence the most prized. Lastly, we collect embroidered shoes, all of which are tiny and exquisite. Bedslippers are particularly priceless. When I ask my lotus-loving friends, all have this obsession with collecting, and even our modes of collecting are similar" (CFL II: 288–89). Such words as "worshipped," "devotion," and "crazed" that Yao and Zhou used sound hollow. No amount of excessive earnestness can disguise the fact that connoisseurship in an age of disavowal is an empty exercise. From reading a novel to collecting words to writing *Picking Radishes,* the only context that can be generated from the production and consumption of texts is more texts, not social experience.

The exaggerated emotions of the connoisseurs were nonetheless heart-felt. Yao Lingxi evoked the transcendental power of love, borrowing the language of both the late-Ming cult of sincere love *(qing)* and the garden of purity in *Dream of Red Chamber* to describe the emotions of connoisseurship: "When human emotions are moved, they would have to be lodged. When the lodged emotions are steadfast, they become an obsession. If your emotions are not lodged, you would feel numb and your heart unanchored, oblivious to the pleasures of living. Not only have I lodged my emotions in this [footbinding], so have many in this world. Why do we lodge our emotions in this? Because it cannot be had. Our longing turns into a disease, to relieve it we have to speak up. Since our obsession is deep, our words are unstoppable." Unlike the late-Ming supreme love, which embodies the power of realization by transcending life and death, this latter-day desire is unrequited as a foregone conclusion.

In the unattainability of the bound foot—its distance and alterity—lies its attraction. Yao continued, "Born after the faltering of the lotus age, we can no longer see the beauty of the lotus hook." This distance accentuates the contrast of an imagined bygone age with the violence that tore China apart in the early decades of the twentieth century. "As we live through this *kalpa* [age] of titanic demons *[Asura]*, we cannot escape the calamities of warfare. . . . Only in the world of the golden lotus can we rest our hearts and lodge our spirits. . . . The beauty of imagination is more enchanting than the excitement of seeing with your eyes or fondling with your hands. I delight in my own delights and seek momentary comfort from them" (CFL IV: iv-v).

INTERVIEWS WITH GRANNY:
FEMALE DESIRES TOLD SECONDHAND

The location of footbinding in the past and the posture of the connoisseurs as impostor created problems for them as narrators of the sex of footbinding: they could not present themselves as a participant in the act. In an age of disavowal, the male experience of footbinding-as-sex can be written about only as nostalgia. A Faithful of Lotus-ism, the admirer of Fang Xuan mentioned above, used two strategies to narrate explicit sexual behavior, albeit not the psychology of sex: childhood memories (and childhood memories of his wife's) and interviews with old connoisseurs.[34]

Similar to Zhou Ying and Yao Lingxi, Faithful described himself as a vicarious connoisseur, born two decades too late to have personal experience of the fragrant lotus. The closest he came was as a boy, when he sniffed the stolen shoes of his cousins in bed. He compared it to gazing at a plum tree to quell a thirst (CFL II: 118). His wife, who started binding at five but let her feet out at eight or nine, recounted fondling her sisters' feet to feel their bones. Faithful also wrote of how she beseeched her young cousin to reverse current fashion and begin binding so as "to quench my [Faithful's] desires," but the girl refused (CFL II: 124–25).

Faithful's interviews with old connoisseurs were presented in two halves; the first consisted of his conversations with a "leftover elder" *(yilao)* or "elder" *(zhanglao),* and the second began abruptly with the connubial delights of a certain "Granny" (*lao,* elder, with radical *nü,* female). The gender of the elder who appeared in the first half was ambiguous: "she" was twice called a "hair-pinned elder" (*jinguo yilao)* who treasured her own arched feet. Her steadfastness was likened to the integrity of a loyalist minister from a vanquished dynasty. Faithful used her to convey a sense of authentic transmission of knowledge, likening her to a white-haired palace-woman from the Tang emperor Xuanzong's court, who recounted intrigues of court life before the An Lushan rebellion shattered the empire and sent the emperor and his entourage into exile (CFL II: 120). Witnesses of the fall, the aging palace-women were the sole custodians of authentic memory of past grandeur. No wonder that the literati impostors likened themselves to them (CFL II: 130; CFL IV: 158).

But at times the elder (as *yilao,* no longer *jinguo yilao*) spoke as a "he." He quoted an ancient's elegy of bedslippers and adopted a monkish voice in condemning forced binding by artificially softening the bones. "He" who discussed the difference between bony and fleshy feet fashioned an all-knowing male voice. But "he" shifted again to a "she" when recounting the training of a maid whose natural endowment in terms of an even distribution of bone and flesh ranked among the top two from hundreds and thousands. The elder taught the girl the art of wrapping, shaping, applying tonic, and burning incense. Graduating to be a "senior disciple," the maid did not take up with any of her numerous suitors until one day her prince arrived with over one hundred pairs of specially ordered embroidered shoes representative of Suzhou, Yangzhou, Fujian, and Guangdong styles. The elder, impressed by his sincerity, sent her blessings by hand-stitching a pair of bed-slippers which fit the maid's "flesh hook" like a glove. They had an orgy for three days and night, "no water nor gruel could sip through." Disheveled, the maid said that she would die without regret (CFL II: 120–21).

If this reads like a martial arts novel, perhaps it was meant to. The selection of a prized disciple, secret recipes, the mother of all weapons, and a finale of combat that would end all combats are familiar tropes, not of the traditional erotic novel, but of the late-Qing martial arts adventures. The sexual encounter, a journey of male desire, appears comical when narrated by a female. Yet only females were privy to the secret knowledge and rituals of wrapping and unwrapping the binding cloth. Hence the gender of the leftover elder's voice was constantly shifting during the interview with Faithful.

The explicit narration of female desires in the second half of Faithful's interviews was assigned to "Granny." Granny, whose husband was an official, once traveled with him to Xianyou, Fujian, famous for its footbound beauties. During her search for prospects to introduce to her husband, she came across several amorous females. "One was a teenage concubine of a prominent family who disdained sexual intercourse, preferring to fondle the penis. She would unwrap her binders when she was aroused and rub her feet around the penis." She delighted in seeing the man making a mess. Another was an ex-courtesan who changed partners every month. "Most curious is a woman who liked to grab her friend's tiny toe in lieu of a dildo. She would not be happy without going through seven or eight [unclear if toes or friends] in a night" (CFL II: 124).

This rare description of a homoerotic tryst between two or more women sounds more credible when told by a woman, Granny. But as one of the three stories of the oversexed and menacing female, it fits the stereotype of the femme fatale authored and consumed by men in erotic novels.[35] Was the bound foot an enticement for female-to-female desires? We cannot be sure. The sexual encounters recorded by Faithful through a nostalgic interview are interesting in his ability to narrate both male and female desires through a shifty, gender-ambiguous voice. This device allows him to broach the subject of female desire from a female perspective but, ultimately, not very convincingly. In spite of, or perhaps because of, the real-life details that

Faithful included, for example the death of Granny in the previous year and his changing her shoes in the coffin, the narrative reads like fiction. Faithful's concoction of his lotus-loving wife, who tried to persuade her young cousin to take up binding and indulged Faithful by planning a trip to Datong, the mecca of footbinding (CFL II: 125), rings false in an age of disavowal. She seems Faithful's female alter ego or, in other words, a figment of his imagination.

The desires of Granny, Faithful's wife, the Xianyou women, and the Plum Girl, as explicit as they may seem, are desires reflected through the eyes of the male connoisseur-impostor. The impostor is the voyeur and also the male ventriloquist. Other occasional narratives of female autoerotic desires in *Picking Radishes* share the same shifty quality of Faithful's retelling of Granny's tales. Not only do they occupy an ambiguous space between the made-up and the real, they also fashion confused narrative voices and points of view. In an extreme example, a neighboring woman's love of her own small feet was completely embedded in, and narrated by, the boy voyeur's curious gaze through a rear window (CFL: 282). Simply put, these secondhand voices cannot be trusted. They bespeak how the bound foot as an object of modern male fantasy was an expression of male nostalgic desires, but tell us little about female views in this matter.

THE SOCIAL LIFE OF SHOES:
YANG TIEYA AND HU XUEYAN

If Fang Xuan, the writing connoisseur, inspired imitative writings that outpaced his own in sexual explicitness, connoisseurs whose deeds were being written about are a different matter. The mimetic connoisseurship they inspired took the form of the invention of gadgets, new and better objects to play with. It is thus no accident that both Hu Xueyan and Yang Tieya, connoisseurs distinguished by their deeds, were associated with the myriad uses and fantastic life of shoes.

Hu Xueyan was a modern connoisseur in that he was not a scholar but a merchant. A Hangzhou banker and philanthropist, he made his fortune by financing the indemnities and military expenditures of the Qing court in the 1860s but went bankrupt in 1883. According to the diarist Li Ciming, Hu "kept as many as a hundred women from good and mean families, many

from raiding."[36] This act, imitative of an emperor, inspired a novel centering on Hu's garden mansion and antique-buying activities, with only rare
glimpses of his footbound harem (he forbade his women to wear skirts, preferring pants which embellish the shape of pointy feet; 38). Hu the wealthy
merchant plays the role of a connoisseur-as-emperor.

The novel, called *The Unofficial Biography of Hu Xueyan* (*Hu Xueyan waizhuan,*) was prefaced 1903 and published around that time. It was attributed to an author who sounds Japanese but is not, Dajiao Shiyu (Ohashi
Shikihane), and was alleged to have been published in Tokyo. It became a
legendary work among the *Radishes* lotus lovers, creating high expectations.
But when such a reader finally came across the book, he was bound to be
disappointed by the formulaic and superficial descriptions of feet.[37] The
paucity of details results from the fact that footbinding served a symbolic
function in the novel, as a relic from history before Westernization. "For
the wind of equal rights between male and female had yet to spread to China,
and footbinding was an elaborate matter in the Hu mansion. They considered it a shame to find one female with big feet in the house, oblivious as
they were of the world of tianzu in the myriad countries and nine continents" (28–29). The fictional Hu Xueyan, who installed telephones in the
sixteen quarters housing his wives and concubines to facilitate his summons,
was indeed a latter-day emperor in a polygynous harem. It is significant that
the historical Hu Xueyan flourished in the 1860s–1870s, decades of the sup-
pression of the Taiping rebels that from hindsight shone as the last restoration of the imperium.

So unsatisfying is *Unofficial History of Hu Xueyan* that lotus lovers took
to embellishing it by fantasizing about shoes. One, Sanyou (Three Friends),
claimed to be fortunate enough to live next door to a Granny who was formerly a maid in the Hu mansion. Granny disclosed elaborate details about
a hierarchy of shoes in the Hu harem: feet three inches or smaller were allowed to be clad in bright red shoes with gold embroidery; four inches or
smaller, pink with embroidered flowers; five inches or smaller, miscellaneous
colors with flowers; bigger than five inches, unadorned blue cloth shoes. Besides hierarchy by size there was also hierarchy by status: maids and concubines both wore red silk bedslippers, but the former could embroider them
only on the tip whereas the latter fashioned embroidery all over. Bedslippers
were also worn in the daytime for Hu's convenient fondling. In the summer, slipper soles were crafted from jade to make them cool to the touch

(CFL: 267). In a subsequent volume, however, Three Friends confessed that he was actually associate editor Zhou Ying and that the details about shoes were gleaned from his memories of a childhood reading of a much more detailed version of the novel (CFL II: 286). There was no Granny. I suspect that neither was there an unabridged *Unofficial History of Hu Xueyan,* since there is no evidence of it whatsoever.

A text of fabricated origins created its own objective reality—or was it the generative power of objects that fabricated texts? Yao Lingxi recorded that one day a friend offered to sell him two leaves of translucent jade with tips that arched slightly upward. Around the edges were rows of tiny needle holes, and the words "shoe sole of the concubine of Hu Qingyu tang" were etched in Small Seal script in the middle.[38] Hu Qingyu tang, as he later learned, was the name of a century-old pharmacy owned by Hu Xueyan in Hangzhou. Yao declined to pay an exorbitant sum for two pieces of "useless object," but through them he came across the Hu Xueyan story (CFL: 158–59). Later, he presented a similar description of the jade soles in a story of Hu, which includes additional details. Hu evidently used the soles, worn by a concubine lying on a couch, to roll tiny balls of opium. Upon learning that the soles were crafted from a jade screen, Yao remarked: "What a waste of natural resources!" (CFL: 181–82).

How ironic that Yao Lingxi, who echoed Tao Baopi's plea that the bound foot should be appreciated as an antique object, would demand utilitarian value from a pair of jade soles. Yao's resorting to the language of "useless objects" and "waste of natural resources" betrays his allegiance to the modern creed of productivity and the utility of the natural body. Curiously, Yao's sneer was also Confucian in tone, frugality being one of the clubs with which literati hit merchants over the head. The danger of mercantile economy has always been its waste and its spectacle: its conspicuous consumption. The most enduring image from the eighteenth-century capitalistic heyday of the salt merchants of Yangzhou is a golden urinal.[39]

Hu Xueyan was also said to use a small shoe as a wine cup, an act so associated with the late-Yuan connoisseur Yang Tieya (Weizhen, 1296–1370) that it was simply known as the Tieya Obsession *(Tieya pi).*[40] Correcting the impression that the famous poet was so vulgar, if not deranged, that he found pleasure in drinking putrid wine, an early-Ming source specified that Yang sipped wine from a cup placed inside the orifice of a small shoe, not directly from it. During the tumultuous last years of the Yuan dynasty, Yang retired to Suzhou and passed his time by drinking and gaming in courtesan houses. Drinking from the shoe was punishment for those who lost a gamble.[41]

Unlike other legendary deeds of connoisseurs, which were shrouded in an aura of fragrance and romance, Tieya's Obsession was honest to a fault in its insinuation of the disgust of bodily odor and filth. Hence as early as the late Ming, the writer Shen Defu shifted the narrative focus from Yang Tieya to his friend and dinner companion Ni Yuanzhen (Zan, 1301–74). Ni, a famous painter whose obsession with cleanliness *(jiepi)* was legendary, was so incensed whenever Yang passed the lotus cup that he would flee the table.[42] The combat of two obsessions, footbinding and cleanliness, draws a chuckle because it exposes the physicality of flesh usually sanitized by the elegance of connoisseurship literature.

The Qing writer Ji Yun (1724–1805) recorded a legend signaling that this supposedly romantic and light-hearted practice of drinking from a shoe had become a cautionary tale. During the ancestral rituals performed on Zhongyuan, the fifteenth day of the seventh month, the head of a prominent family lifted his libation to his ancestors and set it on the table. At that moment one of the glasses cracked open, an ominous sign. The culprit turned out to be his son, who had placed the glass in a courtesan's shoe several days ago. Ji Yun described the Tieya Obsession as "lewd, excessive, and dirty, vulgar to the utmost."[43] In his revulsion he articulated the aesthetic of footbinding before the age of disavowal: averted eyes, indirect representation, and avoidance of the physicality of feet.

Despite longstanding revulsion, or perhaps because of it, drinking from a courtesan's shoe persisted as the most enduring and imitated act of connoisseurship. Its association with Yang Tieya, the first known connoisseur named by contemporary sources, not mythical emperors, firmly linked the appreciation of bound feet with the nostalgic and pleasure-seeking modes of literati culture. Indeed, three of Fang Xuan's five treatises are rules for drinking games, one being "The Moon-Circulating Wine Cup" ("Guanyue cha"), an emulation of the Tieya Obsession.

In the commercialized economies of twentieth-century treaty ports, the uses of shoes multiplied, and the relationship between form and function became ever more fanciful. Yao Lingxi reported that he found in the Zhongyuan department store in Tianjin a new consumer product, slip-on high heels made of cloisonné or red seashell sequined with diamonds. For ten dollars *(jin)* a lady could keep a pair in her purse, slip them onto her leather flats, and hit the dancing floor. Why not try drinking from them, Yao mused (CFL: 170). Craftsmen of the Jingdezhen kilns kneaded porcelain clay into shoe-shaped wine cups and decorated them with erotic pictures.[44] So realistic were they that prostitutes in Jiangxi reportedly wore them to bed (CFL: 187). Another connoisseur recalled that twenty years ago he had seen in Beijing stores outside the Zhenyang Gate a bedslipper fashioned with a rubberized sole in the form of a penis ("Guangdong fake instrument"). Priced at four ounces of silver, the shoe was said to be popular with widows (CFL: 199–200).

Unlike the footbound woman herself, these shoes are not relics from a past age of connoisseurship but are instead products of a new commercialism that associated treaty port culture with sexual license. If, as Zhou Ying explained earlier, a modern-day connoisseur is first and foremost a collector of artifacts and texts, this collecting activity takes the form of purchasing in the modern marketplace. A connoisseur is a shrewd consumer who knows his way around in department stores as in flea markets. No wonder that some entries in *Radishes* read like a shopping guide, as connoisseurs debated the best antique stalls in Beijing to find a bargain slipper (CFL: 202–4).

The commodified nature of the shoe as a fetish object added to its potency as talisman. One man suffering from nocturnal emission cured himself by tying a tiny shoe—smaller than his erect penis—on his penis and testicles before going to bed (CFL IV: 126). In this curious reversal, what used to be an object of wanton desire and enticement for orgasm or loss of self in the bygone days became an instrument of self-mastery in the modern age of disavowal.

As a holder of wine, desired object, or inadvertent loss, the shoe-as-orifice was a receptacle of male fantasies and anxieties in the world of *Picking Radishes*. If the presumed subjects of the connoisseurship discourse are male, the desires and fears are also male-centered. The most poignant expression of this desire, identification with the literati as paragons of male privilege, can reach absurd proportions in an age when dissipation and chaos, not concentration of power and control, were the norm in the body politic. The literati's control of and indeed, monopoly over, the written word must have seemed attractive when runaway wordiness governed the literary world.

THE CONNOISSEURS AS FEMINISTS

If the lotus obsession was a way for modern men of letters to grapple with (or to escape from) the nostalgia of loss and the fragility of modern masculinity, the discourse of footbinding in *Picking Radishes* becomes an alternative one to nationalistic history and its implied masculine subject. Yao Lingxi's or Zhou Ying's mode of identification with women from the past, epitomized in their view of footbinding as antique, set them apart from the prevalent discourse of women as victims of patriarchy and national shame. The connoisseurs thus saw themselves as sympathizers of women, even true feminists.

This difference in mode of identification was often expressed in terms of an overt criticism of nationalist feminism, especially the anti-footbinding movement. One newspaper columnist whose essay was cited in *Radishes,* Lao Xuan (b. 1886), stated his views: "To promote footbinding now is cruel, lewd, and contrary to humanitarian concerns. But to prohibit it is authoritarian, oppressive, and ignorant of human feelings." What he found most objectionable about the anti-footbinding campaign was its rhetoric: "The female is the one who feels the immediate and direct impact of binding; she is imperiled on the spot. . . . Exhortations to give up footbinding should focus on this immediate fact, not some high-sounding slogans about 'strong race' or 'strong country.'" Lao Xuan advocated a bona fide woman-centered agenda that respected a woman's bodily suffering.[45] According to his logic, which is similar to that of the woman educator Xue Shaohui seen in the last chapter, footbinding cannot be eradicated by sociopolitical coercion; it would only die a natural death as its cultural prestige expired. Educate young girls about the ills of footbinding, but leave the old women alone.

Lao Xuan went on to challenge the premise of the nationalistic anti-footbinding rhetoric: "I don't disagree that footbinding has some connection to 'strong race.' But I don't see that the children born to natural-footed mothers in Beiping are necessarily healthier than those from footbound mothers. . . . I'm also sympathetic to the argument that the natural foot facilitates 'strong country.' But I tend to think that the strength of a country depends on the wisdom and courage of its people—a matter of inner heart instead of outward form—and especially not on the shape of women's feet. The bodies of women on the continents of Africa and Australia, as well as the Pacific islands, are much more robust than those of Europe, America, and Japan. So why do the peoples on these two continents and islands fail to build a country, and to the contrary have become slaves of the strong countries and are in danger of extinction?" (CFL: 13). Lao Xuan thus called into question two founding tropes of national feminism: a genetic determinism that says strong mothers beget strong sons/country, and the missionary notion that construes the status of womanhood as an indicator of the advancement of a civilization.

The connoisseur's identification with the footbound woman is inherently limited and one-sided even as he claims to be woman-centered and woman-friendly. The identification of a connoisseur with the object of his desire or appreciation is motivated by self love. Connoisseurs could not represent female desires derived outside of heterosexual unions or without references to men. The problem of shifty voice evinced in Faithful's interviews with the elder and Granny mentioned above bespeaks the difficulties of males speaking *as* females. But they could speak *for* the pitiful woman, which is a mode that literati had heralded.

The pathos of outdatedness was so poignant that it transcended the concerns of the connoisseurs and found its most eloquent expression in a short story by a radical writer, the socialist martyr Hu Yepin (d. 1931). Published in 1929 in the popular magazine *Eastern Miscellany (Dongfang zazhi),* "Two Women in a Small County Town" depicts the psychological anguish of two abandoned wives in their thirties. Never identified by name, the pair of friends shared interchangeable identities: as old-fashioned footbound women in a modern world. On Little New Year's Eve (the twenty-fourth day of the twelfth month), the beginning of festivities that celebrated family union, renewal, and hope, the dejected women tried in vain to drown their loneliness in wine.

The one with a round face recalled that on her wedding night over a decade ago, her husband called her "empress" and adored her tiny feet. After he left for a university education in a metropolis, however, he sent pictures and photos of modern women, admonishing her to change her appearance. Eager to please, she stayed up for three days, soaking her "porcelain-like feet" in cold water in the hope of making them grow. She also forsook the traditional camisole that flattened her breast and "boldly exposed the shape of her two breasts from under her blouse."[46] In spite of her efforts, he left her for a modern woman. Rumor had it that he became a professor at a national university and served on a lucrative committee in the government; he had also fathered a son. She imagined him as having fashioned an "impressive mustache"—in short a perfect modern man who combined intellectual authority, political power, and progeny thus mirroring the successful talented scholar in traditional novels. Unlike the beauties in these novels, however, her investment of early sacrifices did not bring her glory, only a pitiful alimony of thirty dollars a month.

Her friend, a woman with a long face, fared no better. She, too, enjoyed three initial years of conjugal bliss. In fact, so in love was she that she encouraged her husband to go study abroad. "But his advancement means my downfall." On his departure night she suffered a cold, but his madman-like desire was so fierce that she yielded and "satisfied him five times." This is a "filthy memory" that would haunt her for life (104, 105). Her sacrifice was expressed in her bodily and sexual submission, first by binding her feet and then by submitting to his sexual advances. Even after his betrayal, she continued to sacrifice by tinkering with her feet, albeit neither the fickle man nor her own body would perform as she wished. For years she had maneuvered to let her feet out, but they looked all the more like deformed stubs of tulip or bamboo shoot. As the two friends drank themselves into a stupor, the round-faced woman murmured: "Everything else is easy, but there is nothing we can do about [returning bound] feet [to a never-bound state]" (106).

Significantly, what the women saw as self-sacrifice—the giving of their bodies or the aping of fashion—Hu Yepin interpreted as an act of male aggression. Referring not only to the madness on parting night, but also to "that unfortunate and dirty matter" which recurred countless times during the happy three-year marriage, Hu portrayed sexual intercourse as a defilement comparable to rape. This stark assessment of sex, ostensibly made out of sympathy with the woman victim, is all the more stunning because it precludes the possibility of female sexual pleasure even within the context of a blissful marriage, no matter how short-lived it turned out to be. Whatever pleasures she might have experienced she could not keep as memory after the husband's betrayal. Hu insisted on erasing memories of her happiness as he scripted her as the acted-upon with no hope of catching up with the times.

Hu's foreclosure of any possibility of action or pleasure on the parts of the women was couched in terms of the stubbornness of the female body, hence naturalizing their victimhood. In pivoting his story on the physical impossibility of the women's letting their feet out, and hence changing their fate, Hu Yepin dramatized the total dependency of women on men, the only constancy in a changing world. "We are born female, what could we have done?" asked the round-faced one. Her friend tried to console her by envisioning a radical alternative: "Some women, didn't they join the revolutionary party?" "But only because their husbands were revolutionaries?!" the first replied (104). Hu's critique is radical, directed as it was to the historical and present subjugation of women by men, especially by way of the institution of marriage. "Perhaps in the very beginning male and female were the same?" asked one woman. "Maybe," answered her friend. "But all the women we know suffer more indignities than men. Not to mention that we suffer because of men" (106). Hence Hu's "Two Women" is a call to arms in a gender war. Yet it is a one-sided combat, because the old women, who had the most at stake, could not act.

The tragedy of "Two Women" must have struck a chord; one contributor to *Radishes* cited it several years later in his lament over male fickleness (CFL II: 37). Despite their divergent political agendas, the socialist revolutionary Hu Yepin and the connoisseurs concurred in their sympathy for the footbound woman as antique. The male's sympathy and his admission of general male guilt are both predicated on a reassertion of male power: he alone is free to act and take responsibility. The footbound woman, passed over by a changing world, despite her subjective will and efforts to remake her body, appears to be doubly victimized and passive in the final analysis. In her acted-upon subject position she has to be the spoken-for. The connoisseurs and revolutionaries find a fragile common ground in their sympathies for the leftover woman as they vie to speak for her by representing the female body as the obstacle to her liberation. Neither the connoisseur's laissez-faire stance of "let the women be" nor the revolutionary's denouncement of gender inequality leaves any room for the realization of female desires and pleasures, from her own body or another's. If the connoisseurs as ventriloquists cannot narrate female desires, neither can the anti-connoisseur revolutionary.

THE BODY IN PAIN: FEMALE SCREAMS

The female voices that appear in *Radishes* have to be heard against the backdrop of this hegemony of the male in the discursive field as connoisseur, writer, reader, and woman's true friend. Although several letters and songs also appeared under female authorship (marked as such by the gender qualifier "Madam," *nüshi*), most of the female voices took the form of testimonies.[47] Pain figured as the predominant concern, indeed the organizational principle, in these "firsthand" narratives of the footbinding experience.

It is through pain that the female body acquires its textual presence. In a typical testimony entitled "Painful History of Bending Lotus" ("Aolian tengshi"), Madam Axiu registered her complaints with the literati of old, who so loved the bound foot as "curio that they took to embellishing it with flowery words" (CFL: 255). "But for us, generations of women whose bodies are being subjected to this *[shenshou]*, it is no different from a criminal being subjected to the cangue, or worse. As the proverb says of the cruelty of this act, 'a pair of small feet, a tubful of tears.' As one who has personally experienced this *[guolairen]*, I'm willing to express in words [literally, to give shape to] the pain of broken tendons and crushed bones I went through then, so as to awaken all lotus-loving gentlemen of the world" (CFL: 255–56). The association of maleness with flowery words stands in stark contrast with the association of femaleness with the bodily experience of pain, a telling statement of the gendered nature of power inequalities.

When the "curio" or "antique" committed her experience to words, she was by definition contesting her object status. We do not know if Madam Axiu was a woman or a female author subject.[48] As we have seen in the last chapter, such girls as Cai Aihua did speak at school assemblies—albeit at the prompting of her brother—and these words were sometimes reported in newspapers by men. However, it is futile to attempt to discern an authentic female voice or an unmediated female point of view. The import of Madam Axiu's testimony is the novelty of the category of "footbound woman author" and her narratives of bodily sensations. As voices of interiority, female testimonies introduced an element of contest by switching the point of view away from the literati's "flowery words" that constituted footbinding's aura. The realism of the female bodily voice was invented as an antidote to the male voice of privilege.

The subversive potential of women talking back is evinced by Madam Axiu's use of "antique," the main trope of the connoisseurs. As a teenager in the early Republican years, she attended a girl's school and was barred from physical education lessons. "Fellow classmates eyed me as antique and laughed at me" (CFL: 257). From Tao Baopi to Hu Yepin to Axiu, the trope of antique changed hands until the recently dated object acquired a speaking voice and ceased to be an object. Tao Baopi's famous line of "What's wrong with admiring what is already here?" does not seem so innocent or unobjectionable any more.

The female voice tells us nothing new—that footbinding is painful, dated, and irreversible—nor does it add new vocabulary to the male-initiated discourse of antique. But in authoring the inner female body as an alternative birthplace for words, hence a source for truth and authentic experience, female testimonies usher in the last stage of the mode of disclosure that signifies the modern rupture in the footbinding discourse. The dénouement of the cultural prestige of footbinding, hinging as it did before the nineteenth century on textual and visual concealment, is complete.

The language of pain in the hands of Madam Axiu is uneventful, consisting of an overuse of the word pain (*teng*) as noun and adjective. Once she uses a tired simile, "as painful as being sliced by a knife" (CFL: 258) but in the end simply confesses that "in the humidity and dampness after rain, no words can give shape to the pain felt by a footbound person" (CFL: 258). The other two female voices that follow, billed as "self narrations" *(zi shu)* transmitted by scribes, are more colloquial and expressive, but fare no better in linguistic inventiveness. One Madam Jin Suqing reports a "burning hot sensation" upon initial binding, and resorts to the same fire imagery when describing the effect of tight binding in the hands of grandma: "My two feet felt more and more swollen, then burning hot to the point of a continuous piercing pain. I tossed and turned and could not sleep. But I would rather die than loosen the cloth binder a bit. At times I sobbed because the pain was so extreme, but the only way is to clench my teeth and bear it" (CFL: 259–60). Half a month later, she moved to a longer five-foot binder and started to wear soft-heeled bedslippers. As she was on the brink of success, however, both small toes became pustular. She wiped them with cotton wool and proceeded to rebind, when "pain permeated my innards and my whole body shook and trembled" (CFL: 260). Before too long the pain subsided as the feet slowly turned numb.

Madam Jin's iron will resulted at least in part from the toutings of an uncle and other guests at her grandmother's birthday celebration, where she met the Zhang sisters with their immaculate small feet. To monitor her progress, she obsessively measured her feet as she sewed progressively smaller-sized shoes. If the connoisseur's obsession with exact measurements, as we have seen earlier, signaled the triumph of scientism, Madam Jin's obsession signaled the female delight in her own ability to remake her body. The pliancy of the body—and a sense of agency—felt by the woman in the process of binding cut a stark contrast to the stubbornness of flesh and the futility of human effort in the process of unbinding seen earlier.[49] "The fifth toe has come closer and closer to the plantar. I measured the distance: 0.4 inch. The crevice on the sole of the foot *(zuxin)*, too, was getting deeper and deeper. It measured about 0.8 inches. . . . After thirty days of binding, my feet have become as small as 2.9 inches, a shrinkage from the earlier measurement by 0.9 inch!" (CFL: 260). The narrative ended with her public recognition among women from several villages.

Madam Jin did not invent new descriptions of pain, but the accumulative weight of the reiterations allows the reader a glimpse into her body beneath the skin. Her voice came through as vivid and her incentives credible. The bearing of pain figures as the most convincing expression of her agency, and as we hear it told, we begin to realize the extent to which pain is implicated in the female structure of incentives and desires. We can suspend questions about whether it is an "authentic" voice of a "real" woman. We hear it as a female voice, one that is distinct from the male connoisseurs, because the familiar tropes of antique and scientific measurement acquire new meanings in these narratives of the experience of the female body and the creativity of pain.

Madam Axiu's voice inspired imitators because, as one who called himself "Repentant Scholar" (Juefei sheng) noted, "*Picking Radishes* is comprised mostly of poems and songs and precious few are documents of reality *[jishi]*. Madam Axiu's and several others are the only exceptions. They are our wake-up calls *[banghe;* literally, a blow and a shout]" (CFL II: 50). Both the sobriquet and the blow and shout, a zen prop to enlightenment, hark back to familiar tropes in late imperial erotic novels. In these novels, the religious awakening of the repentant male protagonist always serves as fig leaf for blatant narratives of male desires and sexual quests. Repentant Scholar's "Painful Words of the Lotus Hook" in the "Admonitions" section of the second volume of *Radishes* (CFL II: 50–57) too, were distinct male narratives that belong to the same genre of interviews with Granny discussed above, with the same conflation of female desire for her body and male desire for her. The problem of shifty voice is corrected by presenting the female experience in its entirety as a testimony told to a male relative. This allows the Repentant Scholar to narrate female experiences of pain realistically in the third person, the eroticism of which is weakly dismissed by a formulaic male repentance: "Having heard this, my usual love of the lotus suddenly dissipated" (CFXB: 51, 63).

There are, in fact, three testimonies of "Painful Words" penned by the Repentant Scholar, consisting of interviews with his wife, his younger sister, and a neighbor in the former capital of Beiping.[50] His recalling of his wife's experience is innovative in its consciousness of the filter of time: "My wife was born in Tong county, Hebei. Following custom, she had her feet bound at seven. The pain of that initial stage has all been forgotten after all these years. But two events are still vivid today." One is the result of mother's carelessness, who pierced her toe with a needle when she was sealing the binder's end. For days the girl hobbled with a piercing pain, not knowing that her left big toe had been sewn to the cloth binder. The second event was a corrective sitting aiming at reducing the bulging of the arch at age fourteen. Having sat with a pressing iron on her feet for hours, she would further restrain the arch with narrow strips of cloth. The torture lasted two months—but it worked (CFXB: 50–51). The strategy of focusing on these painful events is indeed effective, as it evokes the singularity of the female body through the thread of its internal memory. The residual pain lingers whenever the middle-aged woman remembers these events. Her body also remembers, as she nurses her inflamed foot with bean curd skin or vegetable leaf (CFL II: 51).

Painful words became an industry. Other imitative testimonies ensued, under the titles of "Afterword to Painful Words" (CFL II: 51–54) or the repetition "Painful Words" (CFL II: 57–59), but in the female first-person voice and attributed to authors with female names. Such documentation of pain focuses on the pain of unbinding, hence reinforcing the message of "don't torture them twice; leave the women alone" reiterated by the *Radishes* connoisseurs. Others also proceeded to interview wife (CFL II: 65–66) or old servant (CFXB: 59–63), but both the subject matter of pain and its linguistic expressions have been exhausted. These testimonies sound as tired and old as the practice of binding itself.

The language of pain was recharged in a narrative that appeared in the last anthologized volume of *Radishes,* issued in 1941. In a testimony called "The Experience of Footbinding," attributed to an Elder Sister Wang from Haicheng, descriptions of pain received the precise and taxonomical treatment of a biomedical discourse, complete with attempts of anatomical naming of body parts. The female body in pain is described chronologically through a two-year period, by volume of pain and its duration, as well as in qualitative terms: soreness *(suanteng)* or bloating and snapping pain *(zhangjue teng)* (CFXB: 22–24).

The larger narrative in which this female testimony appeared, "An Overview of Footbinding," is a composite that combines elements from the previous connoisseurship literature and household almanacs: ethnography, origin discourse, Confucian morality, utility, Fang Xuan, female testimonies, tonic recipes, shoemaking instructions, garment-sewing instructions, instructions for arm and leg movement, chamber arts, admonitions to education and a productive life (CFXB: 1–43). Although the isolated elements and data are recycled from discourses of old, this long narrative is distinctly modern and inventive in its comprehensiveness and the use of biomedical terminology (CFXB: 10–11). Even more astonishing is the novel assumption that female education and industry are compatible with footbinding. Having dispensed with matters of deportment, sewing, and sex, the narrator commented matter-of-factly: "after the painful period ended, then you should teach her how to read and write; give her a considerable education" (CFXB: 42). Physical exercise such as strolling and tai-chi were recommended. The narrative ended with a timetable outlining the daily routine of the productive domestic woman, cited from General Zeng Guofan's famous family instructions (CFXB: 43).

It is no accident that the narrative opened with a cultural relativist claim: "Manmade beautification: the use of human efforts to remake the normal [body]. Examples are transformations in the shapes of skull, teeth, nail, and nose of native Americans; small waists of European women; footbinding of the women of our country" (CFXB: 1). This assertion of parity between China and the rest of the world had existed as the underside of the anti-footbinding rhetoric that is the mainstay of the gigantic nationalist history since the late Qing. But the tone is different, because China is no longer defensive about its women's feet. All pretension of criticizing footbinding is dropped because it is no longer necessary. Footbinding is history, and everybody knows it.

The omnipresent narrative point of view and the assumption of the possibility of empirical knowledge—from both inside the female body and out;

from within China and globally—signals the triumph of objectivism which has finally transformed the connoisseurship literature by obliterating the partial and backward-looking literati vantage point. Even the subjective bodily experience of the footbound woman can now be described in an objective tone. The attribution of authorship, "narrated by Madam Lotus Preservation and compiled by Lotus-Appreciating Scholar" (CFXB: 1), recalls a familiar practice of the connoisseurship literature. But the male-scripting-female-experience composite voice assumes new meaning in a world where all that one can play with is narrative voice and perspectives. There is nothing more to be known about footbinding. Safely dead, it can finally be released into the world.

Born of a utopian desire for total knowledge, *Picking Radishes* constitutes an archive in an expanded sense of the word. "The archive," wrote Thomas Richards, "was not a building nor even a collection of texts but the collectively imagined junction of all that was known or knowable."[51] For an archive to work—to be comprehensive and manageable—it has to maintain clear boundaries. This closure became possible only after footbinding ceased to be a culturally viable practice in the early Republican period. Yet the archive can never be completely closed, even after the practice of binding feet it documents is no longer current. There is always the possibility of new knowledge from a hidden text retrieved from a dusty attic, a stowaway shoe brought to light. In between the nostalgic and utopian impulses of Yao Lingxi and his friends lie the pleasures of disseminating knowledge about footbinding in *Picking Radishes.*

Assembled primarily from recycled fragments and old information, *Picking Radishes* is nonetheless an extremely inventive text. Part of its inventiveness—its success in generating new textual forms and meanings—can be attributed to the self-presentation of its modern editors as mimetic literati. A second reason is rooted in the profit motive that governed the marketplace of the 1930s treaty ports. Porcelain kilns and shoemakers produced myriad shoe-shaped objects, often modeled on increasingly fanciful verbal descriptions. Displayed on the shelves of emporiums, these objects inspired renewed rounds of poetic eulogies during drinking parties. Through this word-to-object-to-word generative loop, the archive and the marketplace were littered with superfluous words and things which were thoroughly modern inventions. Both the words and artifacts are "real"—they are still preserved in libraries and museums today—but they are not trustworthy. Neither speaks the "truth" about footbinding in a straightforward manner.

The reality of invented texts, objects, and meanings in and out of *Picking Radishes* complicates our tasks as historians. The archive, as a repository of desires, is not a neutral collection awaiting our exploration. Instead of posing as disinterested investigators, we should read *Picking Radishes* first and foremost to relish the exaggerated emotions and detached artificiality that structured the male fantasy world of the golden lotus. Citations and reiteration release new meanings, but we may do well to remember that seeing the same information thrice does not make it less erroneous. The temptation is great to take the realistic first-person narratives of voyeuristic males and footbound women in *Picking Radishes* at face value, as unadulterated expressions of male desires and female suffering. But the reality of the footbinding experience lies elsewhere, in a yet-to-be articulated space outside the archive.

THE BODY CONCEALED

PART TWO

FROM ANCIENT TEXTS
TO CURRENT CUSTOMS

In Search of Footbinding's Origins

In the three chapters that comprise Part I, we have witnessed the waning of
footbinding's aura in a modern, global world. As the bound foot was de-
mystified and brought into the open for all to see, its images and meanings
were altered by its very availability. Distinctly modern images of footbinding circulated in new textual and visual mediums, acquiring the mantle of
timeless Truth. Most familiar is the prevalent history of the nation authored
by Christian missionaries and Chinese reformers in which the bound foot
symbolized national shame. Equally poignant is the counter-discourse, a nostalgic connoisseurship literature which construed the bound foot as a relic
and antique. Both images signal the unequivocal death of footbinding in
cultural prestige and as social practice.

In Part II, our focus shifts from narrating the end of footbinding to tracing the transmission and perpetuation of its aura in the late imperial period
(sixteenth to early nineteenth centuries), when it was a customary and val-
orized practice. This exercise begins with an appreciation of the exalted status of the written word in the imperial era. In the modern age, multiple ex-
posures of footbinding, especially under the photographic and radiographic
lenses, destroyed footbinding's mystique. To the extent that these new imaging techniques were more powerful in exposing female flesh than was writ-

ing, we may argue that the demise of footbinding coincided with the decline of the written word as an instrument of veracity.

In contrast, in the late imperial period the allure of footbinding was primarily constructed in written discourses and relied upon the latter for its cultural prestige and mystique.[1] My main argument in part II is that textual indirectness, in the form of lyricism or objectivism, functioned in a way similar to embroidered leggings and shoes: as instruments of concealment. Both shifted the gaze from the raw or bare flesh to the ornamentation of culture. Instead of depicting footbinding as a concrete bodily and social practice, Ming and Qing writings worked by inciting imaginations about the hidden body. The reader was teased to visualize and fantasize about that which could not be said.

In this and the next chapter we map the parameters of elite male desires by surveying disparate genres of prose ranging from philological treatises, a forged palace intrigue, notation books, travelogues, and a manual of taste, to vernacular plays. Many are academic in method and tone; some are subtly salacious, whereas others are downright pornographic. Taken together, they served to define "footbinding" as a subject of male inquiry and desire, establish the discursive limits of what could and could not be said about female body parts, and keep the erotics of bound feet alive in male imagination. This chapter documents writers' efforts to comprehend footbinding by locating it in historical time; the next traces their attempts to domesticate it by affixing it to a concrete albeit fantastic landscape.

Instead of condemning these dead Chinese males, our goal is to take the seduction of their words seriously, seeking to understand how they were so effective in perpetuating the mystique of footbinding. At the same time, we strive to glimpse, however piecemeal, the world of local customs and regional cultures, as well as female incentives that these writings inadvertently reveal. Finally, in the last chapter we move from the world of texts to textiles, thus mapping the cosmology of female desires by placing their bodies—of labor, decorum, and fashion—at the center of the worlds they made.

DEFINING FOOTBINDING: THE ARCHED FOOT

Before the nineteenth century, the subject of footbinding was taboo in such official genres as public history, local gazetteers, and didactic texts. The majority of Chinese male scholarly writing on footbinding appears in the form of jottings in notation books (*biji;* literally, brush notes). Jottings are fragmented reading notes, a halfway house between data collecting and systematic analysis. Grouped according to topics (e.g., "the arched foot") they are sometimes categorized according to encyclopedic schemes but often published in random order. Myths, hearsay, and history share the same page and status. Some notations, such as Hu Yinglin's, analyzed below, are learned and serious treatises; others are closer to the fictionalized "small talk" (*xiaoshuo*) on the other end of the spectrum. Given its flexible format, jotting is the prevalent genre in which footbinding can be committed to writing in prose.

All jottings about footbinding before the nineteenth century, a self-referential tradition, are origin discourses. The prototype is a short notation by the Song scholar Zhang Bangji (fl. twelfth century). It also happens to be the earliest extant written reference to footbinding. Zhang asserted at the outset that "[w]omen's footbinding *[chanzu]* began in the recent times; it was not mentioned in any books from the previous eras." Zhang, who completed his book sometime after 1148, was in all likelihood living in an age of footbinding's initial spread.[2] Later scholars often cited his privileged contemporary knowledge to bolster the claim that the beginnings of the practice can be traced to no earlier than the twelfth century.[3]

Curiously, however, instead of his personal authority Zhang appealed to centuries-old histories and lyrics: *History of the Southern Dynasties;* the Yuefu songs and *New Songs from Jade Terrace* (both from the Six Dynasties period, third to sixth centuries); and Tang poetry. The latter three collections of lyrics, replete with references to women's bodies, would become the principal textual evidence to scholars in the subsequent dynasties. Both the Yuefu and Jade Terrace songs are "full of amorous words," explained Zhang. "They depict the stunning beauty of women by visualizing their bodies, and by describing their elaborate ornamentation. They discourse on such body parts as eyebrows, eyes, lips, mouths, waists, and fingers, but there is not a single word on bound feet." One possible exception is a description of a beauty's feet by the Tang poet Han Wo (844–923?), author of a famous collection of amorous poems, *The Fragrant Toilette (Xianglian ji)*. In "Eulogy to Shoes," Han included a line that would stir much controversy: "Glowing, glowing, six inches of succulent flesh" (Liucun fuyuan guangzhizhi).[4]

Before returning to Han Wo, it is important to note Zhang Bangji's logic: if ancient texts, be they poetry or history, fail to mention footbinding, it means that the practice did not exist in those times. The authority of texts

derives in part from the reader's faith that they constitute a complete repertoire of knowledge. Zhang thus ascribed enormous rhetorical and explanatory powers to the written word handed down from the past. This faith in
texts would be renewed every time subsequent scholars debated footbinding's origins by citing more texts. Even when scholars considered such body-
related matters as anatomy, dress, or manners, they assumed that their only
entrance to the realm of corporeality *in the past* was by way of written texts.
The repository of historical truth is presumed to be an archive of texts, not
visual or material cultures.[5]

The scholars' faith in texts is not blind. They were all too aware that even
seemingly unequivocal texts are open to interpretations. Does Han's eulogy,
"six inches of succulent flesh," denote bound feet or not? Zhang Bangji did
not find it conclusive. Since one Tang inch is shorter than a Song inch, he
reasoned, one can deduce from this line that very tiny feet were eulogized
in Tang poetry. But, significantly, "there is no mention of the arched shape
[*gong*, also bow-shaped]." In Zhang's mind, it is not just the size but a particular shape that signifies footbinding. Earlier, in discussing a legend from
the *History of the Southern Dynasties,* he used the same criterion: "The Duke
of Donghun [r. 499–501] of the Southern Qi Dynasty shaped gold leaf into
lotuses and laid them on the floor for his Consort Pan. He made her tread
on them, saying: 'every step a lotus.' But there is no word on whether her
feet were arched and small *[gongxiao]*." Again, footbinding is marked by
small size, Zhang implied, but even more definitive is the arched or bow
shape of the foot.

To most modern minds, footbinding is transparently obvious: we know
what it does and what it looks like. Not so for Song, Yuan, and Ming scholars, who seem perplexed by the definitions and meanings of the mysterious
practice. Their search for footbinding's origins alerts us to its complicated
ontological status, to the difficulties of defining its essential traits. Indeed,
it would not be an exaggeration to argue that it was only through the origin discourse that the parameters of footbinding were discursively formed.
Specifically, Zhang's reasoning implies that by the second half of the twelfth
century two distinguishing characteristics had emerged: small size and an
arch or bow shape. We may deduce that Zhang based his definitions on ob-
serving contemporary practices, but the manner of twelfth-century binding and the exact appearance of "arch shape," which varies from one period

and region to another, are lost to us. In chapter 6, we will make educated guesses by surveying material remains excavated from tombs—the kind of materials that lie outside the philologist's admissible evidence.

OF MYTH AND HISTORY

If Zhang's faith in the textual archives established one enduring feature of the origin discourse, about a century later another Song scholar, Che Ruoshui, supplied the other: a relentless condemnation of the practice. Che's jotting, which appears in a work completed in 1274, bears a striking resemblance to the modern anti-footbinding polemics in its rhetorical strategy:

> The binding of women's feet [chanjiao], one does not know when this
> practice began. A little girl not yet four or five [sui] is innocent and guiltless,
> but infinite suffering was being inflicted upon her. One does not know what
> good does it do to have [the pair of feet] bound into such a small size. When
> Dai Liang of the Late Han [32–220 C.E.] married out his daughter, she was
> [dressed in] a silk upper garment and plain skirt, [holding] a bamboo box
> and [wearing] wooden clogs. That means one cannot blame [footbinding]
> on the ancients. Or, some say that it started with Consort Yang of the Tang.
> But no citations can be found about this either.[6]

The story of Dai Liang, an erudite who retreated to the mountains to escape officialdom, was culled from two ancient books, *History of the Later Han Dynasty* and *Biographies of Ancient Sages from Runan (Runan xianxian zhuan).*[7] If Zhang Bangji looked to what we would now call the "medieval period" of the fifth to sixth centuries for textual evidence of footbinding, Che looked further back to the first and second centuries.

Che's argument that footbinding was not practiced in the Later Han, deduced from Dai's daughter's bridal attire, rests on the same faith as Zhang's in ancient books as a comprehensive repository of knowledge. Likewise, the lack of "citations" about Consort Yang's small feet means that attributions to her were not credible. Che's way of knowing, similar to Zhang's and that of subsequent scholars, works by an incessant impulse to separate history from myth. History refers to stories that can be collaborated and verified with a degree of certainty by *textual* evidence; myths are singular, isolated stories that are beyond verification. Interestingly, for scholars what were judged mythical tales of origins were sometimes found in reliable official historical annals, whereas the stories judged more credible first appear in literary sources.

By the thirteenth century, scholars had relegated at least two stories to the realm of myth. Their sources varied. Zhang, above, mentioned the Duke of Donghun and Consort Pan, which hailed from official history. It gives no indication of footbinding's beginnings, we may recall, because there is no word on whether her feet were both "arched and small." A second myth, mentioned by Che, is that of Consort Yang (717–56). The story of Yang, possibly the most famous femme fatale in history, was transmitted in ballads and tales. She was the favorite of the Tang emperor Xuanzong (r. 712–56) and was forced into exile from the capital by a rebellion. At the post-station of Mawei, Xuanzong's troops mutinied, blaming Yang for their misfortunes and demanding her death. According to a later legend, a granny chanced upon Yang's silk sock by the roadside and made a fortune by charging passersby for a peep.[8] The investment of emotions and voyeuristic value in a cast-off sock led to the rather far-fetched speculation that Yang must have had bound feet. Yet Che was unconvinced because of the lack of contemporary citations.

A third origin story, transmitted by the scholar and bibliophile Zhou Mi (1232–98), identified the originator as Yaoniang, a dancer in the court of Li Yu (937–78; r. 969–75), the last ruler of the Southern Tang dynasty of the Five Dynasties period. "Slender and beautiful, Yaoniang was skilled in dancing. The ruler made a six-foot-tall golden lotus festooned with jewels, ribbons, and garlands of pearls and gems. Inside the lotus he piled five-colored auspicious clouds. He had Yaoniang wrap her feet with silk *[yibo raojiao]*; he had them rendered slender and small *[xianxiao]*, curving upward like the new moon. In plain socks *[suwa]* she danced to the music 'In the Clouds,' her posture was as though she were soaring into the clouds. . . . Later people imitated her, finding arched and slender feet *[gongxian]* wonderful. Thus is the origin of footbinding."[9]

Yaoniang was a fictional character, but her story was fashioned from credible historical circumstances. The ruler Li Yu was an avid patron of Buddhism, a religion popular in his court and society. The golden lotus that he allegedly built for Yaoniang to dance in resembled the bejeweled lotus dais popular in Tang Buddhist statues (see fig. 10). Southern Tang goldsmiths and silversmiths were particularly skilled. Furthermore, Li was a renowned poet, painter, musician, and choreographer; his queen, Zhou, also a historic figure, was an accomplished player of the *pipa*-lute and an innovative choreographer of court dance.[10] The Yaoniang story is thus plausible, although it cannot be substantiated. In the fifteenth century, she would emerge as the most often cited legend that explained the beginnings of footbinding. In the absence of plausible citations in the official histories, a myth performs the cultural work of conveying the meanings of footbinding in a succinct narrative and vivid image.

Indeed, the Consort Pan, Consort Yang, and Yaoniang stories are cut out of the same mold. Taken together, they are more telling than any verifiable historical sources in suggesting that scholars associated footbinding with male power and excess, the femme fatale, and the ephemeral sensuality of harem dancers. The safeguarding of female morality or chastity, so prevalent in modern minds, was cited in neither history nor myth as a possible explanation. To the contrary, in the origin discourse footbinding emerges as an alien and morally dubious subject that invites condemnation.

YANG SHEN'S PHILOLOGY: THE LURE OF THE UNKNOWN

The faith in textual veracity, not to mention the possibility of separating myth from history, was thrown into disarray by the maverick Ming scholar Yang Shen (1488–1559). Son of a Grand Secretary and winner of Optimus at the precocious age of twenty-three, Yang was primed to enjoy an illustrious official career. However, thirteen years later he incurred the emperor's rage in a rites controversy involving the emperor's deceased father. Stripped of his official status, Yang was caned and exiled to a remote outpost in the southwestern province of Yunnan as a common soldier. He never returned to the capital, nor was his status restored when he died at age seventy-one in Yunnan.[11]

Yet there is a silver lining, as two modern biographers have remarked: "The thirty-five years of life in exile afforded Yang the opportunity to become one of the most widely read and prolific scholars in history."[12] Yang Shen's erudition, independent spirit, and virtually unlimited free time made him an ideal candidate to shed light on the mystery of footbinding's origins. Yang chided earlier scholars for "failing to investigate comprehensively" *(weizhi bokao)*, resulting in omission of a number of Tang poems on shoes and socks.

His own examination, in turn, led him to rebut the suggestion that foot-binding originated in the tenth-century harem of the Southern Tang ruler Li Yu. Instead, Yang proposed a new theory, tracing the origins to a much earlier period of the Six Dynasties (222–589).[13]

Based on one dubious Yuefu poem entitled "Double Bindings" ("Shuang xingchan"), Yang's theory provoked debates in the next century, with the majority of scholars siding with Zhang. This debate will be recounted below; suffice it to note here that Yang's theory accords with a common development in origin discourses: the later the writer's period, the earlier becomes the origin. In other words, in a linear progression of time-as-arrow, the distance between the "present" time of the writer and the time of the receding origin tends to increase. Indeed, Yang gestured toward a distant origin as he hinted that one can find references to shoes with "sharp" or pointy toes *(lilü)* in texts as early as the first-century-B.C.E. *Record of the Historian.*[14] But Yang rejected one story that circulated widely in the fifteenth century that placed the origin of footbinding firmly in antiquity. The Shang dynasty femme fatale Daji (d. 1122 B.C.E.?) was a fox, as the story goes, whose feet had yet to change into human form. She thus wrapped them with cloth binders. Not knowing the reason for her disguise, other palace ladies vied to imitate her. Yang dismissed this myth as "pulling the wool over history's eyes," and lamented that some educated people took it for real.[15] Hence Yang shared the scholarly consensus that the existence of solid textual reference distinguishes "history" from "myth."

Yang's search for footbinding's origins is an integral part of his classical studies and literary theory. His attempt to locate the practice not in the recent past but in antiquity resonates with the premise of his classical scholarship. In a vivid analogy that construes geographical space as metaphor for temporal distance, Yang expressed his longing for antiquity by comparing his distance from the profundity of the Six Classics to his distance in exile from the "splendors and riches of the capital." He located Han scholars in the adjacent terrain of Henan and Shandong, whose proximity allowed them to "get it" perhaps 60–70 percent of the time. Song scholars, in turn, were residents of faraway provinces of Yunnan and Guizhou whose comprehension was reduced to a mere 10–20 percent.[16] The simplest interpretation of this analogy is that Yang's veneration of antiquity prompted him to prefer Han learning over Song learning. This was the premise of Qing philological scholarship but a bold assertion in Yang's times, when Song and Yuan commentaries to the classics comprised the Ming orthodoxy.

Yang could not have explained his disdain for Song learning in plainer language: "The Six Classics were composed in Confucius' gate. Since the Han times were not far from Confucius, no matter how untalented were those who transmitted the learning, their readings were still more authentic. Song scholars, on the other hand, were removed from Confucius by one thousand and five hundred years. Even though they were extremely intelligent, how could they discard previous learning and appeal exclusively to their own interpretations?"[17] Much more than venerating the past is at stake here. Yang Shen's attitude toward the past can be understood as a two-part process: first the recognition of incommensurability, then its playful transgression. If "antiquity" means the lifetimes of Confucius and his disciples, it is forever lost. No latter-day reader could hope to understand the classics like the ancients did. The edge that Han scholars had over their Song counterparts was not a function of their abilities or efforts, merely their relative proximity to the classical age. In a sense, we who seek to understand the mysteries of the past are all Yang Shen, the brilliant scholar condemned to a lifelong exile in Yunnan.

Reading Yang Shen, one gets the sense that he knew only too well that the origin of footbinding was unknowable and unverifiable; like Confucius, it was locked in the incommensurable past. This realization, however, enabled him to be playful and inventive with the present and, as we will see, with the historical record. Yang's veneration of antiquity is thus relative, resting as it does on a dynamic understanding of time and an appreciation for the here-now: ancient antiquity is forever lost to us; recent antiquity can be accessed and made relevant to the present by way of "comprehensive investigation." As one of the subjects of such investigation, footbinding opens a small window to the past.

In this dynamic sense, Yang's veneration of Han interpretations of the classics is compatible with his contempt for the "return to antiquity" literary movement that had prevailed since the early Ming. Coining the motto "Poetry can be found in every person and every generation," Yang believed that literature is born of spontaneous and immediate emotions.[18] There could not have been a more forceful statement for the valorization of self-expression and the present that became the hallmark of late-Ming urban culture one century after Yang's death.

Yang's favorite metaphor for natural emotions is none other than the unadorned foot. In the Tang poet Li Bo's oeuvre, Yang found three separate eulogies to a "plain-footed girl" *(suzu nü)* or a silk-washing girl whose "feet are white as frost." When chatting with a decades-long friend, the local literatus Zhang Yushan, Yang mused: "What propelled Li Bo to turn his head and gaze at this plain-footed girl not once but thrice?" Zhang responded in jest: "He surely wrote what came to his mind, didn't he?" Yang was so enchanted with the plain-footed girl that he borrowed Li's imagery and expression to compose a poem of his own. As he stated it, his intention was to express his displeasure with "students of poetry today who are bound by conventions and rigid imitations. In striving to be beautiful, they appear all the more clumsy. It is far better to be natural."[19]

Analogy aside, it is hard to tell what Yang Shen thought of a girl with unadorned feet, or if he construed footbinding as ruinous contrivance.[20] To such modern writers as Xu Ke, the discourse on unadorned foot was proof that an indigenous tradition of tianzu did exist. Yang Shen's admirer-critic Hu Yinglin, in turn, saw Li Bo's poems as evidence that footbinding was absent in the Tang dynasty. The modern critics erred in their anachronism, whereas Hu Yinglin was unconvincing in assuming poetic allusions to be straightforward documents of social practice. In contrast, Yang Shen seems content with insinuations, fragments, and uncertainties.

For all of his diligent reading and notation, Yang's ultimate objective appears to be neither disputation nor drawing the line between myth and history. To Yang, more than other scholars, the search for footbinding's origins is a game. His notations are riddled with contradictions, and he offered no support for his suggestion that footbinding originated in the Six Dynasties period. Instead of proving hypotheses and verifying facts, Yang was more interested in exploring the terms and limits of the philological exercise by asking fundamental questions about the kind of cultural work that written texts perform: How do words befuddle, scintillate, or convey the truth to the reader? His goal was not to instill certainty but to plant the seed of doubt in his readers. How much fun it would be, he seems to be winking to his readers, if everyone realized that the unknown is ultimately unknowable.

HAN FOOTLES: THE MEASUREMENT OF BODY PARTS

Perhaps Yang Shen was playing a practical joke when he eventually took to forging "ancient texts." Perhaps he wanted to poke fun at those who venerated old books. Perhaps he was eager to show off his knowledge of antiquity. One thing is certain: the enigma of footbinding is at the heart of the enticement of his often-cited forgery, *Han Footles (Han zashi mixin)*. As if issuing an open invitation to his readers to be skeptical, Yang presented this short text in a gray zone between probability and improbability. Even in Chinese, half of the title is inscrutable: whereas "Han zashi" can be rendered "trivialities from the Han dynasty," "mixin" is not a recognizable term although "mi" (secrets) and "xin" (name of the eighth of the ten Heavenly stems; spicy hot; suffering; a surname) are common characters. In an afterword signed by Yang, he claimed that he discovered the book in the coffer of a Mr. Dong, a tribal subprefectural magistrate in Yunnan. A seal inscription led Yang to hypothesize that it was brought to the region by an early Ming official, Wang Zichong.[21] It is not surprising that Wang was a verifiable character but Dong was not.

Han Footles narrates the selection of Maiden Ying, daughter of General Liang, as empress during the reign of Emperor Huan of the Later Han dynasty (r. 147–67). In his afterword, Yang Shen made sure that his reader would not miss the climactic scene, which occurs early in the story: "The episode whereby Granny Wu entered the empress's chamber and inspected her body is strange and provocative, albeit too dirty and lewd" (656). This weak disavowal had the predictable effect of hastening the reader's fingers to turn the pages back to the scene, which depicts the sensory world of the maiden's private chamber. The reader gains entry to that space and the maiden's body by identifying with Granny's way of knowing: having adjusted to the light and conducted a visual inspection, she supplemented it with tactile knowledge and quantitative measurements.

The setting: Granny Wu arrives at dawn, when natural light casts a lustrous hue on Maiden Ying's face. She espies Ying's eyes, eyebrows, mouth, teeth, ears, and nose, all perfectly proportioned and aligned. Removing a hairpin, Granny loosens Ying's chignon to measure the length of her hair, which cascades down to the floor; it is long enough to swaddle around the hand/arm eight times. The propensity to submit the maiden's body parts to quantification will become more pronounced and the measurements more precise as the erotics of the narrative intensify.

Granny manages to persuade Ying to disrobe after some resistance; Ying is so shy that she shuts her eyes and turns her back against Granny. Granny goes about her job methodically: "The body emits a fragrance; her muscles are laid out neatly; when slapped her skin is so smooth that it does not cling to one's hand. Her front is round and her back, flat. Her fatty tissue is built like chiseled jade. Her breasts are like sprouting beans; her navel can accommodate a half-inch pearl. Her genitals are protruding, showing off her two buttocks. Her vagina is flush with bright cinnabar red, a reddish gold opal ready to burst into flames." Reading these signs, Granny Wu concludes: "This is a virgin who guards her body strictly with propriety" (651–52). Under Granny's exacting eyes and probing hands, the maiden's body appears in its naked physicality, stripped of not only clothes but poetic allusions.

The physiognomy of the virgin's limbs and genitals is only half of the surprise Yang had in store for his readers. If Granny's inspection of the maiden was "too dirty and lewd" in its suggestive descriptions of the genitals, the subsequent narration of measurements and proportions takes an opposite tact, but is no less provocative: "Granny sizes up Ying's body: her blood embellishes her skin; her skin decorates her flesh; her flesh reveals the bones. In height she is neither too tall nor too short. From head to toe she measures seven feet one inch; her shoulders extend to one foot six inches; her hips are three inches narrower. The tip of each shoulder measures two feet seven inches to her fingers. The fingers are four inches away from her palm, like ten young slender bamboo branches. The length of her thigh to her sole is three feet two inches" (652).[22] The tone of clinical detachment only serves to pique the reader's imagination, infusing the description with an erotic charge.

Finally, the crucial measure: "Her foot is eight inches long. Both the instep and shank are plump. Her sole is flat and her digits are packed together." Then follow two descriptions with curious construction, ambiguous words, and shifty subjects: "restrain/bind/bend—fine white silk—compress—sock" *(yuexian powa)* and "restrain—tie—tiny/concealed/mysterious—simile—forbidden palace" *(shoushu weiru jinzhong;* 652). Various interpretations are possible. If one is inclined to suggest that Maiden Ying has bound feet, then the lines may read: "Her feet were bound in fine white silk and dressed in tight socks. The restriction (or binding) was as mysterious as the depths of the inner palace." Or, an equally plausible reading evokes tight socks and inaccessibility, but says nothing about footbinding: "Her feet are restrained and tucked inside her tight socks of fine white silk. The maiden was restrained and concealed as the resident of the forbidden palace." There are several other possible interpretations.

It seems clear that the possibility of multiple interpretations was intended by Yang. The open-ended quality of the text is embedded in its mysterious title, *mixin,* and accentuated by deliberate contradictions between Yang-the-commentator and Yang-the-author-imposter. As commentator, he signaled his preference for the first interpretation at the end of the afterword: "I have investigated the origins of footbinding but come up empty. Upon reading the words 'restrain—fine white silk—compress—sock' and 'restrain—tie—tiny—simile—forbidden palace,' it dawned on me that footbinding has existed since the Later Han period. Once these words escaped my mouth, even a fast chariot drawn by four horses could not call them back. I thought that I would mention it here in case some readers will find fault with my omissions" (656). Ironically, Yang's unequivocal reading only works to fan the flame of disbelief. For these words are sure to raise a red flag in the minds of readers who recall other descriptions of the maiden's feet earlier in the story.

The reader does not need a long memory to remember, for example, that "Both the instep and shank are plump. Her sole is flat and her digits are packed together." The meaning of "packed digits" is ambiguous, as it could refer to either a bound foot or tight sock. Moreover, physicians in modern times observed that footbound women develop strong buttocks but their shanks are emaciated from lack of use. A "plump shank" is therefore also a sign of the absence of footbinding, although we do not know if that was common knowledge in the fifteenth century. Regardless of the interpretation we choose to adopt, the novelty of this passage is unmistakable. If Zhang Bangji helped transmit the knowledge that footbinding is signified by the arched shape, Yang went further by calling attention to the anatomical effects that binding may leave on different parts of the foot.

Even more befuddling is another factual description, "her foot is eight inches long." Many subsequent writers, such as Yu Huai (1616–96), read it as definitive proof that footbinding was *not* practiced in the Later Han. Yet even such clinical precision is not as unequivocal as it may seem. Yu's friend Fei Xihuang (b. 1664), for example, suggested that eight inches on the Han ruler equaled four Ming inches, and a four-inch foot by Ming reckoning is a bound foot in his eyes.[23] Yang Shen, we may surmise, left openings for future readers to subvert his own suggestion that footbinding in the past can be known by anatomical descriptions and measurements.

Upon closer inspection, even such hallmarks of empirical knowledge as anatomy and quantification are not as certain as they seem when they describe realities in the past and when our *only* access to the body they refer to is by way of the written word. In the end, the reader is left face to face with the futility with which Yang began his search: a futility that arose from a realization of the limitations of the word as the conduit of knowledge from the past. Antiquity, we may recall, is as inaccessible as the splendors of the capital for the scholar in exile. Instead of riding on the historicist faith that the distance between past and present can be bridged by painstaking archival research, factual verification, and logical deduction, Yang Shen dispensed with the pretension altogether that one can return to the distant capital.

Instead of despair, however, Yang rode into the unknown with optimism and a sense of freedom, even mischief. In invading the integrity of the archives as a repository of knowledge and in insisting on a playful reading strategy, he alerted his readers to the lack of one-on-one correspondence between text and meaning. In so doing, he changed the reader's expectations of the kind of cultural work performed by a text. Subsequent scholars, too busy to correct his mistakes, seem oblivious to Yang's main message: that there is life beyond the search for certainty and authenticity.

Han Footles is a milestone in the origin discourse in spite of, and perhaps because of, its dubious authenticity and the layers of ambiguities embedded in the text. The experience of reading and comprehending the story is a lesson in skepticism. Elsewhere, Yang prefaced his own philological exercises with these words: "To believe in the believable, that is no doubt belief; to doubt the doubtful, that is also a form of belief. Ancient scholars established themselves by their propensity to doubt, whereas current scholars work too hard to dispel their doubts."[24] As the ultimate doubter, Yang toyed with the very legitimacy of philological investigations: What if ancient texts, in which we vest so much authority, are in fact modern inventions?

Han Footles demonstrates that seemingly objective quantification may serve unscientific ends; it may even pique erotic imagination. The fetish of numbers and measurements will remain key to the lure of the bound foot for centuries to come, as we have seen in *Picking Radishes*. It seems as though Yang Shen had anticipated those nostalgic connoisseurs from twentieth-century Tianjin and Shanghai. This is a remarkable feat, for the cultural and temporal distances that separated Yang from those residents of modern treaty ports are as insurmountable as those between Yunnan and the capital.

REFUTING YANG SHEN: HU YINGLIN TURNS TO SHOES

Yang Shen's foremost admirer-critic, Hu Yinglin (1551–1602), did not take Yang's insinuations in *Han Footles* that footbinding originated in the Later

Han seriously enough to refute it. But he launched the first concerted attack on Yang's theory that footbinding can be traced to the Six Dynasties, and in so doing sealed Yang's canonical status in the origin discourse. Born eight years before Yang's death, Hu never met Yang. But he was so enamored with the older man's erudition and flair that he devoted three of his own books to correcting Yang's mistakes and omissions. In one, *The Revised Scarlet and Lead Scrolls (Danqian xinlu)*, not only did he adopt the title from Yang, he also quoted Yang's notations verbatim before offering his own learned opinions. It seems as though Yang Shen lived and spoke twice, as an original and in quotations.

Hu Yinglin's works constitute the ultimate tribute by an admirer who took Yang's stricture of "comprehensive investigation" to heart but found Yang's own thoroughness wanting. Together they were recognized by modern scholars as Ming predecessors of the Qing philological movement. Hu Yinglin was even more marginal to officialdom than Yang. Holder of a provincial degree, he had, in fact, never served in the bureaucracy. Hu professed distaste for the rigidity of the examination system, preferring to read widely in history, philosophy, and notations. Son of a successful official, he decided to retire permanently to his private library in a villa at the outskirts of his native city of Lanxi, Zhejiang.[25] As such he fit Benjamin Elman's description of a philological scholar who, sustained by the wealthy urban economy of seventeenth-century Jiangnan, relied on neither an official appointment nor imperial favor for his livelihood.[26] This independence allowed him to depart from the official curriculum of Song learning.

Indeed, the community of scholars that emerged in Hu's lifetime changed the sociological context of the origin discourse. When a new piece of evidence or argument surfaced, it circulated among friends and sooner or later would become citations in another notation book.[27] Previously considered too trivial and private to be spoken of, footbinding's origins emerged as a topic of literati conversation. This currency of footbinding as a subject of informal and scholarly discourses may be a response to its growing popularity as a social practice in the sixteenth century.

The presence of a contemporary audience in part accounts for the location of Hu Yinglin's analytic focus in the here-now. If Yang Shen was preoccupied with the inaccessibility of the receding past, Hu assumed a communion between antiquity and the present. Ancient texts, he believed, could illuminate customary practices in his own times; conversely, current practices influenced his interpretation of the classics. As such, Hu's philological musings can be combed for traces of social history, yielding fragmentary but valuable insights on female attire, male-female difference, and women's handiwork in late-sixteenth-century Jiangnan, as we will see. Above all, Hu's notations suggest that footbinding was perceived as a human institution and hallmark of manmade culture. Moreover, located in the realm of attire and decoration, footbinding defined femininity by marking the female difference.

In fact, it was the styles of female attire and footwear fashioned by Hu's contemporaries that led him to question Yang Shen's theory. Yang's main evidence was a Yuefu song entitled "Double Bindings":

> *A pair of new embroidered silk bindings;*
> *The insteps as glamorous as spring.*
> *Others know not to sing their praises,*
> *I alone know how lovely are the braces.*[28]

The Yuefu songs refer to an eclectic body of ancient songs that can be set to music, including imperial ritual incantations and folk tunes. Some hail from as early as the Han and Wei-Jin periods, whereas others may date as late as the Tang and Five Dynasties (907–60).[29] Yang's contention that footbinding originated earlier than the tenth century hinges on his assumptions that the binding cloths *(xingchan)* referred to in this song are women's foot-binding cloths.

Hu Yinglin, however, observed that there are two vastly different kinds of binding cloth. The *xingchan*-bindings "are what women wore under their socks, or 'leg-binders' *[guojiao]* in today's terms." A crucial difference between leg-binders and foot-binders is that the former were common attire for males *and* females before footbinding *(zazu)* became fashionable for women. In days of old, the only gender difference lay in the fabric: "Men used cloth whereas women used silk, decorated with embroidered patterns to enhance the beauty. But they were hidden under socks, hence the line 'Others know not to sing their praises.'" After women began to bind their feet—whenever that was—leg-bindings became the prerogative of men, as was customary in Hu's times (see fig. 11).[30] Similarly, he observed that cat-tail shoes used to be worn by both males and females in antiquity; in contrast "today they are fashionable throughout the empire. Yet the wearers are exclusively male. Since women have bound feet, they would never wear them." In short, Hu's argument is that footbinding gave rise to gender-specific footwear.[31]

In focusing on differences in footwear style, Hu Yinglin subtly altered the way through which footbinding entered into discourse. Yang Shen's innovative description, in terms of the anatomical parts of Maiden Ying's feet, was not pursued by later scholars. The reason, as he himself put it, is that such a fixation on the body was "too dirty and lewd." In detaching the definition of footbinding from the female body and redirecting the gaze to exterior attire and decoration, Hu Yinglin made the venture more respectable, and more amenable to the methods of philological investigation. We know the existence or absence of footbinding by noting what women wear on their feet.

Faulting Yang Shen for not living by his own creed of comprehensive investigation, Hu found twenty-one new references to female footwear from the Tang times and before. Since none mentioned "arched and slender" *(gongxian)*, he concluded that women did not have bound feet before the Tang. This fixation on shoes, or rather on the textual representations of shoes, could become excessive. For no apparent reason except to demonstrate that Yang Shen failed to cover it all, Hu attached a list of 148 notations on one type of shoes *(lü)*.[32]

THE QUEEN'S SHOES,
WOMANLY WORK, AND THE FEMALE DIFFERENCE

In refuting Yang, Hu has clarified two cultural meanings of footbinding in his times. By the sixteenth century, the arched foot was recognized as the marker of male and female difference. Furthermore, it also marked the distance between past and present, the former being characterized by the lack of substantive difference between male and female footwear. Before turning to Hu's attitude toward historical change and current fashion, it is worthwhile here to expound on gender difference and the making of femininity by analyzing Hu's disagreement with Yang over the interpretation of *The Rites of Zhou* and the nature of womanly work.

The Rites of Zhou, which first emerged in the mid-second-century B.C.E. during the Former Han dynasty, describes the administrative structures, laws, sacrifices, rituals, techniques, and customs in the royal state of Zhou in antiquity. The six sections of the book correspond to the six offices and domains of the Zhou hierarchy: celestial; terrestrial; spring; summer; autumn; winter. The elaborate scheme, wrought of the principles of symmetry and hierarchy, is imbued with cosmological significance. Although we do not know the extent to which they were actually practiced in the Zhou dynasty (1045–256 B.C.E.), these rites were to have an indelible impact on the governmental, architectural, and sartorial institutions of subsequent dynasties.[33]

Of particular interest to philologists searching for hints of footbinding in antiquity is the sixth section, "Winter offices: records of the scrutiny of crafts." A catalogue of the craftsmen attached to the royal court, it describes the technical procedures and component parts that went into the making of the litany of material culture: carriages, weapons, boats, clothing, hats, and shoes.[34] Also relevant is the first section, "Celestial offices: domain of the Prime Minister," which deals with general administrative matters and includes the titles of various keepers of shoes and formal gowns. In particular, Yang Shen's interest was piqued by the office of Keeper of Shoes *(lüren),* who was in charge of the garments and shoes of the king and queen. He mused: "Hmm. Ordering craftsmen to make the queen's shoes—isn't it a lewd thing to do? So what good did the virtue of 'womanly work' [*fugong,* commonly *nügong*] do in antiquity?"[35] Yang implied that women should make their own shoes, the charge of womanly work, and failure to do so would have dire consequences for all.

To illustrate the import of womanly work Yang cited two lines from the second poem in the classic *Book of Songs,* which described women cutting kudzu vine in a ravine and then boiling the fiber. They were engaging in productive work: "Weaving fine and coarse hemp cloth, / Sewing garments comfortable to wear." He concluded: "That was how the Zhou came to prosper. When women did not participate in public work *[gongshi]* and stopped feeding silkworms and weaving, that was how the Zhou collapsed." He added somewhat incredulously: "When the Duke of Zhou institutionalized the system of rites, did he really set up an office making women's shoes?"[36] Yang Shen's attitudes toward the Zhou queen's shoes are curiously contradictory: on one hand, they belong to a realm so private, so close to the queen's skin, that having them made by an officially appointed craftsman is "lewd." On the other hand, what the queen—and by extension all women—made with her own hands is the pillar of public order. Yang's equation of "womanly work" with "public work" endows the women's sphere with enormous public and political significance.

Hu Yinglin came to the Duke of Zhou's defense. He began by noting the anomaly of shoes: all other items in the royal couple's wardrobe were placed under separate, gender-specific charges. Under the Ministry of State *(tian-guan)*, for example, the Inner Master of the Wardrobe *(nei sifu)* oversaw the preparation and maintenance of the queen's formal gowns. The king's gowns fell under the jurisdiction of the Outer Master. The same with headdresses. Why did they share one Keeper of Shoes? The puzzled Hu filed away the question. "Later I examined [sources from] the Han, Tang, and the Five Dynasties to ascertain the origins of women's footbinding. Returning to *The Rites of Zhou* to study the charges of the Keeper of Shoes, I noticed that the shoes of the king and queen, as well as those of titled gentlemen and ladies in and out of the court, are identical in name, shape, and color. It dawned on me that in antiquity [*sandai,* the three dynasties of Xia, Shang, and Zhou], male and female shoes are by and large the same. Therefore it made sense to have the same Keeper oversee them."[37] Hu's way of knowing is typical of philologists: when incongruities stirred his doubts, he went back to examine ancient texts until he arrived at a plausible explanation.

Yang Shen's error, according to Hu, is to impute the gendered division in footwear and the latter's eroticized meanings in *his* times back to antiquity, a bad case of presentism. "For the ancients, [the color and design of ritual] shoes are strictly regimented. In coordination with the [color and design] of headdress, they established clear hierarchical rankings." In fact, Hu maintained that the Zhou was doomed by the confusion of status symbols ("prostitutes and actors wearing the queen's attire") that ensued from the breakdown of hierarchy, not by women's retreat from textile work. In other words, shoes are not trivial and private concerns akin to such "lewd" articles as underwear and lower garments, as Yang had assumed. Without thinking too deeply, Yang lumped the queen's shoes with the "arched and slender shapes *[gongxian zhuang]* that have prevailed in recent times." After a long discourse on the offices of the various keepers of shoes and wardrobes, Hu drove home the point that these items of attire were of public import since they were intended for ceremonial and public functions, not everyday wear. "If the queen's shoes were what women's shoes are today, surely they would lie outside the domain of the Inner Master of Wardrobe, and would have been made by professional tailors."[38]

Hu's complaint, then, is that in his day, women's shoes lost their public significance because of the prevalence of footbinding. Now produced commercially, female shoes have become, as Yang asserted, artifacts of lewdness. Hu's implication seems to be that the female body also experienced a fall from grace: no longer a public vessel, it became a conduit of erotic pleasures. The value of women's labor, too, was degraded. Instead of making hemp cloth, women now either bought many of their everyday shoes from the market or engaged in superficial decoration, such as adding embroidered motifs of flowers and birds to their shoes.[39] In a commercial age saturated with footbinding, femininity had become associated with bodily indulgence, frivolous consumption, and excessive ornamentation. Gaining in textual and social visibility but remaining unavailable to many who could not afford it, footbinding thus attained the height of its erotic potential in the seventeenth century. The implications of this development for urban women and their fashion sense will be examined in the final chapter.

CURRENCY OF THE PRESENT:
FOOTBINDING AND FASHION

Hu Yinglin made many casual remarks indicating that footbinding was a fashionable, conventional, and customary practice in his time. On assessing female beauty, for example, he said: "These days other than the face, the foot is the most essential determinant." Furthermore, "even a child today knows to appreciate and desire the arched shape and smallness of the foot *[zuzhi gongxiao]*." He betrayed a sense of bewilderment at how fast the practice had spread and how far present standards of beauty had departed from those of antiquity. Hence: "In our age footbinding *[chanzu]* has long been practiced. If you did not follow, people would make fun of you. But if you had bound feet during the Six Dynasties, wouldn't you be seen as a human prodigy *[renyao]*?"[40] Rather than footbinding's purported origins, Hu implied, an understanding of the power of convention is more useful in explaining the spread of the practice. Once customary standards of beauty shifted in footbinding's favor, it would spread as a result of emulation.

Another astute insight of Hu's is that at the inception of the practice, literary allusions to silk socks *(luowa)*, dainty feet, and so on were instrumental in changing prevailing standards of beauty, leading to footbinding's popularity. Following Yang Shen's lead, Hu examined a large number of Tang and pre-Tang poems for philological purposes. At the same time, he was aware that literature was more than sociological data: it changes, not just reflects, expectations and experiences. He remarked: "Even in the early years of the Song [eleventh century], the majority of women did not bind their feet. Then in the Yuan dynasty, poems, *ci*-lyrics, songs, and dramas all harped on the subject, leading to its extreme popularity today." Hu grimly added: "We have strayed further from beauty."[41]

Although Hu placed footbinding in the realm of fashion and ornamentation, he did not hide his distaste for the bound foot underneath the concealment of leggings and shoes. Echoing Yang Shen's admiration for Li Bo's "plain-footed girl," he remarked that " 'plain and clean,' or 'plump and beautiful' were standard praises for women's feet in the past. Today, you can say that the bound foot looks good [on the outside], but inside the bodily tissue is dry and petrified, not to mention foul and filthy."[42] This is one of the few admissions made before the nineteenth century that "blow the cover" of footbinding. It exposes a different corporeality than Yang's anatomical and quantifying descriptions of Maiden Ying. It also flies in the face of the preponderance of poetic and dramatic allusions to the eroticized feet, encased as they were in leggings and shoes. Hu described one fashionable item in his day that worked as an instrument of concealment: leggings worn on top of binding cloths that extended up to the knees *(xiku)*, known as "half-stockings" *(banwa)*.[43]

Hu's own theory locates the beginnings of footbinding in the last years of the Tang, which fell in 907, and the period of Five Dynasties (907–60) that ensued. His reasoning, far from systematic, rests on the overriding importance he attached to the adjective "slender" *(xian)*. "Slender" feet are diametrically opposed to natural feet: "If they are said to be slender then the feet are not plain; if they are said to be plain then the feet cannot be slender." This allowed him to read one couplet by the Tang poet Du Mu (803–52) as signaling the beginning of the cultural aura of footbinding, if not the social practice: "Sizing up with a ruler inlaid with gold, shaving off four *fen*, / Slender, slender, jade bamboo shoots wrapped in spring clouds." The slender bamboo shoots, he implied, are allusions to bound feet, whereas the spring clouds refer to beautiful socks. He also mentioned poems by Li Shang-yin (813–58) and in the mid-tenth-century collection *Among the Flowers* (*Huajian ji;* "Slowly shifting the arched sole, embroidering the silk shoe") as supporting evidence. Yet Hu immediately planted seeds of doubt for his own theory, suggesting that "bamboo shoots" might have meant women's toes in Tang times, instead of the arched foot as in his time.[44]

Hu's clearest statement about the evolution of footbinding came in the form of a striking comparison: "Both the printing of books by woodblock and the binding of women's feet began around the end of Tang and the Five Dynasties period; both flourished during the Song, reached extremes during the Yuan, and have reached even newer heights today. The ins and outs of the two stories are extremely similar. It is only that footbinding is a trivial female matter, hence scholars have neglected to study it."[45] Hu's tantalizing coupling of footbinding and printing placed the former in the realm of cultural institution and material practice, a most important insight.

If Yang Shen was more interested in probing the boundaries and limitations of ancient texts, Hu Yinglin was more willing to submit to their authority. He expressed hope that his own tenth-century origin theory might be disproved one day by a more diligent reader: "Books on events in the Six Dynasties are as boundless as the ocean. Perhaps there is a piece of definitive evidence somewhere that can dispel all doubts."[46] Until that happens, skepticism remains the proper attitude. The origins of footbinding, or woodblock printing, for that matter, may not be pinpointed with precision, but the trajectory of its social development can be traced in historic time. So if the quest for origins inspires one to read a few more books and come to better understand institutional and cultural histories, then the lengthy philological exercise would have been worthwhile.

Despite Hu Yinglin's suggestion of a progressive timeline from the tenth to the sixteenth centuries, ultimately footbinding signaled to him the rupture of history. Hu's awareness of the distance between the past and the present prefaces every statement he made about footbinding as a customary practice in his time. This urbane, if not downright modern, celebration of contemporaneity was prevalent in the southern cities in the sixteenth and seventeenth centuries. The present, for all its imperfections such as petrified feet, is the best of times and the only time we can know with some certainty.

Hu Yinglin's sense of historical rupture, celebration of the present, and placement of footbinding in the realm of wearable fashion find their clearest expression in the origin discourse of the scholar-poet Yu Huai (1616–96). Best known as the author of *Random Recollections from the Wooden Bridge (Banqiao zazhi)*, nostalgic memoirs of the Nanjing courtesan quarters before the fall of the Ming, Yu's musings are suffused with an awareness of the distance that separated attire past and present. In particular, high-heeled shoes for the arched foot were inventions "unheard of in the past, and reach their zenith only in the present." Fashionable ladies from the Suzhou area took to increasingly fancy styles: carving the soles out of fragrant wood and covering them with the finest twill damask, or inserting pouches of fragrance in the latticed heel so that every step would leave a floral pattern of fragrant powder on the floor.

Rhetorically Yu called these new styles "dressing the human prodigy" *(fuyao)*, abnormalities believed to be signs of cosmological disorder. His tone, however, conveys not moral sanction but pride in the exquisite tastes of his contemporaries and the fine craftsmanship in the urban centers of seventeenth-century Jiangnan. "These are footwear that poets in the Song and Yuan dynasties failed to eulogize, therefore I am making them known here so that those in this world who wax lyrical about the fragrant toilette and jade terrace can take note."[47] Fragrant toilette and jade terrace refer to poetry that takes women and the feminine as its subjects. Once established, the fashion of high heels was so dominant that three centuries later, as we have seen, Governor Yan Xishan was still troubled by the prevalence of arched wooden soles in the interior of Shanxi.

ZHAO YI AND THE EIGHTEENTH-CENTURY ZENITH

The Qing bibliophile and historian Zhao Yi (1727–1814) enjoyed the last word on footbinding's origins. Zhao, whose life coincided with the height of Qing imperial power and prosperity, was the last philologist whose quest for footbinding's origins appeared more academic than polemical, whose goal was more a quest for understanding than condemnation. From Zhao's notation, "The Arched Foot," it becomes clear that during the century that separated him from Yu Huai, footbinding had become the normative practice of Han Chinese women.

So customary, in fact, that the only noteworthy social historical details in Zhao's notation are exceptions to the norm: "As a current custom, footbinding is practiced all over the empire. But among the people of Guangdong and Guangxi, only those in the provincial capitals imitate it, not those in the countryside. The same is true for the Luo, Miao, Bo, and Yi peoples in Yunnan and Guizhou." The last exception was even more striking: "Females within the city walls of Suzhou value small feet, but country women beyond the city gates all work in the fields in bare feet. They do not bind their feet. We may say that these peoples each follow their own customs and [we] should not make blanket statements."[48] These examples of unfettered feet underscore Zhao's awareness of the spatial, cultural, and ethnic differences in the Qing multi-ethnic empire, as well as the role played by footbinding in making these differences visible. Guangdong, Guangxi, Yunnan, and Guizhou are in themselves peripheral provinces; they are further divided into metropolis-rural and Han–non-Han areas. Also noteworthy is that in Suzhou, one of the wealthiest cities in the heartland, footbinding marked a conspicuous urban-rural gap.

These exceptions do not detract from the fact that during the course of the Qing dynasty, footbinding underwent a 180-degree change: from high urban fashion to customary practice expected of the average woman. Two deliberate policies of the Manchu state might have inadvertently contributed to its popularity among non-elite families: the futile early-Qing efforts to ban footbinding as a signpost of Han Chinese identity and the eighteenth-century promotion of the cotton industry in rural areas.[49] Its seeming omnipresence notwithstanding, the notable exceptions mentioned above led Zhao to conclude that in its eighteenth-century heyday, footbinding was a multiple, not uniform, practice: one should not offer any "blanket statements." That footbinding is a localized, situated practice is a remarkable insight. If footbinding is not one practice but many, it becomes increasingly difficult to presume that its beginnings can be traced back to one point of origin. Although Zhao maintained the faith that ancient texts are repositories of knowledge about past practices, he was all too aware of the futility of the quest for singularity and certainty.

Zhao's notations on footbinding are systematic summaries of existing theories and evidence, and as such provide a convenient closure for the philological quest. All previous explanations, he contended, can be reduced to three: that footbinding originated in the Five Dynasties (907–60); that it already existed in the Six Dynasties (222–589); that it began in the Qin-Han period (221 B.C.E.–220 C.E.). The Five-Dynasties theory, we may recall, was suggested by the thirteenth-century scholar Zhou Mi, developed by Hu Yinglin, and emerged as mainstream opinion by the sixteenth century. The strongest support for this theory, Zhao pointed out, was a negative one: there is no persuasive evidence for the existence of footbinding in the preceding Tang dynasty. Among the myriad pre-tenth-century poetic and encyclopedic references, there was scant mentioning of "slender and small" *(xianxiao)* feet, or of "arched and slender" shoes *(gongxian)*. Zhao's assumption is a familiar one shared by Zhang Bangji, Che Ruoshui, Yang Shen, and Hu Yinglin: if footbinding were indeed practiced in a certain age, then it must have left traces in the written archives. Above all, Li Bo's eulogies of the "plain-footed girl" was positive evidence that footbinding was *not* in vogue in Tang times (655).

The most outspoken advocate for the second theory, that footbinding existed in the three centuries before the Tang, was Yang Shen. Zhao Yi cited Yang's evidence, the Yuefu song on leg-bindings and Han Wo's poem on "six inches of succulent flesh." He added a few other notations, most notable being the story of Consort Yang. The last theory, pointing to the Han dynasty, we may recall, was also proposed by Yang Shen, and found its most direct evidence in his description of Maiden Ying in *Han Footles*. Zhao Yi's assessment of both theories is that, convincing or otherwise, they are noteworthy because they come with textual support *(jieyou suoju)*. But he proceeded to weigh one text against the other: Li Bo's eulogies of the plain-footed girl constitute definitive, positive evidence *(queyou mingju)*, whereas the texts in which Consort Yang's story appeared are untrustworthy forgeries (656).

Zhao Yi's methodical reasoning confirmed that the centuries-old tenth-century theory was indeed the most persuasive. His summation of footbinding's origins: Han Wo's "six inches of succulent flesh" and Du Mu's "Sizing up with a ruler, shaving off four *fen*" poems were written in a time before footbinding emerged as an actual practice. But when poets harped on the long and the short of feet, we may surmise that "the valuing of slender and small *[xianxiao]* feet was gradually gaining ground in prevailing customs." It was not until after the Tang fell, in the Five Dynasties (907–60) period, that footbinding *(zajiao)* became a bodily practice. Zhao's caution that footbinding as an aesthetic ideal is not to be confused for the actual practice of binding feet and that the ideal preceded the practice is remarkably astute.

Also noteworthy are Zhao's views of antiquity and textual veracity. Zhao cited two pieces of support for his chronology: Tao Zongyi's *Notations from Resting the Plough (Chuogenglu)* and the Yuan writer Bai Ting's (1247–1328) notation book *Quiet Words from Deep Water (Zhanyuan jingyu)*.[50] Although these authors did not furnish solid proof, neither support can be dismissed as groundless conjecture because "being Song and Yuan sources, they are not yet distant from the Five Dynasties. These authors must have seen or heard clues that are now lost" (656). This view of the inaccessibility of antiquity recalls Yang Shen's analogy about the capital and Yunnan.

All three origin theories Zhao selected for commentary belong to the realm of verifiable history. He did not find the origin myths about last rulers and their femmes fatales even worth mentioning. Convincing or not, the existence of textual evidence establishes the validity of a theory or claim. The texts he considered acceptable evidence are confined to histories, notation books, encyclopedias, and poetry. Consistently left out of not only Zhao's consideration but also the philological tradition itself is the sizable number of references to footbinding in fiction, drama, and vernacular songs, the genres most instrumental in perpetuating footbinding's aura.[51]

THE BODY DECORATED AND THE BODY REVEALED

The location of Zhao's entry "The Arched Foot" in his notation book is as informative as his sociological and analytic insights. Zhao placed the arched foot in two social and cultural contexts: bodily decoration and deportment, both informed by an acute awareness of gender difference. Immediately following "The Arched Foot" is a notation on the staining of fingernails with red pigment from the garden balsam blossom, allegedly a cosmetic device originating with Chinese Muslim (Hui) women and widely practiced in Zhao's eighteenth century. The procedure is strangely reminiscent of the binding of feet: the petals are ground and mixed with alum, an astringent used in footbinding; the paste is applied to the nails and secured with strips of cloth; after three to four overnight applications the red pigment would stay until the nails grow out.[52]

If varnishing fingernails was always known as a female practice, another article of decoration, a fresh flower as a hairpin, was worn by men in days of old. The distances between past and present, as well as between male and female attire, that had informed the origin discourse of footbinding also structure Zhao's account of hairpin flowers. In Zhao Yi's time, it had become an exclusive female decoration. The top three candidates from the palace examination, however, paraded the streets of Beijing and had gold flowers pinned to their hair, a symbolic gesture of remembering past customs.[53] Footbinding had been viewed as a form of female ornamentation *(nüzhuang)* since the Ming if not earlier, as evinced by its classification in encyclopedias (see fig.

11). Zhao Yi's association of the arched foot with dyed fingernails and hair-pin flowers suggests that this view was still current in his time.[54]

Yet the body is not merely a passive template waiting to be decorated. Being the innovator he was, Zhao opened a new vista from which the origins and meanings of footbinding can be viewed: the body in motion. The body does not always figure in discourses of footbinding's origins. Yang Shen first called attention to the corporeality of the practice by his anatomical descriptions and fetish of measurements. The Maiden Ying that Yang conjured with literary flair, however, is still and passive, more an object under inspection than a volitional agent. Hu Yinglin averted his eyes from the naked body altogether, choosing to locate footbinding in the realm of fashionable footwear. Zhao Yi returned footbinding to the realm of the body by searching for its origins in the history of manners and gestures. The three adjacent entries on the arched foot, fingernails, and hairpin flowers are sandwiched together between a series of notations on sitting, bowing, and other postures that marked the differences between past and present, male and female.

Four issues related to conduct, attire, and furniture are of particular interest to Zhao: What did the ancients do with their shoes and socks in sanctified spaces? When did boots become formal footwear for imperial audiences? Did ancient women prostrate themselves to show respect? What was the posture of repose for ancients: did they kneel or sit? Zhao's investigations into the first two questions led to the realization that the bodily expressions of piety and lewdness are historically contingent. In antiquity, people sat on the floor instead of chairs, and when stepping onto the floor-mat, they would take their shoes off. Zhao asserted that for ancients, the shedding of shoes was a sign of routine respect. The gesture of supreme respect, required for an audience with rulers, was the removal of both shoes and socks, exposing the leg-binders underneath. We have seen that Hu Yinglin argued that these leg-binders *(xingteng, xiefu;* see n. 30) were fashioned by both males and females in antiquity and were not to be confused with foot-binders. Observers in the eighteenth century, Zhao wrote, were likely to frown on the removal of socks as an act of "defilement" approaching "obscenity." How diametrically opposed are customs in antiquity and the present![55]

The Tang dynasty was a pivotal period in the culture of footwear and piety, according to Zhao. In stately sacrificial functions, the removal of shoes and socks was still expected, but officials began to keep their shoes on in routine audiences with the emperor. Furthermore, in the second half of the Tang, leather boots became increasingly common formal courtly wear. Originally a form of non-Sinitic military attire introduced by the Warring States King Wuling of Zhao, leather boots did not catch on in the south but became standard everyday wear in the north. Ironically, after boots gained respectability, shoes became "lewd attire," being associated with bodily privacy, and the removal of socks became unthinkable rudeness. Fashion trends are indeed as changeable as the blowing of the wind, Zhao mused.[56]

Zhao Yi made no direct inference from the shedding of socks to footbinding. But it is tempting to speculate that as bare feet ceased to be the sign of utmost piety during the Tang, and as formal attire called for the encasement of feet in leather boots, the new aesthetics of concealment resonated with the fixation, even eroticization, of female socks and shoes in Tang poetry. When the cultural preference for concealed feet became coupled with the aesthetic ideal of slender female feet, also eulogized in Tang poetry, the aesthetic and ritualistic preconditions for the practice of binding feet were established. Seen in this light, Li Bo's praises of the plain-footed girl are throwbacks to a receding past, whereas Han Wo and Du Mu were fantasizing about the fashion of the future when they fixated on tiny embroidered slippers.

The body that matters to the modern footbinding discourses is either the crippled or the erotic body. Footbinding did alter a woman's posture; the shifting of her center of gravity produced a mincing gait—not unlike that produced by high heels—which was eulogized as "lotus steps" in poetry. But Zhao Yi made the useful reminder that eroticism aside, the material and spatial environments are also crucial to a woman's sense of body and space, and that these conditions, like fashion trends, changed with the passing of time. In other words, her gait and anatomy—the eroticized female body—is not the only body that matters. The gestures and motions of the ritualized body and the social body, in short the constructive effects of binding, are also important aspects of the story that have to be told.

In *The Rites of Zhou* one expression of respectful greeting for women is the "solemn bow" *(subai)*, during which a woman joins her two hands in front of her chest and lowers her forearms. A centuries-long debate since the Song, as vexing as footbinding's origins, centers on the motion of her legs. Was she supposed to also bend her knees in a kneeling gesture? Zhao's answer hinges on a historic change in domestic furniture. In antiquity, when people sat on floor-mats, "kneeling" and "sitting" were similar postures, with the bent leg from the knees down touching the floor. Sitting, a posture of repose, means resting the hips and buttocks on the heels of the two feet, which is how a Japanese today would sit on the tatami mat. In kneeling, a less stable posture, the waist and hips are suspended in air. Hence a sitting woman greeted others by slightly lifting her upper body into a kneeling pose, Zhao reasoned. Later, low platform beds *(chuang)* were introduced for sitting and sleeping, and it was no longer so convenient for women to kneel when sitting on them. They thus stopped kneeling when greeting guests.[57] Again, even a gesture as instinctive as sitting is historically and culturally contingent.

The history of manners has to be sought in the history of material cultures. Zhao Yi narrated but did not date changes in domestic furniture and their profound effects on womanly deportment. Sarah Handler, a historian of Chinese furniture, has studied an early third-century Han tomb painting depicting a feast. "At that time it was common practice for people to sit on mats upon the floor, as low beds and platforms were honorific seats used by the elite and on ceremonial occasions." The canopied bed, elevated and festooned with silk curtains, reached its zenith as ceremonial prop in Tang Buddhist art but its use in domestic homes is less well documented. By about the tenth century, "it became the practice for the Chinese to sit on chairs at high tables rather than upon mats or low platforms" (see fig. 12). This development had an indelible impact on interior space, leading to loftier proportions, walls instead of screens as spatial dividers, and popularity of hanging scrolls as wall decoration.[58]

It is hard to resist the suggestion that without chairs, footbinding might not have materialized. For the first time, people sat with their legs hanging down instead of tucked under, relieving the heel of the foot from bearing the weight of the entire upper body. It is not so much that women had to remove their footwear when sitting on a mat that "prevented" footbinding, for Zhao Yi has informed us that socks were seldom removed except as a gesture of extreme piety. But a shift in posture facilitated by high chairs made footbinding ergonomically possible. Furthermore, the very posture of sitting on chairs facilitates a display of the sitter's feet. If they are so visible, they might as well be decorated according to fanciful suggestions from Tang poetry.

It is less clear if changes in interior space had an impact on the rise of footbinding. The partition of domestic space by more permanent walls instead of screens might have heightened a sense of domestic enclosure, which in turn facilitated the realization of the pre-existing ideal of female seclusion.[59] To modern minds, the safeguarding of female chastity was the very raison-d'être of footbinding. Yet curiously, none of the philologists considered seclusion or morality a plausible explanation. It did not even occur to them that footbinding had any connection with Confucianism. Not only was footbinding absent in the Confucian classics, the practice was also never mentioned, let alone promoted, in any Confucian didactic texts for women.[60] To the contrary, in the philological writings we have examined, footbinding appears as perplexing and morally dubious, associated more with the dangers of sexual license than moral steadfastness.

In short, the tenth century—the last years of the Tang empire and the tumultuous Five Dynasties period after its collapse—emerged as something as close to the origin of footbinding as we can locate in knowable history. There is no smoking gun, but generations of scholars have sifted textual evidence, weighed one probability against another, and used their contemporary knowledge of footbinding to slowly build a compelling narrative. This narrative makes a distinction between the idealization of slender feet and its spread as a social practice, and locates the cultural meaning of the practice in the contexts of fashion, manners, and material culture. During the tenth century, the aesthetic preference for slender and small feet perpetuated in Tang poetry, the rise of concealed feet as a measure of decorum due to changing fashion trends, the availability of chairs that eased pressure on the feet, a new interior architectural space partitioned by walls, perhaps enhancing the appeal of domestic seclusion, all conspired to render the binding of feet not only desirable but also feasible.

QIAN YONG: FROM PHILOLOGY TO SOCIAL CRITIQUE

If Zhao Yi had the last word on the quest for origins by placing footbinding in the context of the body of decorum, three decades later another scholar, Qian Yong (1759–1844), heralded a new—modern would not be an exaggeration—origin discourse. Qian's notation "On Binding Feet" ("Guozu") is a long entry made up of six parts. He echoed the chronology sug-

FIGURE 1. These feet are for walking. ("Women with 'Golden Lilies,'" in John Mac-Gowan, *Men and Manners,* facing p. 249.)

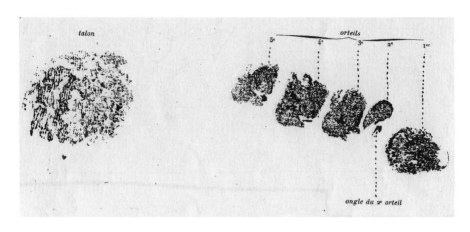

FIGURE 2. Imprint of a bound foot, showing the four folded digits and heel. This sizable foot measures 22 cm (8.8 inches) from toe to heel. The four digits were folded underneath, but the metatarsals were not bent, as in extreme forms of footbinding. The woman's body weight was distributed evenly on the toes *(orteils)* and heel *(talon)*. Dr. J.-J. Matignon's 1899 book, which introduces Chinese culture by way of superstitions, suicide, self-immolation, eunuchs, footbinding, infanticide, abortion, pederasty, and beggary, encapsulates the European fascination with the grotesque and pathological in the Extreme Orient. (J.-J. Matignon, *Superstition, crime, et misére en Chine,* p. 205.)

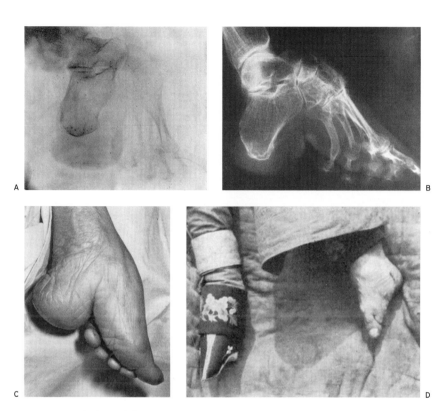

FIGURE 3. The bound foot exposed: photographs in medical reports. (A) X-ray photograph of an extreme arched foot. (J. Preston Maxwell, "On the Evils of Chinese Foot-binding" [1916], facing p. 396.) (B) X-ray photograph of a let-out foot. (C) The cleavage on the underside of the foot. (B and C: H. S. Y. Fang and F. Y. K. Yu, "Foot-binding in Chinese Women"; reprinted from *Canadian Journal of Surgery* 3 (April 1960): 195–202, by permission of the publisher. © 1960 Canadian Medical Association.) (D) Contrast between the naked and the shod foot. (F. M. Al-Akl, "Bound Feet in China," [1932], p. 547.)

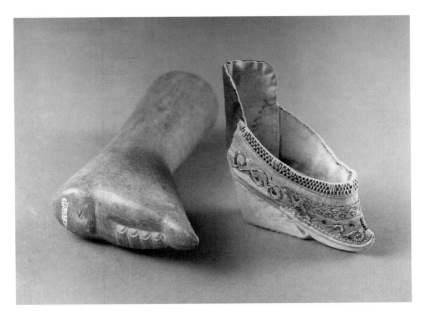

FIGURE 4. Pedagogy of the truncated foot. Wood or plaster models of the bound foot were often used in rallies organized by the natural feet societies, fueling the sensationalist exposure of female body parts. This wooden model and matching shoe were used by the Visual Education Department of the Baptist Missionary Society in Fujian province. (Reproduced by permission of the Government of the HKSAR from the collection of the Hong Kong Museum of History.)

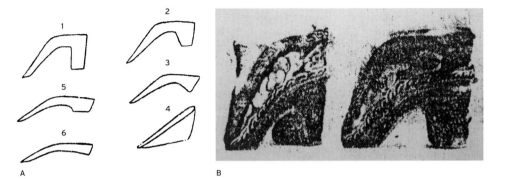

FIGURE 5. Evolution of wooden soles, 1830s–1930s.
(A) The progressive flattening of the arch, shown in a chart with captions by Hu Yanxian, a native of Beijing and a contributor to *Picking Radishes (Caifeilu)*. Hu's captions label the shoes as follows: (1) 1830s style; (2) 1860s–1870s style; (3) 1880s–1890s Shanxi style; (4) 1850s–1860s Jiangnan style; (5) 1890s–1900s northern style; (6) 1920s–1930s current style. (B) 1830s style high-heeled shoes. Hu Yanxian explained that his chart was based on antiquing and interviews with elders:

I once discovered a pair of (1) at an antique stall [shown in (B)]. The uppers are covered with all-over embroidery, the design of which is old and simple. Among the motifs are four animals, perhaps a tiger, lion, elephant, and monkey. The shoe is about four inches long but neither slender nor pointy. Upon consulting with many old men, I realized that this is a very old style. It is not very elegant when judged by today's aesthetic standards.

    I have also seen style (2) in antique stores. I was told that it is a more recent style than (1). The heavy and clumsy look is shed with (3), which is slender, narrow, and delicate. The heel of (4) is like a wedge and extremely tall; the tip of the shoe curves upward. An old man said that this style was not seen in the north. Since the embroidery is elaborate and refined, it must be southern. Style (5) is common in the north in the recent decades. Style (6) is the most "reformed."

    In sum, the older the sole, the higher is [the arch]; the more recent it is, the flatter. As time went on, the arched shoe [gongxie] gradually lost its arch shape. Recently, some shoes have done away with wooden soles altogether. Indeed footbinding is very popular, but the sole of the shoe is now as flat as the earth. (CFL: 227; CFJHL: 130–31)

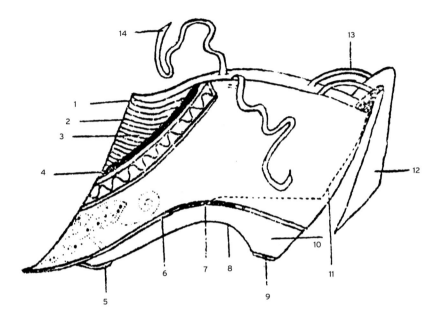

FIGURE 6. (*OPPOSITE*) A drawing of northern-style Kun shoes from the 1920s by Hu Yanxian, who names and describes the parts of the shoe as follows: "(1) moongate or temple gate [the tongue]; (2) ladder rung (mostly made of dark strings in parallel lines; some in crisscrossing lines); (3) mouth-face (the cloth facing underneath the "ladder rung," made of either white cotton or white satin); (4) mouth-tip (sometimes decorated with a colorful silk knotted sash); (5) front heel tab (made of cloth or silk satin in various colors, this was about a half-*fen* [0.05 inch] thick and served to soften the noise of the wooden sole); (6) border piping (this was always white and half- to one-*fen* thick); (7) waist block (ribbon of various colors, marking the middle-back area of the sole); (8) center sole [*dixin*] (place to attach a bell; this part is almost flat in the current styles); (9) back heel tab (same materials as front heel tab); (10) storage area for perfumed powder (with incised floral patterns on the heel); (11) inner high-heel [*ligaodi*] (made of iron, wood, cloth, or bamboo); (12) heel lift (in various patterns, shapes, colors, and lengths); (13) heel lift loop (some are attached to the vamp, not the lift); (14) shoe laces (some are doubled, in fours; mostly red or green)."

In the age of the anti-footbinding movement, the arch became progressively flatter as the regimen of binding became more relaxed. But this did not detract from the fashion statement that the reformed Kun shoes were supposed to make. Hu observed:

The embroidery on the vamp tends to concentrate on the tip of the toes and the edge. The older the style, the bigger the embroidered area. Shoes a hundred years old are covered with all-over designs. The older the wooden sole, the more arched; the more recent, the flatter. Heels a hundred years old look just like the modern [Westernized] high heels.

The tip of Kun shoes comes in all kinds of styles: some curve up like a hook; some are as sharp as an awl; some are very long and pointy, extending far beyond the actual toes; some are short.

The heel lift can vary from two to eight inches in length. Some are practical while others are decorative. The former is made of cloth, seldom silk, so that it is not slippery. After the shoe is fastened on the foot, the heel lift would be turned up and secured under the leg of the pants to prevent the heel of the shoe from drooping. Some heel lifts are purely decorative in function. These delicate tabs trail at the back of the shoes and sway gently as the wearer moves her steps. They are indeed nice ornaments. (CFL: 225–26; CFJHL: 130)

FIGURE 7. The making of Tianjin-style Kun booties, ca. 1904–11: **A-C** show "live sketches" *(shiwu xiesheng)* of three Kun-style booties, 1904 and after, belonging to Bai Jinbao, a Tianjin courtesan famous for her slender feet; **D-E** show the components of the booties. (CFJHL: illustrations between pp. 86 and 87.)

(A) Side view of Bai Jinbao's booties, "waist-piece" decorated with peonies. The lower part of the vamp, faintly decorated with floral motifs, is called a "curved-piece."

(B) Bai Jinbao's booties showing the arched wooden sole and heel tabs, waist-piece decorated with butterfly and melon vines.

(C) Bai Jinbao's booties showing the bamboo heel stiffening, waist-piece decorated with double coins and peaches.

(D) Uppers: decorated waist-piece and uncut curved-piece. *Painted motifs on the waist-piece and curved-piece are the work of professional craftsmen. The drawings on the shaft are bigger and on the latter, more delicate. The more expensive uppers are made of satin; the ordinary ones are made of a starched and polished cotton fabric called "Jingpiao."*

Craftsmen in this profession are all male. They use an apprentice system. Those in training start by drawing the waist-piece and graduate to the more refined curved-piece. After decorated curved-pieces went out of fashion, the craftsmen concentrated on the waist-piece.

When women make their own shoes, they mostly use embroidery; they do not decorate the uppers by drawing. If you see a pair of booties that is not painted but decorated with embroidery or gold couching, it is from a woman's hand.

(E) Wooden soles and small heels.
All booties are attached on wooden soles [mudi] *covered with white cotton cloth. Sometimes a small wooden heel* [xiaodi]*, also covered with cloth, is added to the sole to form the "outer high heel"* [wai gaodi, *in contrast to an "inner high heel,"* li gaodi]*. The wooden sole comes in different sizes; the small heel varies in shape. Normally it is shaped like a truncated oval; occasionally it looks like an apple* [see bottom two drawings here, also bootie on the left in B]*.

Professional wooden sole carvers are all men. Vendors would call them out in alleys; they are also male. They also sell heel stiffening* [xue zhugen]*. It is made of strips of bamboo sheath covered with cloth, like a raft* [see inside of bootie in C]*. When stitched onto the heel area of the bootie, the stiffening prevents it from drooping.*

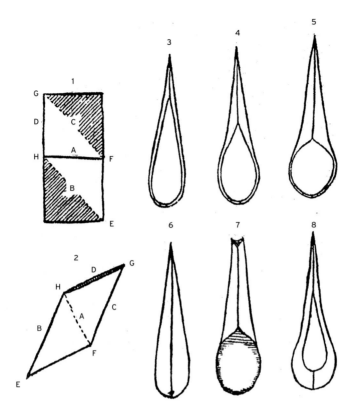

FIGURE 8. Styles of socks in the early twentieth century. Drawing and captions by Hu Yanxian (CFL: 228; CFJHL: 132). Only the bottom views are shown here because the shafts are identical in shape; they differ only in decoration.

(1-2) *Casual socks, 1920s. These simple socks can be made from scraps in five minutes. Take a piece of rectangular cloth whose length is twice its width (proportional to the length of the foot), fold the two diagonals (*B, C*), and sew the two seams together (*EF; BF*). Left as is, the side* D *becomes the opening of the sock. Because the cloth is cut on the bias it conforms to the shape of the foot when worn.* (3) *Kun socks with full padded sole. The sole never extends to the tip, or else it would be uncomfortable.* (4) *Kun socks with half padded sole.* (5) *Socks with padded heel. Women whose heels are fat prefer this style.* (6) *Socks without padded sole. This style is only suitable for those with narrow feet and small heels, or else the sock would look stuffed.* (7) *Socks with cutoff tip and heel. Good for hot summer days and those with sweaty feet.* (8) *Socks with recessed sole.*

FIGURE 9. Playing with footwear fashion, ca. 1905–10: a pair of Shanghai entertainers with feet bound in the more relaxed modern fashion. The cross-dressed "he" wore male cloth shoes while the "she" of the pair wore modern-style socks and flat Mary Janes decorated with pom-poms. Her narrow cigarette-pants, which accentuated the flat, modern silhouette of her feet, represented a sensational style that emerged during the waning years of the Qing dynasty. (Image from the collection of Lewis Stein.)

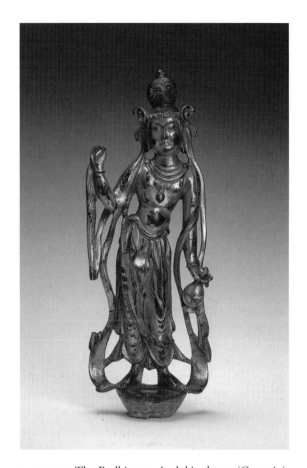

FIGURE 10. The Bodhisattva Avalokiteshvara (Guanyin). The big-footed Bodhisattva appears in a lilting dance pose on a golden lotus in this gilt bronze statue from the Tang dynasty (618–906). Could this image have inspired Yao-niang, or the creation of her myth? (The Avery Brundage Collection, B60B661. © Asian Art Museum of San Francisco. Used by permission.)

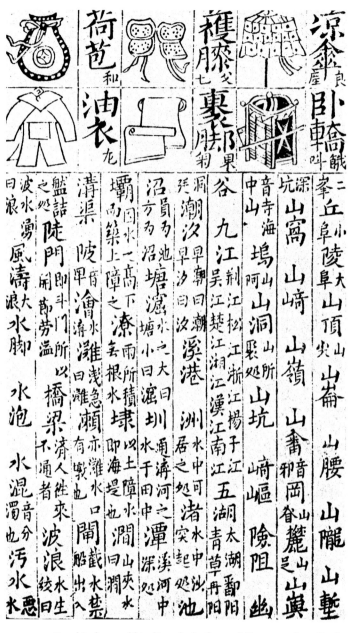

FIGURE 11. Leg-binders and binding cloths from a Ming encyclopedia. In this dictionary of common words and phrases, a pair of leg-binders *(guo-jiao)* is pictured underneath a pair of kneepads (A, illustrations at center top). Both are items for traveling, as are the parasol, palanquin, purse, and raincoat that appear on the same page. On the adjacent page *(not shown)*, are black boots, scholar's shoes, official's hat, head scarf, bow sheath, and

孺 宮娥 公主 古者天子嫁女使公侯
主之故曰公主 同姓主之故曰公主

嬪 宮娥 公主

（right-side columns of Chinese text from the reproduced Ming-edition page）

arrow bag, all unmistakably male objects. In contrast, on another page (**B, illustrations at top right**), a pair of ribbon-like binding cloths *(jiaobo)* appears underneath a face towel, along with three square patches of face powder, two rounds of rouge, and three balls of fragrance, suggesting an association of the binding cloth with items of the female toilette. (*Zengbu yizhi zazi quanshu,* Ming edition, 9.26b, 9.28b.)

FIGURE 12. Tomb mural depicting the landowner Zhao and his wife, resting their feet on footstools, Dengfeng, Henan, 1099. (Su Bai, *Baisha Song mu,* plate 22.)

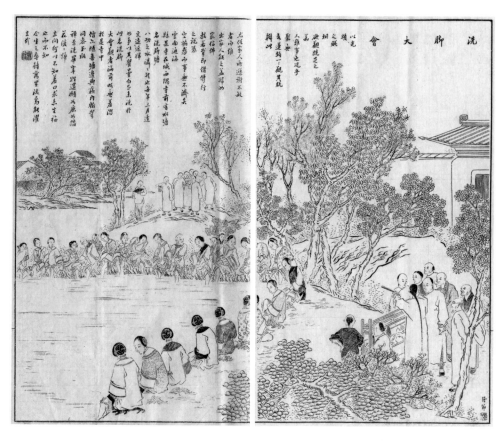

FIGURE 13. Feet-washing festival, Tonghai county, Yunnan province. The captions of this lithograph, which appeared in an 1887 issue of a popular pictorial published by the Shenbaoguan in Shanghai, play on the slippage between the bald heads of the gawking monks (visible on the lower righthand corner) and the bare feet (hidden under water but suggested by the piles of loosened binding cloths) of the tiny-footed women. According to the writer, every spring during the Third Month, women from the vicinity of Tonghai county in Yunnan province would flock to the pond in front of a certain temple on the western corner of the city to wash their feet. When finished they would sacrifice an animal to thank the gods for granting their wishes. Then they would file away like the doe in the Buddhist scriptures who left lotus blossoms with every step she took. When asked, "Why aren't you ashamed?" the women replied, "We're praying for good fortunes in our next lives." ("Xijiao dahui" [A big gathering of feet-washing], signed by the artist, Fu Jie; *Dianshizhai huabao* no. 127, Guangxu 13 [1887], eighth month, 11th–20th day [*zhongyuan*]), 51b–52a; from the collection of Nancy Norton Tomasko.)

femme aux petits pieds
Mongtseu

FIGURE 14. A Yunnan woman displaying her layered footwear fashion, ca. 1910–20. On this postcard, a Han woman appears relaxed but composed in front of a visiting French photographer in Mengzi, a French railway depot in southern Yunnan. Of particular interest is the complex layering of fabric on her feet: the (invisible) wrapping of binding cloth; white socks; crisscrossing wide ribbons accentuating the bent arch; soft "sleeping slippers"; and an outer pair of embroidered cotton shoes that are secured by shoe laces around the ankle. The narrow legs of her white pants, decorated with bold geometric patterns in contrasting colors, were gathered under a shaft-like anklet secured by narrow woven ribbons. Both the conspicuous display of textiles and the dignified expression on her face suggest that the binding of feet was associated with status and wealth in this area as late as the 1910s. (From the collection of Dr. Régine Thiriez.

A

B

C

FIGURE 15. Early Ming footwear: (A) slender shoes with pointy tips, (B) one of a pair of flat, unpadded summer socks, and (C) a binding cloth. (From the collection of the Chinese National Silk Museum, Hangzhou.)

FIGURE 16: Flat-soled female shoes for bound feet, thirteenth to sixteenth centuries.

DIAGRAM	NAME AND DATES	PLACE	SIZE OF FOOTWEAR (L, LENGTH; W, WIDTH; H, HEIGHT)
	Huang Sheng (1227–43)	Fuzhou, Fujian	*L:* 13.3–14 cm (5.3–5.6 in.) *W:* 4.5–5 cm (1.8–2 in.) *H:* 4.5–4.8 cm (1.8–1.9 in.)
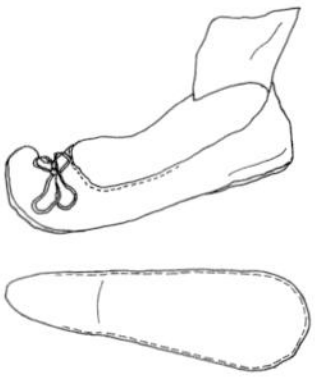	Madam Zhou (1240–74)	De'an, Jiangxi	*L:* 18–2x2 cm (7.2–8.8 in.) *W:* 5–6 cm (2–2.4 in.) *H:* 3.5–4.5 cm (1.4–1.8 in.)
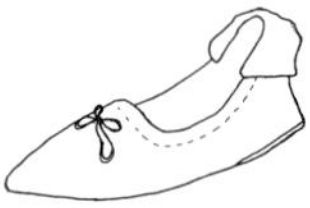	Madam Qian Yu (d. 1320)	Wuxi, Jiangsu	?
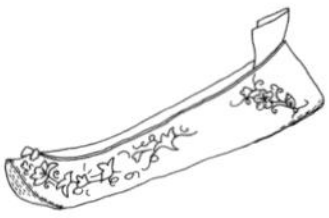	Yuan (before 1362)	Dove Cave, Longhua, Hebei	*L:* 21 cm (8.4 in.) *W:* 5 cm (2 in.) *H:* 5 cm (2 in.)
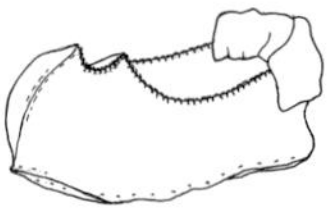	? (Ming)	Yangzhou, Jiangsu	?
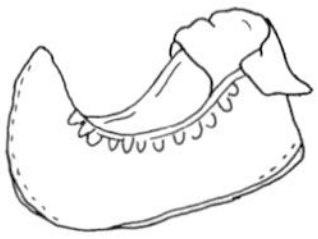	Madam Li (1538–56)	Nancheng, Jiangxi	?
	Madam Sun (1543–82)	Nancheng, Jiangxi	*L:* 13.5 cm (5.4 in.) *W:* 4.8 cm (1.9 in.) *H:* 2.5 cm (1 in.) *Soles:* 1.5 cm (0.6 in.) thick

HEIGHT OF WOMAN	DESCRIPTION OF FOOTWEAR	REMARKS	SOURCE
?	6 pairs of shoes; 16 pairs of socks	Huang died at age seventeen, hence the smallness of her feet.	Fujiansheng bowuguan, *Fuzhou Nan-Song Huang Sheng mu.*
152 cm (5 ft. 1 in.)	7 pairs of shoes; 7 pairs of socks		Jiangxisheng wenwu kaogu yanjiusuo and De'an xian bowuguan, "Jiangxi De'an Nan-Song Zhoushi mu qingli jianbao."
?			Zhou Xun and Gao Chunming, *Zhongguo lidai funü zhuangshi*, p. 305; Zhou and Gao, *Zhongguo yiguan fushi dai cidian*, p. 704.
?	Embroidered lotus, peony and plum blossoms on green silk tabby. Lined with white silk tabby. Sole stitched with hemp threads into lozenge pattern.	Found in a package of Yuan documents and textiles hoarded in a cave.	Zhao Feng, ed., *Fangzhipin kaogu xinfaxian*, p. 162.
?			Zhou and Gao, *Zhongguo lidai funü zhuangshi*, p. 304.
?	Yellow brocade vamps	Li was first wife of Zhu Yiyun, Prince Yixuan of Ming.	Jiangxisheng wenwu gongzuodui, "Jiangxi Nancheng Ming Yixuan-wang Zhu Yiyin fufu hezang mu."
?	Yellow brocade vamps	Sun was second wife of Zhu Yiyun, Prince Yixuan of Ming.	Zhou and Gao, *Zhongguo lidai funü zhuangshi*, pp. 298, 306.

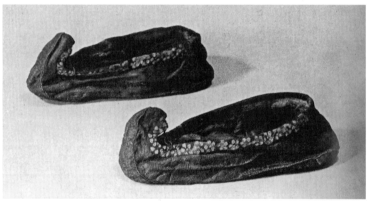

FIGURE 17. The curled-toed socks and shoes of Huang Sheng (1227–43). (Fujiansheng bowuguan, ed., *Fuzhou Nan-Song Huang Sheng mu,* plates 62–63, p. 45.)

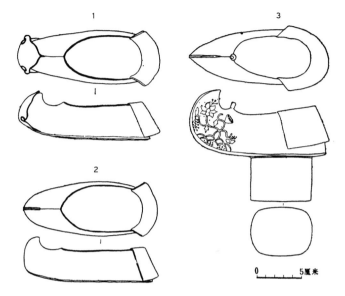

FIGURE 18. Empress Xiaojing's shoes. The drawing shows three pairs of shoes found in her tomb: (1) cloud-tip flat shoes, found in a box of jade ornaments and shoes that belonged to Empress Xiaoduan and Empress Xiaojing; (2) phoenix-head flat shoes, one of four pairs found in Xiaojing's coffin; (3) transitional phoenix-head high-heeled shoes, found in a box of Xiaojing's shoes and children's clothes at the southern side of her coffin. Apparently shoes like (3) were made by attaching cylindrical heels to shoes like (2). (Zhongguo she-huikexueyuan kaogu yanjiusuo et al., eds., *Dingling,* 1: 122.)

A

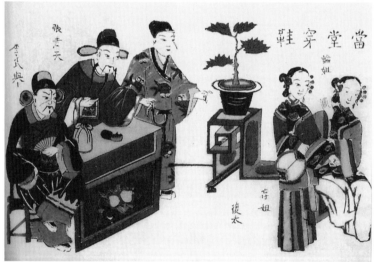

B

FIGURE 19. "If the shoes fit, you must acquit": two court scenes from a popular Shandong drama, *Wang Dingbao Borrows to Pawn (Wang Dingbao jiedang)*. Adapted from the northern ballad "The Embroidered Shoe" ("Xiuxieji"), the drama depicts the poor student Wang Dingbao's troubles with shoes. His cousin and fiancée Spring Orchid lent him her wedding attire so that he could pawn the items to pay his way to his exam in the capital. Ruan Li, who desired Spring Orchid, accused him of stealing (A). His wise and brave fiancée defended him in court, proving that she was the rightful owner of the shoes by slipping them onto her feet in front of the judge (B). (From a set of three New Year prints by artists in Yangjiapu, Weifang, Shandong; from the collection of Gao Jianzhong, reprinted in Zhang Daoyi, ed., *Lao xiqu nianhua*, pp. 107–9.)

A   B

FIGURE 20. Patterns for children's shoes in the eighteenth-century compendium by Tanmian daoren, *Precious Mirror of Feminine Virtues (Kunde baojian):* **(A)** pattern from *Kunde baojian*, 1777 edition, 8.38a (reprinted with permission from the Harvard-Yenching Library); **(B)** pattern from *Zhengshan kunde baojian,* nineteenth-twentieth-century edition 4.39a (from the collection of Don J. Cohn). As noted in the text, the *Zhengshan kunde baojian* is a hand-done replica of the printed original. That the two are almost indistinguishable attests to the copyist's skill and the fact that he or she had access to the original.

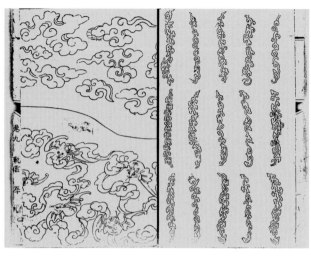

FIGURE 21. Embroidery designs for booties in *Precious Mirror of Feminine Virtues*. **(A)** Generic cloud motifs and first half of cloud-and-bat designs for the shaft of booties (*Kunde baojian,* 1777 edition, 9.49b–50a). **(B)** Second half of shaft booties and appliquéd cloud designs for shoes (*Kunde baojian,* 1777 edition, 9.50b–51a; see also *Zhengshan kunde baojian,* nineteenth-twentieth-century edition, 5.42b–44a; **(A)** and **(B)** reprinted with permission from the Harvard-Yenching Library).

FIGURE 22. Fashion cycles of Tianjin footwear, 1894–1911: arched-sole styles (1894–1911) are shown in **A-F**; a flat-soled style (1897/8–1911) is shown in **G** (CFJHL: illustrations between pp. 87 and 88). The original captions have been rearranged into outline form with new headings and occasional comments by the present author.

(A) Arched sole, stage 1: 1894 (style A).
The "double footwear" style *(fulu):*

Outer shoe *[taoxie],* with wooden sole that retains the classical arched shape to facilitate walking.

Soft-soled slipper [*ruandi xie,* not visible in this drawing], sometimes worn between binding cloth and outer shoe all day. If this slipper was not used, the wearer would remove the outer shoe and change into soft-soled slippers [or sleeping-shoes, *shuixie*] at night.

Legging *[kutui'er]* with stirrup strap and edged with houndstooth stitching covers the outer shoe.

Leg-binder *[tuidai]* secures the legging at the ankle.

A long skirt covers all but the tip of the outer shoe. The top of the foot is bulged; there is a crevice in the instep; and the tip of the toe dips slightly downward.

(B) Arched sole, stage 1: 1894 (style B).
The layered "bootie" *(xuezi)* style:

Soft-soled slipper [or changing slipper, *huanjiao xie*] on top of binding cloth.

Bootie-liner *[xue dengzi]* on top of soft-soled slipper, usually made of blue *[gangkao se]* cotton. The slightly ruffled edge of the liner peeks out from the bootie.

Bootie on top of bootie liner. Bootie is made of three parts:

Waist-piece [*xue yaozi,* the shaft], decorated here with chrysanthemum flower and leaves;

Curved-piece *[xue wanzi],* the lower part of the vamp that meets the curved sole;

Moongate [*yueliangmen,* the tongue], a small triangular piece made of white cotton or silk.

Leg-binder secures the ankle.

FIGURE 22 *(CONTINUED)*

(C) Arched sole, stage 1: 1894 (inside style B).
Two styles of bootie-liner:

1 (upper figure). Stirrup bootie-liner which resembles the stirrup legging, made of printed cotton cloth [indigo with white flowers here].

Changing-slipper inside bootie-liner is usually red, occasionally purple.

Binding cloth *[guojiao, zuchan]* peeks from underneath changing slipper.

Small drawing at upper left: The back of the changing-slipper showing heel-tab.

2 (lower figure). Plain bootie-liner with cut-off toe and heel, made of blue *[gangkao se]* imported cotton fabric.

(D) Arched sole, stage 2: 1898.
The layered "bootie" style.

Changes from 1894:

The tip of the bootie is more curved.

Moongate tongue changed from long oval to pointy triangular shape.

Bootie decoration:

Tiny embroidered or painted flowers on tip of curved-piece vamp next to moongate tongue.

Waist-piece shaft either decorated with embroidered or painted motifs or plain.

If waist-piece is plain, curved-piece would be either red or purple.

If waist-piece is decorated, curved-piece would be turquoise blue.

Changing slipper exposed after bootie liner is shed:

Mostly red in color, occasionally green or purple.

Edged in black.

Shoelaces in red, shown crisscrossing on the arch of the foot and around the ankle.

Heel lift at the back, usually white.

Worn on top of binding cloth [depicted as six horizontal strips] to bed at night.

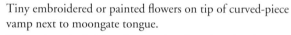

(E) Arched soles, stage 3: 1902.
The layered bootie style.

Changes from 1898:

The bulge becomes flatter.

The tip of the toe curves ever so slightly upward, but surface is flat.

The leg-binder creeps up, reaching almost the knee.

Undecorated bootie in vogue; especially enticing are same-colored waist and curved pieces.

Some waist-pieces double-trimmed on the upper edge.

The flatter bulge and toes reflect a more relaxed binding style in response to the anti-footbinding edict issued by the Qing court, as do the plainer footwear styles, but there is no relaxation on the meticulous attention lavished on the fashion of layered footwear.

The changing slipper:

Some feature cascading thin strings at the toe area, some do not.

Simplified shoe laces.

Heel lift disappears.

Tiny sock—a new item—worn between changing slipper and binding cloth.

(F) Arched soles, stage 4: 1908–11.
Simplified layers: The "inside-out" shoe style.

Changes from 1902:

Women middle-aged and older stick to booties; younger women vie to wear shoes.

Outer shoes are shaped like the former "changing slippers" but with wooden soles.

Older women stick to changing slippers; younger women skip it and wear three layers: binding cloth, socks, shoes. At night the younger woman takes off the outer shoes and keeps the socks on as sleeping slippers.

The new shoes (upper figure):

Plain or decorated with stitched or embroidered motifs at the tip.

Tip decorated with pom-pom made of silk floss.

Most fashionable look is pink pom-pom on lapis blue shoes.

The new socks (lower figure):

White cotton.

Sometimes decorated with stitched black motifs but often plain.

FIGURE 22 *(CONTINUED)*

(G) Flat sole style, 1897/8–1911.

Shoes are worn over socks. Although the shoes are flat-soled, the feet are still tightly bound. The trend is to gradually let the feet out; the three-inch golden lotus is no longer necessary.

gested by Hu: "Since the Yuan and Ming periods, footbinding has been practiced in gentry and common families. It seems as though feet cannot be left
unbound, for it supplements the face in establishing a female's beauty." His
interest, however, lies not in locating the origins in history but in using the
past to condemn a living practice.

The present, in Qian's mind, leaves much to be desired. In the late eighteenth and early nineteenth centuries, footbinding had become a craze especially in the north. Qian confirmed Zhao Yi's suggestion that footbinding was a localized practice with significant regional variations. The smallest
feet were found in the northern provinces of Hebei, Shanxi, Shandong, and
Shaanxi. The mothers had become experts in miniaturization, encouraging
girls to begin walking at the nominal age of two to three. When the girls
reached four or five their feet would be "blocked by strips of cloth" (*yi bu-
tiao lanzhu*) so that they would cease to grow in length and size. By the age
of six or seven, the feet would be "segmented" (*yicheng pianduan*) and "di-
minished in size" without the usual binding process. It is difficult to ascertain what he meant by "segmented," or the difference between blocking and
binding. Qian's point, however, that footbinding was so prevalent in the
north that northern women had developed special binding methods, is well
taken. In contrast, in the south footbinding was less pronounced. In such
provinces as Guangdong, Guangxi, Hunan, Hubei, Yunnan, and Guizhou,
"not all daughters from elite families have bound feet."

In the heart of Jiangnan, in the four prefectures of Suzhou, Songjiang,
Hangzhou, and Jiaxing famed for silk and cotton production, female feet
were the biggest. According to Qian, this is because mothers had too much
sympathy for their daughters' pain and delayed binding until seven and eight.
"By then the feet are already grown, as the mothers knew full well. But without thinking too deeply, they bound their daughters' feet even more tightly
so that they would become small. The daughters, screaming and crying from
pain, would be whipped. The neighbors could not bear to listen."[61] The
economic historian Li Bozhong has argued that from the seventeenth to the
first half of the nineteenth centuries, cotton spinning and weaving were so
lucrative that daughters from the Jiangnan countryside could earn 70 to 80
percent of the daily wages of a male hired hand. A peasant woman made
about 3.6 *shi* of rice annually if she performed textile work for 130 days out
of the year, enough to feed herself. If she doubled her workload to 260 days,

she would bring a considerable cash income to the family. The importance of female labor to the domestic bursary contributed to an improvement in women's status in family and society.[62] In his anecdotal remark, Qian made an implicit acknowledgement of this economic fact, but attributed the persistence of footbinding in spite of the women's economic contributions to the mother's mindless adherence to convention.

Even more important than what Qian said in his ethnographic account is how he said it. Whereas Zhao Yi's descriptions of exceptional areas appear in the form of a random list, Qian's survey of the regions of the empire is systematic and explicitly comparative. Although an awareness of north-south difference in the styles of footbinding existed as early as the seventeenth century, as we will see in the next chapter, Qian was the first to adopt an omniscient viewpoint to produce an ethnographic survey. Having divided up the empire according to a geographical schema, he then compared the units for the allegedly representative size of bound feet. The assumption was that the author knows; he travels from one region to another and has a means to measure and aggregate data in each region. The empire (later nation) is thus envisioned as a sum of comparable parts. This way of knowing would structure the anti-footbinding discourse in the age of nascent nationalism.

Previous philological treatises were all negotiations of the distance between antiquity and the present, and Qian's was no exception. But his interest was so strongly focused on the present that he opened with the assertion: "Footbinding of women is mentioned neither in the classics nor histories" of antiquity, let alone the suggestion of its attractiveness. In contrast, "today, everybody follows the custom, and every family binds its daughters' feet. It seems as though unless you have small feet, you cannot be a person, you cannot be a female" (23.14a, 15b). Footbinding was essential to definitions of womanhood in the eighteenth and nineteenth centuries, and as such the degeneracy and corruption of womanhood was complete. Qian ended his summary of theories about footbinding's origins with a social sneer and a moral indictment: shoes for bound feet were invented for palace dancing and as such were "attire for mean people" *(jianzhe zhifu)*.[63]

Although stating the absence of footbinding in the classics is an old trope, Qian's emphasis is not the authority of the classics as repository of knowledge but the possibility of political intervention. If footbinding is not sanctioned by ancient texts, it can and should be stopped. He made his intentions clear in the end: "The reason I have gone to such lengths is because this matter is crucial to the well-being of all under heaven. The search for origins is not simply an academic exercise" (23.16a). In fact, Qian was the first philologist to suggest an action program: Have the local authorities issue a prohibition compact. Have prominent families, as well as educated and genteel households pledge their allegiance to the "Manchu way" of unfettered feet, which he pointed out was in accordance with antiquity. Prostitutes, actors, and illiterate families can all be spared. In ten years' time, the prevailing custom can be reversed (23.15b).

Qian's program is interesting, for it happens to be exactly what the local natural feet societies that sprang up in the last decade of the nineteenth century tried to do. Furthermore, in suggesting that illiterate families can be left alone, he showed an understanding of the cultural dynamics that propelled the spread of the practice: lagged emulation. If we can change the elite cultural ideal, we can intervene in reforming the practice. This, too, was the strategy of the missionary and nationalist reformers during the early stage of their campaigns. Indeed, in rhetoric and action program Qian Yong had anticipated the modern anti-footbinding movement.

THE UNFETTERED, LABORING FEMALE BODY

In denigrating footbinding, Qian articulated a new definition of womanhood that was at odds with prevalent popular standards. "In terms of female virtue, the most important is a calm and obliging disposition; second is a sedate and dignified appearance. The size of feet should be irrelevant." The way she walked is also important: "Regardless of the size of the feet, or whether she uses a lift or not, the most valuable is a small first step and slow, deliberate footsteps. . . . If she stumbles in walking, showing all kinds of ugly postures, what good would smallness do?" (23.15a). A "lift" *(gaoxie)* is a wooden block that ancient dancers wore on their soles for a tapping sound. Women in Qian's times supplanted it at the heel area inside the shoe to create an illusion of smallness. Qian's remark bespeaks the single-minded fixation on footbinding in the nineteenth century. So prevalent was it that Qian fully endorsed the aesthetics of dainty and deliberate steps that footbinding was supposed to foster.

Qian's ideal woman is one with a mature laboring body, an instrument in the service of the dynasty or the state. "In antiquity there were the ideals of *dingnan* and *dingnü*," referring to adult males and females fit to be conscripted by the state. Footbinding is detrimental to the formation of these ideal subjects, leading to the downfall of the state. *Dingnü,* the robust adult woman, signals Qian's insistence that female bodies are given to both productive and reproductive labors (23.16a). The articulation of the uses of female bodies is one of the most interesting products of discourses of footbinding. The seventeenth-century writer Chu Jiaxuan has suggested that an integral and symmetrical female body was perfect for the service of the patriarchal family.[64] Qian Yong, however, was the first to author the modern discourse that the female body, once liberated, was to be an instrument of the state.

To underscore the public import of female feet, Qian merged the origin discourse with dynastic history, inventing a zigzag narrative that oscillates around the pivotal figure of the femme fatale. The Southern Tang, which practiced footbinding, was conquered by the Song, which did not practice it. When the Song began to bind, it was conquered by the Yuan; when the Yuan began to bind . . . and so on. Overcome by wishful thinking, Qian contradicted his earlier remark of "every family binds its daughters' feet" to proclaim that the Qing dynasty, which prohibited footbinding, would surely last unto ten thousand generations (23.16a).

The integrity of the female body and national fortune is conjoined because of the public import of maternity. "When women have bound feet, their heavenly and earthly bodies are out of sync. The boys and girls they give birth to are bound to be weak. When that happens, everything falls apart"(23.16a). This is a shrewd prognosis. What Qian Yong had anticipated is perhaps not the collapse of the Qing imperium per se, but the reasons attributed to that downfall by anti-footbinding reformers. With this argument for the importance of motherhood to the national pursuits of wealth and power, the philological search for origins became virtually indistinguishable from the tianzu discourse examined in chapter 1.

The search for origins is the most prevalent way by which scholars could write about footbinding in a respectable manner. What has been called "philology" in this chapter for the sake of convenience is a bit of a misnomer. It is undeniable that Che Ruoshui, Yang Shen, Hu Yinglin, and Zhao Yi were erudite and respected scholars, albeit Yang and Hu were marginal to officialdom. It is also true that the methods they used largely follow those of mainstream philology: comprehensive investigation, skepticism, and the authority of textual evidence. Yet the subject of footbinding, shrouded in taboos and deficient in textual allusions, is incongruous with the philological approach to truth and certainty.

Unlike such serious investigations as the authorship and dating of classical texts, footbinding remained a dubious subject in formal scholarly disputations before the nineteenth century. Yang Shen let us into the mindset of his sixteenth-century contemporaries when he suggested that having an official managing and making the Zhou queen's shoes was "lewd." Hu Yinglin's rebuttal of Yang confirmed that since the advent of footbinding, female footwear had become charged with erotic connotations and direct descriptions of feet were too provocative to enter respectable discourse.

So strong is this taboo against exposed feet that as late as the eighteenth century, Zhao Yi described the contemporary view of taking off one's socks as "defilement" bordering on "obscenity." If it was difficult to write about naked feet without sounding too lewd, it might also have been just as taboo to look at them in the bedchambers. Surely, it would be an exaggeration to say that no man had ever laid his eyes on them. In all likelihood, the stronger the taboo, the more insistent voyeurs would become in unwrapping the binding cloths of wives, concubines, or prostitutes.[65] But it is important to note that the search for footbinding's origins was conducted with averted eyes as well as on the margins of decency and scholarship. It is an attempt to find explanations in defiance of not only the unknowable but also the unspeakable.

In naming the unspeakable, the philologists established the parameters and definitions of footbinding. In the process of searching for its origins, they wrote a coherent subject into existence. We have already seen how the arched or bowed shape *(gong)* emerged as the defining trait of footbinding in such a process. The variety of other names used to describe footbinding alludes to either the desired shape (slender *[xian]* and small *[xiao, xi]*) or the swaddling *(chan, za, guo)* required. A bound foot is known by its exterior shape, size, or the packaging; none of the names provide any clue to the flesh underneath. These names in themselves served as instruments of concealment.

Without exceeding the bounds of decency, the origin discourse focused the reader's gaze on female body parts. The citation of a cluster of lyrics from the fragrant toilette tradition in notation books and their status as admissible evidence gave these provocative poems a degree of respectability. These lyrics, like the vernacular plays and other prose writings discussed in the next chapter, played no small part in perpetuating the erotic appeal of footbinding through the centuries. Although almost all of the philologists who wrote about footbinding found it deplorable or inexplicable, in recycling these materials they inadvertently perpetuated the cultural aura of the practice.

5

THE EROTICS OF PLACE

Male Desires and the
Imaginary Geography of the Northwest

In stark contrast with philologists who perpetuated the mystique of foot-binding with downcast eyes, less academically inclined male writers from the seventeenth and eighteenth centuries were unabashed in their fascination with the subject. In travelogues, notation books, vernacular plays, and songs, they depicted the bound foot as an alien object that is alluring but dangerous. We will see in this chapter that the visceral appeal of this image was part and parcel of an exotic landscape called the Northwest. More than a geographical location, the Northwest was a cultural imaginary in which indecent male desires could find concrete and socially acceptable expressions.

By tracing five recurrent tropes—female competition; the bureaucrat's journey to the Northwest; the courtesan (and her maids) from Datong; north-south differences; and the fashionable female pilgrim—this chapter maps the cultural and social unevenness that structured both the prevalent image of footbinding and male desires for it. We begin with writings adopting a distinctly masculine point of view and shift to those incorporating female points of view toward the end of the chapter. The former presupposes the male privilege to size up, grope, judge, and rank women whereas the latter showcases women's interior sense of body-self and the usefulness of footwear fashion to their self-presentations to the world.

FEET CONTESTS IN THE WILD WEST

In the last decades of the Qing dynasty, when the aura of footbinding began to dim in the coastal cities, the northwestern city of Datong in Shanxi
retained its centuries-old reputation as the mecca of footbinding. Datong
boasted its own style of lotus shoes, whose arched wooden soles seem more
curvaceous and embroidered motifs more risqué than other regional styles.
The plunging topline of the vamp, an exercise in visual drama, directed the
viewer's gaze to the tip of the wearer's toes.[1] Even more spectacular were
Datong's "Feet Contests" *(saijiao hui)* held every spring and autumn, the
seasons of temple fairs. The writer Li Hong, who published martial arts novels
under the pen name Huanzhu louzhu (Master of the Returned Pearl Pavilion), recounted:

> In the past, footbinding was a popular folk practice in northern Shanxi. Every
> eighth month, feet-airing festivals were held in areas around Datong. Long
> wooden benches, aligned like staircases of a grandstand, were placed in fair
> grounds or open squares. Hundreds upon thousands of women sat there, show-
> ing the twin hooks under their skirts. Any passer-by could savor the sight and
> make comments. Ladies from respectable families *[liangjia guixiu]* mingled
> with others; their slippers were sometimes festooned with pearls and made of
> embroidered fine silk. These shoes were so delicate that they did not even fill
> one's palm, and the workmanship was exquisite. Profligate men took advan-
> tage of the situation, and debaucheries recurred during those days.[2]

As with the origins of footbinding, the beginning of these affairs was shod
in mystery. A mid-nineteenth-century encyclopedia recorded that in Zhangjiakou, a border town just south of the Great Wall, respectable women with
tiny feet were allowed to show off during a "Tiny-Feet Festa" *(xiaozu hui)*
around the third and fourth months. Likewise in nearby Xuanhua and Yongping, Zhili (present day Hebei province), during the ten days before and
after the Qingming festival, women from opulent and deprived households
alike decked themselves out in their finest and sat by their front gates, proudly
displaying ("airing") their feet. Qingming, ten days after the spring equi-
nox, brought families outdoors for tomb-sweeping and picnics. As if emboldened by the advent of spring, passers-by could judge, rank, and even
touch the feet without reproach from the women's fathers and husbands.[3]

In the 1930s, a Japanese ethnographer, Nagao Ryūzō (b. 1883), mentioned
similar gatherings in Xuanhua, Yongping, and Ruzhou, in Henan province.

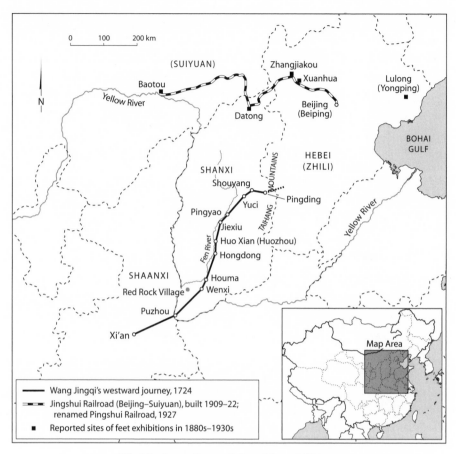

*The Northwest: Reported sites of feet exhibitions,
the Pingsui Railroad, and Wang Jingqi's westward journey.*

Nagao, a former employee of the Southern Manchurian Railway, compiled his monumental record of customs in China by interviewing sojourners in Fengtian, the capital of Manchukuo, and Beijing. It is unclear if the information about the feet contests was verified.[4] Local sons educated enough to be enlisted in the editorial committees of gazetteers, however, seemed reluctant to allow their native place to be associated with such an unseemly custom. Hence gazetteer "reports" of feet contests were often couched in terms of a *denial* of rumors perpetuated by a misinformed outsider.[5]

Feet contests allegedly took various forms and were sighted in regions far removed from the Northwest. According to an 1887 pictorial, in Tonghai county of the southwestern province of Yunnan, women from local villages and afar gathered by a pond in front of a temple every Third Month for a "Feet-Washing Festival" *(xijiao dahui)*. Believing that this act of devotion would bring them good luck in their afterlife, the captions suggested, the women carried on "in front of hordes of spectators without a bit of embarrassment or shame." Instead of a competition, the viewer was treated to a rare display of the forbidden flesh in the name of piety (see fig. 13). The words for "bare feet" *(xianzu)* and "washing feet" *(xizu)* resemble each other in shape and sound.[6]

Indeed, semantic slippage is the common denominator uniting disparate accounts of feet contests or displays. First *sai* (to compete) mutated to *sai* (to air under the sun; sometimes a synonym *liang* was used). Then *jiao* (feet) traded places with *jia* (armor). One often-cited legend traced the origins of feet festivals to an armistice between the Khitan-Liao and Song armies in 1004. Having laid down their arms, the soldiers aired out their armor before putting it away. Somehow people in posterity got confused and took to airing women's feet in the open.[7] It seems as though playing with words lifted taboos surrounding women's bodies, creating a carnivalesque atmosphere on the page. In precious few other spaces could women be imagined as exhibitionists, vying to attract the male gaze in public. Indeed, if feet contests are signified by a willful self-display of female bodies, writers in the 1930s observed, women in areas throughout China could be said to enjoy occasions that are "feet contests in reality albeit not in name."[8] Did women from Datong or Tonghai really deck out to air or wash their feet in public? There is no conclusive evidence. Feet contests belong to the realm of urban myths which everybody talks about as if they were present but no one seems to have actually seen.

MYTHS OF ORIGINS

The connoisseur Yao Lingxi was skeptical about the reliability of reports of feet contests if not the events themselves. He traced the glut of accounts to a serial discussion in a Shanghai tabloid, *Fengren,* in the 1920s instigated by its editor, Gong Dafeng, and a writer named Hengsan, both Yao's friends. The passages reprinted by Yao were replete with ethnographic details: the favorite grounds for the contest in Datong was the temple of Guandi, the God of War; women who used high arched heels to create an illusion of smallness shied away for fear of mockery; in nearby Weizhou (Zhili) women stood on stones carved for the occasion that were as tall as the spectators' shoulders, and so on. Empiricism aside, in *Fengren* feet contests figured first and foremost as instruments of conversion: one official had loathed small feet so much that he founded an anti-footbinding society in his teens. Later, when stationed in Datong he chanced upon a feet contest. So enamored was he that he took one such beauty as his concubine. Yao was dismissive of the authenticity of such stories, saying that Hengsan had never been to Datong and Gong, who had traveled there, reported only hearsay.[9]

Yao preferred a different kind of mythmaking, concocting a three-staged history of female self-display that is suffused with nostalgia. The golden age of feet contests was the Ming dynasty, also the golden age of footbinding according to Yao. When small feet constituted a sign of status and prestige, women loved showing off their feet. Yao located the agency only in the women: "Feet contests in those days were no different from beauty pageants in Europe and America today: women took the opportunity to eye each other and learn new tricks; young girls took the opportunity to goad each other; men took the opportunity to feast their eyes."[10]

During the golden age, feet contests were part of a naturalized landscape where human actions and desires were punctuated by seasonal rhythms. "The climate in the northern borders lagged behind that of the heartland. The shriveling chill lingered as late as the third month, as the wind wiped up dust against one's face." Busy in anticipation, women embroidered slippers behind closed doors and away from each other's prying eyes. Finally, when spring arrived in full force in the middle of the fifth month, sisters and neighbors brought out their stowed-away slippers and rode donkey carts to the countryside, resting their feet on carpets red as gibbon blood and feasting from picnic baskets. It was prime mating season: profligate men fluttered about like butterflies; the women sometimes took out mirrors and flirted with their suitors not by direct gaze but by way of their reflections.[11]

This primordial scene of sexual license suffered a decline when the moral authorities cracked down. In the second or degenerate stage of Yao's history, women were domesticated and took to sitting outside their homes on the day of the contest. The shy ones hid their faces behind curtains, exposing only their feet by resting them on benches. No longer could they mingle freely with men. Yet the standards of the contests were still high: even those who boasted of three-inch feet enjoyed no guarantee of being selected Optimus. A final stage set in after the establishment of the first Republic in 1912—and the growth of railroad networks. Although Yao did not mention it, the completion of a railroad from Beijing westward to Zhangjiakou (1909) and Datong, later extended to Baotou in Suiyuan province (1922), opened the northwest interior to the speedy, modern ways of the coastal metropolis.[12] Feet contests fell out of favor and disappeared entirely upon the success of the Northern Expedition, which reunified China and established a second Republic in 1927.[13]

In other words, according to Yao Lingxi, by the time the bulk of "ethnographic reports" of feet contests appeared, the custom had already fallen prey to the march of progress. His own "history," with its fanciful details about blood-red carpets and flirtatious mirror images, is almost certainly a fabrication. Its chronology fits too neatly into his pathos of nostalgia— footbinding as the haunting of modernity—discussed in chapter 3, and the details are too fictitious to warrant verification. Yet can we dismiss altogether the numerous accounts in notation books since the nineteenth century or the weight of persistent disavowals in local gazetteers? Surely these tantalizing stories, kept alive for over a century, had the power to inspire imitative behavior in life.

Suspended between doubt and certainty, feet contests in modern China are less an ethnographic event or tourist attraction than an invitation to wonder.[14] Whether they were true or not is less important than the kind of vicarious pleasures they afforded readers in the 1920s and 1930s. The interior— only beginning to be penetrated by speedy travel or the ideology of foot liberation—remained in the reader's imagination an elemental place rife with sexual energy, far removed in time from the treaty ports where they resided. However untrustworthy, reports of feet contests convey a different veracity in their tone of ethnographic realism, one that anchors the alleged female desires to self-display and male desires to gawk and narrate in a distinct northwestern landscape.

The rest of this chapter probes the prehistory of feet contests by focusing on the erotics of the Northwest as a place in the seventeenth and eighteenth centuries: how geography structured male desires of and fantasies about the female body in three disparate texts: a manual of taste, a journal, and a collection of vernacular plays.[15] What twentieth-century observers have subsumed under "feet contest" is an amorphous and centuries-old cultural phenomenon wrought of four elements: male eyesight; male privilege to travel, judge, and narrate; competition among women; and female self-presentation. This chapter traces how they constituted the cultural imaginary of Shanxi—and Datong especially—as the embodiment of both the sublime and the mundane aspects of footbinding.

My thesis is that men's experience of footbinding was by definition an encounter with a body not their own. Mediated by sensory perceptions, the pleasure was always ephemeral and elusive. Therein lies the impulse to affix it to the concrete coordinates of a place and to submit it to writing. In contrast, to a woman the binding of feet was first and foremost a corporeal affair directed to oneself. Toward the end of this chapter and in the next we will see that although no less sensual, this experience was mediated not by the geography of place but by the materiality of the things that women made, wore, exchanged, and consumed.

Since as early as the seventeenth century, travelogues by scholar-officials, novels, and popular songs have told of a bureaucratic journey to the Northwest that led an unsuspecting traveler to an amorous encounter with beauties with tiny feet. In these stories the temporary suspension of inhibition as well as the inversion of gender and sexual norms dramatized by feet contests are integral to the wonder of the Northwest. Also prevalent is the juxtaposition of the civil and the military, the former symbolized by the embroidered slippers and the latter, by various martial elements associated with feet contests as we have seen: the airing of armor, martial arts novels, and the temple grounds of Guandi the God of War, to name a few. In much the same way, the unabashed behavior of tiny-footed village women was both alluring and dangerous—lurking behind the refinement of their craft was a threat of violence and death. As will be seen in the stories that follow, domesticity and concealment turned inside out unleashed a desire that, like the women, could not be easily contained.

THE COURTESAN OF DATONG

Perhaps it is no accident that Datong figured as the birthplace of feet contests in many modern accounts. In popular imagination, the city had been the home of northern beauties since the Ming emperor Wuzong (reign name Zhengde, r. 1506–21) raided virgins for his harem from Datong and Xuanhua.[16] Legends embellished through time play an important role in the identity and image of the city. More importantly, the allure of a place—any place—solidifies only upon comparisons with other, less memorable places. Hence in stories about Datong courtesans, the narrator-arbiter had to be a seasoned traveler with a bird's-eye view: a masculine subject position. The narrator typically appears as a traveler along a route of towns stretched out on a synchronic landscape, much like the "profligate men" going from door to door during a feet contest. If modern reports of feet contests operate on an exaggeration of female agency in self-display—at the same time that the women were being pinned to a place—in earlier adventure stories the power and mobility of the male scholar appear in full force. From this perspective, feet exhibitions are less contests of female skills than of male knowledge and tastes.

The seventeenth-century maverick writer Li Yu (ca. 1610–80), no stranger to the itinerant lifestyle, revealed the terms of male contests in clear relief in an essay "Hands and Feet" ("Shouzu"): *"Having traversed all four corners of the empire,* I have come to see that in terms of having the smallest feet that are not burdensome *[lei],* and having the smallest feet that are still functional *[yong],* it is hard to top Lanzhou in Shaanxi, and Datong in Shanxi." Li's comparative knowledge was presented with the immediacy of personal experience: "The feet of Lanzhou women measure at most three inches, some even smaller. Their steps are agile and quick—like flying—sometimes outpacing even the men. Yet when you remove their socks and fondle the feet, you tend to feel the hard and soft parts in equal proportions. By chance you may discover feet so soft that it feels as though they are entirely boneless, but they are rare in Lanzhou. In Datong, however, the majority of courtesans are like that. Lying in bed with them, it is hard to stop fondling their golden lotus. No other pleasures of dallying with courtesans can surpass this experience."[17]

Li Yu's comments appeared in his *Casual Expressions of Idle Feeling (Xianqing ouji),* a collection of three hundred short essays presented in eight sections: writing plays, staging plays, feminine beauty (literally, "voices and faces"), houses, furniture, food and drink, flowers and trees, health and pleasure. Li's no-nonsense advice on a breathtaking array of subjects has led many to consider the book, first published in 1671, a manual of taste or a guide to everyday sensuality for the status-conscious reader in the urban culture of the time. The average reader would have found more useful knowledge from the later sections than the first three. Comments on courtesans' feet served a different purpose: advertising the author's authority as a connoisseur of women in part to secure future employment.[18] Specifically, they were part of the section on "Feminine Beauty," which follows "Writing Plays" and "Staging Plays," areas in which Li enjoyed a justified reputation as both a practitioner and a theoretician.[19] Together they comprise a guide to selecting and training household entertainers and, by extension, concubines. These standards of artistic and corporeal accomplishments were not intended for wives.

Li mentioned that a wealthy patron engaged his service to "procure [literally, size up] concubines" *(dai yi guiren xiangqie)* in Yangzhou.[20] No doubt he had potential patrons in mind when he boasted of his expertise in such matters: "When in the capital I told many people about [the secret of Datong courtesans], but they were incredulous. One evening two courtesans showed up at a banquet, one a native of Shanxi and one, Hebei. Neither had much face to speak of, but both had extremely small feet. I challenged the unbelievers to test the feet for themselves, and as expected, Shanxi beat Hebei handily. Stiffness and softness made a world of difference." Li's own newly acquired actress-concubines, Miss Qiao and Miss Wang, whom he proceeded to educate using the methods he outlined, may have served as models for the sections on acting and feminine (read concubine) beauty.[21]

Modern readers are likely to be incensed by Li Yu's objectification of teenage girls as well as the system of concubinage he both practiced and exploited for employment. I intend to neither defend nor condemn. Instead of an emotional and moralistic response to the text, I prefer to offer an analytic one by focusing on its singularity. The two essays "Hands and Feet" and "Shoes and Stockings" constitute the only unabashed statement of appreciation of bound feet *in prose-essay* from the seventeenth century. All other essays on footbinding take the form of either a morally neutral origin discourse or condemnation, as we have seen in the last chapter.[22] Li Yu's unique and influential voice as an essayist—Patrick Hanan has called him "the best-selling Chinese author of his time"—thus deserves a hearing.[23] His obsession with stylistic invention as a writer might have emboldened him to break a generic taboo; his devotion to taste as an expression of the self may in turn account for the unapologetic tone of his connoisseurship. The attitudes and standards of appreciation of bound feet he revealed, however, had resonance among urban readers of his time.

SEDUCTION OF THE EYES:
LI YU'S AESTHETIC OF FUNCTION

At the heart of Li's connoisseurship of feet is what I would term an "aesthetic of function," which gives pride of place to agility of movement, not size. Feet bound so small that they crippled are a "burden" *(lei)*, whereas properly bound feet, although small, serve their "usefulness" or "function" *(yong)* in altering the gait and enhancing the grace of the woman. His preferences are dictated in part by the requirements of performance in singing, dancing, and acting, and in part by his love of naturalness. Hence he parodied a "Miss Carry," whose feet were so tiny that she had to be carried around, as a "clay figurine" that would cost no more than a few coppers from the street vendors, not the thousand pieces of gold that her patron had allegedly paid. "The Creator gives us a pair of feet so that we can walk. When ancient poets waxed lyrical on beautiful women . . . they emphasized that a woman has to be able to walk on her bound feet, so much so that it feels as though she would walk right into a painting." Miss Carry bespoke a fixation on size that had gone terribly wrong. In a competitive environment, the pursuit of extreme beauty had grown so excessive that it became not only unnatural but outright anti-human. The aesthetics of function was antidote to a fetish of measurements in vogue in the seventeenth century.

Incredibly, Li Yu has stood our modern sensibility on its head: In his times the binding of feet for both respectable wives and concubines was such a conventional practice that to bind was "natural," and not to bind was *unnatural* for these classes of women.[24] Furthermore, among women who did bind, the difference between "natural" and "unnatural" hinged on a subtle gradation of options, a spectrum that the connoisseur has to navigate with faculties of eyesight, smell, and touch, as well as discernment. Li's advice to the potential client: "The best way to 'test' a woman's feet is none other than asking her to walk about back and forth. Observe if her motion is agile or stiff, natural or forced, and you get a very good idea. A pair of feet that is bound straight is agile, if crooked it would be difficult to move about. If properly balanced *[zheng]*, the pair of feet is natural, if lopsided *[wai]* it is contrived. Feet that are straight and well-balanced in shape are not only beautiful and conducive to walking, they are also far less likely to be foul. Putrid smell stems from a contrived artificiality."[25]

Li Yu was brutally honest. For all his emphasis on female agility, he did not cover up the fact that the women were pinned down, lined up, and sized up as objects of desire that can be bought and sold. It is thus all the more intriguing that his definition of "natural beauty" requires the woman—having been rendered an object and commodity—to gaze back. In a preceding essay on "Eyebrows and Eyes," Li made a subtle revelation that altered the terms of the connoisseurship of "sizing up" *(xiang)* when he discussed how much of a woman's heart, intelligence, and fortitude—her interiority—was revealed in the shape of her eyes, the proportion of black and white, and the way she moved her eyeballs. Movement of the eyes, in turn, was integral to her gait. Instead of fetishized body parts, Li Yu preferred a full body in movement; his erotics of place is wrought of a simultaneity that situated the woman's body and his sensory faculties in the same space and in real time. Therein lies the singularity of his connoisseurship in the context of his time.

This simultaneity required careful choreography on the part of the man. To catch her natural eye movements, suggested Li, the connoisseur has to reverse the social hierarchies of active/passive and high/low; physically trading places with the woman: "Stay passive and wait for her to move; lie low so that you can watch her from below. When the body turns, the eyes would naturally follow. No one can sway her body while the eyes remain fixed. Let her walk back and forth in a succession of half-steps, while you look at her by going around her eyes. Without her moving her eyes deliberately, you would see them move. This is one way. Furthermore, a woman is shy and tends to cast her eyes downward. If I stand taller than she is, and she looks down, there is no chance that I would see her eyes. So I put her in an elevated place, either on a set of stairs or in front of a pavilion, and watch her as her body descends. Since she cannot go any lower, she would have to swirl her eyes to avoid my gaze. . . . The difference between class and vulgarity, or beauty and the lack thereof, lies in how naturally her eyes move."[26] Agility and naturalness of a woman's bodily movement, knowable from the same in her eyes, defined "class."

The nature of the encounter remained economic, if one wants to be crass about it, but the terms of the game have changed. Li Yu has let us into a sophisticated dance of seduction in which a shy beauty "gazes back" by trying to avoid the gaze. No longer were the women lined up like dolls awaiting selection, like contestants of feet exhibitions on benches or grandstands. Compare Li's passage with modern accounts of feet contests or other seventeenth-century essays on the meat market-like scene of procuring girls, and the difference that Li's aesthetics of function makes is obvious.[27] The modern distinctions we make between "object" and "subject" seem too dichotomous and mechanistic to capture the dynamic relationship between these women and their viewer. From within her object status the woman exercised a form of subjectivity; to be an "object" properly she was to have interiority and agility, as well as the ability to gaze and to return a gaze naturally (while pretending to be too shy to do so).

Having discoursed on "naturalness" as a choreographed dance between the viewer and the viewed, Li Yu proceeded to offer tips on playing with the artifice of fashion that would further the pleasure of the eyes. This is done not by manipulating the body—tightening the binding cloth—but by manipulating the viewer's gaze. Hence "the fashionable colors for socks are white and pink; for slippers a darker red. Now midnight blue *[qing]* is also in vogue." Most notable is shoe design: "High-heeled slippers can make small feet look even smaller, slender feet look even more slender." Yet big-footed women desperate to win feet contests often sought to deceive, and true winners took to wearing only flats. Li recommended, "No need to give up on high heels altogether, just do not go to extremes. Women with slightly large feet should wear thick instead of thin soles; if too thin the shape of the foot would be exposed." Decoration is also important; most clever was the recent fashion of festooning the tip of the slipper with a pearl no larger than a grain.[28] These remarks highlight the extent to which footbinding was implicated in the competitive and anxiety-ridden regime of fashion in the seventeenth century.

The message from all of Li's practical advice is clear: With ample money, enough leisure, and a little help from Li Yu, any master can learn to enjoy a concubine as alluring as the legendary courtesans of Datong. By way of an aesthetic of function, the erotics of Datong as a place was unhinged from its geographical moorings and became portable. Embodied in a well-groomed concubine who seemed to have walked out of a painting, the joys of Datong— unsurpassed in the empire—found their way into every patriarch's house.

WANG JINGQI'S WESTWARD JOURNEY

The trope of an amorous bureaucratic journey found an unlikely hero in Wang Jingqi (1672–1726), a fifty-two-year-old private advisor seeking employment from the powerful Nian Gengyao (d. 1726), general of the West-

ern Armies. In the second month of 1724, Wang set out on a westward journey from Zhili (modern Hebei) that would take him past the Taihang Mountains, through a string of towns and villages along the Fen River in Shanxi
and across the Yellow River into Shaanxi, before arriving at the ancient capital of Xi'an, Nian's headquarters (see map, p. 147).[29]

Wang Jingqi went down in history as the unlucky man who incurred the
Yongzheng emperor's wrath in the first of four literary cases during the emperor's short reign. The prime target was General Nian, once Yongzheng's
favorite, whose arrogance and power became too threatening.[30] On the eve
of his arrest, Nian had supposedly burned his papers, but carelessly left Wang's
missives, bound into two thin books, in a pile of loose papers. Incensed by
Wang's disrespectful remarks about his father, the Kangxi emperor, Yongzheng
scribbled on the cover of the first book, "Seditious and wild to the utmost!
To my extreme regret I did not see this earlier. Save it for another day. A man
of his ilk will not be allowed to slip through my fingers." Thus Wang and
his son were executed in 1726, and his wife exiled to be a slave; his brothers,
nephews, and relatives within the five mourning grades all received their due.
A full two centuries later, after the last emperor, Puyi, vacated the palace in
November 1924, inventory takers from the Palace Museum found Wang's first
book and a small portion of the second in a locked box in Maoqin Hall in
the palace.[31] Twice forgotten, the text has thus miraculously survived.

To modern eyes, Wang's missives, published as *Jottings on My Westward
Journey (Dushutang xizheng suibi)* in 1928, are less about sedition than seduction. Wang, who won a provincial-*juren* degree in 1714, seemed more
adventurer than scholar in temperament and taste. His extant assortment
of about thirty-five entries, mostly scripted on the road and bearing dates
ranging from the sixth of the second month to the twenty-eighth of the
fifth month, 1724, includes a few letters, prefaces, and poems—requisite public genres for the bureaucrat. More unusual are anecdotes about high
officials, prostitutes, women bandits, and soldiers, dotted with lewd and scatological humor. There is, for example, the story of a Yangzhou male prostitute, Wang Sizhong, who rose to become Assistant Prefect *(tongpan),* courtesy of a bribe on his behalf by his lover. Or Vice Minister Zhang Pengge,
whom Kangxi had likened to an actor. Among Zhang's riotous deeds, besides putting makeup on his face: one day he returned home from his morning audience at court; still in his ceremonial attire, he headed straight to a
serving woman and pushed her onto her bed, stripped her naked, placed

her feet on his shoulders, and proceeded to penetrate her when his wife showed up with a whip. Adding insult to injury, the serving woman's feet were each "over one foot long."[32]

Often these stories bear the mark of those swapped with boisterous friends over a jug of wine at dinner. Wang Jingqi delighted in exposing the unseemly underbelly of bureaucratic life, especially among holders of the metropolitan-*jinshi* degree (Presented Scholars) in high office: not only the corruption but also the unspoken hankerings and corporeal desires that no amount of symbolism or toggles on the ceremonial court robe can tame. He offered these stories to Nian probably without a second thought, assuming that the general would find both truth and comic relief in them.[33] He also probably thought that no one outside Nian's close circle would set eyes on them. It is in this spirit of men's locker-room humor, camaraderie, and competition that we should read the stories of Wang's encounter with the Datong courtesan Lightning Steps (Buguang) and the three mysterious ladies from Red Rock Village.

Lightning Steps came to him as a surprise, the recommendation of an innkeeper at Houma, a town that Wang did *not* name as one of the ten famous gathering places for prostitutes in Shanxi.[34] Wang admitted that "by nature I loved whoring" until an illness in 1721 forced him to restrain himself. But while on the road, he gave in to the lure of the unknown. At once fragile and virile, Lightning Steps announced herself as a contradiction. Taken aback by her haughty air, Wang went on a verbal offensive: "Since you are already lost in the world of wind and dust, shouldn't you lighten up? You have to hang out with vulgar people all the time, so why make it difficult on yourself?" She thought for a moment, then threw back her head and laughed, "You seem to know who I am." Glancing at Wang's bow resting on the wall, she turned the table on him. "Why would a gentleman carry this around?" He said, "I heard that you are a skilled archer. May I have the pleasure?" She stepped into the backyard, planted a rod on the ground, stepped back scores of steps, and hit the target three times. The verbal and physical dueling set the tone for the night. Lightning Steps sang a bitter song she composed, accompanied by the *pipa*-lute, and told Wang about her betrayal by a *jinshi*-degree holder from Jiangnan (the Yangzi delta region; literally, south of the river). She sang another song, and they were both in tears. Wang Jingqi and Lightning Steps lit a lamp, sat up and chatted until dawn, then bid their tender farewell.[35]

The journey that took Wang to this encounter with the Datong courtesan was similar to those of Li Yu some fifty years earlier: a bureaucratic journey through a synchronic string of towns for livelihood and adventure. Lightning Steps made her entrance in a way that we have come to expect from Li's connoisseurship: with agility, etched in her name and dramatized by her archery demonstration. Also familiar is the contrast between her civilized and martial personas, an aesthetic we have identified in the feet contest reports. But Wang's bantering, not to mention all the tears, bespeaks a seduction of a verbal and sentimental nature, in contrast to Li Yu's flirtatious gazes and groping for bonelessness. Lightning Steps is dramatically different from the Datong courtesan we have met in one crucial aspect: Wang did not once mention her feet. Wang was no prude and had in fact an excessive interest in women's feet, as we will see. But for him the Datong courtesan stood for another erotics of place, not as the embodiment of sublime pleasures but as the perpetual victimized other of Jiangnan.

Being a southerner himself (Wang was a native of Hangzhou), Wang Jingqi was attuned to the northern difference embodied by Lightning Steps from the start. He couched his first impression of her in terms of a local mountain, Gushe, which appeared in the Daoist classic *Zhuangzi* as the dwelling place of a deity whose skin is bright and translucent as ice and whose countenance is fair as a maiden's.[36] Surely, "the deity of Gushe Mountain" was a standard allusion for a beauty, and Wang's use might have meant nothing more than literary showmanship. But it was the first of a string of signs that betrayed Wang's sensitivity to north-south differences in geography, culture, and distribution of power.

The courtesan was equally sensitive to the unevenness of place. Most striking were the three songs that Lightning Steps wrote and sang, which Wang recorded verbatim. Set to the tune of "Taotao ling" in the tradition of "Zhenggong diao," they are full of reiterative locution *(dingdingdongdong)* and auxiliary words *(er, wu)*, creating a crisp diction that sounds harsh to southern ears. Lightning Steps, twenty years old, sounded apologetic about her northern upbringing. Daughter of a military officer who died while stationed in southern Yunnan, she returned home at age nine to Datong with her birth mother, a concubine, and the first wife. When her birth mother, too, passed away, Lightning Steps was sold to a brothel. "What I have just sung for you is a vulgar sound of the north, please do not laugh."[37]

It was in her betrayal by the Presented Scholar that the Datong-Jiangnan difference assumed the unequal exchange of local-metropolis. The scholar, who remained unnamed, traveled north to await an appointment. He made a detour to Datong, hoping to call on a friend who was serving there but was rejected. Lightning Steps, then sixteen, fell in love with him although he was destitute. Over the curses of her foster mother at the brothel, she let him move in with her and pledged herself to him. After one year, he had to make his way to the capital, and she financed the trip with all that she had saved up. Two years later, when he still had not sent for her, she tracked him down, a newly appointed magistrate in Henan. He had these words to say: "As an official, of course I cherish my name and integrity. Why would a lofty magistrate take a whore as concubine?"[38]

Wang Jingqi was so moved by Lightning Steps's spiteful song that he shed tears, lamenting that, "I, too, am at the end of the line." His sympathy is indicative of his own marginal existence in the male official world: although a southerner, he toiled on horseback in the north. Although his father served as Vice Minister in the Ministry of Revenue and his elder brother was a Presented Scholar, Jingqi's *juren* degree was too meager to land him a formal bureaucratic post.[39] In *Westward Journey* he reiterated resentment against Presented Scholars: "Alas, this xx-scholar was down and out when Lightning Steps gave him money; she earned every cent of it on her bed. He used this money to gain his appointment, to travel to his post, to feed his parents and wife, and to procure another concubine. . . . I don't know what kind of heart is his. I call him xx-scholar instead of his real name. How come this man can be a Presented Scholar? Isn't it pathetic?"[40]

As Wang Jingqi headed for Wenxi, his next stop on the road, Lightning Steps fretted that the authorities were cracking down on prostitution so relentlessly that she would have to return to Datong. Datong for the courtesan was not a portable garden of pleasures, but a place on a loop, a home that offered no solace and no way out. The physical and social mobility that, by contrast, figured as the hallmark of the southern scholar's privilege was to become even more pronounced in Wang's next adventure.

RED ROCK VILLAGE: THE DOMESTIC IN THE WILD

After Wenxi, Wang Jingqi journeyed to Dashiutou, some forty *li* down the road, where he was stricken with bouts of hernia. He sent off the slower contingent of his servants with a horse-drawn cart carrying the bulk of his luggage, planning to catch up with them after a rest. A gust kicked up a sandstorm by the time he set out with a lone attendant; they missed the official road and overshot by some twenty *li* to the south. Debilitated by a second hernia attack, Wang rode into a village about one *li* to the east and saw a south-facing door of a house ajar. Someone by the road told him he was in Red Rock Village.

Neither the sand in his eyes nor the excruciating pain in his entrails could dull Wang's keen ethnographic observation. Behind the open front gate a sizable compound presented itself, with five south-facing rooms, two eastern rooms to their left, and a stable on the west housing four horses. Three women in the middle room, the most private and elevated space in the compound, scurried to hide in the side building upon seeing the invasion of two strange riders, screaming, "What do the guests want?" The master of the house appeared, an old man of about seventy by the name of Li, who fixed his gaze on Wang and after a pregnant moment said, "Ah, a Mr. Scholar *[guanren]* from the south!" Wang's southern origins, which he denied earlier in self-pitying sympathy with Lightning Steps, announced his status without his uttering a word.[41]

Wang's attention to the interior architecture—indeed, the domesticity— of the Li household is rivaled by *their* fascination with his outsider's privileges as a southerner. His first physical contact with the three women occurred in tandem with a noisy negotiation among themselves over sanitation. Wang was pinned to his saddle by pain and could not dismount. The three women rushed to hold and guide him to their middle room upon the beckoning of Old Li. The elder woman called out, "Baby Jade, go get your pillow and coverlet." Baby Jade hesitated, "Maybe Mr. Scholar would find them too dirty, what to do?" The elder retorted, "Are you afraid that they would mess up Mr. Scholar's clothes? The *kang*-platform bed is very cold. No matter how dirty the bedding, isn't it better than putting him on straw mats made of reed?" On the verge of passing out, Wang felt the bedding underneath, and evidently heard the conversation, but did not give the women his characteristic scrutiny.

Old Li was about to borrow a stove, firewood, and a cake of tea from a neighbor to make a jug of tea. Before leaving with Li, Wang's attendant whispered to his master in a lilting Wu dialect from the heart of Jiangnan: "You are not in the pleasure quarters; these beauties are from a respectable household. My master should be careful with his loose mouth, for you never know how unruly these people out west can be." He left Wuyi tea, a delicacy from Fujian, on the table before taking off to catch up with the horse-drawn cart. Hangzhou natives, famously picky about their tea, were likely to find tea brewed from cakes stiff as a brick unpalatable. This episode exposed not only how Wang was addicted to certain southern comforts, but also how both master and attendant were acutely aware of their linguistic and cultural differences while traveling in the north.

Wang began to wake up, and saw that the elder woman, who was holding a baby, had eyebrows and eyes "as pretty as a picture." The younger one, Baby Jade (Yuwa), was a bit over twenty. The youngest, no more than sixteen or seventeen, was particularly bewitching. "The twin arches of all three are smaller than three inches." He addressed the elder woman as "Wife Li," who told him that Baby Jade was her daughter-in-law and Little Cloud (Xiaoyunwa), her daughter. The verbal exchange broke the ice, and soon Wife Li was insisting that hernia can be cured only by a massage. She ordered the two to "serve Mr. Scholar" *(fushi guanren)*, which we may note is an honorific used by prostitutes or maids; "to serve" carries a connotation of tending to the corporeal comforts and pleasures of the master. Wang was placed on his back on the *kang*. Baby Jade sat on the edge and held one of his hands; Little Cloud crouched from behind with her back leaning on the western wall (thus facing east) and held his other hand. They then proceeded to massage the spots where he felt pain while taking turns to wipe the sweat from his face.

Wang did not fail to note that Old Li returned with the stove and was pleased with the attention his women gave the visitor. Li was solicitous himself, soon leaving again to buy steamed buns. The reader may begin to notice Wang's meticulous recording of the coming and going of people. This narrative strategy marked the boundary of the domestic place while animating the interior by human movement and action. Amidst the flurry of activities, the southerner—the perpetual outsider—alone remained still at the center of the room.

Noticing the pot that Old Li had left on the stove, Wang remarked that it was so huge that it would take ages for the water to boil. Wife Li laughed, "Mr. Scholar, don't be surprised. All the men in this place are stupid; not a single exception!" Wang asked whose baby was this, and was told that it was Baby Jade's. He inquired, "Is it your grandson or granddaughter?" Li sighed, "Every boy born in this village is ugly; every girl is fetching. She is a girl." Her husband, son, and son-in-law were all so ugly that even their wives loathed seeing them. They worked outside the village, leaving the harem-like household in the hands of the women.

The flirtation turned overt when Baby Jade verbalized the south-north difference: "Mr. Scholar, are there mismatches in the south?" Wife Li started to reminisce about a similar conversation with a Scholar Shen, a southerner who came through under circumstances similar to Wang's. All of a sudden, the two younger women gazed at each other and exclaimed, "Why, Mr. Scholar has really soft hands!" and held his hands up to show to Wife Li. Wang went along, "You ladies don't seem to have stiff hands yourselves?" Wang's attendant returned, announcing that the cart was waiting at the entrance of the village. Wife Li invited the servant to the side wing with a jug of tea. Wang wasted no time in asking Baby Jade, "Since you loathe your husband's company, it must be quite a chore having to deal with him those long nights when he is around." And she replied, "I hate it whenever my husband returns. His whole body reeks of mud and sweat, stinking you to death. I have nothing to say to him, and sex is not what we're about. My mother-in-law has often told us that southerners are soft and lovely; hearing their voices and glancing at their smiling faces, you cannot bear to let them go. I and my little sister-in-law have never met a southerner, and we have often prayed that we would be born in southland in our next lives. Today finally we managed to lay our eyes on a southerner, and indeed my mother-in-law is right!"

The seduction was conducted in tandem with a discourse on chastity. Earlier, Wife Li insisted that despite the charm of village daughters, for several hundred years Red Rock Village had never seen an unchaste woman. Now, Little Cloud chimed in with a secret: the Scholar Shen whom Wife Li remembered so fondly was a lost traveler who knocked on their door some twenty years ago and was invited to stay in this same room. A native of Jiaxing, at the core of Jiangnan, he served as a private advisor for the magistrate of Pingyang. He became very cordial with Wife Li, got her husband drunk, and after everybody fell asleep went over to knock on the eastern wing door. Giving in to temptation, the young Wife Li rose to open the door. But the brightness of a starry sky put a chill in her, stopping her in her tracks. She often told the story to the two young women, warning them to guard against temptation.

The segue to the topic of chastity is odd in the middle of a flirtation that is showing no sign of abetting. Wang asked, "Since your mother never had sex *[wujiao]* with Scholar Shen, how come she misses him so deeply after twenty years?" Baby Jade said, "Why do we need to have sex *[youjiao]* to remember? We, too, will never forget Mr. Scholar in our hearts." When Little Cloud got off the *kang* to sip tea, Wang started to fondle Baby Jade's breasts. Baby Jade said, "Mr. Scholar is wrong." Little Cloud chimed in with a doggerel before returning to her former position on the *kang:* "Blue sky, bright sun, a face with two sides, / Living, lively, how wrong can it be?" As Baby Jade got off the *kang* to kindle the charcoal on the brazier, Wang patted Little Cloud's buttocks and tugged at her foot. It was stiff as iron and immobile as a rock. Wang loosened her with words: "By chance I meet you and have no other [improper] thought. I am so fond of you that I just want to play with you a bit. Why do you use your mighty power *[shenli]* to shut me out?" Little Cloud relaxed and placed both feet on Wang's knees. Unexpectedly Wang slipped off her shoes. Little Cloud changed color, saying: "Isn't Mr. Scholar afraid that I would be angry?" Baby Jade mocked Little Cloud's doggerel: "Blue sky, bright sun, a face with two sides, / Living, lively, how afraid can he be?" The three eyed each other and laughed.

Wang asked, "Jade Lady and Li'l Lady, do you want to be reborn in the south [alt., do you want to give birth to a southern fruit]?" Little Cloud admitted, "Indeed the thought has crossed my mind." Baby Jade said, "Wouldn't it be my great fortune if I get to be Mr. Scholar's maid-concubine in my next life?" Little Cloud: "How dare I want Mr. Scholar. I'd be happy to be Mr. Scholar's maid-concubine." Wang: "I'm an old man with white hair and beard, what does Li'l Lady see in me that makes her so devoted?" Baby Jade: "Whenever we meet local men we treat them like pigs and dogs. After our meeting with Mr. Scholar today, we won't be able to forget." Little Cloud: "Not just the two of us; mother would also place you in her heart and at the tip of her tongue after you leave."

Wife Li entered and began to urge Wang to leave. She and Baby Jade left to fetch good water for a farewell cup of tea. Seeing that he was alone with Little Cloud, Wang forced her to lie down with him, "frolicked with her, stopping at nothing." Little Cloud responded in kind without resistance. "But she guarded her genitals with her hands, saying: 'Definitely not here. I have too much strength in my hands and do not wish to hurt Mr. Scholar.'" Wang offered Little Cloud pieces of gold he had tucked inside his boots, but she refused: "I'm a woman and have no way of spending it. Don't let others see it lest they have evil thoughts." She caressed Wang, on the verge of tears: "We will probably never meet again. Even a brief encounter like ours is destiny. Please keep Little Cloud in your thoughts. Maybe we will be together in our next lives."

Baby Jade returned and divulged a secret. Both her father-in-law and her husband were horse thieves. Of the nine women in the village, three were in the Li family, and all three practiced martial arts since they were young. Although there was no livelihood in Red Rock, Wife Li had made a pact with the other village women that they would not prostitute themselves. Instead, they donned male attire and became bandits. But they promised each other to leave southern men unharmed. Wang started to feel the gravity of the situation, but could not bear to leave the two ladies. Little Cloud voiced a standard line of the sacrificial woman: "Mr. Scholar has ten thousand miles of future ahead of him. Do not throw it away for two women."

Wife Li returned, sent the two younger women to pack a bag of grapes for Wang, and revealed yet a deeper secret. "Both of them want you to stay, and you don't seem to want to leave either. But you can't linger. Even I, a middle-aged woman who is like dead ashes and dry wood, still find your voice and laughter irresistible. How could the two of them resist, being so young?" Seeing that Wang did not move, Wife Li pulled him up: "So you think the two are charming? They are in fact women who would kill without batting an eyelash. If you sleep with them, how can they let you go? If they ambush you on the road and kidnap you, are you strong enough to fight them?"

They bid their farewells in the courtyard. Wife Li urged, "Mr. Scholar, please hurry." Baby Jade explained: "Not that my mother-in-law wants to be rude to Mr. Scholar. Mr. Scholar likes it here, and the two of us can surely find someone to serve you in bed. There are no unchaste women in this village, and if there were, she would not come from our family. We know that Mr. Scholar is full of passion, but the circumstances do not allow us to keep you here." Little Cloud added: "Now please hurry, Mr. Scholar. We will come to your cart to see you off." Wife Li warned: "Make sure that you go as far as Niudu Village before resting. There is no friendly territory between here and there. Be careful; be careful." All three saw him off by the cart. Little Cloud held on to the curtain of the cart. "If Mr. Scholar passes through here again, make sure that you stop for tea." As he hit the road, Wang overheard Wife Li telling the two: "I have always told you how wonderful southerners are. Now that you have seen one, wouldn't you think about him day and night?" They disappeared behind the closed door.

When Wang arrived at Niudu Village, it was past midnight. There he found that one of the women had slipped a blank journal bound in red satin and inlaid with gold into the package of grapes they had given him. He sighed, "How strange, just like the dream of Huai'an." A popular story, the dream of Huai'an tells of Chunyu Fen, who fell asleep under a scholar tree *(huai)* and dreamed that he married the princess of a kingdom of Huai'an and was appointed the magistrate of Nanke. Having luxuriated in life's riches for thirty years, he woke up to find that the kingdom was but a large ant hole by the root of the tree and Nanke, an even smaller hole beside it.

EROTICS OF THE NORTH AND SOUTH:
DUELING MALE AND FEMALE DESIRES

Wang recorded his encounter with the three women in his journal on the thirtieth of the second month, 1724. Following the convention of porno-graphic novels, Wang appended an afterword of remorse and warning. Ad-monishing himself, he admitted to twelve mistakes, which included letting a woman touch him and not suspecting that such bold behavior contradicts the mores of a respectable family. Although he seemed to suggest that the women initiated the flirtation, he also put the blame squarely on himself for giving in to his lust, which blinded him to the repeated warning signs. At the same time, he held on to his conviction that all three women were virtuous in intention and behavior, "they are motivated by sincerity, stop at righteousness, and guard themselves with propriety." He believed that he was saved by the women's virtues.

It is hard to read this story today without a foreboding sense of dramatic irony. We know that Wang was to be executed a year later and would not take up Little Cloud's invitation for tea. Did she hold him dear in her heart the rest of her life? Did the three women talk about Wang as they robbed other men—northern men, stupid and ugly like dogs and pigs? Were they really bandits, warriors with bound feet? How much social and geographic existence did they have outside of Wang's head? This last question is im-portant; whether we interpret the flirtation and seduction as social custom or male fantasy—or both—in the early eighteenth century depends on how believable we find the story. The key to an attempted answer lies in our recognition of a tension between the ethnographic concreteness of Wang's narrative stance and the ephemeral effect of his writing.

The thick description of sites, sounds, and sentiments is characteristic of Wang—as we have seen in the Lightning Steps story—and is also evident in other entries in *Westward Journey*. Wang had keen eyes and ears. His description of a place is always precise and graphic, replete with cardinal directions and measurements. The mapping of his lost bearings, the Li house, and Little Cloud's eastward-crouching position on the *kang* are good examples. With economy Wang evoked the pictorial cosmology of a place, revealing the patterns and structures of a macrocosmic order that frame human actions and are in turn animated by the latter.[42] The pictorial quality of place is also wrought by a vivid musicality of tones and voices: the diction of Lightning Steps's northern songs, Baby Jade and Little Cloud's doggerel, and the colloquialism of the dialogues.

Also characteristic of Wang's prose is his awareness of his corporeal presence in space. Immobilized by pain, first on his horse and then on the *kang*, Wang's narrative was propelled by his gradual awakening: first his ears, then eyes, then hands and fingers, and finally his mind. In this progressive pedagogy of the senses, the Li house assumed a layered and dynamic existence, unfolding its secrets to the visitor gradually but ever so partially. A full comprehensive view was possible only in the beginning, when the narrative opened with Wang walking through a door ajar. The longer he stayed, the less he knew and the less he trusted his sensory faculties. The narrative ends with the three women disappearing behind a closing door. At the end of an intimate and disarming encounter, the Li residence and Red Rock Village retain their alterity, with the exotic and untamed stereotypical character of the Northwest further mystified.

This alterity accounts for the dreamlike quality of the episode, one that permeates the Red Rock narrative, even without Wang's overt reference to the "dream of Huai'an" at the end. The elusiveness of Wang's experience stands in tension with his precise and vivid ethnographic observations. The Northwest as a dreamlike landscape recurred in *Westward Journey*. Later, in a poignant scene entitled "Remembrance of things seen on the road," Wang opened with his desire to see for himself the reality of courtesans from Shanxi and Shaanxi in situ, having heard of their fame and experienced a few— out of their place—south of Beijing. But his desires were dashed by strict anti-prostitution policies then in force. After he entered Shaanxi at Tong, he heard that in slightly off-track areas about one to eight *li* from inns and thoroughfares, women gathered in circular settlements *(bu)* called "picture houses" *(huafang)*. Riding on horseback with a local guide, he found a bewitching scene that rattled his senses so much that he could not judge which prostitute was superior.[43]

Even more surprising, "on the way I saw respectable women *[liangjia nüzi]* riding on stallions with gold bit on the reins and brightly colored saddle cushions. They covered their faces with light gauze. No one had feet bigger than three inches; nor did they have rouge and powder on their faces. But their colors, bodies, air, countenance *[taidu]*, smiles, and facial expressions are out of this world."[44] Similar to Li Yu, Wang located beauty in something as elusive as a woman's air and movement of her body. The ladies' opulence created an erotic presence that was dense and moist, accentuating the barren and arid landscape. The contrast recalls a similar depiction by Yao Lingxi of the golden age of feet contests in Datong. Like Yao's nostalgic recollection, Wang's brushing encounter with ladies on horseback assumes a dreamlike quality, like the fluttering gauze on their faces. The more he sought the reality and fixity of pleasures tied to a specific place, the more elusive the place became. However memorable, the pleasures of a foot connoisseur were ephemeral.

The reader is left with unanswerable questions: How did Wang know that these women were from respectable families? And surely he did not measure their feet to ascertain that they were no bigger than three inches? But empirical veracity was the last thing on his mind. The pleasure of writing—and reading—about footbinding in the Northwest was afforded by the seduction of the senses and the suspension of belief: in short the suspension of the mind which created a sense of wonder. The erotics of place is thus inseparable from the pleasures of the text.

In a subsequent entry, Wang recorded a conversation in Puzhou with a Student Chang, who corroborated much of what the three Li women had told Wang. A prolonged drought coupled with corrupt bureaucrats had bankrupted all local families; women with no shame turned to prostitution whereas women with a sense of righteousness became "rouge bandits." They would rob only wealthy passers-by, taking no more than twenty to thirty percent of their goods, and they would not kill lightly. A gang of twenty-some rouge bandits led by nine woman warriors lived in Red Rock, and the three Li women were their leaders. Wife Li, nicknamed "Flash of Light," was quick as lightning when wielding her long spear on horseback; Little Cloud was "Cloud of Snow," feared for her snow-white muscles and the snow-white flash of her fifty-catty knife blades; Baby Jade was an archer who could pull a heavy bow and shoot long-distance arrows, a "divine-shouldered bowman."[45] Although the specificity of names and deeds adds a historical heftiness to the three women, in itself it does not "prove" their reality outside of Wang Jingqi's head and text. It will remain a mystery to us. What rings true from *Westward Journey* is the poignancy and futility of male and female desires that structured the cultural imaginary of unevenness between the north and the south.

Student Chang's information about the rouge bandits enhances the menacing alterity of Red Rock as a place. Central to the erotics of the Northwest, as we have seen in the reports of feet contests and Lightning Steps's prowess in archery, is a sense of lurking danger cloaked in sweetness: the very allure of female sexuality according to the bedchamber arts tradition. This tension was epitomized by a martial arts tradition whose practitioners were bewitching girls who would not hesitate to kill. Wang's initial fixation on a limited, southern sign of the three women's femininity—their tiny feet—led him to misread a more complex and menacing northern femininity. This misreading in part accounted for the belated awareness of the danger he was in.

Wang's lust for flesh and skin was matched by the three women's relentless romanticizing of the south, which assumed an airy, imaginary hue—their own erotics of the south as a counter-discourse. Wife Li's remembrance of Scholar Shen, compounded by Baby Jade and Little Cloud's repeated promises that they would never forget Mr. Scholar's sound and face, reduced the southern man's corporeal presence to a fantastical one. In a gender reversal he lived in his sensory and desiring body and was, in fact, troubled by his body. The women, in turn, lived in their heads, a surrealistic world of secondhand mental images and anticipated memories of the south. Scholar Shen's and Wang's bodies served as visceral conduits to a place that the northern women had not visited and would never see. They thus fetishized the scholar's body, making it a synecdoche of a utopian order they could only hope to enter in their next lives.

Wang's lust began with the eyes—he was enticed by the women's pretty faces and bodies. The size of their feet was a key marker of their beauty. His physical assault began with Baby Jade's breast, advanced to Little Cloud's buttocks and then feet, and further took the form of his removing her slippers. Wang was fascinated by the layering of female footwear. In an entry that imitates the style and content of philological investigation heralded by Yang Shen and Hu Yinglin discussed in the last chapter, Wang inserted his own observation: "[Besides the binding cloth] women in the Northwest often wear soft slipper-socks *[ruan xiewa]* next to their skin; perhaps it is the same as what people call 'soft slippers' *[ruan xie]*. Even matters as trivial as this should be subjected to the [Confucian demand of] 'investigation of things' *[gewu]*."[46] But just as male desires were kindled by a progression of sensory priorities, the women held onto a hierarchy of privacy of body parts: breast, yes; feet, yes; undressed feet, yes when pressed; genitals, no. The genitals remained the last frontier of female propriety.

Echoing Li Yu's aesthetic of function, a pair of bound feet was by no means an impediment to movement in Red Rock Village. The three leaders had feet smaller than three inches, as we have seen; another bandit, Jueyun'er, was said by Student Chang to have feet only two-and-some inches. She donned leather shoes and could run alongside horses.[47] In a later entry, Wang supplied more ethnographic information on how the northern difference was epitomized by ways of binding feet: "In Shaanxi, Shanxi, and Hebei, girls start to bind their feet at age two to three. Their feet are naturally slender and small, and they do not bind into an arch shape. They laugh at arch-shaped *[gongxing]* feet, calling them 'goose-head feet' *[etoujiao]*. In these areas, I have seen women with very tiny feet, measuring only 2.7 or 2.8 inches on the ruler. The sole of the foot is flat. Those who call the bound foot 'arched foot' *[gongzu]* are uninformed outsiders."[48] The term "arched foot" was a euphemism for footbinding, as we have seen in the last chapter. Wang alerted us to regional variations in name and style, if not in "natural" bodily endowment as he alleged.

The footbound women warriors of Shanxi were in control of their bodies if not, ultimately, their destiny. When Wang tried to fondle her foot, Little Cloud denied him access to her erotic body by stiffening her muscles into an iron pellet. But in the end, the erotics of the south that provided a fantastic escape from their impoverished lives could be sustained only as long as they kept up with Mr. Scholar's game of seduction. The memento one of them had long prepared for the day, the blank journal bound in red satin, was a material expression of the woman's secret longing: Wang might not have realized that red satin decorated in gold is a fabric reserved for making wedding shoes.[49] For all of their agility and fertile imagination, marrying a scholar who could write was the women warriors' only way out of Red Rock Village.

PU SONGLING'S VERNACULAR PLAYS:
LOCAL TONGUE AND THE UNEVENNESS OF PLACE

Both privileged southerners, Li Yu and Wang Jingqi were attuned to the alterity of Datong and the north-south difference embodied in a pair of bound feet. Datong and Shanxi acquired a different air when the writer himself was from the north, albeit not a local. In his vernacular plays (*liqu*, literally popular songs), the Shandong native Pu Songling (1640–1715) presented different pictorial and social cosmologies of footbinding and the erotics of the north. Pu, a prolific writer famous for his collection of nearly five hundred tales, *Records of the Strange from Liaozhai (Liaozhai zhiyi),* wrote a series of less-well-known song-prose, of which fifteen are extant. These "vernacular plays" are diverse in format and style: three are dramas with designated roles, others are looser compositions wrought of unrhymed prose, rhymed prose, and tunes popular at the time.[50] Dotted with colloquialisms in the dialect of Zichuan, Pu's hometown in the northeastern province of Shandong, the ballads have a prosaic quality that evokes neither competition nor mutual fantasy between north and south. Instead, they bespeak a mundane materiality and a subtle unevenness in the local landscape that footbinding has come to be an unremarkable part of.

The pleasures of Datong and the beauty of its courtesans received iconic treatment in one vernacular play, "Song of Blissful Clouds, Revised and Expanded" ("Zengbu xingyun qu"), adopted from legends about the adventures of Ming emperor Zhengde, or Wuzong. Bored by bureaucratic routines, the emperor slipped out of the capital alone, disguised as a military officer. His destination:

> *Shanxi tops the thirteen provinces,*
> *What a scene in the city of Datong!*
> *The men are pretty without peers,*
> *And the women, oh so exquisite and romantic.*
> *Such outstanding talent, all dazzling.*

Three thousand in the pleasure quarters of Xuanwu yuan [Court of promoting
    martial virtues],
Each one rivals the fairies in the sky.[51]

For three months he dallied in the courtesan quarters, won the heart of Fo
Dongxin (Even-the-Buddha-skips-a-heartbeat), and dueled with a local
ruffian, Dragon Wang, son of a Minister of War. Finally, Zhengde revealed
his identity, had Wang executed, and made his triumphant return with his
new consort.

This long play sustains audience interest primarily by way of dramatic irony:
a shabbily dressed emperor determined to have fun at the expense of his un-
witting companions. Pretending to be oblivious to the fine arts of whoring,
he made one faux pas after another. In a play that extracts comic relief from
the villain's snobbery, status distinctions embedded in the minutiae of everyday life—in speech, dress, and bodily movement—are magnified for the
audience to savor. Toward this end footbinding serves as a useful rhetorical
device. Its main function is to mark status distinctions among local women,
not north-south difference as we have seen in the writings of Li and Wang.

The theme of female competition is announced early on, in a scene of
the emperor's entrance into the pleasure quarters:

All the beauties look like fairies,
The tips of their feet peeking out from curtains.
Intent on seducing men,
Their musky bouquet envelops your heart.
One by one they stand by the door, greased coiffure and powdered face,
Throwing you a smile and a glance.
Even if you are an immortal,
Would you remember the magical grottoes and mountains?[52]

The twin themes of brothel women competing for male attention and men
adjudicating the latter's ranking is perhaps as old as whoring itself, but the
tantalizing scene of women lining up behind curtains with their feet peeking out may have anticipated the late-Qing and early Republican feet contest accounts discussed earlier.

The aesthetics of feet mediates two kinds of contests among women in
the Datong pleasure quarters. The first is status ranking among courtesans.
Fo Dongxin, the exquisite courtesan who would be at home in Li Yu's cos-

mopolitan world, was introduced as having "tiny, tiny gilded lilies, no more
and no less than three inches." Later, a vernacular song coveys her full-body
glamour in motion:

> *Ascending the small pavilion to meet the military man,*
> *She blossoms like a flower.*
> *One smile of the red lady is worth a thousand pieces of gold.*
> *On top she wears a padded red jacket,*
> *At bottom, a green silk skirt with gardenias,*
> *Slender embroidered slippers, only half a zha in size.*
> *With a face that greets an immortal she faces him,*
> *Oh my, this lady is beautiful.*[53]

A *zha* is a handy measure in Shandong dialect, the length between the thumb
and middle finger of an outstretched hand. "Half-a-*zha*," or "not even half-
a-*zha*," a standard expression that recurs in Pu's vernacular plays, is the local equivalent of "three-inch golden lotus." In the hierarchy of the Datong
brothels Fo Dongxin belonged to the highest class, signified by her ability
to entertain her suitors with an elegant *Kunqu* aria. Further down the scale,
a wineshop waiter told Zhengde, one could save money by calling on girls
who were "a bit heavy with the bottom board" (*diban chen xie*), which he
explained is "feet a bit on the big side" in local parlance.[54]

In a more sophisticated choreography of agility and taste that recalls Li
Yu's aesthetic of function, footbinding marked a second distinction among
brothel women: between courtesans and maids. Unwilling to entertain a
shabby military man, Fo Dongxin initially sent her maid, Golden Stool, to
Zhengde in her stead. Golden Stool hiked upstairs on her large bound feet,
"one step deep and the next step shallow, / her legs quiver as her heart pon-
ders." On her way to curtsy to Zhengde, she tripped and fell flat on her
face. When Zhengde looked up he saw "A 'slender gilded lily' half a foot
big, / Nostrils like a chimney above the stove." But what gave her away were
her clothes:

> *An old jacket cut into a vest,*
> *Showing big patches and white stitching.*
> *A chestnut brown cotton skirt, billowing like a tent,*
> *A ripped kerchief, colors faded.*
> *Shoes made of coarse purple cotton cloth, a flower pinned on top,*
> *A chignon smaller than a jujube nut.*[55]

The second maid, Jade Dais, also failed to convince because "unable to change her Meixiang way of walking, she opens her legs wide. Like a horse galloping, a donkey hitting the trough, she runs upstairs with a ping and a pong."[56] "Meixiang" was a generic name for maids. Contrary to our modern expectations, the ability to run signified not freedom but inferiority. Surely the size of feet mattered, but more subtly it was the grace of footsteps and the fabric of footwear that marked the difference between servant and mistress. The clumsiness of the maids, etched on their bottom-heavy names, betrayed their lesser upbringing and doomed them to subservient status. In another play, a Shandong proverb conveyed the assumption that it was not unusual for maids to have bound feet, but it was not to be taken too seriously: "Xiao Lamei binds her feet." Xiao Lamei is another generic name for maids. Locals immediately understood it to mean: "a pro-forma performance" (*you kuaikuai zoushi liao;* literally, a bit lumpy would suffice).[57]

TWO KINDS OF FEMALE LABOR

Another vernacular play, "Immortals with Riches and Honor" ("Fugui shenxian"), seems to have scripted or anticipated Wang Jingqi's journey twenty-some years later in its four basic elements: a westward journey of a Mr. Scholar down on his luck; his seeking shelter from a strange, all-female household; the seduction of a beauty with bound feet; a denouement in which the amorous encounter was revealed to be illusionary or deceptive. In the case of "Immortals," a Scholar Zhang ran afoul of the law. A fox spirit, Shi Shunhua, rescued him and lived with him conjugally for five years. When Zhang became homesick, Shi sent him back to his wife. But he killed a ruffian the night after he returned home. Shi again came to his rescue and delivered him to a ward in Shanxi. After much travail, Zhang was reunited with his son in the examination hall, where both captured high honors.

In "Immortals," footbinding marks a third female difference, that between Shi the fox spirit and Zhang's mortal wife, according to a variant of the spectrum of burden-function (*lei-yong*) that Li Yu had proposed with his aesthetic of function. In a bifurcation that parallels the bifurcation of female sexuality into temptress and saint, the "function" of footbinding is split between the provocation of the senses and the economic productivity of the body. Fox Shi's temptress charm is signified by her bound feet in much

the same way as with the Datong courtesan. When she first appeared, Scholar
Zhang gasped:

> *There she is, a fairy from heaven,*
> *Only eighteen, such a tender age.*
> *An apricot-yellow jacket,*
> *Over her lazy waist that rivals Xiaoman.*
> *Her long skirt flutters,*
> *A pair of tiny gilded lilies,*
> *Whenever her foot shifts, the silver flower hairpin trembles.*
> *A blossom of white peony* that can walk,
> *As if her face can only be found in a painting. (emphasis mine)*[58]

(Xiaoman was a concubine of the Tang poet Bo Juyi, who immortalized
her willowy waist in a poem.)

Later, when she went to seduce Zhang, who was sitting in bed reading a
book, Shi Shunhua's presence was announced by the sounds she made as
she walked:

> *Suddenly, a string of jade rings chimes ding-dong,*
> *Is it the trembling of the bed curtain hook?*
> *Someone is inside the room,*
> *I hear her high-heeled slippers lightly resting.*

Shi's agility was highlighted in a later rescue scene in which she appeared to
snatch Zhang away from the two guards who had taken him prisoner. With
Zhang in tow, she leaped onto a mule: "The lady lifts up her skirt, tilts her
small foot upward to step on the stirrup, and mounts the saddle before
Zhang."[59]

In contrast, Zhang's wife, Madame Fang, was stationary, a posture that
befit a chaste wife. Her domesticity was symbolized by a second "function"
of footbinding: economic productivity. Hence when she saw her long-lost
husband, "ping-g-g she drops the embroidered slipper in her hand," which
she has been sewing, and "one can hear the scuffle of her gilded lilies as she
hurries" to the door.[60] That both wife and temptress had bound feet is in
itself unremarkable. It is the use to which their feet were being put that
marked subtle distinctions in female social roles and status. In a similar scene
of bifurcation of female labor in "Song of Blissful Clouds," emperor
Zhengde fell victim to a practical joke. Instead of the courtesan quarters he

was led to a spinster's hall, where the old women spun cotton, made soles for footwear, and mended old clothes.[61] In Pu's vernacular plays, the erotic body of the temptress was associated with the consumption of fashionable clothes, whereas the productive body of the domestic woman was associated with sewing. Furthermore, among the latter a hierarchy of female labor was expressed in the fabric and nature of the garments: respectable wives embroidered and made their own shoes; spinsters under public care spun, stitched sheets of cotton into soles, and mended old clothes.

THE MUNDANE MATERIALITY OF FEMALE BODIES

Pu Songling's use of bound feet as a marker of unevenness in female bodies, function, and status is perceptive if not altogether intentional. "Immortals with Riches and Honor" is adopted from a tale in *Liaozhai zhiyi*, "Zhang Hongjian," which made no reference to footbinding at all. Shi was only described as "a beauty" *(liren)*, her goodness signified by her acts of loyalty in rescuing Zhang.[62] There is no room in this long but sparely told tale for peripheral details or rhetorical embellishment. More curious is "Song of Tribulation" ("Molan qu"), a vernacular play twice as long as "Immortals" and based on the same Zhang Hongjian story. The reduction of references to feet to perfunctory remarks in this longer play can be explained by differences in genre and theme between the two vernacular plays. "Tribulation" is a drama written for three designated role types: male lead *(sheng)*, female lead *(dan)*, and clown *(chou)*; the plot, replete with dramatic twists, is propelled more by dialogue and action than storytelling. Furthermore, "Tribulation" is more of the Scholar's tale than the fox spirit's; Zhang's personal drama is set in the context of rural immiseration in the north, and fascicles 29–35 focus on Zhang's bureaucratic career and military exploits. In this virile tale, as if the lure of women's feet would be distracting, Pu Songling expunged line by line any mention of them in the seduction, riding, and homecoming scenes.

From the absence of footbinding in "Zhang Hongjian" we may infer that a pair of bound feet was so customary in Pu Songling's world that there was no need to single it out as the site of exceptional beauty or virtue. Its perfunctory existence in "Tribulations" reinforces this impression. As Judith Zeitlin has observed in her insightful study of the *Liaozhai* tales, "bound feet, those man-made fetishes that had become the locus of the erotic imagination in late imperial China, are transformed into a *natural* and *immutable* proof of true femininity."[63] The matter-of-fact existence of bound feet in the local landscape is even more pronounced in the vernacular plays, in which references to them are often made by dwelling on the materiality of female body and its labor. As a result, the binding of feet appears in a prosaic and less erotic guise.[64]

This difference in emphasis between the tales and the plays is epitomized in the way the filial daughter Sanguan is revealed to be a cross-dressing avenger toward the end of the tale "Shang Sanguan": "When they move Yu's [Sanguan's] corpse to the courtyard, his stockings and shoes feel hollow. When the footwear is shed they see a plain slipper *[xie]* the shape of a hook. So he is a she." The same episode in the vernacular play "Song of the Cold and the Dark" ("Hansen qu") lavishes attention on the material accouterments on her body: "Old Wang [the magistrate] rises to examine [the corpse]. He has her shoes taken off, and pulls out a bundle of cotton wool. Then a pair of gilded lilies comes to light. She wears a midnight blue Taoist robe, her legs are wrapped in felt stockings, and her shoes are filled with cotton wool. Her body is tied up in ropes, a leather belt tightens on her waist and on it a leather knife sheath hangs." The quotidian quality of bound feet is emphasized by highlighting the mundane materiality of her body. If the stripping of feet, a taboo subject, affords the reader momentary flights of fantasy, the exposure of cotton wool (*mianhua taozi,* a local expression for ginned cotton) returns his imagination to the tediousness of women's textile work. The fluffy balls of cotton, the tentlike robe, felt stockings, and belt add bulk to her body, reminding the reader that this is a body of production, not eroticism.[65]

That footbinding was a mundane and customary practice for prostitutes, wives, and often their maids in early-Qing Shandong is most evident in the play "The Pleasures of Marriage" ("Qinse le"), where it figures as a part of the female toilette and as a token of exchange. Told in monologues and songs by a bride in first-person, this most provocative of the vernacular plays narrates her psychological state before, during, and after her wedding. Even in this provocative ballad, Pu Songling refrained from fully exploiting the erotic potential of bound feet. One of the songs of the bedroom scene describes the foreplay:

That man I know is young in age,
But his face looks mature.

Refusing to stay still,
He caresses my face before fondling my feet.
Fooling around in a hundred ways,
He bites my cheeks lightly.
My hand letting go for a second,
And my pants become undone.[66]

The fondling of feet was serious flirtation; the only episode in the disguised emperor Zhengde's adventure that hints at the erotic potential of feet is one in which he teased a tiny-footed maiden who offered him water by a well by "squeezing the tip of her toe."[67] But the seduction of feet ends here; it figures neither in the bride's sexual fantasies nor the groom's action in "The Pleasures of Marriage."

Instead, footbinding appears most frequently in the play as an essential part of a well-groomed woman's toilette. The prospective bride sang:

Hearing that mother-in-law is coming to inspect [xiang] me,
I redo my coiffure and bind my feet anew.
Brush on rouge,
Apply powder and pin a flower [in my hair],
Tidying myself up, fresh as a flower.

Tending to the hair and feet is shorthand for techniques of adorning one's full body. The same sensitivity to the term of self-presentation was evident the morning after her wedding night. Rousing herself out of bed in a daze, her limbs were so listless that she wondered:

Where did my soul go?
How am I to comb my hair and bind my feet?
Forcing my attention to the dressing table,
Piling my hair to the left and to the right but it comes undone.[68]

The rearrangement and tightening of the binding cloth reestablishes order and control after dishevelment.

The term "tidying up," or *zaguo* (literally, swaddling and binding; also *zagua*) in Shandong dialect, is used by both males and females to refer to the daily management of the body and its social image.[69] It implies not only the importance of personal hygiene, but also the social nature of adornment. In contrast to the male connoisseur's overriding concern with ephemeral pleasures, the recurrence of "tidying up" in Pu Songling's vernacular plays suggests other seventeenth-century perspectives on the body-self, especially those of a woman: the body had a physical presence and a material heft, the binding of feet required assiduous maintenance, and doing it right was integral to the presentation of the female self to the world. Furthermore, *zaguo* connoted self-respect and respect for the solemnity of social intercourse; as such it was a measure of the woman's moral discernment and worth.

The moral import of *zaguo* is evinced by an exchange between the two protagonists in "The Wife and Her Mother-in-Law" ("Gufu qu"), a vernacular play about a filial young bride, Shanhu, and her overbearing mother-in-law. One early morning, when Shanhu tended to the shrew, the latter eyed her face and cursed, "You are done up *[zagua]* like a witch *[yaojing]*." The word *yaojing,* often used to name a temptress, also named her crime as one of over-ornamentation. From that day on, "Shanhu rose every morning, day after day she piled her hair into a coiffure neither beautiful nor ugly, draped on a garment neither clean nor dirty, and changed into a pair of shoes neither too new nor worn out."[70] Her moderation in attire, which involved more difficult choices than if she were to dress to stand out, announced her moral fortitude. In particular, a pair of shoes neither too new nor worn out implied a calculated control over one's own body and its image.

TOKENS OF EXCHANGE

Besides being parts of a routine toilette, the artifacts associated with footbinding also mediated a woman's place in her world by serving as tokens in economic, ritualistic, and sentimental exchanges. In one play, a matchmaker was enticed by the reward offered by a magistrate: "He promised to 'tear' *[lie]* me a half-foot piece of binding cloth *[banchi bu de guojiao]*. Let me go make the rounds. If I manage to make this match, having gotten this piece of cloth, besides 'tearing' it into foot binders I may even have leftovers for a pair of insoles."[71] So conventional was footbinding that a length of binding cloth served as currency in a business transaction. The verb "to tear" suggests that this seldom-discussed item of intimate female attire was made of plain-weave cotton, for which ripping would have left an edge straighter than cutting with scissors. But the meaning of "half-foot piece" is ambiguous. Since "half a foot" was hardly long enough to bind feet, it is likely to refer to the width.[72] The consumption of binding cloth, not to mention the frequent need to replace the insoles of shoes, recalls the emphasis on daily maintenance in the discussion of footbinding-as-toilette. Small feet might indeed have been spectacular objects of desire for men, as Li and Wang suggested, but for the women who needed to putter around on them, it was the materiality of body and footwear that consumed attention.

The materials for binding feet were but a fraction of the products of the sewing woman's hands. Textile objects mediated other social or familial relations for women besides business transactions. In another play, Fan Hui-niang, a bride from a powerful old family of scholar-officials in Shaanxi, visited her new mother-in-law and elder sister-in-law at the Qiu family manor for a formal gift presentation: "Elder Sister sat down with her, and [Hui-niang's] maid made the presentation: for mother-in-law, embroidered slippers, pillow ends, and four bolts *[duan]* of silk *[chitou]*; for Elder Sister, embroidered slippers, pillow ends, and two bolts of silk."[73] Standard northern pillows are shaped like an elongated rectangular box; "pillow ends" *(zhending)* refers to a pair of embroidered squares, about seven by seven inches each, that adorn its two ends. Often of red silk embroidered with elaborate patterns of flowers, butterflies, chubby babies, and operatic figures, they symbolized the young woman's wish for an amorous and fertile marriage. Both slippers and pillow ends made discreet references to the sensuous pleasures of the boudoir. As such they were standard bridal gifts to the women of her marital family; these specimens of needlework skills were received without fanfare.

But delicate negotiations over the bolts of silk fabric ensued. The Qiu were a small landlord family who ran a family farm. They were well-off enough to rent their property out to tenant families, but the patriarch had been kidnapped by bandits, and the family fell upon hard times. The Qiu second son, an outstanding student, caught the attention of Huiniang's father, who arranged for an uxorilocal marriage. The status consciousness of the Qiu women was palpable:

> *Elder Sister said, Oh, but we can't accept the fabric. . . .*
> *Our family cannot even offer you a glass of water,*
> *My brother is causing enough difficulty at your house.*
> *My mother would be saddened if she accepted your silk.*
> *Go ahead and show them to mother,*
> *See what she says.*

As if on cue the latter resisted: "It's all reversed! / How come *your* parents have to go to such trouble?" Both mother and daughter acknowledged the unevenness or the reverse flow of the exchange: they should be giving her gifts, if only they could afford it.

Huiniang refused to budge:

> *My father said, Two bolts [pi] of tabby silk [chou], two bolts of gauze [sha],*
> *Let Mother make an outfit.*
> *How dare I take it back?*
> *If I do, my father and mother would scold me.*
> *This is nothing really precious anyway.*

Thus the rhetoric of filiality and humility allowed Huiniang to prevail over her mother-in-law. But Elder Sister held out: "Mother may accept, but I absolutely cannot." Huiniang switched to a rhetoric of moral economy: "Elder Sister, please accept them. In the future I'd have many occasions to beg your help."[74] With this promise that the unequal exchange will be redressed in the course of time, Elder Sister gave in.

Later, Huiniang dispensed generous gifts of a three-foot length of red satin and two hundred coppers *(qian)* to each of the tenant wives—domestic helping hands for the landlord family—who scurried over to pay respect.[75] We get the impression that four bolts of silk represented a generous and, strictly speaking, unnecessary, gift to a mother-in-law. The verbal negotiation transformed the excessive gifts from a reminder of their already obvious status inequality to a token of sentimental give-and-take, a reciprocal exchange to be realized in the future. Huiniang's rejoinder that the gifts were mandated by her parents notwithstanding, this material and sentimental exchange between the bride and her new marital female relatives was a private affair between the women.[76] The negotiation of a gift comprised of such finished products as slippers and pillow ends and raw materials of uncut fabric bound the women into a symbolic loop of production-consumption of each other's labor.

In sum, in Pu Songling's vernacular plays, the figure of the Datong courtesan, the erotics of the north and northwest, and the trope of the westward journey are mapped on the axes of bodily labor and mundane materiality. In lavishing attention on the bodies and things of plebeian men and women, Pu conveyed an unsentimental reality of footbinding that is radically different from those of Li Yu and Wang Jingqi. Although written by a man, the plays come close to illuminating female perspectives on the burdens and utilities of footbinding in the early-Qing period. The functions of footbinding exceeded the sensual seduction that Li and Wang fixated on: it afforded women a "natural" feminine identity, a medium for self-presentation, and a means of negotiating the social gradations and unevenness that overarched their lives. The undeniable erotic charge of footbinding coexisted with female concerns for ritual propriety, self-adornment, and the mundane business of having to live in a body. Within the boundaries of male-authored discourses and tropes, Pu Songling thus opened a window into the footbound women's cosmology of place, which was constituted by the density and tactility of things they produced and consumed corporeally.

FASHION, STATUS, AND FEMALE ANXIETY

The vernacular plays also documented intense female anxieties in a world of economic disparities coupled with heightened status awareness.[77] From the import of eyesight to Li Yu's connoisseurship of women and Wang's practice of it, we have already gleaned the growing emphasis on visuality in this environment. In particular, dress constituted a medium of not only private pleasures but also social negotiations over status ranking and gendered identities. In a visually oriented society, the surface of female bodies—especially the adorned bound foot—acquired significance as "social skin," a boundary between self and others as well as between social classes. Highlighting the increasingly sensory, especially visual, terms of social intercourse, the historian Kishimoto Mio has called the visceral awareness of social unevenness that permeated Ming-Qing society "status sense" *(mibun kankaku)*. Everyday life became anxiety-ridden as dress, vehicles, and terms of address came not only to signify social difference but also to constitute it.[78]

Status anxiety affected men and women differently. Surely the wayward students, small landlords, and struggling merchants had their share of worries and envies. But social unevenness had a more visceral impact on women because it was inscribed on their bodies for all to see. To show that they were desirable brides, moral beings, or bearers of the status of their families, women subjected themselves to constant scrutiny: hence the frequent use of the verb "to size up" or "inspect" *(xiang)* in the writings of Li Yu and Pu Songling. In an age saturated with visual messages, it was incumbent upon the women to "tidy themselves up": to dress right, to perform correctly, and to look the part. The opportunities for female adornment and self-presentation thus came with a flip side, the tyranny of visual scrutiny and sartorial correctness.

The opportunity for social climbing and fears of being exposed culminated in anxieties about posing. The impostor syndrome must have been so familiar to Pu Songling's audience that one of the surest ways to draw a chuckle was to joke about ugly feet. Really big, never-bound feet brought far less comic relief than poorly bound feet, the owner of which suffered a litany of names: "Half-squeezed-foot" *(ban lanzi jiao)*; "Half-blocked-foot" *(banlan jiao)*; "Little-crooked-bone" *(xiao wailagu)*. The literal meaning of these colloquial terms of address was less important than their harsh, deprecating sound. Another spate of expressions focused on the horsey or donkey-trots of women with poorly bound feet, as we have seen in Golden Stool and Jade Dais, the two maids who tried to pass themselves off as their mistress. A related complaint was the terrible noise such a woman made as she walked: "zhuo-da-zhou-da." Even worse was ugly feet coupled with wastefulness. Hence a husband taunted his shrewish wife: "Keeping you around we would have no jacket and pants to wear; why, a pair of your shoes uses up three feet of cloth."[79]

Both the desire for the glamour of fashion and the fear of appearing shabby accounted for the seriousness with which women prepared for a visit to the temple, one of the few excuses for a respectable woman to parade herself in public. In a vernacular play, the chef of a well-off household expressed his pride in his wife's appearance: "My master feeds me everyday and pays me every month; we have money to spare. For my wife I had tailored a bright red jacket and bright green cotton pants. When she is put together *[zagua]*, she looks as fetching as a colorful pigeon, and everybody marvels at how handsome she looks. Yesterday she wanted to go burn incense but had no shoes, so I sold a catty of sesame oil for her to buy a half-foot length of silk *[sanling]*. Also I gave her a catty of ginger and half a catty of peppercorns to exchange for a knotted silk sash *[koushi daizi]*. Shouldn't these things also count toward what I make from my good master?" A knotted sash may refer to a wide ribbon with tassels on both ends. Longer ones were used to fasten a skirt. Its mention here after footwear may mean a leg sash, a shorter version that northern women tied around their lower calves and ankles to accentuate their arched shoes.[80]

The trope of an incense-burning wife dressed to the hilt for her pilgrimage is so emblematic of the visual age that it recurs in folk songs from other regions of the empire. Indeed, seventeenth-century songs from the Wu-dialect area in Jiangnan expressed the same anxieties about gender and status boundaries in a fluid society that we have seen in Pu Songling's northern songs. In the south, too, women with poorly bound feet were ridiculed with more ferocity than those who never bothered to bind; the specter of *failed* social climbing was all the more poignant because it was familiar. A typical example is the song "Country-Mama Wants to Make an Offering to the Bodhisattva." Following the standard pattern of starting with the head and moving down the body, the narrator ended with her footwear and gait:

> *From neighbor to the east she borrowed binding cloth,*
> *From neighbor to the west she borrowed socks to wear on top [taowa].*
> *Bright red shoes with green heel-tab,*
> *Stepping forward, with a jerk.*

Seeing her skidding on a stone-paved road, passers-by had a good laugh.[81] Echoing the emphasis on "tidying up," a pair of fresh binding cloths was a standard requirement for the toilette.

An earlier example of the trope is a spectacular play, "The Incense-Burning Wife" ("Xiaoxiang niangniang"), in the seventeenth-century collection of Wu tunes, *Mountain Songs (Shan'ge)*, compiled by the Suzhou writer Feng Menglong (1574–1646).[82] One unusual feature of this lengthy ballad is the reverse flow of pilgrimage—here, the wife of a merchant family was traveling from city to village. As a consumer of fashion, she was less parodied than paraded. One warm day in spring, aching to go sight-seeing, the wife came up with a plan to burn incense in a bodhisattva temple in Qionglong Mountain. The urban-rural contrast was highlighted at the outset: "Country people are honest to a fault; city people are rash and reckless." Her reck-lessness is first manifested in her audacity in overruling her father-in-law's objection by cursing him and threatening to hit him. But the family business was in the red, the rice in the pantry was about to run out, and the house was in disrepair. In a frenzy she plotted a strategy of assembling a re-spectable wardrobe with the help of two neighbors. If she was reckless, she was to be a reckless consumer of fashion.

The headgear and coiffure required the most effort: "There is no other way, then, but to cover my head with a pearl-studded velvet hairpiece; go borrow one. A hibiscus-brocaded damask scarf for the head; go borrow one. An orchid-shaped jade hairpin; go borrow one. Lilac earrings; go borrow a pair." Fortunately, the women had perfect knowledge as to whom to turn to for help: "The wife in charge of the Xu family has a jade-studded Guanyin-shaped gold pin for the sideburns. The young daughter-in-law of Chen-the-butcher has a pair of phoenixes picking golden peaches; Elder Sister Zhang has a gold-plated butterfly; Li San's mother has a green-spotted grasshopper." What they could not borrow they would procure from the market: "Take four coppers cash, and buy me a red cord to bundle my hair into a screw-knot; find some rouge [*lujiaocai,* siliquose pelvetia] to brush my cheeks."

The regimen began with grooming the head and ended with tidying up the feet, as in the northern songs: "Beg for a bar of round and fragrant soap for washing my body. Get two sticks of benzoin incense to perfume my clothes. That should do for the head. Now let's see what shall I wear. Borrow a brocade top lined in pink for the inside, top off with an unlined jacket—either chestnut blue or willow yellow would do. A patterned silk one-piece dress and a fringed cape, need one each. A pair of white shoes piped in blue and a pair of loose trousers, need one pair each. And borrow a pair of white, washed foot binders." With her neighbors gone, she rushed to wash and starch her underwear. Thus there was more to self-fashioning than ostentatious display. Although concealed, the tidiness of these intimate items was important to her inner sense of self. Sending her aunt and nephew to the pawnshop completed the preparation. For two wine ewers with bronze spouts and two patched-up garments she obtained silver and copper cash for the candles, incense, temple donation, lunch, and transportation. And a bundle of pine branches for a nice hot bath that evening.

The following morning, the pilgrim set off by boat and then rode a palanquin to the mountains. She had a splendid time before hurrying back by sunset. The two neighbors promptly seized and returned the borrowed goods; within seconds she was stripped naked. The play concluded with a lament: "A while ago she glittered in gold, like a newly minted bodhisattva statue on Chengshu mountain. . . . Now she looks like a stinking fortune-telling hag dragging a turtle [as oracle] from door to door."[83] In a visually oriented society, a woman's fashion or "social skin" defined her social status and persona: without fashion she was nothing.

The gap in wealth between the north and south, personified in the three Red Rock women's adoration of southern scholars, is here dramatized in the visual disparity between the chef's wife in the northern song and her southern counterpart. Attuned to the subtleties of color coordination and the varied textures of silk, the merchant's wife belonged to a fashion regime superior to that of the chef's wife, a colorful bird in her green cotton pants. Southern refinement is also evinced by the attention given to bathing, perfuming the body, and fumigating the clothes as part of the toilette. Jiangnan, the center of sericulture, led the rest of the empire in terms of the materials and styles of attire as well as the knowledge of the consumer.

But in the final analysis, the two pilgrims occupied a similar socioeconomic position: the upwardly (and potentially downwardly) mobile urban commoner. Although by no means members of the privileged literati, by dint of employment or residence they enjoyed limited access to the requisite cultural resources to pull off a studied imitation. The channels through which they obtained their items of fashion and accessories, however, betrayed their incomplete participation in the economy of wants. Both the silk sash bartered with ginger and peppercorns and the wardrobe put together from loans, pawning, and other circuits of recycling bespeak the women's circumscribed means. Their desires, always exceeding their world of things, were to remain ultimately unfulfilled.

The figure of an incense-offering pilgrim—neither refined nor elite but resourceful enough to know how to pose—returns us to the public space in front of temples with which we began this chapter. The temple ground, alleged stage for rapturous feet contests in the Northwest, appears to be a different place from the eyes of the fashionable woman now standing at its center. Secure in her inner knowledge that her binding cloth was clean, she courted the gaze of other women and men with her exterior splendor. Female competition was no mere male fantasy; it was a daily reality for the status-conscious women whose bodies shouldered much of the anxiety of an urban commercialized society. But with the anxiety also came new opportunities to fashion selves that exceeded old social distinctions. In making decisions about what fabric to purchase, what garments to have made, as well as what shoes and jewelry to wear to the temple, the incense-burning wife partook in the making and remaking of the erotics of place which we had taken to be the prerogative of the male writer-traveler.

6

CINDERELLA'S DREAMS

The Burden and Uses of the Female Body

What traces does the body leave behind after life expires? What remain of the sensations and sentiments that render each life singular and each woman with bound feet the mistress of her universe? These questions flashed in my head as I turned to examine with white-gloved fingers the exhibits in the conservation room of the National Silk Museum in Hangzhou. A pair of shoes, two pairs of socks, and one set of binding cloths from the Yongle era (1403–24) of the Ming dynasty sat on two felt-lined trays, recent discoveries from a lady's tomb in Jiangsu province (see fig. 15).

Slender and delicate, the ivory-colored shoes are in good condition. At a length of 21.75 cm (8.7 inches) they are not tiny, but their extreme narrowness bespeaks an aesthetic that prefers reshaped feet to unfettered ones. The edge of the vamp and the toe area are decorated with cloudlike "as you wish" *(ruyi)* and floral motifs that were outlined in black ink and then embroidered. The underside of the recessed toes is reinforced with evenly spaced backstitching to bind the satin upper to its lining. The original fabric sole has corroded, exposing a layer of curly felt-like fiber that once was the cushion inside the sole.

The unlined summer socks and the padded winter ones are flat with a loose, straight shaft, as is typical of Chinese socks since the Han dynasty.[1]

The socks are each wrought of two pieces of fabric cut into the silhouette of a foot with contoured toe and heel areas, with the toes dipping slightly downward. Their length is 22 cm (8.8 inches), which is longer than the shoes but is in effect shortened when the bulk of a three-dimensional foot was fit into what was essentially a two-dimensional space.

The dead woman was apparently buried with the binding cloths on her feet. A long strip of cotton or silk gauze about 6 cm (2.4 inches) wide, the Ming binding cloth is similar to its modern counterparts in size, but the method of binding differs. Instead of concealing the starting end of the cloth by binding over it, here it was left loose around the instep. The last loop stretches horizontally across the toes, compressing them into the narrow and pointy style of the shoes. The finishing end of the cloth is secured by tying it in a knot with the starting end. A blackish speck no bigger than 2 mm, possibly a fragment of a toe bone, was found in the fold. Collapsed onto itself, the flat bundle of fabric remembers the silhouette of the foot and the space it once inhabited.[2] The body is gone, but a tactile imprint on a piece of intimate fabric—like the shroud of Turin—hints at the reality of its presence.

In the previous five chapters, we have approached the history of foot-binding primarily through the writings of men. This is necessary because male concerns and emotions have to a large extent shaped the subject and our knowledge of it. The modern nationalist's feelings of embarrassment and shame, the connoisseur's pathos of nostalgia, the philologist's curiosity and disapproval couched in a disinterested tone, the traveler's fantasies about the northwest, the adventurer's quest for the most exquisite pair of feet: these very real passions have constituted the figure of "woman with bound feet" in our minds as well as theirs.

To put it bluntly: Were it not for male emotions and desires, there would have been no women with bound feet. A pristine, isolated subject called "footbound woman" does not exist. Male desires and female desires are intertwined; hence to understand the latter we have to go through the former. This is not to deny that in each male-to-female encounter—in text and in life—their interests, positions, and experiences differ. I have read male writings backwards and sideways, paying attention to gaps and silences, to illuminate that gendered difference. The humiliation felt by the older women during the anti-footbinding drive, the futile longings that consumed female bandits in the miserable countryside, the incense-burning pilgrim's anxieties about not looking sharp enough: these emotions are no less poignant than male ones. Each woman with bound feet lived in a complex world, each facing a changing constellation of motives, choices, sufferings, and rewards. Whenever possible, I have sought to view the world from her eyes.

Toward the end of this book, I harbor a lasting regret. The crux of the matter—the bodily sensations of premodern women with bound feet—is ultimately unknowable.[3] My quixotic goal in this chapter is to get as close to their bodies as possible. These bodies once occupied a temporal and cultural space, leaving behind material imprints and traces which rarely took literary forms. However fragmentary, shoes, socks, binding cloths, foot powder, medicinal recipes, and embroidery patterns provide clues to the vanished body, its subjective experiences, and the histories of which they were a part. In focusing on the things that women made and the things that made them women, this chapter places the burdens and uses of the female body at the center of footbinding's history from the fifteenth to the nineteenth centuries.

FROM FLAT SOLES TO CURVED ARCHES

Nothing is known about the fifteenth-century Jiangsu lady who wore silk slippers in life and in death. But her sartorial remains, seen in the context of the evolution of female footwear, tell a significant history. Her narrow, pointy, and flat-soled slippers are typical of an early stage in the history of binding feet which lasted through the Song and Yuan dynasties, and seems to have lingered into the early- to mid-Ming.[4] Excavated female footwear from this period conform to two subtypes (see fig. 16): the first, as in the specimen here, is shaped like a kayak, narrow and sleek with pointy toes that dip slightly downward; the second, shaped like a canoe with a high stem, features turned-up toes that were sometimes called "phoenix heads" *(fengtou)*.

The aesthetic appeal of the former style is an elegant slenderness, whereas the visual focus of the latter is the curvature of the toes, which can soar to a dramatic height of 7 cm (2.8 inches). Although "bow-shaped shoes" *(gong-xie)* is a generic term referring to any slippers for bound feet, these curved-toe shoes might have been its original namesake.[5] The length of either type of footwear from the thirteenth to fifteenth centuries ranges from 13 to 22 cm (5.2 to 8.8 inches)—by no means small by latter-day standards.

Characteristic of both styles is the sole: whether thin or platform-like, it is of even height. The body weight is thus distributed evenly on the bottom of the foot. The fabric sole often serves as a cushion for soft landing: witness the curly fiber on the bottom of the pair I examined or the embroidered shoes of Madame Sun (1543–82), consort of a Ming prince, excavated in Nancheng, Jiangxi province (see fig. 16h). The yellow brocade upper, 13.5 cm (5.4 inches) long and 4.8 cm (1.9 inches) wide, was stitched onto a platform sole of stacked cotton cloth that is 1.5 cm (0.6 inch) thick; the inside was fortified with an insole padded with fluffy silk fiber.[6] Although delicate, these shoes were made for walking.

In chapter 4, we have seen that the scholar Zhang Bangji identified an "arch or bow-shape" as the quintessential sign of footbinding in the second half of the twelfth century. Successive scholars in the thirteenth and fourteenth centuries also referred to feet that were "arched and slender" in their origin discourses. But we should beware of readings that are too literal, for "arched foot" *(gongzu)* is a generic term that encompasses a range of shapes and degrees of curvature. It is most likely that the kayak and the high-stem-canoe shapes were fashioned to accommodate two different ways of binding feet. The former required reducing the spread of the toes, possibly by folding the four digits downward. An anecdote relates that in the court of the Southern Song emperor Lizong (r. 1225–64), consorts "tied their feet into a straight and slender shape" *(shuzu xianzhi)*; the style was given the moniker "Quick-mounting" *(kuai shangma).* In his fable of Maiden Ying discussed in chapter 4, the Ming scholar Yang Shen depicted her feet in terms of "packed digits and flat sole."[7] In these cases, the term "arching" is misleading because the bound foot was straight.

The high-stem-canoe-shaped shoes, in turn, might have entailed an upward bending of the toes to conform to the curved tips of the shoes. The remains of two Southern Song ladies provide tantalizing but inconclusive material evidence for this style of binding. The muscles and ligaments of Huang Sheng (1227–43), wife of an imperial clansman buried near Fuzhou, Fujian, had decomposed, but the bones of her feet were wrapped in a long strip of plain gauze. Both the socks she was wearing and the fifteen pairs in her wardrobe feature curved upturned toes, as do the shoes on her feet and the five pairs stored in a pouch (fig. 17). A daughter of the supervisor of foreign trade in Quanzhou, Fujian, Huang Sheng was buried with a wardrobe of 201 pieces of clothing and 153 pieces of silk fabric, attesting to the sophistication of the Fujian coast as centers of silk manufacturing and fashion.[8]

Curled-toed shoes may be merely whims of cosmopolitan fashion, but the unadorned socks are constructed with the wearer's comfort in mind. There is no other compelling reason for the socks to have upturned toes than to conform to the shape of the body.

Even more suggestive are the remains of Madam Zhou (1240–74), interred in De'an, Jiangxi, who was a daughter and wife of scholar-officials. Her body was found intact and a published photograph of it, stripped bare, shows her toes curling upward. When found, her feet were wrapped in binding cloth made of pale yellow gauze. And, similar to Madame Huang, both the gauze socks and shoes she was wearing feature curled toes, as do the seven pairs of socks and shoes in her wardrobe.[9]

The stylistic similarities of the footwear of the two southern ladies suggest that upwardly curled toes might have been a regional fashion that began in the mid-thirteenth-century.[10] Future excavations from other regions and periods may reveal divergent binding styles and techniques. From the two types of footwear discovered thus far, we may conclude that in the Song, Yuan, and early-Ming periods the goal of footbinding was to make the foot narrower and the tip of the toes sharper. The toes might have been curled upward in some cases and folded downward in others, but the arch of the foot was not tampered with. A flat sole was the norm. The sizable shoes and the choice of silk, a fabric less sturdy than cotton, for the two Song ladies' binding cloths are suggestive of a relatively relaxed regimen in the initial stage, when the binding of feet was associated more with aristocratic delicacy than arduous labor.

Modern observers have taken the quest of excessive smallness and its corollary, the bulged arch—epitomized by the name "three-inch golden lotus"—to be a timeless trait. In fact it gained currency only in the later stage of footbinding's history that unfolded with the advent of high heels in the sixteenth century. In an essay discussed in chapter 4, the writer Yu Huai (1616–96) commented on the novelty of arched heels favored by fashionable Suzhou women, carved out of fragrant wood and covered with the finest silk: "The engineering of high heels *[gaodi]* was unheard of in the past, but nowadays they are exquisite."[11]

Heeled footwear facilitated a new visual pleasure, as explained by the scholar Liu Tingji (b. 1653): "The heel area of the shoe is elevated by a small cylindrical piece of carved wood, called high-heel *[gaodi]*. The tip of the toes thus touches the ground at an angle, appearing all the more arched and tiny *[gongxiao]*."¹² We have seen in the last chapter that the seventeenth-century connoisseur Li Yu made a similar remark: the unfair advantages of high heels were so pronounced that some women with truly tiny feet, not wanting to be accused of cheating, took to wearing flats. The birth of high heels bespeaks a craze for miniaturization that began in the late-Ming period.

More than affording an optical illusion, high heels also brought about a sea-change in the method of binding underneath the seemingly timeless label of "arched feet." Besides folding the four digits under, the new regimen pushed the base of the metatarsal bones and the adjoining cuneiforms upward, forming a bulge at midpoint on the top of the foot (see fig. 3a). The distance between the back of the heel and the tip of the big toe was thus reduced drastically. Bending the arch stretched and weakened the tendons and the extensors of toes on the instep. The metatarsal bones became atrophied, but no fracturing was required, as is often imagined. The compression of the fifth metatarsal bone toward the heel bone created a cleavage on the underside of the foot, which was surrounded by thick fatty pads. This cleavage became the locus of erotic excess. When the connoisseur Li Yu bragged about the feet of Datong courtesans that are as soft as if they were boneless, he was referring to the pads around the crevice.

The new triangular foot has often been compared to a lotus bud or bamboo shoot, which evokes the shape of a gently curved heel tapering off to sharp, pointy toes. The bulge on the top of the foot enabled a reduction in the length of the foot, but it was unsightly and recurred as the subject of ridicule. The goal of this strenuous binding that did away with the flat sole thus appears to be an overall shrinkage in volume, a utopian melting away of the body mass. High-heeled shoes redirected the wearer's body weight onto a tiny tripod-like area consisting of the tip of the big toe, the folded toes, and the back of the heel. However unsteadily, heeled footwear provided better support than flats for these feet.

The extreme way of binding gave rise to a new adjective for feet, "arched and curved" *(gongwan)*, which became another euphemism for the bound foot. Hence Yu Huai said of a famous late-Ming Nanjing courtesan, Gu Mei, that her "curved arches *[gongwan]* were slender and small."¹³ At first glance the statement is curious in Chinese for it is comprised of a succession of four adjectives: arched—curved—slender—small *(gongwan xianxiao)*. The uncompromising demand of the new fashion regime is thus conveyed.

THE CULT OF THE GOLDEN LOTUS

Although "golden lotus" (*jinlian,* also gilded lily) had been a euphemism for women's feet in Song poetry and Yuan drama, it was not until the fad of high heels appeared that footbinding could rightly be called "the cult of the golden lotus."[14] With this obsession with smallness at the expense of movement, standing and walking became increasingly precarious. This cult and its attendant eroticization of bound feet in the sixteenth and seventeenth centuries were products of the commercialized, competitive, and fashion-conscious culture in Jiangnan, a subject already discussed in the context of Hu Yinglin's sense of historical rapture in chapter 4, personified by the incense-burning wife toward the end of the last chapter, and elaborated on below. Once established, however, this extreme way of binding gradually became normative for countless women throughout the empire into the twentieth century. Li Yu's parody of "Miss Carry," doctors' reports of gangrene, and the litany of crippling effects recounted by the late-Qing abolitionists all refer to this latter-day fad that made high heels not only desirable but also necessary.

Although the cult of curved arches prevailed, neither the ideal nor the practice was universal. Ye Mengzhu, a Shanghai literatus who was the most astute observer of fashion trends in early-Qing Jiangnan, remarked that the new regimen was initially a mark of status distinctions: "The preference in making arched shoes *[gongxie]* has long been the smaller the better. But judging from what I see, this perhaps applies to only daughters from elite families *[shizu zhi nü]*. As for others, servants and maids from the marketplace, they often strive for narrowness. Therefore, their shoes are flat-soled—the shoes could be decorated with gold embroidery and pearls, but they do not wear high-heeled shoes in the shape of bamboo shoot *[gaodi xunlü]*."

Ye corroborated the observations of Li Yu and Yu Huai that high heels facilitated an optical illusion of smallness. The style thus began to spread through the social ranks in the second half of the seventeenth century. Ye continued: "In the waning years of the Chongzhen reign [1628–44], even small children from the alleyways bound their toes into a slender shape, hence half of the shoes worn in respectable families *[neijia zhilü]* followed the fashion of high heels. Those with narrow and tiny feet can thus show off, and those with sizable feet can hide their defect. Women in our dynasty have followed this custom."[15] Even as high heels became de rigueur, the old way of binding—compressing the digits without bending the metatarsal bones—never completely disappeared.

More pronounced than status differences were regional diversities. The Hangzhou writer Tian Yiheng remarked in 1609 that the binding style of contemporary women harked back to the mythical Yaoniang, whose feet wrapped in silk gauze curved upward like the new moon. As for poetic names, "Nowadays in the fragrant toilette genre and indecent verses, when people eulogize dainty feet they say 'sprout of bamboo shoot' *[xunya]* or 'half-fork' *[bancha]*. In colloquialisms they say 'three-inch-three-*fen*' *[san-cun sanfen]*. These are very elegant. In contrast, ancients sang praises of arched shoes *[gongxie]*, which were curved and turned over like a drawn bow *[wanzhuan rugong]*. It is the manner of northern women today; southerners laugh at such feet, calling them 'keeled-over feet' *[fantou jiao]*, or 'groping the stem of the boat' *[chuai chuantou]*. These are vulgar sights unworthy of mention."[16] It is difficult to discern the shapes from verbal descriptions alone, but it appears that the desirable southern feet were characterized by straight, pointy toes and gently curved insteps—a bamboo shoot—whereas overzealous arching in the north often yielded unsteady bulging feet that doubled up onto themselves.

Northern women returned the compliment by deriding bulging feet from the *south*. When the adventurer Wang Jingqi made his fateful trip to the northwest in the 1720s, he found that Shanxi women dismissed southerner's bow-shaped *(gongxing)* feet as "goosehead bumps." Northern bound feet featured flat soles, Wang added, hence should not even be called "arched feet" *(gongzu)*. Wang might have read an almost identical description in a notation book by the scholar Gao Jiangcun (Shiqi, 1645–1704), who stated that: "By 'gongzu' we refer to binding the foot by breaking the middle, curving it like an arched bow. Little do we know that girls in Hebei and Shanxi [Yan-Zhao] started binding at age three or four. Their feet are *naturally* slender and small, and do not show an arched bow shape. Those who do are being ridiculed as 'goosehead bumps'; the latter is not treasured" (emphasis mine).[17]

Tastes may differ between north and south, but the ultimate goal—a perfect pair of tiny feet—remains elusive. The contradictory descriptions of north-south difference may in part be due to a century-long time lapse from Tian to Wang, but more importantly, they bespeak the impossibly high standards that the aesthetic of curved arch had set. Although unsightly, the bulge was inevitable because however vigorous, binding merely rearranged the bones, tendons, and muscles. As Cinderella's stepsisters were painfully aware, the body mass did not simply disappear, human will and effort notwithstanding. The more popular the cult of the golden lotus became, the more ugly bulges there would inevitably be. Just like the toes of lesser women, the entire practice of footbinding was vulgarized as it keeled over and turned onto itself.

In the nineteenth century, a connoisseur of the pleasure quarters in Yangzhou voiced his disenchantment with the profusion of ugly feet camouflaged by arched wooden soles: "If a pair of feet is not [as slender and curved as] lotus petals, and the woman forcefully fashioned them into a curved-arch shape, I'd prefer a pair of plump white feet [i.e., unbound; the kind that Tang poet Han Wo immortalized in his line] 'glowing, glowing, six inches of succulent flesh.'" Neither were high heels panaceas. They would make small women appear all the more fragile and lovely, but the sight of tall and robust women—especially those whose bound feet were sizable—tottering on dainty heels was laughable.[18]

Implied in the criticism is the lament that the playing field was uneven; only a minority of naturally small-bodied and small-boned women was born to look good on the curved arch. At the height of its popularity, foot-binding as a ladder of success for women thus mirrored the fate of the civil service exam, a similar vehicle for men: as more people joined in the fray and the competition became impossibly fierce, the belief that winners and losers were born, not made, gained currency. This fatalism softened the humiliation of defeat, upheld the prestige of an increasingly ridiculous system, and thereby enticed even more people to participate.[19] With the cult of the golden lotus, footbinding became a virtual religion as it came to be discussed increasingly in the language of divine intervention and the chosen few in the eighteenth and nineteenth centuries.

The early style of binding resurfaced en masse as a by-product of the anti-footbinding movement in the twentieth century. Many women who let their feet out did so by relaxing the arch but retaining the narrowness at the toe area. Some mothers also proceeded to bind their daughters' feet in this manner from the start (see figs. 2, 3b). By then it was too late. A new view of the machine-like body created in the image of the Christian god had taken hold. Regardless of the women's subjective wishes, both the utopian and the mundane manners of improving upon one's body had become hopelessly dated.

THE SUBJECT OF MEDICAL ATTENTION

One sign of the growing obsession with size in the fifteenth and early six-teenth centuries is the heightened medical attention paid to women's feet and the ailments brought about by improper binding. Male physicians rarely mentioned treatment of diseased female feet in their case books, but an early and revealing case was recorded by Xue Ji (1487–1559), a doctor famous for his knowledge of Song classics in external medicine *(waike)* and the treat-ment of women *(fuke)*: "There was a twelve-year-old personal attendant *[shinü]* whose face was rather fetching. But her new master found her feet too big, so he recklessly took some binding cloth and tightly bound them, and then he sealed off the end with needle and thread." The maid com-plained of excruciating pain but to no avail.

After half a month, the master agreed to unseal the binder upon seeing that putrid fluid was oozing from the cloth. He summoned Dr. Xue, who saw that "the front of the feet had completely rotted and turned black, both the bones and muscles are dead." The rotting was halted by a washing of scallion broth and an application of ophicalcitum powder *(huajuishi)*, a rock mineral commonly used to dress wounds. Rubbing a red-jade tissue-generating ointment *(shengji yuhong gao)* on the wound and ingesting a por-ridge of rice and ginseng restored the girl's vitality and stimulated new tis-sue growth. But she never regained full use of her feet.[20]

In all likelihood this case hailed from the early- to mid-sixteenth century, when Xue maintained a private practice in Nanjing. The master had probably procured the attendant at a considerable price, hence his willingness to spare no expense in summoning the famous doctor when his investment was im-periled. Xue's biting tone and use of such adverbs as "recklessly" *(renyi)* be-tray his sympathy for the maid and disdain for the master's follies. So crazed was the master by the cult of miniaturization that the maid's "fetching face" did not suffice. This new standard of artificial beauty clearly left much to be desired in the doctor's mind. Also implied in "reckless" is a judgment more medical and physiological in nature: twelve is too advanced an age to begin a regimen of vigorous binding. Furthermore, sealing up the binding cloth without regular disinfection and cleaning was downright irresponsible.

If the master had cared enough to look, he would have found a range of recipes for tending to the binding of feet in the household encyclopedias of his times. First appearing in two seminal almanacs, *Essentials of Domestic*

Living (Jujia biyong shilei, ca. 1260–94) and *Comprehensive Compendium in the Forest of Affairs (Shilin guangji,* compiled after 1233 but before 1279), these recipes were reprinted in subsequent editions or anthologized in other encyclopedias that Ming readers seem to have had a boundless appetite for.[21] As established by the two thirteenth-century almanacs, this tradition of pharmaceutical knowledge consists of two portions: a liquid for soaking the foot to soften the bones before binding and an ointment or powder to keep the foot dry, soft, and corn-free. Both the initial binding and subsequent everyday maintenance became the subject of meticulous medical attention.

The liquid portion assumes fantastical names. *The Forest of Affairs* named it "Xishi's bone-shedding broth," after a Warring States consort who personified feminine beauty. To make this broth, mix half an ounce each of frankincense and apricot kernel; have two ounces each of crude mirabilite *(puxiao)* and the root bark of white mulberry, and divide each ingredient into five portions. Place one portion of the apricot kernel and bark mixture into a new jar, add five bowls of water, and reduce it to half by boiling. Add one portion of each of the other two ingredients, seal the jar with a tape, and boil it for another hour or less. Remove the tape and place the two feet on the jar to soak up the gush of steam. When the liquid has cooled enough to touch, pour it into a basin and soak the feet in it. Return the liquid to the jar and repeat the procedure in two or three days. Each portion is good for three treatments. When all five portions are used up, the feet will become "as soft as cotton wool, putting up no resistance to swaddling and tying. It is very efficacious."[22]

Even more miraculous is the infusion in *Domestic Living,* labeled "An inner palace's shortcut to shrinking the lotus steps." Prepare a thick dark broth by boiling the ashes of buckwheat stalks while mixing together the fine powder of sal ammoniac Sal, white poris cocos *(fuling)*, and ligusticum rhizome. Apply heat to 0.3 ounces of the powder and three bowls of the ash broth in a clay pot. After several boilings, wash the feet in it, reheating if necessary. Several washes would ensure that the feet are "naturally soft and easy to bind." The recipe originated from "a supreme being; its wonders cannot be exhausted with words." With its help, even a thirty-year-old woman can attain her heart's desires.[23] This recipe appeared under the category of "Boudoir Matters" ("Guige shiyi"), alongside such advice as ways to cure pimples, prevent hair loss, or blend fragrant face powder. The binding of feet and their care has become a matter of routine toilette.

Although not without medical grounding, both recipes belong to the realm of magic. The repeated evocation of five in the first recipe and three in the second recalls Taoist exorcist rituals, as does a broth of ashes. The attribution to "Xishi" and "a supreme being" from the "inner palace" places the origin of secret knowledge in the harem, the exclusive pleasure garden of male privilege and the birthplace of footbinding in popular imagination. Like the anti-wrinkle creams peddled by today's cosmetics companies, these infusions promised miraculous transformations.

In contrast, the second type of recipe, a foot powder, is pragmatic and no-nonsense. Grouped under the rubric of "Steady steps for the golden lotus" are recipes of different ingredients. The *Domestic Living* manual recommends an application of the root bark of Chinese wolfberry pounded with safflower, which would hasten the scarring over of corns within a day. *Forest of Affairs* offers a fine powder made of the bark of cork tree, the ear of *jingjie (schizonepeta tenuifolia)*, the rhizome of Chinese goldthread, and yellow lead. Ingrown nails causing "unbearable pain" and crevices between the toes too swollen or rotten to be wrapped up in binding cloth would be cured instantaneously.[24]

Copied verbatim or in modified form, this handful of thirteenth-century recipes was transmitted widely in Ming and Qing household almanacs, remaining part of a standard lexicon and knowledge associated with the caring of bound feet until the twentieth century.[25] We do not know the extent to which such standardized, formulaic knowledge was put to practice several centuries after their initial codification. Women in various locales, too, were likely to have employed their own local remedies that were not committed to writing. The emergence and transmission of a tradition of pharmaceutical attention to feet tell us less about actual domestic practices than about two perceptions of the female body that might have accounted for the arching of feet and, as a result, their heightened medicalization.

The bone-softening and shedding tonic evokes a fantastical corporeal state of bonelessness—a Cinderella's body—that is pliable and responsive, readily submitting to one's will and desires. It is a body of the chosen few whose feet are so small that it seems as though they did not occupy any space. The foot powder, in turn, ministers to a multitude of bodies fettered by gravity and physicality—the stubborn body of Cinderella's sisters and the rest of humanity. Perhaps the incessant impulse to remake the latter into the former led to the intensification of footbinding around the fifteenth century.

In a status-conscious society, an initially reasonable desire to improve upon one's given station or body and to out-small the neighbors could easily run amok. Be that as it may, the binding of feet, in its milder or extreme forms, was motivated by a utopian desire to overcome the material, stubborn body.[26]

ENTERTAINING URBAN WOMEN: FASHION AND STATUS IN THE CHANTEFABLES

A nagging complaint about the burden of a stagnant and immobile body ruined by footbinding recurred in a host of fifteenth-century texts, the most graphic of which is a chantefable, "Judge Bao Judging the Case of Imperial Uncle Cao" ("Xinke shuochang Bao Longtu duan Cao Guojiu gongan zhuan"). The discovery of this and ten other chantefables (*shuochang cihua,* also called verse ballads) in 1967 in Jiading, near Shanghai, filled a missing link in the history of Chinese popular literature as in the history of footbinding. In the tomb of a Madame Xuan, wife of a Ming scholar-official, peasants found twelve book-like bundles, the pages caked together with lime and dirt. The peasants were terribly disappointed: other than the old books, the tomb yielded only porcelain shards. The books languished on the shelves above a pile of firewood in a farmhouse. Five years later, buyers from a bookstore bought the lot and sent them to the Shanghai Museum. Upon being steamed and washed, the bamboo paper yielded a goldmine: eleven chantefables and one southern drama *(nanxi)* that had been unknown and unread for five hundred years.[27]

Printed between 1471 and 1478, these works of popular entertainment were deemed too vulgar by scholars at the time to be preserved in their libraries or literary compilations. Madame Xuan evidently loved them so much that she went to the grave with them. Anne E. McLaren, a specialist on chantefables, has argued that in presentation style and readability they lie midway between the "performance-style" format of Yuan *zaju*-drama and "desk-top" drama editions printed by the late-Ming literati. The chantefables were performed in wealthy households, and the printed text allowed the audience to read and sing aloud in the family circle, thus serving to "render the complete performance experience" to audiences who had enjoyed them on stage. Although the "authorship" is male, to a large extent these chantefables reflect and shape the tastes and worldviews of their predominantly female audience.[28]

"Imperial Uncle Cao" is a long episode in a series featuring the beloved

Judge Bao, a wise and incorruptible avenger of injustice. Set in the reign of the Northern Song emperor Renzong (r. 1023–63), the story opens with the travails of Scholar Yuan. Admitted into the roster of a special metropolitan examination, he happily set off with his wife, née Zhang, and infant son from Chaozhou, in the far southeastern edge of the empire, to the eastern capital of Kaifeng. Their first experience of the capital, a typical country-bumpkin-coming-to-town scene, was narrated with a characteristic energy that must have made the chantefable so enchanting to its audience:

> *The eastern market spilling over to the western market,*
> *The people on the southern street gawking at people on the northern street.*
> *The cotton fabric store sitting opposite from the silk satin store,*
> *The door of the teahouse facing the door of the wine shop.*
> *A medicine shop sells dry herbs and prepared tonics,*
> *Flower sellers calling out to flower buyers.*[29]

The series of oppositions establishes the grid-like political cosmology of imperial cities while conveying a sense of the commercial hustle and bustle that threatens to upset such symmetrical order. In barely a few lines the audience is transported to the urban streets in which the sensory faculties of the body dominated.

A visual curiosity did the scholar in. The following morning he could not wait to take in the sights (*kanwan,* look and play). In a quickening passage propelled by reiteration of "to look" (*kan),* the audience follows the family of three to tour the stores, government offices, and city gates. Then they ran into the entourage of Imperial Uncle Cao, younger brother of the empress:

> *From his horse he [Cao] saw [kanjian] with his own eyes,*
> *With his eyes he saw the figure [shen; literally, body] of the wife,*
> *He saw that her face was beautiful as a flower,*
> *Her body more tender and bewitching than the Bodhisattva Guanyin. (4b–5a)*

Conduit of his lust, Cao's eyesight was also an instrument of his ruthless power. He tricked and strangled the scholar; the infant son he beat to death and threw into a well. Threatened with death herself, Zhang became Cao's wife and was taken to his new post in Zhengzhou. There was no mention of Zhang's bound feet in this scene of fatal attraction.

The storyteller directed the audience to Zhang's feet at her second appearance in the Cao mansion, when she had just received a summons to join Cao for a drink. She intuited that Cao, who had become worried about Judge Bao's investigations, was plotting to kill her at the table. Determined to maintain an upper hand by looking her best and remaining sober, she gazed into her dressing mirror:

> She paints her brows skillfully and applies lipstick lightly,
> She piles a high coiled dragon chignon on her head,
> Twelve gold hairpins, one for each hour.
> She wears a headdress of gold phoenix and pearls,
> Her two sidelocks as dark as the clouds.
> For the top she puts on a golden-yellow jacket of Sichuan damask [shexiang
>   chuanling ao]
> On her waist she ties on a Wave-on-River-Xiang skirt [xiangjiang shuilang qun].
> On her feet her slippers [gongxie] are only three inches long,
> Gently shifting her lotus steps she leaves the room.

Her beauty was accentuated by her elevated status, marked by scores of maids holding golden censers leading the way. Cao found the spectacle of her presentation as enticing as her person (18a–b).

In this formulaic description, footbinding—represented by two standard tropes, three-inch slippers and lotus steps—was part of an expensive and elaborate attire fit for a princess. To a large extent, the entourage of finely appointed attendants was the outermost layer of the attire, a moving extension of her privileged self. The significance of this formula, which recurs in the chantefables, has to be assessed in the context of the latter's entertainment mandate. The storyteller routinely invoked a vivid image and conveyed the social circumstances of a character by lavishing attention on the clothing, makeup, hairstyle, and jewelry.[30] The audience could thus visualize the character by concrete, bodily signs, not as mere abstractions.

Witness, for example, the deliberate gradations made between the appearance of a princess and her attendants in another chantefable. The princess, younger sister of the emperor, is introduced to the audience in almost identical terms as the ill-fated Woman Zhang: phoenix headdress, lotus-root silk skirt, west-brook *(xichuan)* red brocade jacket, pearl pendant earrings, twelve gold hairpins, and "embroidered slippers on her feet, three inches long." Identical, too, is the gentle manner in which she walks: "A bold step no more than five inches, / A dainty step she makes is no more than three inches."

Like Zhang, the princess's opulence is accentuated by her impressive entourage of thirty.

The maids were put in their place by visual contrast. They wore clothing
good enough to impress the pedestrians: west-brook ten-motif brocade *(xichuan shiyang jin)* jackets, purple gauze skirts, beaded headdresses, and a
peony on the sidelocks. But the sheer brevity of description and the lack of
footbinding announced their servitude to the princess.[31] This pattern re-
peats itself in the presentation of a princess in another chantefable. The only
non-noble women with bound feet to be described in the chantefables are
an entertainer who appears in a pair of "arched shoes embroidered with colorful clouds" and the wife of a hereditary master weaver who decked herself out for a pilgrimage to a temple.[32]

Both three-inch slippers and lotus steps, consistently attached to princesses
and other females who serve high-status men, constitute a stereotype. Stereo-
types acquired power from regularity and repetition; having enjoyed enough
chantefables, the audience learned to interpret cultural codes in life by the
same rules. It would be erroneous to infer that all princesses, entertainers,
and weaver's wives had bound feet in fifteenth-century China. The characters in the chantefables do not "represent" social reality or practice. Rather
their presentation or representation constructed the audience's sense of female beauty, social status, and desirability, linking it firmly to footbinding.
In this way, the chantefable performances served as a vehicle in the transmission of Cinderella's dreams among their audiences.

STUBBORN BODIES:

THE BURDEN AND USES OF FOOTBINDING

With this knowledge we may return to the saga of Imperial Uncle Cao and
Woman Zhang, who feigns drunkenness and is resting in bed. Cao, who
could not bear to kill her himself, dispatches a sword-wielding servant. Out
of the blue an Old Man Zhang, an incarnated deity, comes to the woman's
rescue. He takes the time to administer a sobriety test, telling her that he
will whisk her away only if she is sober enough to walk on the rim of the
well counterclockwise three times and then clockwise three times. "Without a single misstep" and "as airily as a cloud" she passes the test (19b). In the
dark the old man leads her to the rear garden gate, telling her to flee to Kaifeng in the morning, where she can (and does) seek redress from Judge Bao.

But surely she is not to get to the good judge so easily. The latest obstacle is her bound feet: "Her feet small and her shoes pointy, it is hard to walk, / The wild wind blows until her face turns red" (20a). The White Gold Star Venus appears in human form with a wheelbarrow and escorts her to Kaifeng. Referring to this scene, Anne McLaren has observed that "in Ming chantefables and nüshu writings one commonly finds bound feet depicted as an impediment to the actions of women." According to McLaren, both chantefables and nüshu writing, a form of texts in female script found in twentieth-century Jianyong, Hunan, belong to the same oral tradition of non-learned women in which footbinding was a source of complaint and an outright burden.[33]

In the context of the chantefables, McLaren's conclusion is not wrong but one-dimensional. It fails to take account of the complex constellation of meanings associated with footbinding within and without the text of the chantefables. In the entire set of eleven chantefables, this is the only instance where footbinding is depicted in a negative light. Indeed, bound feet do constitute an impairment to Woman Zhang's action as she flees the palace of her murderous "husband" in the dark, hovering by the roadside alone. But it is more accurate to say that bound feet become an impediment only to a woman who has fallen from grace; the nuisance of bound feet signals the pain of downward mobility.[34]

Contrast her circumstances with those of Cao's sister, the empress, who upon hearing that Judge Bao has seized both of her brothers, races to Kaifeng in a dragon-and-phoenix palanquin borne by eight bearers, accompanied by an entourage of three thousand flower girls and eight hundred female attendants (32b–33a). The empress's mother, too, is conveyed in a speedy eight-man palanquin (30b). If footbinding—or, to be exact, three-inch slippers and lotus steps—is a stereotype in the chantefables, it derives its rhetorical power from a social attitude that associates bound feet with women of privilege. Hence in the chantefables, footbinding recurs as a sign of upward mobility. The perils of Woman Zhang could only reinforce this prevalent association of bound feet with high status. Footbinding was useful for social climbing, not mountain climbing.

The chantefables contain contradictory messages about the physical mobility of women with bound feet. Such stereotypical expressions as lotus steps, three-inch steps, or gently shifting steps remind the reader that a woman with bound feet realizes her beauty in motion, albeit in dainty steps.

Woman Zhang's success in circumnavigating the rim of the well also attests to the desirability of nimbleness. In contrast, the expression "Her feet small and her shoes pointy, it is hard to walk" *(jiaoxiao xiejian nanxingzou)* and its variant "Her shoes are arched, her feet tiny, and her steps difficult" *(xiegong jiaoxiao bunanxing;* 20a) recall the nuisance of corns, bunions, and ingrown nails that a growing repertoire of foot tonics and powders ministered to.

The complaint about tiny feet and restrictive footwear that impeded walking is a trope common in the fifteenth century. In another southern drama *(nanxi)* contemporary with the chantefables, "The Embroidered Jacket" ("Xiuru ji"), an old prostitute mouthed it on a mountain path as an excuse to part ways with a poor scholar: "My feet are tiny and my shoes arched *[jiaoxiao xiegong]*; the path ahead is winding and uneven, I am not used to walking on this kind of road."[35] The expression might well have enjoyed a life off stage. In the "Wedding rites" section of a 1597 household almanac, there appears a series of auspicious chants that the master of ceremony was to utter at each stage of the wedding ceremony. One of the chants recommended for the arrival of the bride is:

> *Look, the bride alights the palanquin,*
> *In a flash we glimpse her matchless countenance.*
> *Her feet tiny, her shoes arched, and her steps unsteady [jiaoxiao xiegong xing-*
> * buwen],*
> *Let the jade maidens hold her by her side.*[36]

In both of these usages, the line appears to be less a bitter complaint than a straightforward statement of a fact of womanhood. Although agility was valued, the crippling effect of binding feet came to be taken for granted. In the wedding incantation, unsteady steps constitute not a source of complaint but celebration.

This heightened awareness of the perils of footbinding and the conflicting desires about the extent and manner of physical mobility manifested in the chantefables are emblematic of a transitional age that witnessed the initial spread of the cult of golden lotus. There seems to be general agreement that small feet and ornate footwear were markers of privileged status—the sign of conspicuous leisure—but there was also a growing unease if not malaise about the crippling effect of the increasingly strenuous way of binding. This ambivalence was in fact voiced during the entire span of footbinding's life as an actual practice, beginning in the twelfth century. The more popular and demanding the practice became, the more vocal was the opposition. The futility of the male literati's protests was in no small part due to the success of such performing arts as the chantefables in conveying both the burdens of footbinding and its glamorous image to their female audiences.

THE BURDEN AND USES OF THE BODY

A profusion of the word *shen* (body) is instrumental to the visceral appeal of the chantefables. The usages of *shen* are both familiar and unexpected to a modern reader. In "Imperial Uncle Cao," for example, Cao's brother urged him to "hurry up and kill the body of Woman Zhang" (17a). Cao began his confession by recounting, "Her husband is the body of a government student *[xiucai]*" (19a). Stranded in the dark during her escape, Zhang "Blames the body of her husband over and over" for "bringing ruination to this unworthy body of mine *[wo nu shen]*." Her savior with a wheelbarrow "comes across the body of the woman by the road" (20a). Grammatically superfluous, the recurrence of *shen* highlights the presence of a material body that can be seen, disposed of, or spoken of by others. It also connotes a sense of self in lieu of, or in addition to, the first-person pronoun. *Shen* is thus more accurately rendered "body-self."

Shen evokes a different way of being than the one prevalent in post-Enlightenment Euro-America, which construes the body as a container of the self or as a property owned by the self. Hence the expression "having a body." In contrast, *shen* bespeaks a phenomenology of "being a body." Suzanne Cahill, who has detected a similar use of *shen* in the poetry of Tang Daoist women, has suggested that for these women, such disciplinary practices as fasting, ingesting drugs, or abstinence from sex constitute the only way to approach immortality. To transform the body one must begin by disciplining the body with seemingly destructive measures. Synonymous with the self, the body is at once a hindrance to and a means of deliverance.[37]

These insights on the ironic status of the body-self put the perils of footbinding in a different framework of understanding. Beginning with the premise that self and body are separate entities, such modern critics as Reverend MacGowan viewed the binding of feet as an act of mutilating the natural (God-given) body, as seen in chapter 1. To them, it is inconceivable that any woman would have maimed herself out of her own free will. In the world of the chantefables and Tang Daoist practices, however, the concept of a "natural body" was alien. Men and women achieved their goals—be they religious, material, social, or sensual—by working their bodies. Reflecting this premodern Chinese view, the connoisseur Li Yu placed the "burdens and uses" *(lei* and *yong)* of the body on a continuum, a formulation which is more useful than the modern discourse of "natural versus crippled body." According to the latter framework, one has either a natural or a deformed body; according to the former, every self *is* a body that is open to, or even requires, various degrees of manipulation.

Li Yu's formulation, we may recall from the last chapter, is part of his "aesthetics of function." His original usage focuses narrowly on bound feet. Praising courtesans from Datong, he wrote of their "having the smallest feet that are not burdensome; having the smallest feet that are still functional." When applied to women with or without bound feet, the discourse of burden-and-use allows us to view their bodies as they viewed them from the inside, as both an obstacle and a vehicle to achieving whatever aspirations they may have had, without our dictating for them what these goals are to be.

In the remainder of this chapter, I seek to understand the women's perspectives and desires from their self-presentations—presentations of their body-selves—by focusing on the footwear they produced, purchased, and wore from the seventeenth century to the turn of the twentieth century. In taking stock of how women worked with and against their bodies, we map the changing constellation of the burdens and uses of the female body during the heyday and eventual demise of the cult of the golden lotus.

FRIVOLOUS BODIES: A NEW URBAN FASHION REGIME

Empress Xiaojing (1565–1611), consort of the Ming emperor Wanli (r. 1573–1620), was buried with a striking pair of high-heeled shoes, the best material evidence of the new taste for miniaturization that has survived from the Ming period. Made of pale red satin, the shoe uppers are rather small, measuring only 12 cm (4.8 inches) in length (see fig. 18, no. 3). The slightly turned-up toes retain the silhouette of the bow-shaped shoes from the previous dynasties, whereas the 4.5 cm- (1.8 inch-) tall cylindrical heels announce a new fashion regime. Embroidered lotus blossoms and leaves decorated the vamp, and at the underside of the tip of the toes, embroidered pine and bamboo. The oval heels, 7 cm (2.8 inches) long and 5 cm (2 inches) wide, are made of layers of thick straw paper, stitched together with plied silk yarn and covered with plain red satin.[38]

Empress Xiaojing was a posthumous title awarded to Consort Wang, who began her career in the inner palace as a maid in the chambers of Wanli's mother. In 1582, she was promoted to Imperial Consort two months before giving birth to Wanli's first son, the future heir apparent and emperor. By then Wanli's attention had turned elsewhere, and his futile efforts to install the son of his favorite Consort Zheng as heir brought court life to ruination. When Consort Wang died lonely and despondent in 1611, her body was interred in a separate site. But as the mother of the new emperor upon Wanli's death in 1620, she was granted the privilege of resting alongside Wanli and his official wife, the Empress Xiaoduan, in the magnificent Ding mausoleum.[39] Xiaojing was a classic Cinderella, albeit she did not live happily ever after.

Xiaojing was buried in her coffin with four pairs of flat "phoenix-head" (*fengtou*) shoes, 12.9 cm (5.2 inches) long (see fig. 18, no. 2). In a box placed at the southern edge of her coffin were two pairs of "cloud tip" (*yuntou*) shoes, only 10.5 cm (4.2 inches) long (similar to fig. 18, no. 1).[40] The empress's high heels were made of uppers similar in shape to these flat-soled shoes with curled tips; there was no indication of the arched wooden soles that contemporary writers marveled at. It is likely that Xiaojing's high-heeled shoes were a prototype, marking the transition to a new fashion regime that embodied the opulence and contradictions in Emperor Wanli's world. The infusion of silver money from the New World in exchange for silk and porcelain rocked the moral foundation of the empire, as historian Timothy Brook has described in his splendidly titled book, *The Confusions of Pleasure*. The sexual provocation of women's footwear epitomizes the allure and dangers of the money economy.

The splendor of arched wooden heels in the urban fashion regime found its most vivid expression in *The Plum in the Golden Vase (Jinpingmei cihua; also known as Golden Lotus)*, a novel that was first published in 1618 but that had circulated in manuscript form since 1596. The literature specialist Shang Wei has remarked on the quotidian quality of the novel as the very emblem of its modernity. Like an encyclopedia, the novel evokes the vivid everydayness in the polygynous household of a merchant named Ximen Qing, his six concubines, and a multitude of servants, maids, and hangers-on, in an anecdotal and fragmentary manner. As such the novel epitomizes the profusion of desires and words that characterized the cultural market-place in Wanli's world.[41]

The encyclopedic quality of *Plum in the Golden Vase* is evinced by the details that the author lavished on objects as prosaic as shoes. The three re-lated themes of female-male seduction, female advancement, and compe-tition among women that are so central to the rise of the cult of the golden lotus—and the novel itself—find concrete expressions in the minutiae of footwear in several legendary scenes. In chapter 4, Ximen Qing and Pan Jinlian, a married woman, were flirting ferociously as they sat drinking in Dame Wang's teahouse. Cutting to the chase, Ximen deliberately brushed a pair of chopsticks to the floor, which rested next to Jinlian's feet.

> Ximen Qing quickly stooped down to pick them up. Behold:
>> *The up-turned points of her tiny golden lotuses,*
>> *Barely three inches long,*
>> *But half a span in length,*
>> *Peeked out beside the chopsticks.*
>
> Ximen Qing ignored the chopsticks but gave a gentle pinch to the embroidered tip of her shoe.
>> The woman laughed out loud. "There's no need to beat around the bush, sir.
>> *If you've got a mind to it,*
>> *I've got the will.*
> Are you actually trying to seduce me?"

Embroidered slippers had acquired such an erotic charge that even a pinch at the tip was immediately understood to be sexual provocation.

> At this juncture, right there in Dame Wang's room, the two of them:
>> *Took off their clothes, undid their girdles, and*
>> *Enjoyed each other on the same pillow.*[42]

Jinlian's beauty, especially her tiny feet, was her ticket to success. She mur-dered her vendor husband to become Ximen's fifth concubine, sowing seeds of retribution that brought her violent death toward the novel's end. Mean-while, in Ximen's household, Jinlian met her match in Song Huilian, the wife of a servant with feet smaller than hers.[43] Their contest comes to the fore in chapter 23. Having refused to let Ximen use her bedroom for a tryst with a lowly servant's wife, Jinlian eavesdropped on the two as they spent the night in a grotto in the garden.

"It's frigid in here!" [Huilian] continued. "Let's go to sleep. What are you so intent on examining my feet for anyway? You'd think you'd never seen anyone with small feet before. The only thing is I don't have any shoe uppers. Couldn't you contrive to buy me a pair tomorrow? I see other people making shoes all the time, but I can't make any for myself."

"My child," said Ximen Qing, "that's no problem. Tomorrow I'll buy you several mace [coppers] worth of different patterned uppers. Who would have thought your feet are even smaller than the Fifth Lady's?"

"There's no comparison," the woman said. "The other day I tried on one of her shoes and found that I could wear it over my own. But it's not size that matters so much as the stylishness of the shoe."[44]

Huilian has mouthed the ultimate put-down, and Jinlian was understandably incensed. In the end, Huilian's exquisite feet did not win her a berth in Ximen's entourage of "wives," symbolized by the privileges of a room of her own and the leisure to design and sew stylish footwear. In this episode, however, the failed Cinderella won a prize in the form of purchased, pre-embroidered shoe uppers. She has moved up in the world.

In Ximen's household there was a hierarchy of shoemaking labor. Huilian and other servants stuck to the chore of stitching shoe soles, interstitial labor that was the fact of life for countless farm women. Not much had changed almost three centuries later when Ida Pruitt watched her neighbor in rural Shandong sitting in her courtyard,

pasting the scraps of cloth—all left-over pieces, all the bits from worn-out clothes—on a plank. After the pasteboard had dried on the plank leaning against a sunny wall, she would pull it off and cut it into shoe-sole sizes. Sewing these lifts together with hempen twine was the work forever in the hands of every woman. The half-done shoe soles with the long steel needle stuck in one of the holes, the small drill and a loop of hempen twine, lay on every window sill, ready to be picked up when there was time for a stitch between other duties.[45]

By contrast, the mistresses of the house took to designing and making shoe uppers with great seriousness and care. The opening scene in chapter 29 of *Plum in the Golden Vase* describes their preoccupation with magnificent details:

The story goes that the next morning Pan Jinlian got up early and sent Ximen Qing on his way. Remembering that she wanted to make a new pair of red shoes for herself, she took her sewing box into the garden with her and sat down on the stylobate of the Kingfisher Pavilion, where she began to sketch the design to be embroidered on the vamps of her new shoes. She sent [her maid] Chunmei to invite [sixth concubine] Li Ping'er to join her.

When Li Ping'er arrived, she asked, "What's that you're sketching, Sister?"

"I want to make a pair of shoes," said Jinlian, "out of scarlet iridescent silk, with flat white satin soles, the toes of which will be embroidered with the motif of 'A Parrot Plucking a Peach.'"

"I've got a square of scarlet variegated [ten-motif] silk," said Li Ping'er. "I'll make a pair just like yours, except that I want high heels on mine."

Thereupon, she fetched her sewing box, and the two of them sat down to work together.

When Jinlian had finished sketching the pattern on one vamp, she set it aside, saying, "Sister Li, sketch the other one for me, will you? I'm going to the rear compound to fetch Sister Meng the Third. She told me yesterday that she was going to make a pair of shoes too."

She went straight to the rear compound. Meng Yuelou was in her room, leaning on the bedrail, stitching away at a shoe that she held in her hand.

When Jinlian came in the door, Yuelou said, "You're up and about early today."

"I got up early," said Jinlian, "and sent Father off to attend the farewell party for Battalion Commander He outside the South Gate. I've arranged with Sister Li to do some needlework together in the garden while it's still cool in the morning. In a little while the sun will be too hot, and we won't be able to continue. I've just finished sketching the design for one shoe and asked Sister Li to do the other one while I came straight over here to invite you to join us. The three of us can do our work together.

"What kind of shoe is that you're working on right now?" she went on to ask.

"It's that pair of jet silk shoes you saw me start on yesterday," Yuelou replied.

"What a fine fellow you are," exclaimed Jinlian. "You've managed to finish one of them already."

"I stitched that one yesterday," said Yuelou, "and I've already done a good deal on this one."

Jinlian asked to have a look at it and said, "What kind of decoration are you going to put on the toe?"

"I'm not to be compared with you youngsters," said Yuelou, "with your flashy fashions. I'm too old for that. I'll have gold-spangled toes, with a motif of white mountains around them, stitched out with sand-green thread, white satin soles, and high heels. How does that sound?"

When Meng Yuelou arrived at the garden she asked Jinlian:

> "What are you making flat-soled red shoes for? They don't look as nice as high-heeled shoes. If you're worried that wooden heels are too noisy, you can put felt on them, as I do, and they won't make a noise when you walk."
>   "They aren't for everyday wear," said Jinlian. "They're sleeping shoes."

The night before, one of Jinlian's red sleeping shoes had been stolen by a servant's son and soiled, hence she had to wear "a pair of sand-green pongee sleeping shoes with scarlet heel lifts" to bed. Ximen, who adored red shoes, urged Jinlian to make a new pair.[46]

Meng Yuelou's suggestion of putting felt on wooden soles is the kind of insight that would occur only to a woman. More than any of the notations we have surveyed, this scene conveys not only the splendor of high heels but also the fact that the architects of the fad were none other than the women who designed, made, and wore them.[47] The women's attention to choice of fabric, color coordination, and design of the vamps bespeaks the importance of shoes to their wardrobe and the pleasures they derived from them. Also evident are the way that shoemaking was enmeshed in the women's everyday lives and that this activity facilitated both female companionship and competition.

I have not been able to locate any high-heeled slipper with a wooden sole from the seventeenth century, and this scene helps explain why. For all the attention lavished on their design and production, high-heeled shoes were objects of frivolous consumption. They soiled and wore out easily, but even before they did they had often become dated. In two days the entrepreneurial Meng Yuelou managed to replenish her wardrobe with a new pair. The pre-embroidered uppers that Ximen Qing was to procure from the market for Huilian must have given the domestic women an impetus for stylistic innovation. Caught up in the vicissitudes of the fashion cycle, the embroidered slipper, an object so central to women's self-presentation and men's erotic imagination, was thus essential but ironically disposable and ephemeral.

Jinlian's eagerness to make a new pair of red sleeping shoes is a useful reminder that there is no reprieve from the tyranny of fashion day or night, indoor or outdoor. Not only the embroidered slippers but the full regalia of footwear, from the sleeping shoes to leggings, were essential in lending the golden lotus a splendid and mysterious aura. Sleeping shoes, which are not so different from flats for outdoor wear except that the former are soft-soled, acquired the same connotations of privacy and provocation as bras and panties in the West: not that they were never taken off, but the concealment and subsequent undressing is more interesting than the exposure itself.[48]

Even more unmentionable was a loosened binding cloth. At the height of the cult of the golden lotus, bare feet constituted such a taboo that for all the risqué sex scenes in *The Plum in the Golden Vase,* only one hints at the spectacle of naked feet. In a drunken orgy, Ximen "took off [Jinlian's] red embroidered shoes, unwound her foot bindings, and amused himself by using them to suspend her two feet from the grape arbor overhead."[49] In breaking a visual and textual taboo, this scene in chapter 27 is one of the most famous (and infamous) in the novel, an emblem of the sexual license and excesses in Ximen's household. The connoisseur Li Yu, in his erotic novel *The Carnal Prayer Mat,* written in 1657, explained that the naked foot is a taboo because it is the ultimate turn-off. In a bedroom scene, the protagonist Vesperus took off all of Jade Scent's clothes, "including her underwear and breastband, everything but her leggings." Li commented: "In the last resort tiny feet need a pair of dainty little leggings above them if they are going to appeal. Without leggings, they would be as unsightly as a flower with no leaves around it."[50]

As designers, makers, and wearers of sleeping shoes or arched high heels, the women engineered an artifice of concealment and illusion, thereby manipulating the viewer's gaze. Their skill is one of condensing, of reducing the messiness of the disintegrating world into their bare essentials—red satin or white damask? Gold couching or green chain stitching? In lavishing so much detail onto something as minuscule as the edge of the vamp, sole, and especially the tip of her slippers, the shoemaker focused the boundless desires and fascination of the world onto her body-self.

PRODUCTIVE BODIES:
SHOEMAKING AND THE MARKETPLACE

The philologist Hu Yinglin (1551–1618) complained that contemporary women no longer made their own shoes, entrusting the job instead to "needle-workers who specialize in such a task" *(dangzhi zi fengren).*[51] Although information on the economy of shoemaking is scarce, anecdotal data suggest that the "needle-workers" were seamstresses or craftsmen for hire to wealthy families, making shoes to order. Unlike men's shoes, female footwear did not develop into a full-fledged commodity sold in stores until the modern period.

Commercial production of myriad household goods and personal items became increasingly common from the sixteenth century on. Fan Lian, a native of Songjiang and a keen observer of fashion trends, noticed a seismic change in the production of men's footwear: "At first commercial shoe-making was limited to the operations run by palanquin-bearers from Nanjing; there were absolutely no shoe stores nor straw-shoes stores in Songjiang. Since the Wanli reign [1573–1620], we began to see men making shoes. The styles they made gradually became lighter and more refined, and they established a cluster of stores to the east of the county seat. The palanquin-bearer's operations have thus become the lowest in the pecking order."

The flourishing of commercial shoemaking was fanned by the ease of travel and regional migration. A shoemaker by the name of Shi moved to Songjiang from nearby Yixing and created a fad of straw shoes with the expertly braided ones he sold. "Thereupon Yixing shoemakers opened stores in blocks of five or six in the city. These stores now number several hundred; their prices are so cheap that the natives can feel the heat of competition."[52] "Men making shoes," or the end of shoemaking by domestic women, is synonymous with its commodification. From Fan's description, however, it is clear that these commercial shoes were styled for men.

The Portuguese Dominican friar Gaspar da Cruz, who visited the southern city of Guangzhou (Canton) for a few weeks in the winter of 1556, described a thriving shoe market there decades before the reign of Wanli. Impressed with the abundance of shoes, which was to his mind emblematic of the material wealth of China, he opened his chapter on "mechanical craftsmen" and "merchants" with footwear: "And because shoes are the thing that most is spent, there are more workman of shoemakers than of any other trade. In Cantam are two particular streets of shoemakers very long, one where they sell rich shoes and of silk, another where they sell common shoes of leather; and besides these two streets, there are many workmen scattered about the city." A pricing structure had developed: "The rich boots and shoes are covered with colored silk, embroidered over with twisted thread of very fine work; and there be boots from ten crowns to one crown price . . . [s]o that the rich and the very poor may wear shoes, and the rich as they list. The shoes of three pence, or of a rial, are of straw."[53]

Besides workshops catering to local costumers, a regional footwear trade also prospered. A 1599 almanac coached itinerant merchants on the merits and demerits of footwear that various villages and cities specialized in: "The cloth-soled cotton shoes from Flintstone Bridge, Zezhou, and Yangzhou are very tight; the cotton shoes with straw- or hemp-braided soles from Fengxiang prefecture, Fenzhou, and Luzhou, in turn, are loose. Silk shoes from Nanjing are uneven in height, and those from Suzhou tend to be only so-so. But the platform-soled shoes *[lü]* from Nanjing are made of fine materials with soft linings; they last. Those from Yangzhou have stiff linings and inferior materials; they won't last."[54] Fengxiang, Fenzhou, Luzhou, and Zezhou are in the northwestern provinces of Shaanxi and Shanxi; Nanjing, Suzhou, and Yangzhou are in Jiangnan. Commercial shoemaking, which was not dependent on any rare raw materials, thrived in the heartland as well as the periphery of the empire.

The almanac also encouraged local entrepreneurs to experiment with new products and explore markets further afield: "Reed shoes from Jiangyin may provide a viable living. Gather and sun-dry the reeds in early spring, seal them with heavy paper, and store in bundles by the window or door. Be careful, for they may discolor if exposed to wind or develop yellow spots if rained on. After late autumn they are ready. The frequent traffic to Hunan and Guangdong would guarantee a 50 percent profit." Jiangyin is a river port on the banks of the Yangzi. Another good location was the intersection of the Yangzi and the Grand Canal: "Guazhou hemp shoes may provide another viable living. Gather the hemp fibers around the turn of the year and air them dry. Package the fine items with the coarse ones. The goods would find their way north and south; traders are bound to show up and buy them."[55]

Although the writers made no mention of the division of labor in the shoemaking families, we may surmise that regional specialization and long-distance trade in footwear provided an additional means of livelihood for women in farming households, alongside the spun yarn and other piece goods they produced to supplement domestic income. The commercialization of male footwear and the attendant rise of male professional shoemakers did not end women's careers as shoemakers.

The circumstances of women as consumers of footwear are murky for lack of textual and material evidence. It appears that the clientele of the shoe stores in Songjiang and Guangzhou, as well as the itinerant wholesalers, were men. The only hint that respectable women wore store-bought shoes was made by the Suzhou native Shen Fu (b. 1763). When his wife, Yun, desired to attend a lantern festival dressed as a man, Shen suggested: "In the street they sell 'butterfly shoes' *[hudie lü]* in all sizes. They're easy to buy, and afterwards you can wear them around the house. Wouldn't they do?"[56] Although favored by stylish women as casual wear (and when they cross-dressed in public), "butterfly shoes" were flat-soled footwear intended for men.

In the first decade of the nineteenth-century, a native of Yangzhou remarked that workshops in his hometown produced butterfly shoes far superior to those in Suzhou and Hangzhou. The soft sole was stitched from ten to twelve layers of fine felt, and the vamps were fashioned from plain satin, imported wool, or silk crepe in purple or grey. The tip of the toes was reinforced with an appliquéd jet-black felt or satin butterfly, hence the name. When he was young, the writer remembered "buying" butterfly shoes for 0.5–0.6 ounces of jet silk, but by the late eighteenth century the stores were asking 1.2–1.3 ounces of silver for a pair.[57] Sturdy and comfortable, they remained popular informal male footwear. It is conceivable that shoes for women without bound feet were available in the stores alongside butterfly shoes and other male footwear. It seems unlikely, however, that shoes for respectable women with bound feet, which are vested with such power of provocation, could be procured in such a manner.

This assumption is supported by the fact that in the Qing law courts and theater, the embroidered slipper, especially the sleeping shoe, was such a synecdoche of a woman's sexuality that its very possession by a man other than her husband sufficed to intimate illicit union (see fig. 19). The murder case of the twenty-three-year-old Woman Wang in Jinzhou in 1737 turned on the key evidence of her green cotton sleeping shoes. Wang's husband, a vegetable peddler, borrowed money from Zhang Da, a thirty-three-year-old friend, a vendor. On the morning of June 10, Zhang showed up and got into a fight with Wang after her husband had left the house. Wang, stabbed in her face, neck, and abdomen, told county investigators that Zhang came to reclaim his money and, upon seeing that she was alone, tried to rape her but she resisted. Later in the day, she died from her wounds.

Caught by the couple's landlord at the scene, Zhang was thrown in jail. During his reexamination by a new magistrate he offered a new line of defense, saying that he had long been Wang's lover. On June 9 he chanced upon her having sex with another lover, Wu. He flew into a rage when Wang refused to sleep with him the following morning. As proof for his affair with

Wang he directed investigators to the sleeping shoes stowed in his inventory box. Adding to Zhang's credibility, Wu confessed to his illicit affair when interrogated. But the green shoes stood as the sole evidence for an alleged affair between Zhang and the now dead woman. Wang's mother admitted that she recognized them as "shoes that my daughter had made for herself." Wang's husband, however, had never seen them. The judge opted to believe Zhang.[58]

In another case from 1743, even a pair of outer shoes stowed in a man's luggage constituted cause for suspicion. Yu Qi was escorting his recently married younger sister back to her new family after a natal family visit when they passed through a village in Yongcheng, Henan, around midnight, and sought lodging. A local boxer and ruffian named Li, looking for an excuse to cause trouble, cornered them and searched Yu's bags, finding a pair of female shoes tucked inside his bedding. Li claimed that this was sufficient proof to him that Yu was trying to elope with his illicit lover. The case ended up in court after the young bride, having been raped by Li, committed suicide. The judge did not buy Li's excuse, which in any case did not mitigate his criminal act.[59] However forced, Li's defense attests to how commonplace it was to construe women's shoes as extensions of their private parts. If they were commodities readily available in the marketplace, the frequent argument that they were tokens of illicit love would not have washed.

STYLISTIC CHANGES
AND TRANSMISSION OF KNOWLEDGE

In the seventeenth and eighteenth centuries, women's footwear was produced at the intersection of the market and domestic economies. The advent of high heels brought an end to the domestic production of female shoes according to the classical requirements of "womanly work" as the foundation of a self-sufficient agrarian economy. In theory, a pair of shoes made of cotton, hemp, or silk could have been the product of domestic women's hands in its entirety, untouched by market transactions. But the wooden sole required carpentry work that could only be procured from outside the boudoir. The late-Ming courtesan Liu Rushi (1618–64) was said to have commissioned famous artisans to carve her wooden soles, including the most sought-after bamboo carver of his day, Pu Zhongqian.[60]

The shoemaking scene from *Plum in the Golden Vase* suggests that domestic women did not stop making shoes. For everyday footwear, urban women from households with cash to spare bought the components—the wooden soles and pre-embroidered uppers—and assembled them at home. There is also evidence that among the domestic help engaged by wealthy families were teams of seamstresses who labored in the family compound to supply the needs of family members.[61] Such special-occasion shoes as wedding shoes, gift shoes for in-laws and friends, and votive shoes offered to the gods did not belong to the realm of frivolous fashion but were extensions of the body-self; they were inevitably made by the wearer or devotee from scratch.[62] The aura of handmade artifacts could only be enhanced in an age of commercial production, hence the design and embroidering of shoe uppers, in contrast to stitching fabric soles, were deemed genteel women's work in Ximen Qing's household.

Market tastes began to intrude into the boudoir by way of uncut pre-embroidered uppers in the late Ming. We do not know the selection of vamps that Ximen Qing was able to buy for Huilian, but the cross-fertilization among the tastes of the marketplace, brothel, and boudoir is evident in a tendency toward over-ornamentation. Song and Yuan shoes for bound feet were monochrome, in such muted neutral colors as pale yellow and embroidered in outline stitching with floss of the same color. Although more dramatic, Empress Xiaojing's pale-red high heels are also single-colored. Sometimes made of textured damask or brocade and decorated with a tiny bow, the earlier shoes are quiet, with a fine aesthetic sensitivity that focuses the eyes on the shimmering light of the thread that reveals subtle variations in texture.

The handiwork of the ladies in Ximen Qing's household announces a new multicolored palette featuring primary colors. Red or black vamps are contrasted with white soles or green heel tabs; gold couching stands out on purple vamp. Peach red uppers are edged in gold leather. Tian Yiheng (fl. 1609) confirmed that gilded lamb skin was a new material that shoemakers of his day used lavishly for women's slippers.[63] The palette became more variegated and the color combinations more striking as time went on, and by the end of the Qing embroidery stitching in a cascade of contrasting color was the norm.

The profusion of auspicious symbols on every surface of Qing material culture, from porcelain and paintings, to textiles and robes, was also evident on shoe designs. The games of visual punning became increasingly sophisticated; a bat *(fu)* standing for fortune *(fu)* no longer sufficed. Fertility and conjugal happiness, two ardent desires that undergirded almost every motif embroidered on shoe uppers and soles, found concrete expressions in a colorful array of images: lotus, butterfly, pomegranate, double coins, melon and vine, goldfish, peach, and the eight immortals. As if seeking a reprieve from this overload of good wishes, commercial uppers became spare, vague, and abstract toward the dynasty's end. The even and expertly executed stitching coupled with formulaic floral designs found on the majority of late-Qing slippers attests to the fact that footwear, after all, is a mundane business. When embroidery became too tiresome, brush-painting on shiny starched cloth vamps mass-produced a new look in 1904–11 (see fig. 7d).[64]

Domestic assembly of purchased components remained the dominant mode of production for bound-foot shoes during the Qing dynasty. In the nineteenth century, professional carpenters made wooden heels and soles in standardized sizes and styles, and male peddlers hawked them along with heel stiffenings and other sewing implements, calling out, "Come buy wooden soles!" as they went (see fig. 7e). In Jiangsu, peddlers carried carving knives to make adjustments, in a procedure known as "lathing wooden soles" *(che mudi)*. A wood file was a standard tool in village households in the Tianjin area for fine-tuning. According to a rare report about the trade in late-Qing Hebei and Shandong in *Picking Radishes,* three types of pre-made wooden soles were available, in descending order of popularity: heels, front taps, and full heel-to-toe soles.[65]

The standard sizing of pre-made shoe components gives a rough indication of the average sizes of bound feet. The full sole came in sizes 1 (7.6 inches) to 10 (3.3 inches). The heels, which extended to the mid-point of the shoe, also came in ten standard sizes, in increments of 0.3 inch, with size 1 at 4.8 inches, size 2 at 4.5 inches, down to size 10, 2.1 inches. The carpenters generally sold the heels at wholesale in strings of ten pairs, one each of the ten different sizes. Retailing vendors, however, would sell the bigger ones at a higher price. Most readily available were the middling sizes 3–7 (4.2 inches to 3 inches, which means shoes 8.4 to 6 inches long), and the biggest sizes of 1 and 2 tended to be the first to sell out.

The pricing structure was also standardized, at least for the northern region where data are available. If the vendor desired additional pairs of sizes 1 and 2, he would have to add a forty percent premium to the wholesale price. Carpenters also made soles of specific curvatures and sizes to order.

If the design required additional lathing on the top, bottom, and sides of the standard soles, he would charge five times the wholesale price. If only one side of special lathing was needed, the price was doubled. In Jiangsu, a standard pair retailed at 4 coppers *(wen)* in the 1880s. By the 1900s the price had doubled, but business soon tapered off as the anti-footbinding movement spread.[66]

The making of shoe uppers was less commercialized. The earliest extant examples of mechanically reproduced shoe patterns appear in a household almanac entitled *Precious Mirror of Feminine Virtues (Kunde baojian)* published in 1777.[67] Gathered in the last two fascicles (*juan* 8–9) are a wealth of sewing and embroidery patterns in actual sizes, covering the span of small personal effects for men, women, and children. Fascicle 8 features primarily objects for men's use, to be given to men as souvenirs, or for children: male hats, children's hats, four styles of purses, toothpick holder, fan cases, pincushions, powder puffs, paper bags, pillow ends, children's shoes (fig. 20a), men's shoes. Fascicle 9 focuses on female clothing: headbands, kerchiefs, children's headbands, women's collars, straight lapels, big sleeves, small sleeves, skirt panels, trim for the bottom of pant legs, floral embroidery motifs for shoes, cloud embroidery motifs for shoes, cloud embroidery motifs for the shafts of boots (fig. 21a), cloud appliquéd motifs for shoes (fig. 21b).[68]

The other seven fascicles of the almanac are fashioned entirely from recycled materials culled from two textual traditions: moral instruction books and such practical household encyclopedias as *The Forest of Affairs* and *Essentials for Domestic Living.*[69] The compiler, Tanmian daoren (Taoist adept who sleeps in a jar), stated his purpose: "Women may use this book in their fragrant pavilions or leave it by their sewing boxes, so that the two can keep each other company day and night. May their hearts be stirred just by looking at the book, so that they would know the teachings of 'thrice following' and the 'four virtues.' May they know that such household chores as drawing water, grinding grain, and needlework are not just the preserve of the poor and the mean, but should not be ignored even by daughters of privilege." The rhetoric places *Precious Mirror* in the tradition of didactic texts admonishing women to adhere to their domestic calling. At first glance, the almanac seems to decry the degeneracy of the commercial age; women had neglected the requisite womanly work for so long that they needed to be taught anew the skill of drawing patterns.

Underneath and against its own rhetoric, however, *Precious Mirror* has far less to do with domestic virtues than with the culture of the market-place. Issued by a commercial publisher, it is in itself a commodity. Surely the sewing and embroidery patterns could have been an inspiration for ladies in the boudoir, but they were likely to be more helpful to a class of minimally educated daughters who desired to produce value-added piece goods for the market but suffered from a lack of artistic education. It is no accident that all the patterns are small and the design of the clouds, flora, and fauna generic. There was an enormous market in such small personal effects as purses, fan cases, and children's hats, all standard gifts and requisite social lubricants for friends and strangers. Small textile goods in the form of collars or sleeve facings were the mainstay in embroidery stores *(xiuzhuang)*, which sold them to the busy housewife or tailor to fashion into finished garments.

Instead of being an instrument for reviving domestic textile production as claimed, *Precious Mirror* is a testament to the intrusion of the market into the former and to the formulaic modular designs that dulled the viewer's mind that resulted from it. In this light, it is significant that although generic designs for embroidering women's shoe uppers proliferated, no outline pattern of the shoes themselves was included. The latter appeared in printed form only in the last decade of the Qing dynasty, suggesting that until then, the skills of designing, cutting, and assembling shoes for bound feet remained knowledge transmitted from one seamstress to another by personal example. They had remained, in other words, embodied female knowledge.

Precious Mirror of Feminine Virtues must have met a fervent demand, for it remained in circulation into the nineteenth century in the form of an almost identical copy of the two chapters of patterns meticulously traced by hand using an extra-fine calligraphic brush (fig. 20b, 21c-d). The single handmade copy, which is in fact more exquisite than the original, must have consumed an inordinate amount of time.[70] Perhaps this is only natural, for by the turn of the last century any material production or reproduction that bears a tactile imprint of bodily traces appears precious, a mirror into the bygone days when women embroidered and stitched an entire world into existence.

THE LAST FASHION CYCLES

The invention of high heels created a frivolous, urban fashion regime and ushered in the cult of the golden lotus in the fifteenth and sixteenth centuries. Paradoxically, footwear fashion reached the second summit of its creative power during the demise of the golden lotus at the turn of the last century (see fig. 9). By then perfected as an integument of concealment, "basic footwear" comprised three or four layers: binding cloth, sock, soft-soled slipper, and outer shoe or bootie. Leggings, leg-binders, ankle bracelets, and pants or a long skirt completed the ensemble at the lower body (see figs. 14, 22).

Shoes had become the keepers of the exterior presentation of the body-self. Be they exposed and accentuated by leg binders that extended from the ankle to the knee or peeking demurely from under a long skirt, their design, color, and fitting were crucial to the overall "look" that a woman desired to achieve. In the transitional decade of the 1890s to 1900s, the popularity of Kun-style shoes and booties with a gently relaxed arched sole reflected the adaptation that the fashion regime made to the anti-footbinding movement (see figs. 6, 7). Kun shoes derived their allure from the residual aura of high heels, but at the same time they announced the end of the era of the golden lotus. The arch of the shoes, like the arch of the foot, became progressively flatter as the twentieth century advanced. In the 1920s and 1930s, stylistic and technological innovations in female footwear were driven by the incorporation of Western structures, designs, and materials. Kun shoes and booties are the last elegant heeled footwear for bound feet produced in the Chinese shoemaking tradition.

Underneath the shoes, socks or sleeping slippers are akin to the modern camisoles: their main function as "underwear" is less as body-shaper than as a frontier of provocation. They add a layer of intrigue to the admirer's eyes and present a barrier in disrobing, prolonging the pleasure of anticipation. This is why in the 1890s, when prostitutes led the fashion cycle in footwear as harbingers of change, much of their creative energy was focused on the design and positioning of the sleeping slippers, changing slippers, and socks. The arrival of sleeping slippers worn as outer shoe in 1908–11, on the eve of the collapse of the imperium, signaled the end of the old order of seduction. There is nothing more to expose and nothing more to hide.

As intimate textile next to the skin, the binding cloth was the most essential foundational garment. Like a straight-fronted corset in the Art Nouveau period (1890s–1900s) that helped reshape the wearer's body into the fashionable S-curve, the binding cloth molded the foot into the requisite shapes and silhouettes according to the whims of fashion: a bulged arch with rounded tip at the toes this year; a flatter arch with straighter toes next year. As the retroactively reconstructed chronology in *Picking Radishes* (see fig.

22) shows, the wheels of footwear fashion turned at a robust pace during the years from 1894 to 1911, at the height of the official anti-footbinding movement. New styles and silhouettes appeared every three to four years.

The binding cloth performed its feat without alterations in its physical design or structure; therein lay its difference from corsetry in a most important way. The cloth binder manipulated the presentation of the body-self not by the insertion of whale bone stays or padding. It remained the long strip of fabric that it had been since the beginning of footbinding's history, as evinced by the remains of the mid-thirteenth-century ladies Huang Sheng and Zhou discussed above. The fabric had changed with the increasingly arduous binding regimen in the Ming and Qing periods; plain woven cotton with a slightly rough touch to the hand—which would neither slide nor give—became the fabric of choice.[71] Observers have reported that the binding cloth was among the last articles that women hand-wove on domestic looms in Yunnan and Taiwan.[72] Imported white cloth was also used when available. The width, length, and color of the binding cloth may vary with the age of user and the occasion; young girls, for example, sometimes used indigo-dyed cloth to enhance healing. But the basic design and principle had remained constant for centuries.

The foundation for changes in the fashion regime is far more subtle: it inheres in the user, not the implement. In *Picking Radishes,* someone using the pseudonym of Plain Girl explained the incredible burden this material fact placed on the nimbleness and skill of the woman. Because variations in the dimensions of the binding cloth are slight, choosing the right size required nuanced understanding of one's own bodily conditions and the desired stylistic effect. The length of the cloth, she explained, can range from five or six feet to seven or eight feet; some are even longer than ten. But any cloth shorter than five feet would not suffice for the requisite five or seven wrappings. The optimal width of the cloth is six-tenths of the length of the foot; in practice three inches is the average width. Any cloth narrower than two-and-a-half inches or wider than three-and-a-half inches would be difficult to manage.

Even more unforgiving is the manipulation of the binding cloth. The traditional seven layers of wrapping involved dexterity of fingers and an intimate, intuitive understanding of the anatomy of one's own feet. First, position the binding cloth under the ball of the foot, bring it up to the top and fold the four digits downward, leaving the big toe unfettered. Second, bring the cloth up and restrain the middle of the foot sideways. Third, wrap around the big toe and work backward to the heel. Fourth, push the heel forward and work upward to the big toe, this time leaving it unbound, to apply a second wrapping on the folded digits. Fifth, cross to the pushed heel, secure it and apply a second sideways wrapping to the middle of the foot. Sixth, reinforce the big toe and work backward. Seventh, bring the cloth to the inside arch of the foot after a final wrapping of the heel and secure the end with needle and thread. Controlling the tension of the cloth at each step served to mold the foot into desirable shapes.[73] When footbinding was a viable practice, such measurements and procedures would have been intuitive knowledge to the women. Only at the end of footbinding's history would it be necessary to commit such knowledge to writing for the curious outsider and posterity.

But that is the historian's perspective, not the women's. Anti-footbinding measures came and went; as did the tides of fashion. Deft fingers continued to wield the binding cloth day after day, shaping and reshaping the foot to fit into the new flat pointy tips, the tiny satin Mary Janes, or the triangular leather oxfords in the 1920s and 1930s. The body could be stubborn and the binding of feet burdensome, but when the fingers were at work all else was forgotten. Shoes and socks could easily be store-bought, worn and discarded; they are merchandise in a commercialized regime of fashion. A pair of bound feet, however, was inalienable. Once bound, they required assiduous maintenance according to the demands of hygiene and fashion. A pair of shapely bound feet was the lifelong handiwork of the woman.

The least eroticized among the implements for footbinding, the binding cloth was also the last item taken off the domestic loom. Although indispensable, it did its work virtually unseen, from the inside, and without decoration. More than the flowery words of men and the spectacular but hollow shoes, the binding cloth remained the preserve of the woman's productive, private body-self.

RESIDUAL MEMORIES

I arrived in Liuyi village in Yunnan province early in the morning, and I was too late. The vast courtyard in front of the village's senior center was empty, rendering the huge couplet on the side wall all the more eye-catching: "The last song of the golden lotus; / Stepping to the dance as the rooster crows" *(jinlian juechang, wenji qiwu)*. The sign marks the performance soon to begin exclusively for me as a tourist site, the same way that notable inscriptions announce the entrance to the Song pavilion in nearby Elegant Hill. Since the 1990s tourism magazines and television programs have promoted Liuyi as "Footbinding Village," the last bastion of the practice in China.[74] During peak tourist season there would be several dance performances every week.

Tonghai county, of which Liuyi village is a part, was settled by Han soldiers brought by the powerful Mu family from Nanjing during the early years of the Ming dynasty. Having defeated the indigenous Yi, Bai, Tai, and Hani peoples, the Han immigrants established six camp-like villages on the southern shores of Lake Jilu. Local legends attribute the beginnings of footbinding and a high level of civility in the area to the settlement (see fig. 14).[75] In the mid-1980s there were five to six hundred women with bound feet in the predominantly Han village. Today, Liuyi is a prosperous exporter of napa cabbage and other fresh produce to cities as far away as Beijing. Among the population of over nine thousand there remain only about eighty golden-lotus ladies.

Ma Qiaofen, a physical education coach at the senior center, told me that footbound women in the village have danced for visitors since 1985 (for a negotiable fee). Ma, a congenial and robust Yi-minority woman who married into the village thirty years ago, does not have bound feet. In 1984, about one hundred fifty of the tiny-footed women took the initiative in organizing a senior sports association, gaining instant fame when their croquet team beat the big-footed contingent from the county seat. Since then they have competed in regional and national tournaments. The disco-on-bound-feet routine they developed also became a media sensation.[76]

Inside the main hall, seven women in blue polyester tunics trimmed in red sat on low benches, quietly awaiting their spectator. Underneath balloon-shaped white pants they wore white cotton socks and flat embroidered slippers made of bright red polyester in Mary Jane style. I noticed that the majority had "liberated feet" that were flat and without the bulge, much like the style in the initial stage of footbinding's history. The only two with triangular arched feet—which retain the shape after "liberation"—were, not surprisingly, also the oldest: Xiao Xiuxiang is eighty-four and Pu Jifen, seventy-eight. Tonghai county was famous for its handwoven cotton cloth in the first half of the twentieth century.[77] Xiao and Pu are both old enough to have worked at the loom for their families. Pu Jifen retains the reputation among her friends as the best embroiderer and shoemaker.

The dancers filed into position, each holding a bamboo flute as the music sounded from a cassette recorder. No prompting was needed; the repertoire must have been familiar. Gliding across a spectrum from the civil to martial arts, they followed the flute dance with a sword dance and a tai-chi dance which looked remarkably like the exercise routine seen in early morning parks across China. Their steps steady and stately, their bodies surprisingly supple for their age, the women showed no expression on their faces. It looked as though they were either engrossed in the present moment or dancing a dance that belonged to a life and time far removed from their own. Afraid to break the spell when the music stopped, I applauded with muffled hands.

To break the ice, I asked casually if they still do textile work. No, someone replied, the family loom was taken down and turned into firewood eons ago. Xiao Xiuxiang and Pu Jifen flashed a playful grin. Without missing a beat, they both raised their left arms into mid-air as if they were sitting in front of a loom. Their pair of arched feet stepping on what would have been treadles, they moved their right arms back and forth as if shuffling a shuttle cock in perfect coordination. Neither the croquet nor the dances they learned in the recent past have displaced or erased the earlier regimen of productive labor. Their bodies remember.

A way of life has become history: the hand-weaving technology is obsolete, the livelihood nullified along with it, and the culture of binding feet is vilified. Yet the body remembers. When the body expires, the sediment of residual memories, the layers of history that the body bears witness to, and the repertoire of skills that have woven colorful and textured worlds will disappear along with it. With my mind's eye, I took a snapshot of the two old women working their imaginary looms, and in that instant I knew that not only had I collected my trophy souvenir but I had also witnessed the conclusion to this book.

EPILOGUE

The pursuit of beauty, status, sex, culture, money: footbinding is implicated in every one of these human desires, but in themselves these drives for *self*-betterment or gratification cannot account for the ferocity with which footbinding spread, sprouting a surprising array of literary forms and material cultures along the way. Envy, cruelty, violence, objectification: these horrible things that men do to *others* are also part of the story, but they are inadequate explanations for the longevity of the practice and the stubbornness with which women embraced and perpetuated it. At once beautiful and ugly, neither voluntary nor coerced, footbinding defies a black-and-white, male-against-female, and good-or-bad way of understanding the world.

As conclusion to this book I can offer no convenient culprit, facile explanations, or neat narratives. The parts are bigger than their sum; the history of footbinding does not add up. It has to be sought in the incongruities, repetitions, and omissions in the textual and material archives. The whole millennium-long history is a bit out of kilter, if not downright absurd: In the beginning, the word preceded the deed; toward the end the deed exhausted and exceeded all justifications. In between these two extremes, women lived in the mundane realities of their bodies while aspiring to a better life.

The aesthetic ideal of tiny feet and dainty steps first appeared as poetic allusions to enchanting but distant goddesses in the Six Dynasties period. Eulogies of brocade slippers and shoelaces became increasingly graphic and acquired an erotic charge in the boudoir poetry of the Tang dynasty. The poet's imagination was translated into material forms in subsequent dynasties, as "every step a lotus" heels or "echoed hallway" soles became prized items in fashionable women's wardrobes. But the absence of contemporary criticisms and the lack of archaeological remains suggest that the binding of feet had yet to be realized as an actual practice before the fall of the Tang.

Although male desires for bound feet were born of and perpetuated by poetic allusions, the written word enjoyed far less persuasive power among women. A handful of literate women in the Ming and Qing dynasties did participate in poetic exercises, but women learned about the burdens and uses of footbinding primarily from the performing arts and material culture—realms that were influenced by the world of the literati but were by no means contained by it. For this reason I have sought female perspectives not from women's poetry, but from ballads, vernacular plays, household almanacs, and the material remains themselves. However dominant, male desires and tastes cannot account for the longevity let alone the geographical and social scope of footbinding.

In seeking female incentives I have avoided the language of "free choice." Modern critics often imagine that traditional Chinese women would have rebelled if given a choice, and the fact that they did not attests to the draconian success of Confucian patriarchy. This erroneous view derives from a modern, individualistic valorization of free choice that structures our desires but not theirs. It is true that from the sixteenth century on, women did not have a "choice": any daughter from Han Chinese families whose economic circumstances could remotely allow them to bind would. Even those who could not afford to did. Footbinding was not merely an announcement of status and desirability to the outside world, but also a concrete embodiment of self-respect to the woman herself.

Gayatri Spivak has construed "free choice" as "the radical and voluntary rearrangement of desires." Female desires were so "rearranged" by the fashion regime and sediments of culture in the late imperial period that *not*-binding became unthinkable, in the same way that choosing to bind is unthinkable to us. Instead of resisting, the women applied their imagination and skills to the pursuit of perfect pairs of footwear and the most advantageous angle of presentation, vying to outdo their sisters and neighbors in the choice of fabric, novelty of style, and workmanship. To them, the appeal of footbinding is located in the fantastic lives of shoes as fashionable and ritualized objects. Without the participation of women, footbinding would not have spread so far in the face of persistent and vehement opposition by moralizing and pontificating men.

Although the exact mechanisms of transmission remain dimly understood, during its spread across geographical and social boundaries, the practice of binding feet sedimented in local cultures and acquired a concrete reality in the minutiae of everyday life—rituals, colloquialisms, footwear styles, and gestures of the body. In due time, a once alien practice that belonged to the "other woman" became a matter-of-fact way of living in one's body. On both the collective and personal levels, the persuasive power of footbinding was rooted in this power to switch perspectives, to create novel views on a familiar body, to inculcate a new "common sense," and indeed to remake the world.

In light of this localized, embodied nature of footbinding's reality and its propensity to change, I stated my thesis at the outset that there is not one footbinding but many. Instead of offering blanket statements or a comprehensive history in this book, I have presented my readings of what I take to be the most intriguing texts and objects produced during footbinding's long history. In structuring the chapters so that they introduce a succession of local, partial, and often conflicting viewpoints, I hope to create an open-ended space in which each reader will not only come to his or her own conclusions but also continue to reassess them.

Footbinding began as an act of embodied lyricism—to live as the poets imagined—and ended as a ridiculous exercise of excess and folly. In the final analysis, self-contradiction—the ability to encompass conflicting desires and the tendency to turn against itself—is the only enduring trait of footbinding as a social practice and as a subject of knowledge. For this reason, it continues to both repel and fascinate long after it has ceased to be a viable practice.

NOTES

1. Stephen West uttered these two words in a casual conversation at Columbia University, Oct. 2002.

2. A notable exception in English is Howard S. Levy's *Chinese Footbinding: The History of A Curious Erotic Custom* (Taipei: Nantian shuju, 1984). The rhetoric of disavowal that Levy adopted is a thinly veiled disguise of his fascination and longing. This stance is remarkably similar to that of Yao Lingxi, the compiler of the encyclopedic *Caifeilu* (Picking radishes). The fragmentary structure of Levy's book is modeled after *Caifeilu,* which also supplies much of his substantive data. For the complicated stance of Yao and Levy as well as the generation of new knowledge and desires from textual imitation, see chapter 3 of the present book. An exception in Chinese is Gao Hongxing's *Chanzu shi* ([A history of footbinding] Shanghai: Shanghai wenyi chubanshe, 1995), which is less a historical than an ethnographic study, based almost entirely on information culled from *Caifeilu.*

3. One consequence of my decision to focus on footbinding as a lifelong process in this book is that footbinding often appears as something that women practiced on themselves. For the dynamics of transmitting footbinding from mother to daughter, see my *Teachers of the Inner Chambers: Women and Culture in Seventeenth-Century China* (Stanford, Calif.: Stanford University Press, 1994), pp. 169–71.

4. Sigmund Freud, "Fetishism," in *Sexuality and the Psychology of Love,* ed. with an introduction by Philip Rieff (New York: Collier Books, 1963), pp. 214–19. See also Julia Kristeva, *About Chinese Women,* trans. Anita Barrows (New York and London: Marion Boyars, 1991), pp. 81–85. Rey Chow has critiqued Kristeva's reading

of footbinding as female castration in her *Woman and Chinese Modernity: The Politics of Reading between West and East* (Minneapolis: University of Minnesota Press, 1991), pp. 6–7. On the related issue of female fetish, I have learned more from my former undergraduate students at Rutgers Stephanie Capneau and Samantha Pinto than from published volumes.

5. Thorstein Veblen, *The Theory of the Leisure Class* (New York: Penguin Books, 1994), pp. 148–49. This classic was first published in 1899.

6. Hill Gates, "Footbinding and Homespinning in Sichuan: Capitalism's Ambiguous Gifts to Petty Capitalism," in *Constructing China: The Interaction of Culture and Economics,* ed. Kenneth G. Lieberthal, Shuen-fu Lin, and Ernest P. Young (Ann Arbor: University of Michigan Press, 1997), pp. 177–94. For the petty capitalist mode of production, see her *China's Motor: A Thousand Years of Petty Capitalism* (Ithaca: Cornell University Press, 1996). Delia Davin is the first to explain the popularity of footbinding by the mode of economic production. In the north, where dry-field agriculture dominated, footbinding flourished, in contrast to the wet-rice regions in the south (*Woman-Work: Women and the Party in Revolutionary China* [Oxford and New York: Oxford University Press, 1978], pp. 117–18).

7. Laurel Bossen, *Chinese Women and Rural Development: Sixty Years of Change in Lu Village, Yunnan* (Lanham, Md.: Rowman & Littlefield, Inc., 2002); quote from p. 45. See also pp. 73–75 for Bossen on the correlation between the history of technological change and footbinding from 1800 to the 1950s. For "cultureless custom," see Gates, "Footbinding and Homespinning," pp. 180–82.

8. These interviews were conducted in Beiping before 1938 and were first published in 1945 (Ida Pruitt, *A Daughter of Han: The Autobiography of a Chinese Working Woman* [Stanford, Calif.: Stanford University Press, 1967], p. 22). Pruitt (b. 1888) spent the first twelve years of her life in Penglai, a village in Shandong. In her memoir *A China Childhood* (San Francisco: Chinese Materials Center, Inc., 1978), Pruitt related how footbinding was practiced by all but the most deprived women in this part of the country in the 1890s, from the daughter of the local physician to Dada, her peasant caretaker. Dada's youngest daughter did not have bound feet, and was called "a prostitute" (89). So prestigious was footbinding that the daughter imitated the sway of women with bound feet, and a refugee woman had "token binding" (158). I am grateful to Sarah Scheenwind, who brought this book to my attention.

9. For an overview of the history of an enduring European fascination with footbinding since the sixteenth century, see my "Bondage in Time: Footbinding and Fashion Theory," *Fashion Theory: The Journal of Dress, Body, & Culture* 1, no. 1 (March 1997): 3–28. For an in-depth investigation of one chapter of this history, see Sandra May Adams, "Nineteenth Century Representations of Footbinding to the English Reading Public," Ph.D. diss., University of Macau, 1993. I thank Dr. Chi-sheng Ko for making this study available.

10. Another often-cited explanation, that footbinding kept women in the house by crippling them, is a distinctly modern theory that gained currency during the

anti-footbinding movement. The didactic work *Nürenjing,* in which this reasoning was articulated, is a modern text that has no bibliographic and textual traces before the late nineteenth century. The logic of the construct and its premise that mobility is desirable are modern biases. It could not have provided a plausible explanation for footbinding's spread during the imperial times. Not only was the virtue of binding feet never mentioned in the Confucian didactic literature, it also flies in the face of empirical evidence that footbound gentrywomen did travel outside of their homes without detriment to their moral respectability. I have argued that the relationship between footbinding and Confucianism is extremely ambivalent. For the women, footbinding amounted to the achievement of Confucian goals (modesty and civility) using an anti-Confucian means (maiming the body). See my "Footbinding as Female Inscription," in *Rethinking Confucianism: Past and Present in China, Japan, Korea, and Vietnam,* ed. Benjamin Elman, John Duncan, and Herman Ooms (Los Angeles: Asia Pacific Monograph Series in International Studies, UCLA, 2002).

11. Joan Wallach Scott, *Only Paradoxes to Offer: French Feminists and the Rights of Man* (Cambridge, Mass.: Harvard University Press, 1996), p. 2.

12. Bill Kirby first planted this question of finality in my head at the end of a talk I gave at Harvard University in March 1992. For the past decade it has guided my approach to footbinding's history, and I would like to acknowledge his inspiration.

13. Feminists who believe in a universal patriarchy may disagree. Mary Daly, following Andrea Dworkin, sees the oppression of women today in the form of plastic surgery as synonymous with footbinding, female genital cutting, and Nazi medical experiments. See Daly, *Gyn/Ecology: The Metaethics of Radical Feminism* (Boston: Beacon Press, 1978). See also Dworkin, *Woman Hating* (New York: Plume, 1974). I have articulated my disagreement in an earlier article, "The Sex of Footbinding," in *Good Sex: Women's Religious Wisdom,* ed. Radhika Balakrishnan, Mary E. Hunt, and Patricia Beattie Jung (New Brunswick, N.J.: Rutgers University Press, 2001).

1. GIGANTIC HISTORIES OF THE NATION IN THE GLOBE

1. "Xiaojiao beige huashang xiuzhifu" (The sad song of small feet has come to a full stop), *Xinmin wanbao,* Nov. 22, 1999. Production of these pointy shoes started only in 1991, "using old designs and traditional handwork techniques." It is not clear if the shoes were leather or fabric. Silk or cotton shoes—the predominant traditional Chinese footwear—required no lasts for stretching the upper onto the soles, only for ironing the vamp. Orders poured in from throughout the country. A dispatch from the Xinhua News Agency (dateline Beijing) on Oct. 26, 1998, stated that in the first two years of production, over two thousand pairs of shoes were sold annually (http://www.sfmuseum.org/chin/foot.html). For photographs of four single modern leather shoes made for (once-)bound feet, see my *Every Step a Lotus: Shoes for Bound Feet* (Berkeley and Los Angeles: University of California Press, 2001), p. 135.

2. See, for example, Zhang Zhong, *Xiaojiao yu bianzi* (Taipei: Youshi wenhua shiye gongsi, 1995); Dai Qing and Luo Ke, *Chanzu nüzi: Dangdai Zhongguo nüxing wenti* (Hong Kong: Mingbao chubanshe, 1996); Wang Zijin, *Bozu diguo: Zhongguo chuantong jiaotong xingtai yanjiu* (Lanzhou: Dunhuang wenyi chubanshe, 1996). The title of a popular book of Qing cultural history by Wang Dongfang says it all: *March to Modernity: Braid-Cutting and Feet-Liberating* (*Maixiang xiandai: jianbian yu fangzu* [Shenyang: Liaohai chubanshe, 1997]). See also Liang Jinghe's substantive section on anti-footbinding in his unabashedly polemical book, *Jindai Zhongguo lousu wenhua shanbian yanjiu* ([A study of the evolution of the culture of undesirable customs in modern China] Beijing: Shoudu shifan daxue chubanshe, 1998), pp. 204–22. Although published in English, Fan Hong's *Footbinding, Feminism, and Freedom: The Liberation of Women's Bodies in Modern China* (London: Frank Cass, 1997) is informed by the same liberationist rhetoric and dichotomous view of history. Two other books from the same period on the ethnography of footbinding, by Gao Hongxing and Yao Jushun, are exceptional in adopting an objective tone. Although Yao's *Zhongguo chanzu fengsu* (Shenyang: Liaoning daxue chubanshe, 1991) was presented as an original work, the first nine chapters are in fact verbatim translations of Okamoto Ryuzō's *Tensoku monogatari* (Tokyo: Tōhō shoten, 1986 [first published 1963]). On reflections on culturalism, tradition, and modernity during the mid- to late-1980s, see Xudong Zhang, *Chinese Modernism in the Era of Reforms: Cultural Fever, Avant-Garde Fiction, and the New Chinese Cinema* (Durham and London: Duke University Press, 1997).

3. For state prohibitions, see Sun Yat-sen's 1912 edict in CFL II: 39. Lin Qiumin has pointed out that it was never implemented on the national level ("Yan Xishan yu Shanxi de tianzu yundong," *Guoshiguan guankan,* fukan [new series] 18 [June 1995]: 143). Using primarily missionary and foreign accounts, Christena Turner has unearthed remarkable local variations in the practice of binding feet and the timing of its end. She has argued that such variations expose the fragility of the veneer of cultural integration that bound "China" together into a meaningful entity. It also destabilizes the integrity of "footbinding" as a category ("Locating Footbinding: Variations across Class and Space in Nineteenth and Early Twentieth Century China," *The Journal of Historical Sociology* 10, no. 4 [Dec. 1997]: 444–79).

4. Two surgeons studied the feet of women with bound feet in Hong Kong in the 1950s and produced a report that is remarkable not only in its documentation but also in its sympathy for Chinese cultural practices and the women. See H. S. Y. Fang and F. Y. K. Yu, "Foot Binding in Chinese Women," *Canadian Journal of Surgery* 3 (April 1960): 195–202. The surgeons attested to the fact that footbinding did not break bones: "Individual bones of the foot alter but slightly in shape, yet the distortion is considerable." Furthermore, "The joints of the outer four toes which are acutely flexed into the sole, have adapted to their deformed manner and cannot be straightened, even by force" (199). Footbinding is irreversible.

5. Susan Stewart, *On Longing: Narratives of the Miniature, the Gigantic, the Souvenir, the Collection* (Durham and London: Duke University Press, 1993), p. 71.

6. For an introduction to the works of and modern scholarship on Qiu Jin, Ding Ling, and sixteen other women writers, see Amy D. Dooling and Kristina M. Torgeson, eds., *Writing Women in Modern China: An Anthology of Women's Literature from the Early Twentieth Century* (New York: Columbia University Press, 1998).

7. One ironic outcome of this containment is that despite the rhetoric of sexual liberation, the corporeality of the female body is erased. Lydia Liu has been one of the first scholars to focus on the suffering female body in nationalist discourses ("The Female Body and Nationalist Discourse," in *Scattered Hegemonies: Postmodernity and Transnational Feminist Practices,* ed. Inderpal Grewal and Caren Kaplan [Minneapolis: University of Minnesota Press, 1994], pp. 37–62).

8. In an attempt to rethink the history of the Chinese enlightenment, Wang Zheng has used oral history to recover the voices of another group of women whose voices were submerged or contained by official communist historiography, bourgeois career women. See her *Women in the Chinese Enlightenment: Oral and Textual Histories* (Berkeley and Los Angeles: University of California Press, 1999).

9. Gail Hershatter was the first to make this observation. See her "The Subaltern Talks Back: Reflections on Subaltern Theory and Chinese History," *positions: east asia cultures critique* 1, no. 1 (Spring 1993): 103–30, which discusses *Small Happiness.* For interviews with footbound women in the 1930s, see the *Caifeilu* volumes (discussed in chap. 3); for interviews conducted in Taiwan in 1960–61, see Howard S. Levy, *Chinese Footbinding: The History of a Curious Erotic Custom* (Taipei: Nantian shuju, 1984), chap. 10. One particularly informative interview was that of Lu Zhilan (b. 1915). Lu, a native of Lu-Family Village in the vicinity of Ji'nan city, Shandong province, had her feet bound in 1922. All the girls from the more than three hundred families in the village had bound feet (Yao Jushun, *Zhongguo chanzu fengsu,* pp. 158–65). A latest and possibly last attempt is by Yang Yang, son of a footbound mother from Liuyi village, Yunnan province, who related the stories of twenty-six women in his *Xiaojiao wudao: Dian-nan yige xiangcun de chanzu gushi* (Hefei: Anhui wenyi chubanshe, 1999), pp. 91–168.

10. John MacGowan, *How England Saved China* (London: T. Fisher Unwin, 1913), pp. 25–26. Although the Reverend stayed in China for fifty years and compiled a dictionary of Amoy colloquiums, it is not clear if the couple spoke the local tongue when they first arrived. For an account of their trip from London and their initial impressions of Amoy ("I am going to take you in imagination a very long journey to the far-off land of China, that we may see with our eyes the strange people that live there") see MacGowan, *Beside the Bamboo* (London: London Missionary Society, 1914), quote from p. 9. Coincidentally, MacGowan erroneously attributed the origins of footbinding to the Duke of Donghun of Qi (Tung Hwun Hau, 499–501 C.E.). See his *The Imperial History of China* (Shanghai: American Presbyterian Mission Press, 1906), p. 225.

11. MacGowan, *How England Saved China,* pp. 46–68. The speech of the "tall, handsome-looking woman" is from pp. 59–60. The Heavenly Feet Society was to meet twice a year. Many men showed up and spoke at its next meeting (pp. 70–74).

Alison Drucker has placed the first meeting in 1874 ("The Influence of Western Women on the Anti-footbinding Movement, 1840–1911," in *Women in China: Current Directions in Historical Scholarship,* ed. Richard W. Guisso and Stanley Johannesen [Youngstown, N.Y.: Philo Press, 1991], pp. 187–88). Here I follow Lin Weihong's deduction of 1875 from the date of publication of Baozhuo zi's essay in 1878–79 ("Qingji de funü buchanzu yundong [1894–1911]," *Guoli Taiwan daxue lishi xuexi xuebao* 16 [1991]: p. 155).

12. MacGowan, *How England Saved China,* p. 21.

13. Ibid., pp. 34, 64–65.

14. This posture of "going native" is not always egalitarian in intent or result. John MacGowan donned a "Viceroy's official robe" in a photograph with sixteen Chinese elders from the Amoy churches. The photograph was taken to mark his fiftieth year in Amoy. All the Chinese wore plain "riding jackets," and MacGowan stood out as the most authoritative (*Beside the Bamboo,* image facing p. 177).

15. It is unclear if Macgowan's Heavenly Feet Society had a Chinese name at its first meeting in 1875. The name "Jie chanzu hui" first appeared in an article by Baozhuo zi, "Xiamen jie chanzu hui," *Wangguo gongbao,* vol. 11 (1878–79): 406–408, reprinted in Li Youning and Zhang Yufa, *Jindai Zhongguo nüquan yundong shiliao,* pp. 836–40. See also Lü Meiyi and Zheng Yongfu, *Zhongguo funü yundong (1840–1921)* (Henan Renmin chubanshe, 1990), p. 43. A Xiamen Tianzu hui was founded in 1904; its manifesto is in Li and Zhang, *Jindai Zhongguo,* pp. 880–81. None of the early anti-footbinding societies founded by Chinese reformers, beginning with Kang Youwei's 1883 Bu guozu hui, adopted the name "tianzu hui." Bu chanzu (Don't bind feet) or Jie chanzu (Quit binding feet) predominated, both being a negation of a native category, *chanzu* (footbinding). Tianzu hui (Natural feet society) became a common name across the country only in the early 1900s. See Lin Weihong, "Qingji," pp. 160–63; Lin Qiumin, "Jindai Zhongguo de buchanzu yundong (1895–1937)," master's thesis, Guoli Zhengzhi daxue, 1990, pp. 52, 60–61. Even then, "jie chanzu" remained current in the press. In 1902, an essay in *Dagong bao* by that title was translated in Taiwan, then a Japanese colony, in an interlinear format. See "Kai tensoku setsu," *Taiwan kanshū kiji* 2, no. 11 (1902): 43–49 [887–93].

16. In an earlier article "Footbinding as Female Inscription," I have discussed a striking anti-footbinding polemical essay by the early-Qing writer Chu Jiaxuan in which he wrote a natural geometric body into being. In its Confucian context, this natural body was to serve the patriarchal family. For the body in imperial discourses, see Angela Zito, *Of Body and Brush: Grand Sacrifice as Text / Performance in Eighteenth-Century China* (Chicago: University of Chicago Press, 1997).

17. Baozhuo zi, "Xiamen jie chanzu hui," in Li and Zhang, *Jindai Zhongguo,* pp. 839–40. As Lin Weihong has shown (citing Virginia Chau), in the early 1870s Christian communities in China debated whether footbinding was a categorical sin and if women had to let their feet out before they could become Christian. An 1878 meeting resolved that footbinding is not a doctrinal matter, and that the family of

believers has the right to choose the best course of action (Lin Weihong, "Qingji," pp. 152–53). For summaries of these debates in *The Chinese Recorder* between 1869 and 1870 (by Dr. Dudgeon, H.G., J. C. Kerr), see Lin Qiumin, "Jindai Zhongguo de buchanzu yundong," pp. 30–32; see also Virginia Chiu-tin Chau, "The Anti-Footbinding Movement in China, 1850–1912," master's thesis, Columbia University, 1966.

18. Baozhuo zi, "Xiamen jie chanzu hui." In contrast, the reformer Liang Qichao drew on a Chinese tradition of anti-footbinding polemics ["Lanling nüzi"] in blaming the "despicable man" who committed a wrong that lasts a thousand generations so that he can indulge in "one day's worth of desire" ("Jie chanzu hui xu," in Li and Zhang, *Jindai Zhongguo,* p. 841).

19. The flourishing of anti-footbinding societies in 1895–98 has been the most studied aspect of the anti-footbinding movement due to the abundance of sources. In this chapter I focus on its pre-history and its re-reading by such Republican writers as Xu Ke (see below). Almost all of the documents pertinent to the founding of the Tianzu hui in 1895 and local societies in 1898–1911 are reprinted in Li and Zhang, *Jindai Zhongguo,* pp. 480–542, 836–909. For interpretive histories, see the works of Lin Qiumin, Lin Weihong, Lü Meiyi and Zheng Yongfu, Julie Broadwin, Alison Drucker, and Sakamoto Hiroko. See also the fascinating memoirs of Mrs. Little on the work and local reception of the Tianzu hui in her *The Land of the Blue Gown* (London: T. Fisher Unwin, 1902), pp. 305–70.

20. The trope of the body-as-machine, so prevalent in missionary discourses, is part and parcel of a larger valorization of circulation (of air, ideas, and so on) as the basis of hygiene. In educational meetings organized by the Natural Feet Society, members would use a tube of rubber hosing to demonstrate the importance of unobstructed blood circulation (Kikuchi Takaharu, "Futensoku undō ni tsuite," *Rekishi kyōiku* 5, no.12 [1957]: 35).

21. Joan Judge has analyzed the contradictory message about women's value and potential in the discourses of women's education during the 1898 reform period ("Reforming the Feminine: Female Literacy and the Legacy of 1898" in *Rethinking the 1898 Reform Period: Political and Cultural Change in Late Qing China,* ed. Rebecca E. Karl and Peter Zarrow [Cambridge, Mass.: Harvard University Asia Center, 2002], pp. 158–79). The view that women were "mere playthings preoccupied with making up their faces, binding their feet, and piercing their ears" was prevalent in the writings of such leading intellectuals as Yan Fu, Kang Youwei, and Liang Qichao (in Li and Zhang, *Jindai Zhongguo,* quote from p. 161) in the 1890s and 1900s.

22. Traditional historiography emphasizes foreign initiatives. Jialin Bao Tao's revisionist essay argues strongly for a cooperation of equal footing ("The Anti-Footbinding Movement in Late Ch'ing China: Indigenous Development and Western Influence," *Research on Women in Modern Chinese History* 2 [June 1994]: 141–73). Lin Weihong, in her pioneering study of local anti-footbinding societies ("Qingji"), emphasizes instead that the earlier Christian movement and the subsequent Chi-

nese local movements stemmed from separate rationales and social dynamics. Both were external to women's concerns for their own benefits. Lin Qiumin concurred in arguing that the missionary motive was "religious" whereas the reformers' motive was "political" ("Jindai Zhongguo de Buchanzu yundong," p. 51). For a rare study of the role of female Protestant missionaries in the anti-footbinding movement, see Takashima Kō, "Kyōkai to shinja no aida de: Josei senkyōshi ni yoru tensoku kaihō no kokorumi," in *Chūgoku kindaika no dōtai kōzō*, ed. Mori Tokihiko, pp. 273–309 (Kyoto: Kyōtō daigaku jinbun kagaku kenkyūjo, 2004). I thank Ono Kazuko Sensei for sending this essay to me.

23. Xu Ke, "Tianzu kaolüe," in Xu Ke, ed., *Tiansuke congkan* (Shanghai: Shangwu yinshuguan, 1914), 1a. For details about the myriad anti-footbinding societies that sprang up around 1898, see the convenient summary in Lin Weihong, *"Qingji,"* pp. 155–66.

24. Xu, "Tianzu kaolüe," 1a–b. Xu, "Zhizu yu," in Xu, *Tiansuke biji shisanzhong*, vol. 2 (Hong Kong: Zhongshan tushu gongsi, 1973), p. 139.

25. Xu, "Tianzu kaolüe," 1a–b; see also "Zhizu yu," p. 139.

26. The Bu guozu hui, among the earliest Chinese anti-footbinding organizations, was co-founded by Ou Eliang in Kang's hometown, Nanhai, Guangdong province. See Lü and Zheng, *Zhongguo funü yundong*, pp. 76–77; Lin Weihong, "Qingji," pp. 155–56. Kang Youwei's famous memorial to the Guangxu emperor, admonishing him to ban footbinding ("Qingjin funü guozu zhe"), is in Li and Zhang, *Jindai Zhongguo*, pp. 508–10.

27. Xu Ke, *Chunfeiguan ci*, 31a, 34b, in *Tiansuke congkan*. The assassinated friend was Xia Chuifang, a founder of the Commercial Press.

28. Tang Yisuo, "Xu Zhongke xiansheng 'Tiansuke yuwan tu' xu," 22b–23a. Appendix to Xu Ke, *Chunfeiguan ci*, in Xu, *Tiansuke congkan*.

29. Liang Qichao, "Lun nüxue," in Li and Zhang, *Jindai Zhongguo*, pp. 549–56; quotations from pp. 549–50. Although often cited independently, this is a section of a longer essay, "Bianfa tongyi." Joan Judge has pointed out that the arguments and tropes of this essay served as a blueprint for subsequent reformist writings on women's education ("Reforming the Feminine," p. 170). Rebecca Karl has analyzed Liang's trope of "women as slaves," which was part and parcel of the trope of all citizens as slaves (*wangguo nu*, colonized subjects) in "'Slavery,' Citizenship, and Gender in Late Qing China's Global Context," in Karl and Zarrow, *Rethinking the 1898 Reform Period*, pp. 212–44.

30. "Nüzi ziqiang," plate 553, in Wang Shucun, *Zhongguo minjian nianhuashi tulu* (Shanghai: Renmin meishu chubanshe, 1991), p. 542. The same themes of women's economic independence and equality of classes recur in the essays of Xu Ke's daughter Xu Xinhua (New China). They were published after her death at age twenty-one as *Tongfenshi wen* and *Tongfenshi biji*, in Xu Ke, *Tiansuke congkan*.

31. Tang Yisuo, "Xu Zhongke xiansheng," 23a.

32. Ibid. The early cotton mills were established in Shanghai after 1895. By 1919, almost half of the 181,485 factory workers in Shanghai were in the cotton mills (Emily

Honig, *Sisters and Strangers: Women in the Shanghai Cotton Mills, 1919–1949* [Stanford, Calif.: Stanford University Press, 1986], p. 23).

33. According to Shi Meng *Huang Xiuqiu* was first serialized in 1905 in vol. 2 of *Xin xiaoshuo* and issued as a separate title by the same publishers in 1907 (*Wan-Qing xiaoshuo* [Shanghai: Shanghai guji chubanshe, 1989], p. 109). The editors of a modern Taiwan reprint give the dates 1904 and 1906, respectively. See "Huang Xiuqiu tiyao," in Tang Yisuo, *Huang Xiuqiu,* in vol. 15 of *Wan-Qing xiaoshuo daxi* (Taipei: Guangya shuju, 1984), 1. The confusion may rise from the fact that the year of publication of *Xin xiaoshuo* ceased to appear after vol. 2 no. 6 (Tarumoto Teruo, *Shinmatsu shōsetsu kandan* [Kyoto: Hōritsu bunkasha, 1983], p. 12). Ying Hu has analyzed this novel by focusing on the meetings between Huang Xiuqiu and Madame Roland in the novel, which she construes as a metaphor for the encounter between Chinese nationalism and the universalism of European Enlightenment (*Tales of Translation: Composing the New Woman in China, 1899–1918* [Stanford, Calif.: Stanford University Press, 2000], pp. 153–96). Hu has also traced the novelist's subjugation of women's education to nationalistic concerns to Liang Qichao's essay, "Lun nüxue" (pp. 162–69).

34. Tang Yisuo, *Huang Xiuqiu,* pp. 23, 54.

35. Joan Scott has argued that this paradox is inherent in liberal feminism (*Only Paradoxes to Offer: French Feminists and the Rights of Man* [Cambridge, Mass.: Harvard University Press, 1996]).

36. Zhang Xiushu, "Qingmo minjian ertong duwu," in *Sichuan wenshi ziliao xuanji* (Chengdu: Sichuan renmin chubanshe, 1979), 20: 185.

37. Ibid., pp. 184–85.

38. Ibid., pp. 187–89.

39. *Nü xuebao* 7 (Sept. 1898), 1b. The illustration is the work of a woman artist, Liu Qing (Keqing), and is reprinted in Nanxiu Qian, "Revitalizing the Xianyuan (Worthy Ladies) Tradition: Women in the 1898 Reforms," *Modern China* 29, no. 4 (Oct. 2003): 420.

40. The *Dalu* magazine is discussed in Zhang Nan and Wang Renzhi, eds., *Xinhai geming qian shinian jian shilun xuanji* (Beijing: Sanlian shudian, 1978), *juan* 1, p. 967. This cover is reproduced at the beginning of *juan* 1, no page. The Globe Society is mentioned in Wang Shu-Hwai et al., eds., *International Union List of Chinese Journals Relating to Women* (Taipei: Institute of Modern History, Academia Sinica, 1995), p. 57.

41. Xiao Yun, "Tianzu shuo," *Xiaoshuo congbao* 3, no. 8 (1917): 2.

42. Ibid., pp. 2–3. The author was more interested in showing off various allusions to *tian* and *chanzu* than in writing a polemic against footbinding. The essay ended with a plea that as commendable as the Tianzu hui may be, reformers should concern themselves with issues more serious than women's feet.

43. Madame Roland (1754–93) was a leader of the Girondists who was put to the guillotine. For her popularity in late-Qing China, see Ying Hu, *Tales of Translation,* pp. 153–96. The way Madame Roland introduces her name in *Huang Xiu-*

qiu resembles that in a long biography of the heroine serialized in two 1902 issues of *Xinmin congbao,* suggesting influence by the latter ("Jinshi diyi nüjie Luolan furen zhuan," in Li and Zhang, *Jindai Zhongguo,* pp. 318–31). One of the three books is *Yingxiong zhuan,* in an alphabet script; another is a translated geography textbook. The third, also an alphabet, is unnamed. Tang Yisuo's attitude toward the West, as mirrored in Huang Tongli, is ambivalent. Tongli thinks that Madame Roland, a member of the White clan, is condescending to Xiuqiu because she is from the Yellow clan (23). Throughout the novel he criticizes the Westernization model represented by Shanghai as going too fast too far, to the point of compromising "Chinese" identity. Hence he questions the motives of some members of Shanghai natural foot societies (73, 76).

44. It is not clear if the doctor's big feet are the product of her Cantonese connections or foreign education. Ying Hu has seen in Tang Yisuo's way of ascribing the undetermined origins of Dr. Bi's natural foot "a narrative awareness of a larger China"("Re-Configuring Nei/Wai: Writing the Woman Traveler in the Late Qing," *Late Imperial China* 18, no. 1 [June 1997]: 82–83).

45. Wang Tao sojourned in England in 1867–70, during which time he also visited France and Russia. He founded the *Xunhuan ribao* (Circulation daily) in Hong Kong in 1873. Zheng Guanying handled foreign enterprises for Li Hongzhang. See Paul A. Cohen, *Between Tradition and Modernity: Wang T'ao and Reform in Late Ch'ing China* (Cambridge, Mass.: Harvard University Press, 1987).

46. For the importance of the transnational world in the making of modern Chinese nationalism, see Rebecca E. Karl, *Staging the World: Chinese Nationalism at the Turn of the Twentieth Century* (Durham and London: Duke University Press, 2002).

47. Wu Guoqing, *Wentan guaijie Gu Hongming* (Changsha: Yuelu shushe, 1988), p. 151. Lydia Liu has analyzed Gu's "sovereignty complex," one manifestation of which was his loyalty to the anti-reformist Empress Dowager ("The Desire for the Sovereign and the Logic of Reciprocity in the Family of Nations," *Diacritics* 29, no. 4 (1999): 160–69).

48. Hui-min Lo is the only scholar who has painstakingly sifted through history and myth to reconstruct Gu Hongming's upbringing and early career. Gu was said to have been born on the estate of the second-generation colonial planter Forbes Scott Brown, who was of Scottish descent. As guardian and benefactor, Brown later financed Gu's education in Europe. See Lo, "Ku Hung-ming: Schooling," *Papers on Far Eastern History* 37–38 (1988): 46–47. Gu's great-grandfather Gu Lihuan (d. 1826) was present to welcome the vanguard of British Captain Light when he landed in Point Pennager. When Penang was colonized and renamed Prince Wales Island in 1786, Gu Lihuan was appointed "Kapitan" in charge of Chinese affairs. One of Lihuan's sons, Guocai, accompanied Stamford Raffles on his trip to colonize Singapore. See Wu Guoqing, *Wentan guaijie,* pp. 46, 186–87. Hui-min Lo identified Zhou Zuoren as the first one who asserted that Gu's mother was European. Although this remains unverified, Lo described a permissive society governed by neither Confucian nor Victorian morality, with rampant extramarital affairs and illegitimacy.

Forbes Scott Brown's mother was Malay or Chinese ("Ku Hung-ming: Schooling," pp. 47–48).

49. Two events in 1879–81 served as triggers for Gu's "conversion." One was a missionary incident in Fuzhou. Lo has located an English poem by Gu which suggests that he first set foot in China in late 1879, when he arrived at Fuzhou, Fujian. Gu gave up his naïve faith in European Enlightenment values and became a Chinese nationalist, as evinced in the last stanza of his poem: "We want no priest to help us in our need, / Priests we have shaven and unshaven both; / We want no mumblings of an outworn creed, / But science we want and knowledge of our growth, / And Rules with unselfish hearts and just, / To sweep you from our land as whirlwind sweepeth dust." The second trigger was a meeting with the Fujianese scholar-translator Ma Jianzhong (1844–1900), a French-educated Roman Catholic, in Singapore in 1881. According to unverified accounts, Gu was then serving in the Colonial Secretary's Office in Singapore. The legendary meeting took place at the Strand Hotel, and according to Gu's recollections over forty years later, they conversed in French because Ma's Mandarin was poor. Inspired, Gu resigned from his post three days later and prepared to sail to China by growing a queue and wearing Chinese clothes, hence "coming back into the fold of Chinese nationality" (Lo, "Ku Hung-ming: Homecoming, Part 2," *East Asian History* 9 [1995]: 67, 73, 83–89; poem on p. 73). See also Wen Yuan-ning, "Gu Hongming," *T'ien Hsia Monthly* 4, no. 4 (April 1937), reprinted in Zhu Chuanyu, comp., *Gu Hongming zhuanji zhiliao* (Taipei: Tianyi chubanshe, 1979), 2: 2–3. In 1882, Gu enlisted as interpreter for a British surveying expedition to Yunnan and Burma. By then he seems to have had working knowledge of Cantonese and Mandarin and "reasonable reading ability in Chinese" (Lo, "Homecoming, Part 2," pp. 90–93; see also Wu, *Wentan guaijie,* pp. 188–89).

50. Information on Gu's knowledge of Malay and Amoy dialect is from Lo, "Ku Hung-ming: Homecoming [Part 1]," *East Asian History* 6 (1993): 167.

51. On *Analects* tutors, see Huang Xintao, *Xianhua Gu Hongming* (Haikou: Hainan chubanshe, 1997), pp. 24, 28, 40. The *Kangxi Dictionary* episode and the student's report of misshapen characters are in Wu, *Wentan guaijie,* pp. 173, 15. The scrawls of his calligraphy are in Zhu Chuanyu, comp., *Gu Hongming zhuanji zhiliao,* 1: 47. Judging from Gu's calligraphy as reproduced as frontispieces in volume one of his *Gu Hongming wenji* (Haikou: Hianan chubanshe, 1996), these observers are right.

52. Huang Xintao, *Xianhua Gu Hongming,* pp. 34–38. In another version Gu was said to read an English newspaper upside down (Sang Rou, *Gu Hongming de youmo* [Taipei: Jingmei chubanshe, 1985], pp. 43–44). A variation on the same theme: when Gu ran into a German professor in the hallways of Peking University, he would criticize Germany in German, and could do the same in English or French in accordance with the identity of his hapless colleagues (Wu Guoqing, *Wentan guaijie,* p. 161).

53. Representative of Gu's views on classical Chinese is "Fandui Zhongguo

wenxue geming" (Opposing the Chinese literary revolution), in *Gu Hongming wenji*, 2: 165–70. This essay was first published in *Millard's Review* on July 5, 1919, two months after the May Fourth incident that launched the New Culture Movement. The poignant tribute was transmitted by a woman writer, Ling Shuhua, a neighbor of the Gu family whose father was a close friend of Gu Hongming (Wu, *Wentan guaijie,* p. 138).

54. The "badge and insignia . . . " are Gu's words, quoted by Hui-min Lo, who has also argued that when Gu left Penang for his schooling in Scotland sometime in 1870 or 1871, he was definitely wearing a queue, but he cut it off before sailing from Edinburgh for Penang and China in 1879 ("Schooling," pp. 50, 62; see also "Homecoming [Part 1]," p. 169). Others are less certain that Gu had a queue in Penang. Wen Yuan-ning, who did not disclose his source, wrote that Gu started to grow a queue only after he was "converted" by Ma Jianzhong in Singapore sometime between the late 1870s and early 1880s (Zhu Chuanyu, *Gu Hongming zhuanji zhiliao,* 2: 2). Gu cherished telling the stories of his being ridiculed in Europe because of his pigtail. See Wu, *Wentan guaijie,* p. 5; Huang Xintao, *Xianhua,* pp. 17–18.

55. Gu Hongming, "Zhao xiang" (Taking a photograph), in *Gu Hongming wenji*, 1: 453–54. See also Huang, *Xianhua,* p. 216; Sang Rou, *Gu Hongming de youmo,* pp. 158–60. Gu Hongming was very sensitive to the social snobbery of Victorian Scotland (Lo, "Schooling," p. 53).

56. Gu, "Ri-E zhanzheng de daode yuanyin" (The moral cause of the Russo-Japanese War), in *Gu Hongming wenji,* 1: 201.

57. Gu, "Zhongguo funü" (Chinese women), in Gu, *Zhongguoren de jingshen,* trans. Huang Xingtao and Song Xiaoqing (Haikou: Hainan chubanshe, 1996), pp. 96–98. Gu expressed the same admiration for the quiet virtues of a queen in "the state of Italy," a commoner daughter who earned her exalted place by passing a test imposed by her king. Gu stated that he translated the biography of this virtuous foreign woman from "classical Italian" (Yi-da-li guwen; "Yi-da-li-guo xianfei zhuan," in *Gu Hongming wenji,* 2: 241–44).

58. Lo, "Homecoming [Part 1]," p. 176; "Homecoming, Part 2," p. 90.

59. The memoirs of Hu Shi, Zhou Zuoren, Luo Jialun, and a host of Gu's students can be found in Wu, *Wentan guaijie, passim*. The story of Gu's wife and concubine first appeared in Chen Zhang's biography of Gu, in Gujintan zazhi she, ed., *Gujin mingren zhuanji* (Taipei: Gujintan zazhishe, 1972), pp. 109–17. See also Huang, *Xianhua,* p. 180. Gu's daughter had unbound feet and loved to go dancing with Gu's students (Wu, *Wentan guaijie,* p. 153; see also Sang Rou, *Gu Hongming,* p. 248). It is not surprising that these rather titillating stories are widely anthologized. See, for example, Sang Rou, *Gu Hongming,* pp. 79–84; Zhu Chuanyu, *Gu Hongming zhuanji zhiliao,* 2: 8–9. The seven-word mantra and the rotten egg sayings are recounted in Wu Guoqing, *Wentan guaijie,* p. 36, and Zhu, *Gu Hongming zhuanji zhiliao,* 1: 17, 78. These seven words were in fact those of another alleged lotus lover, Fang Xuan, to be discussed in chap. 3.

60. The first three items of feudal customs are from Huang, *Xianhua,* pp. 81–84.

The list is longer in Sang Rou, *Gu Hongming,* p. 247. For a classic summary statement of the missionary discourse, see Dr. J.-J. Matignon, *Superstition, crime, et misére en Chine: souvenirs de biologie sociale* (Lyon: A Storck & Cie, 1899). Matignon
was an officer of the French Legation; his list of "miseries" is given in fig. 2 of the
present book. I am grateful to Steffani Pfeiffer for giving me a copy of this book
and for her insightful analysis.

2. THE BODY INSIDE OUT

1. Kang Youwei, "Qing jin funü chanzu zhe," in Li Yuning and Zhang Yufa,
Jindai Zhongguo nüquan yundong shiliao (Taipei: Zhuanji wenxue chubanshe, 1975),
pp. 508–10. Kang condemned footbinding on five grounds: it is a form of corporeal punishment; it detracts from parental love; the broken bones make the women
frail; it weakens the Chinese army by weakening their seed (*zhong,* race); and the
barbaric custom makes China a laughing stock in the eyes of other nations. Kang's
sense of embarrassment at being subjected to global gaze is palpable. He ended the
memorial with the prediction that if footbinding is successfully outlawed, "the foreigner's ridicule that we are barbaric will subside" (510).

2. Xue Shaohui's husband, Chen Shoupeng (1857–ca. 1928), and his brother Chen
Jitong (1851–1907) were editors of the reformist newspaper *Qiushi bao.* Jitong's wife
went by the Chinese name of Lai Mayi. The initial organization meeting took place
on Dec. 6, 1897, and the girls' school opened in May 1898. Seventy girls registered
during the two years of its operation. The journal began publication on July 24,
1898, and the last issue, the twelfth, appeared on Oct. 29, 1898. Only eight issues
are extant. See Nanxiu Qian, "Revitalizing the Xianyuan (Worthy Ladies) Tradition: Women in the 1898 Reforms," *Modern China* 29, no. 4 (Oct. 2003): 399–454.
See also Qian, "Qingji nü zuojia Xue Shaohui jiqi 'Waiguo lienüzhuan,'" in *Ming-
Qing wenxue yu xingbie yanjiu,* ed. Zhang Hongsheng (Nanjing: Jiangsu guji
chubanshe, 2002), pp. 932–56. I am indebted to Nanxiu Qian, who generously made
her drafts and copies of Xue Shaohui's writings available to me.

3. Xue Shaohui, "Fu Shen nüshi shu," in *Daiyunlou wenji, juan xia,* 20b–21a;
in Xue, *Daiyunlou yiji* (Fujian: Chenshi jiakanben, 1914). Nanxiu Qian brought
this letter to my attention. Shen's original letter is no longer extant. According to
Nanxiu Qian (personal communication, Dec. 2002), Xue's response was not published in the eight extant issues of *Nü xuebao,* but it is likely that it appeared in one
of the four issues that are no longer extant. Xue criticized Kang's memorial, using
similar wording, twice in her letter. Her rebuttal of the femme fatale argument is
also a direct response to an essay by Yong Jiaxiang, who won an essay contest held
by the Tianzu hui in 1898 (Li and Zhang, *Jindai Zhongguo,* pp. 510–13). Hence it
is likely that the original publication date of Xue's letter was late 1898. Like the male
philologists before her, Xue Shaohui erred in mistaking poetic allusions for social
practice. See chap. 4 for a discussion of the philological way of knowing.

4. Xue Shaohui sought to reestablish the "talented women" genealogy in modern times. She adopted the Confucian terminology of *nüde* (female virtue) and *fu-*

dao (the way of a woman), but argued for a radically new content of women's education. For the curriculum of the girls' school, Xue favored a combination of "venerating Confucius" *(zun Kong)* and Western languages and sciences. Two teachers
recruited by Liang Qichao, Dr. Kang Aide (Ida Kahn) and Dr. Shi Meiyu (Mary
Stone), signed an open letter criticizing the school's Confucian orientation. See Qian,
"Revitalizing." For Kang Aide, see Hu Ying, "Naming the First 'New Woman,'" in
Rethinking the 1898 Reform Period: Political and Cultural Change in Late Qing China,
ed. Rebecca E. Karl and Peter Zarrow (Cambridge, Mass.: Harvard University Asia
Center, 2002), pp. 180–211.

5. Xue's comments on the rapidity of changing tastes capture the ambiguous
beauty standards in a transitional period. Decades after footbinding was being condemned as shameful, many women continued to find bound feet beautiful whereas
unbound feet were merely convenient. Ida Pruitt, a missionary's daughter born in
Shandong in 1888, expressed this attitude *(A China Childhood* [San Francisco: Chinese Materials Center, Inc., 1978], pp. 89–90). Kwei-lan, a gentry daughter in Pearl
Buck's first novel, *East Wind: West Wind,* struggled with the reversal of standards.
She was crestfallen when her Western-educated husband showed her an X-ray of
the "ugly" foot but eventually agreed to unbind her feet to please him (*East Wind:
West Wind* [London: Methuen & Co., Ltd., 1934; first published 1930], pp. 47–48,
67–76). The historian Yang Nianqun has discussed an identical story in the context of the introduction of discourse of biomedicine. His source was a story translated from a German magazine and published in the influential Chinese journal
Funü zazhi in 1927 (13, no. 3: 1–6). In Yang's essay Kwei-lan's (Guilan) story was
presented as a real event that happened in a commoner household ("Cong kexue
huayu dao guojia kongzhi: Dui nüzi chanzu you 'mei' bian 'chou' de duoyuan fenxi,"
Beijing dang'an shiliao 4 [2001]: 248–51). See also scattered remarks made by old
women whom Howard Levy interviewed in Taiwan in 1960–61 (*Chinese Footbinding: The History of a Curious Erotic Custom* [Taipei: Nantian shuju, 1984], pp. 246,
267, 278). Yang Xingmei and Luo Zhitian have analyzed this change in standards
of feminine beauty brilliantly in their study "Jindai Zhongguoren dui nüxing xiaojiaomei de fouding" (paper presented at the Symposium on the History of Health
and Beauty, Institute of History and Philology, Academia Sinica, Taipei, Taiwan,
June 11–12, 1999).

6. Early efforts by local male elite were concentrated in the three reformist provinces of Guangdong, Jiangsu, and Hunan. Only in Hunan did the Hunan Buchanzu
hui (1897) receive official support from Huang Zunxian, the Surveillance Commissioner *(ancha shi)*. See Lin Qiumin, "Jindai Zhongguo de buchanzu yundong,"
master's thesis, Guoli Zhengzhi daxue, 1990, pp. 52–58. Chinese-initiated anti-
footbinding societies proliferated on the local level around the turn of the century.
Lin Weihong, who has based her arguments on the years of formation of the local
Tianzu hui's, identified 1898 as their peak. She has also observed that they were
ineffective in ending footbinding, populated as they were by a minority of local
leaders who rallied to curry favor with their superiors. These local official and semi-

official organizations lacked broad-based support among the local elite, who remained overwhelmingly conservative ("Qingji de funü buchanzu yundong [1894–1911]," *Guoli Taiwan daxue lishi xuexi xuebao* 16 [1991]: 177–78). In contrast, Lü Meiyi and Zheng Yongfu (*Zhongguo funü yundong [1840–1921]* [Henan: Renmin chubanshe, 1990], pp. 162–63) saw initial setback for the local tianzu movement after the fiasco of 1898 and the Boxers; they identified 1901–5 as the period of renewal of local anti-footbinding activities.

7. For a list of titles and prices of the pamphlets available in 1904, see Li and Zhang, *Jindai Zhongguo,* pp. 872–73. For essay contests, see pp. 840–41. See also Lü and Zheng, *Zhongguo funü yundong,* pp. 163–64. In one Natural Feet Society meeting in Hankou alone, Mrs. Little gave away two thousand leaflets and tracts to the invited Chinese officials for further distribution (Little, *The Land of the Blue Gown* [London: T. Fisher Unwin, 1902], p. 306).

8. Thiriez has written that "Women unbinding their feet for the photographer . . . were poor models fulfilling the demands of a market. The fact that few negatives were actually taken was a measure of the impropriety of this Western fantasy" ("Photography and Portraiture in Nineteenth-Century China," *East Asian History* 17/18 (1999): 77–102; quote from p. 97; see also p. 93). These photographs focus on the pair of feet; often showing one bound and the other unbound. Before the 1890s, every commercial photographer would have several images of the bound foot, mixed in with other "Chinese customs" such as the rickshaw, the bamboo pole, the 360 occupations, and so on, for customers to choose from. At least one photo studio in Shanghai had two large display windows, hence Chinese passers-by would also have access to some of these images. This and other information on photo albums, commercial photographers, and their customers is from Thiriez (personal communications, Feb. 2003). I thank Dr. Thiriez for taking the time to answer my questions and for generously sharing her materials and expertise.

9. One of the earliest medical reports illustrated by both X-ray and regular photographs is J. Preston Maxwell, "On the Evils of Chinese Foot-Binding," *The China Medical Journal* 30, no. 6 (Nov. 1916): 393–96. Dr. Maxwell practiced in Yongcun, southern Fujian. See also the X-ray drawings and photographs of naked feet in F. M. Al-Akl, "Bound Feet in China," *American Journal of Surgery* n.s. 18, no. 3 (Dec. 1932): 545–50. Two X-ray radiographs taken in 1920 and 1922 by the Department of Radiology at the University of California are reproduced in Ilza Veith, "The History of Medicine Dolls and Foot-Binding in China," *Clio Medica* 14, no. 3/4 (1980): 255–67.

10. Kang, "Qing jin funü chanzu zhe," in Li and Zhang, *Jindai Zhongguo,* p. 508.

11. Much of the anti-footbinding propaganda worked by the technique of visual exposé. According to a Tianzu hui 1904 report, a poster with a photograph "A New Way to See Through Bones" was posted in and around Beijing (Li and Zhang, *Jindai Zhongguo,* p. 872). On the X-ray mode of penetration as a means of social critique, see my "The Subject of Pain," in *From the Late Ming to the Late Qing: Dynastic Decline and Cultural Innovation,* ed. David Wang and Wei Shang (Stanford,

Calif.: Stanford University Press, forthcoming). A "Tianzu huabao she" (Natural feet pictorial) was advertised in 1912. See Lin Qiumin, "Jindai Zhongguo de buchanzu yundong," p. 96.

12. Thiriez, "Photography and Portraiture," p. 97.

13. Although speech making dominated the meetings of the Tianzu hui, it heralded various rituals to enhance audience participation. In its 1904 meeting in Shanghai, several pairs of shoe models were exhibited on stage at the end of the meeting, and the female guests were invited to cast red strips of paper inside the shoes to "vote" on the most popular styles. Shanghai Zhongguo Tianzu hui, *Tianzu huibao* no. 1 (Summer 1907): 17.

14. *Jingzhong ribao*, Dec. 30 and 31, 1904, in Li and Zhang, *Jindai Zhongguo*, pp. 881–82. The reporter's coining of "Fangzu commemorating assembly" *(fangzu jinian hui)* highlights its ceremonial nature, staged *after* the fact of Cai's unbinding.

15. According to Lin Weihong, four anti-footbinding societies were founded by women: 1895 in Shanghai; 1903 Hangzhou; 1903 Liuyang; 1904 Lili ("Qingji," p. 167). The Lili buchanzu hui was housed in a private tutorial school, the Qiuwo mengshu (Selfhood-seeking school). Mrs. Ni's manifesto (dictated to Liu Yazi) is in Li and Zhang, *Jindai Zhongguo*, pp. 867–69. The anti-footbinding movement gave elite women a forum to make speeches and exercise their leadership skills. For the speeches of Mrs. Gao Baisu in Hangzhou, see Lin, "Qingji," p. 147. For female speech making in general, see those of Xue Qinjin in Zhangyuan in 1901, in Amy D. Dooling and Kristina M. Torgeson, eds., *Writing Women in Modern China: An Anthology of Women's Literature from the Early Twentieth Century* (New York: Columbia University Press, 1998), p. 84, and cf. p. 9. See also the formation of a Funü xuanjiang hui in 1911 (Li and Zhang, *Jindai Zhongguo*, pp. 971ff, 1535).

16. A similar set of instructions for young girls and older women, "Fangzu liangfa," was reprinted in Zhongguo Tianzu hui, *Tianzu hui nianbao* (Shanghai: Meihua shuju, 1908), pp. 12–13. The *Fangjiao hui* in Shaoxing emphasized that once they let their feet out, females should refrain from wearing shoes with pointy tips, and should instead advertise their "civilized state" by wearing shoes with round tips (ibid., p. 15).

17. "Suzhou fangzu hui yanshuo fangzu zhi fazi," in ibid., pp. 71–77. These informative instructions circulated widely beyond Suzhou. A slightly abridged version, without the twenty names and the address of the Suzhou fangzu hui, appeared as "Yanshuo fangjiao zhi fazi," in *Shuntian shibao*, Aug. 19 and Aug. 23, 1905; in Li and Zhang, *Jindai Zhongguo*, pp. 535–37. The *Shuntian shibao* instructions concluded with an admonition absent in the *Tianzu huibao* version: "Women from foreign countries do not bind their feet, therefore their bodies are strong and solid and they are capable of performing a hundred tasks. We have made one mistake before and should better make up for it now. Let it out! Let it out! Don't delay! Don't delay!" (537). As late as 1928, a much shortened version of these instructions appeared in the newspaper *Yishi bao* (Aug. 14, 1928), cited in CFL II: 32–33.

18. For a photograph of inner high heels, see my *Every Step a Lotus: Shoes for*

Bound Feet (Berkeley: University of California Press, 2001), p. 102. An informative ethnographic study of the fangzu campaigns in Taiwan describes a similar process of fangzu that hinged on gradually lowering the height of the heels so that the instep of the foot could flatten. In Taiwan, a special kind of shoes with exposed wooden heels and rounder tips was made. As the arch flattened, the heels would be sawed down, until eventually the woman could wear flats. See Hong Minlin, "Chanjiao yu Taiwan de tianranzu yundong," *Taiwan wenxian* 27, no. 3 (Sept. 1976): 148, 156. In *Every Step a Lotus,* I have erred in suggesting that these were training shoes for binding feet (62).

19. The commingling of Christian miracle and personal efforts also structures a conversion story related by Reverend MacGowan. A Christian woman who had bound her feet for forty years decided to let them out. "The men and women of China had never yet dreamed of the subtle power that Nature possessed of touching with her magic fingers the poor distorted feet and of restoring them to the natural shape which God had originally designed. It was reserved for a Christian woman, a member of the Heavenly Foot Society, to show that the convictions of the women and the deductions of science as given by the medical man were entirely wrong" *(How England Saved China* [London: T. Fisher Unwin, 1913], p. 80; the entire story is on pp. 80–86).

20. For this proclamation, see CFL II: 39. On the mobilization and training of people's bodies for the Republic, see Andrew Morris, *Marrow of the Nation: A History of Sport and Physical Culture in Republican China* (Berkeley: University of California Press, 2004).

21. In the last decade of the Qing dynasty, authorities in Sichuan province promoted fangzu. Their approach, however, was admonition and did not involve the threat or exercise of state power to inspect and to punish. See Yang Xingmei and Luo Zhitian, "Jindai Zhongguoren," pp. 3, 14, 21.

22. Lin Qiumin, "Yan Xishan yu Shanxi tianzu yundong," *Guoshiguan guankan, fukan* n.s. 18 (June 1995): 130.

23. Yan Xishan, comp., *Shanxi Liuzheng sanshi huibian* (n.p. [Taiyuan]: Shanxi cunzhengchu, 1929), *xuanyan* 1a, 2a–b. For the grouping of "Three Ills," see 3.3b. The "women comprise half our population" statement is a rhetorical flourish. In a 1919 speech, Yan referred to a census report that put the male to female ratio as approximately 7 to 5. He attributed the shortage of females in part to footbinding *(Zhi-Jin zhengwu quanshu chubian* [Taipei: Yanzhai, n.d. (1960)], p. 721).

24. The "horrid sight" quote is from Yan, *Shanxi liuzheng,* 3.4a. The term "ordinary people" is from 1.4b.

25. "Jinzhi chanzu gaoshi," in Yan, *Zhi-Jin zhengwu,* p. 1523. The passage cited here recurred as a mantra in many of Yan's edicts and proclamations. See, for example, his order to the Taiyuan police bureau *(Shanxi liuzheng,* 3.78b). This notice was not dated, but from the other dated edicts I deduce that it was promulgated before April 1918. The figure of one hundred thousand copies in the first printing is in *Shanxi liuzheng,* 1.4b.

26. Yan, *Zhi-Jin zhengwu*, p. 721.

27. Ibid., pp. 717–24. *What the People Should Know (Renmin xuzhi)* is a basic text for mass education to be read to the illiterate. Written in a colloquial style, it includes a list of "don'ts" (footbinding, female infanticide, teenage marriage) and lessons on world geography, races on the globe, and unequal treaties. A revised version is appended to Shanxi cunzheng chu, comp., *Shanxi cunzheng huibian* (n.p. [Taiyuan?]: Shanxi cunzhengchu, 1928). In the preface of a second reprint dated Jan. 1919, Yan mentioned that a total of 2.7 million copies of the primer were printed (Preface, *Renmin xuzhi,* no page).

28. Yan admonished these lawmakers to promote civilization and progress upon returning to their native districts. "How can we, Shanxi people, bear to see China following the footsteps of India and Poland?" (*Zhi-Jin zhengwu*, pp. 1521–23). Outer appearance as a conduit of inner beliefs is a constant theme in Yan's orders and speeches: "The changing of outward form can orient people's hearts and minds" (*Shanxi liuzheng, xuanyan* 2b).

29. "Gexian sheli Tianzu hui jianzhang," Sept. 25, 1917, in *Shanxi liuzheng*, 2.56b–57b; cf. Shanxi cunzhengchu, comp., *Shanxi cunzheng huibian*, 1.39b–40b. The membership figure was cited in Yan's report to the president of the Republic, see *Shanxi liuzheng*, 1.4b.

30. "Xiuzheng yanjin chanzu tiaoli," in *Shanxi liuzheng*, 2.55b–56a; *Shanxi cunzheng*, 1.42b–43a. In the former source the decree is dated Nov. 29, 1916; in the latter Dec. 27, 1916. The same, undated but entitled "Yanjin chanzu tiaoli," also appears in *Zhi-Jin zhengwu*, pp. 1503–4. As early as 1899, a manifesto for the Shanghai Tianzu hui had suggested imposing a fine according to a sliding scale: the smaller the feet, the heavier the fine ("Tianzu hui chenci," in Li and Zhang, *Jindai Zhongguo*, pp. 854–56).

31. *Zhi-Jin zhengwu*, pp. 1523–24.

32. For the March 1918 order against the manufacturing and selling of wooden heels and copper bracelets, see *Shanxi liuzheng*, 3.78a; *Zhi-Jin zhengwu*, p. 1512. Some Kun-shoes, especially those sold in stores, had wooden soles. As the arched shape went out of style, the firm support of a wooden sole was no longer needed, and leather or cotton soles became common. Some Kun-shoes were also domestically made. Variations of the style remained popular unto the 1930s. One variation is the *zaoxie,* a flat shoe with a one-piece vamp construction instead of two (CFJHL: 93, 113). For a photograph of a vendor's set of arched wooden soles outlawed by Yan, see Ko, *Every Step a Lotus,* p. 85.

33. *Shanxi liuzheng*, 3.78b–79a; Yuwu zhen is in Tunliu county. Yan responded to a letter from a lawmaker in 1918 who pointed out that "The militant heroine in traditional attire dramas is always clad with [stilts that] imitate bound feet, as if unless she has bound feet she cannot represent a heroine. . . . So when the audience idolizes the heroine they also idolize her bound feet. Has it occurred to anybody that since the ancient heroine is so militant, how can she possibly have small feet? This strange phenomenon is invented by some busybody; it is not the true image of the

ancient heroine. In fact, it brings her shame." The provincial Tianzu hui scripted new operas but the dialogues proved too difficult for the actors (*Shanxi liuzheng*, 3.80a–b; *Zhi-Jin*, p. 1514). In Beijing, male actors playing female roles often wore stilts *(qiao)* to signify bound feet, and a great number of taboos surrounded the use of the stilts on stage and their storage offstage. Mirroring the decline of footbinding as a social practice, *qiao* also fell into disuse in the decades after 1902. For this fascinating history, see Huang Yufu, *Jingju, qiao he Zhongguo de xingbei guanxi, 1902– 1937* (Beijing: Sanlian shudian, 1998).

34. In the Lu'an area (Lu'an was a prefecture in the Ming and Qing; its seat is present-day Changzhi city in southern Shanxi), a good bride was one with "a tidy head and tiny feet," whereas a good husband was one who was wealthy (Wang Ji- aju, "Lu'an diqu hunsang zhidu zai Xinhai geming qianhou di biange," in *Shanxi wenshi zhiliao* [Taiyuan: Wenshi zhiliao yanjiu weiyuanhui, 1984], 7: 104).

35. *Shanxi liuzheng*, 3.79b.

36. "Tianzu diaocha biao" and "Tianzu baogao biao," in *Shanxi liuzheng*, 5.37a–38a.

37. "Xuning gexian quzhang . . . " March 13, 1919, in *Shanxi cunzheng*, 2.47a.

38. CFL: 275.

39. The hiring of female feet inspectors was stipulated in a March 19, 1919, order; in *Shanxi cunzheng* 2.47b. For the impropriety of mixing female bodies and the body politic, see *Zhi-Jin zhengwu*, p. 720.

40. *Shanxi liuzheng*, 2.57b.

41. "Nü jichayuan guize" and "Nü jichayuan fuwu guize," both Nov. 22, 1919, in *Shanxi liuzheng*, 2.57b–58b; *Zhi-Jin zhengwu*, p. 1507; *Shanxi cunzheng* 1.41a–b.

42. Both statements are in speeches by Yan. The first (Jan. 1919) is in *Zhi-Jin zhengwu*, p. 719; the second, in a public notice dated 1921, is in ibid., p. 1525; see also *Shanxi cunzheng*, 5.36a.

43. The rumors about women soldiers and fear about docility were transmitted by Yan in the 1919 speech to students; in *Zhi-Jin zhengwu*, p. 720; see also pp. 715–16. The problem of conservative local gentry was the most daunting obstacle, as Yan pointed out in repeated directives; see the ones for Shaoyang county (*Shanxi cun- zheng*, 2.49a) and Datong (*Shanxi liuzheng*, 3.81a–b). The rumors about the immu- nity of brides are related in two directives: one for Huguan county in 1923, the other for Lucheng in 1926; both are in *Shanxi cunzheng*, 2.48b–49b; and *Zhi-Jin zhengwu*, pp. 1519–20. Huguan was a particularly recalcitrant county. In 1918, Yan admon- ished the county authorities to begin the "publicity—persuasion—enforcement" process (*Shanxi liuzheng*, 3.80b), but as late as 1923 Yan lamented that "the results are negligible."

44. For Yan's polemics against early marriage, see, for example, *Xiuzheng renmin xuzhi*, 16b, appended to *Shanxi cunzheng*.

45. The three duties and the 30/70 percent stipulation are in *Zhi-Jin zhengwu*, pp. 993 and 1524, respectively.

46. *Shanxi liuzheng*, 3.79b–80a.

47. For Yan's complaints about the Tianzu hui, see *Shanxi cunzheng,* 2.48b; *Zhi-Jin zhengwu,* p. 1518. For abuses in Pinglu, see *Shanxi liuzheng,* 3.84a. For abuses in Shouyang, see *Zhi-Jin,* pp. 1520–21; *Shanxi cunzheng,* 2.49a.

48. "Quan sheng xuesheng buqu chanzu funü hui jianzhang," Aug. 29, 1918, in *Shanxi cunzheng,* 1.40b–41a; *Zhi-Jin zhengwu,* pp. 1506–7; this constitution was not included in *Shanxi liuzheng.* In a directive to county magistrates and school authorities the same day, Yan encouraged them to establish a sports club together with the Refusing to Marry club (*Shanxi cunzheng,* 2.46b; *Zhi-Jin zhengwu,* p. 1513). A badge made of paper for members in the Refusing to Marry club in Jiexiu county is in the collection of Dr. Ko Chi-sheng. On the front it says, "I won't marry a foot-bound woman." On the back a name is inscribed (Ren Shuming) with a date (Min-guo 8 [1919]). A photograph of this badge is in Ke Jisheng, *Qianzai jinlian fenghua* (Taipei: Guoli lishi bowuguan, 2003), p. 139; see also Yan's appointment letter for a feet inspector dated 1918 (139) and the receipt for a fine imposed on an "uneducated" wife Li, dated 1933 (140).

49. *Zhi-Jin zhengwu,* p. 719.

50. *Shanxi liuzheng,* 3.83a–b; Yan's warning against "empty words" is at 3.79a.

51. For the commemorations in Xiangling and the Fanshi magistrate's wife and daughter, see *Shanxi liuzheng,* 3.80a and 3.82a, respectively.

52. *Zhi-Jin zhengwu,* pp. 1524–25.

53. Ibid.

54. Ibid.

55. *Shanxi liuzheng,* 1.4b, 3.79b.

56. Ibid., 3.81b–82a. The recruitment of Yanshi female teachers is at 3.79a–b.

57. Zhou Songyao, *Chanzu* (n.p., n.d.), pp. 20–21.The subject positions of the female inspector and the footbound woman were so far apart that stories about their budding friendship were literally the stuff of fiction. In the 1936 anthology *Picking Radishes (Caifeilu),* for example, a Mrs. Meng from Tongxian told of her encounters with one female inspector from the Tianzu hui. The latter became so sympathetic to her inability to unbind that they became close friends, "sisters with different surnames" (CFL II: 59). It is hard to ascertain if this anecdote is from a woman's hand or that of a male ventriloquist. For the problems of female testimonies in this anthology, see chap. 3.

58. The resistance of the older women is in Yan's order to county authorities, May 25, 1920. He admonished the latter to focus on persuading the former so as to eradicate footbinding by the end of the year (*Shanxi liuzheng,* 3.83b–84a). The shifting focus on fangzu among women older than sixteen was mandated in an earlier notice dated Dec. 20, 1919, in *Liuzheng* 3.82b; see also its attendant announcement in which Yan addressed the women directly, in *Zhi-Jin zhengwu,* pp. 1524–25.

59. *Zhi-Jin,* p. 1518. See also repeated notices to counties in 1923, 1924, 1926 (*Shanxi cunzheng* 2.48b–49b; *Zhi-Jin,* pp. 1519–21).

60. The percentage figures are cited in Lin Qiumin, "Yan Xishan yu Shanxi tianzu yundong," pp. 141–42. The 1932–33 figures are in Yang Xingmei, "Nanjing guomin

zhengfu jinzhi funü chanzu de nuli yu chengxiao," *Lishi yanjiu* no. 3 (1998): 125. Also cited in Ryūzō Nagao, *Shina minzoku shi* (Tokyo: Kokusho kankōkai, 1973), p. 824.

61. In his 1664 edict to ban footbinding, the Kangxi emperor targeted only girls born after 1662. He did not mention the unbinding of older women. It was retracted in 1667 or 1668. The prohibition failed for political reasons: ironically the ban turned footbinding into a desirable marker of Han Chinese ethnicity. See my "The Body as Attire: The Shifting Meanings of Footbinding in Seventeenth-Century China," *Journal of Women's History* 8, no. 4 (Winter 1997): 8–27.

62. For example, on April 19, 1927, a "fangzu yundong dahui" (rally of the fangzu movement) was held in Hankou; around May, one was held in Lanzhou. Later that year a "Xihu nüzi yundong dahui" (rally of the women's movement by the West Lake) was held in Hangzhou. See *Shenbao* reports cited in CFL II: 28–31. Andrew Morris (personal communications, Sept. 1998) has noted that the organization of the Hankou rally was similar to that of a sports meeting, with departments *(gu)* handling publicity, general affairs, and publications.

63. The cloth binders had symbolic value to both a civilizing regime and the women themselves. In 1899, a plague broke out in Honolulu's Chinatown. Before burning Chinatown to the ground, American authorities forced women to unwrap their binders and burned them (Rebecca E. Karl, *Staging the World: Chinese Nationalism at the Turn of the Twentieth Century* [Durham and London: Duke University Press, 2002], p. 78). Women wove their binding cloth using a simple loom. Laurel Bossen has reported that in Yunnan, long after machine-woven textiles had replaced domestic production, "one of the last remaining handwoven products in one of the villages I visited in 1996 was the long thin cotton binding cloth that the old ladies still use to bind their tiny feet" (*Chinese Women and Rural Development: Sixty Years of Change in Lu Village, Yunnan* [Lanham, Md.: Rowman & Littlefield, Inc., 2002], p. 71). Dr. Ko Chi-sheng has reported a similar situation in Taiwan (personal communications, June 1999).

64. Stages two and three were combined later (Lin Qiumin, "Jindai Zhongguo de buchanzu yundong," p. 127). Deng, a trusted lieutenant of Feng Yuxiang, was transferred to Henan in 1928 to head up a new "fangzu chu" (Office of letting-out-feet), where he applied the same binding-cloth-based fangzu tactics. See Yang Xingmei, "Nanjing guomin zhengfu," pp. 126–27; Hong Renqing, "Minguo shiqi de quanjin chanzu yundong," *Minguo chunqiu* 6 (1996): 19.

65. For "bare-legs-tiny-feet," see "Shaanxi yanjin nüzi chanzu zhi quwen," *Shenbao,* Feb. 22, 1928; cited in Lin, "Jindai Zhongguo," p. 128. The pageant was called "bare-feet-tiny-feet" and the *Shenbao* source was dated 1927 in CFL II: 26–27. For the shoelace mount, see CFL II: 2, 31, 281; the number 25,400 is from p. 29.

66. CFL II: 27.

67. Ibid., p. 28.

68. Ibid., p. 52.

69. CFL IV: 251–52. The term *jiefang* (liberation) used in this story is different

in connotations from the *jiefang* (to unwrap [the binding cloth] and let [the foot] out) used in the fangzu discourse earlier. For contestations over the term *jiefang* in early communist discourses of the 1920s and 1930s, see Harriet Evans, "The Language of Liberation: Gender and *Jiefang* in Early Chinese Communist Party Discourse," *Intersections: Gender, History, and Culture in the Asian Context,* inaugural issue (Sept. 1998): 1–20.

70. There are two notable exceptions to the almost universal celebration of the anti-footbinding movement. Lin Weihong, in her pioneering study of the late-Qing anti-footbinding societies at the local level ("Qingji de funü buchanzu yundong"), has questioned their effectiveness in the face of severe opposition from the conservative gentry. She has also criticized their male bias, and has striven to document the involvement of elite women. But she did not illuminate the subjectivities of the women who bound their feet. Yang Xingmei ("Nanjing guomin zhengfu"), in assessing the anti-footbinding efforts of the Nanjing regime, has focused on the incentive structures that made the binding of feet reasonable to the women. This is an important paradigmatic shift.

3. THE BOUND FOOT AS ANTIQUE

1. In Tianjin Yao and his family lived at no. 58, Yiqing li, Mengmai lu (Bombay Road, Yiqing Lane). Ruth Rogaski (personal communications, Dec. 2000) has informed me that this residential area in the British Settlement was primarily for Chinese lower-middle-class families. Almost nothing is known about Yao Lingxi (courtesy names Xunqi, Dansu) in published documents other than what he revealed in *Caifeilu*. I have had the good fortune of examining a number of Yao's handwritten poems, letters, and miscellaneous manuscripts in the collection of Dr. Chi-sheng Ko, the unsurpassed authority on Yao. After the communist revolution, Yao remained active in a poetry society and wrote poems to celebrate such occasions as Women's Day (March 8) and Labor Day (May 1). His birth date (the thirtieth day of the eleventh month, 1899) is mentioned in a poem from one of his friends, Xu Zhenwu, written in 1961. The last poem by Yao is dated 1959. I thank Dr. Ko for his generosity.

2. *Tianfeng bao* was published from 1930 to 1938 and as a pictorial, *Tianfeng huabao,* from 1938 to 1939. I am grateful to Kwan Man-Bun for his help in identifying this and other Tianjin materials. A total of two volumes was planned for the sixth venture, *Caifei jinghualu,* but the second volume was never printed. I do not have circulation figures. The list price for the first volume *(Caifeilu [chubian],* 1934; cited as CFL) was $1.50 *(guobi,* national currency), which was about ten times the price of an average book. Yet it sold well enough that a reprint appeared in Jan. 1936, one month before the sequel was issued. *Caifeilu xubian* (1936; cited as CFL II) was listed at $1.50. *Caifeilu sanbian* (1936; CFL III) was priced at $1.20, and *Caifeilu sibian* (1938; CFL IV) at $1.50. *Caifei xinbian* ($3.80; CFXB) and *Caifei jinghualu* ($3.50; CFJHL) were both published in 1941.

3. Materials in the published volumes are grouped in sections: Foreword,

Colophons, "My Reactions to *Caifeilu*," Evidential Studies *(kaozheng)*, Jottings, Elegant Words, Opinions, Special Works, Snapshots, Banters, Admonitions, Misc. Notes, Humor, Appendix. There is no apparent logic to the classification, and the order is not always followed. Each individual volume of *Caifeilu* is thus similar in format to a traditional jotting or notation book *(biji)*, which contracts and expands according to the availability of materials.

4. Tao was a prolific writer agile in various genres. One essay of connoisseurship of feet shows an intimate knowledge of regional styles and local customs (CFL: 127–34). See also his poems and songs, probably composed as drinking games with friends (CFL: 100–109, 116; CFL IV: 82ff). He was rumored to have authored a million-word *Lotus History (Lianshi),* but the manuscript was burned by his wife after his death (CFL: 290–91, 355–56; CFL III: 185–88). He also authored a review article entitled "Qian-Qing de xiaoshuo yuekan," (Xiaoshuo periodicals from the bygone Qing Dynasty), published in a 1922 issue of the magazine *Youxi shijie.*

5. Zhou Ying is the pen name of Zhu Chengyu. The last surviving member of the *Caifeilu* team, he remained in Shanghai after 1949 and later retired as a shopkeeper. Unfortunately, he passed away in 2001 before I had a chance to interview him. I am grateful to Mr. Yang Shaorong for identifying his whereabouts.

6. The song is "Valley Wind" ("Gufeng"), in the "Airs of the Wei" ("Weifeng") section of the *Book of Songs.* Arthur Waley thus rendered these lines: "He who plucks greens, plucks cabbage / Does not judge by the lower parts" (*The Book of Songs,* trans. Arthur Waley [New York: Grove Press, 1996], p. 30). Scholars have concurred that the voice of this song was that of an abandoned wife, but they disagree on whether the root or the leaves of the vegetables were the more desirable parts. See the Chinese text and commentary by Wang Fuzhi in Jin Qihua, trans., *Shijing quanyi* (Jiangsu: Jiangsu guji chubanshe, 1996), pp. 76–79. The reading of *xiati* as genitals was heralded by Li Yu *(Xianqing ouji* [Shanghai: Shanghai guji chubanshe, 2000], p. 146); see also quote by Zhou Zuoren in Shuwu, ed., *Nüxing de faxian* (Beijing: Wenhua yishu chubanshe, 1990), p. 240. Both Fang Xuan and Li Yu played with the ambiguity between lewdness and canonical respectability in using the term "picking radishes."

7. For the triumph of positivist scientism in the 1920s, see D. W. Y. Kwok, *Scientism in Chinese Thought, 1900–1950* (New Haven: Yale University Press, 1962); Charlotte Furth, *Ting Wen-chiang: Science and China's New Culture* (Cambridge, Mass.: Harvard University Press, 1970); and Prasenjit Duara, *Rescuing History from the Nation: Questioning Narratives of Modern China* (Chicago: University of Chicago Press, 1995), p. 93. See also the warning in *Caifeilu* that eyes are unreliable (CFL: 9–10).

8. Each *Picking Radishes* volume, as loops of quotations, recalls Benjamin's comment that collection of quotations illustrates the infinite and regenerative seriality of language. See Susan Stewart, *On Longing: Narratives of the Miniature, the Gigantic, the Souvenir, the Collection* (Durham and London: Duke University Press, 1993), p. 156.

9. In time the *Picking Radishes* columns and anthologies shifted focus. In the beginning, more excerpts from traditional sources and scientific surveys were featured, and the writing tended to be of higher quality. Understandably, good sources ran out, and the entries became more superficial in tone and content. There were more first-person narratives, often with sexual exposé. The Lotus-Seeking Club can be seen as an effort for the editors to broaden their readership while improving the quality of coverage. In an announcement, the club invited women with bound or once-bound feet (*nü tongzhi,* female comrades) to mail in questions about the decoration and hygiene of feet, claiming that an expert, Madam Chen Jingyun, would answer them in private (CFL IV: 366). It is not known if any women did so.

10. Yao insinuated that scores of young readers of his newspaper columns did become enticed to bind (CFL IV: 343). One was an ailing male student who wanted to bind his own feet as talisman. Yao brought a physician friend to their appointment but he did not show up (CFL: 220). Another was a fifteen-year-old girl who asked for express recipes that would help shrink her feet at once to placate her itinerant father who was soon to return home. Having determined to his satisfaction that she was not an impostor, Yao wrote his friends for instructions, which he then published (CFL: 356–61). This is an extreme case of a female voice that is presented as authentic, but the very nature of the request is so incongruous with the age of disavowal that it generates its own skepticism. For a spectrum of female voices in *Caifeilu* and the problem of authenticity, see below in this chapter.

11. Playing or gaming *(youxi)* and whiling away of leisure time *(xiaoxian)* are dominant modes in the world of late Qing fiction. They figure as the raison d'être of the Suzhou-based weekly *Libailiu* (Saturday, named after the U.S. *Saturday Evening Post*), often known as the home of "Mandarin duck and butterfly" fiction, a popular form of urban entertainment. Another fiction writer, Li Baojia (1867–1906), called himself the Master of Gaming (Youxi zhuren) and founded the *Youxi bao* in 1897. In the same year, another major novelist, Wu Woyao (1866–1910), founded the *Xiaoxian bao.* See Teruo Tarumoto, *Shinmatsu shōsetsu kandan* (Kyoto: Hōritsu bunkasha, 1983), pp. 5–8, 252.

12. The miniature, as Susan Stewart reminded us, is linked to the nostalgia for childhood. The diminutive lends itself to domestication and manipulation *(On Longing,* p. 69).

13. Late Qing fiction is a mega-genre that enveloped drama and poetry and was distinguished from earlier fictional genres in the speed with which written manuscripts hit the newsstand (Kang Laixin, *Wan-Qing xiaoshuo lilun yanjiu* [Taipei: Da'an chubanshe, 1986], pp. 239–56). David Der-wei Wang has argued that the late Qing was the beginning of the literary modern in China (*Fin-de-Siècle Splendor: Repressed Modernities of Late Qing Fiction, 1849–1911* [Stanford, Calif.: Stanford University Press, 1997]).

14. Tao Anhua [Baopi], "Xiaozu juan" (Excising small feet), *Yueyue xiaoshuo* 1, no. 6 (Feb. 1907): 177–86, quote at p. 177. *Yueyue xiaoshuo* was published from 1906 to ca. 1908. In 1907, when Tao's story appeared, its editor was Wu Woyao (Taru-

moto, *Shinmatsu*, p. 13). Anhua in Hunan province, Tao's native place, became one of his courtesy names.

15. This penalty scheme, which implies that six inches was the size of a never-bound foot, is modeled after "Tianzu hui chenci," published in the first 1900 issue of *Wanguo gongbao;* cited in Li Yuning and Zhang Yufa, *Jindai Zhongguo nüquan yundong shiliao* (Taipei: Zhuanji wenxue chubanshe, 1975), pp. 854–56.

16. Life imitates fiction just as fiction imitates life. Yao Lingxi reported an official-in-waiting Xu in Hubei who apparently drafted a memorial similar to the one Tao described. It is not known which came earlier (CFL IV: 155, 171).

17. As such, "Excising Small Feet" belongs to a genre of exposé of the literati world as it was breathing its last. The definitive genre of the 1900s, this literature is represented by the more famous and much longer *Exposing the Corruptions of Officialdom (Guanchang xianxing ji)* (1903-?) by Li Baojia; *The Travels of Lao Can* (1903–4; continued 1906–7) by Liu E; and *Strange Events Witnessed in the Recent Two Decades* (1903; 1906–10) by Wu Woyao.

18. I have argued in an earlier article ("Bondage in Time: Footbinding and Fashion Theory," *Fashion Theory: The Journal of Dress, Body, & Culture* 1, no. 1 [March 1997]: 3–28) that this split between form and content, or representation and inner truth, was the result of a modern metaphysic of seeing. Timothy Mitchell has identified this split as the primary mode in which "colonizing power" operates (*Colonising Egypt* [Berkeley: University of California Press, 1991]).

19. This textual symmetry is also found in one of the earliest anti-footbinding tracts, *Quan fang jiao tushuo,* published in 1894 by a group of Presbyterians in Shanghai. According to Yao Lingxi's description, this tract comprises eighteen double leafs, each with a drawing and captions. The first nine sets depict connoisseurship subjects such as "ancient beauties," whereas the other nine deal with anti-footbinding subjects such as "the pain of footbinding" and so on (CFL: 239–40). One set, "Yaoniang chanzu," is reproduced in CFJHL. For a third example, see Jia Shen, *Zhonghua funü chanzu kao* (Beijing: Xiangshan ciyouyuan, 1925). A fourth example is Qiu Weixuan's "Chanzu kao," followed by "Tianran zu kao," in his notation book *Shuyuan zhuitan* (1897; an excerpt is reprinted in the collectanea *Xiangyan congshu,* as *Shuyuan zhuitan jielü,* in vol. 8, *juan* 3).

20. The corollary of this phenomenon of verbatim quotation of connoisseurship writings in anti-footbinding literature can be found in the titles of some anti-footbinding tracts which advertise "Studies of Footbinding *[chanzu]*"—not tianzu. A well-known example is Jia Shen's *Zhonghua funü chanzu kao;* another is Zhou Songyao's *Chanzu* [n.p., n.d.], the two earliest anti-footbinding treatises published in book form. Neither the titles nor substantive portions of the text communicate the authors' polemical intent. There are also many poems with titles like "Praises for the Beauty's Feet" or "Elegies for Footbinding" that are full of such nationalistic slogans as "natural-born limbs" or "equal rights between male and female" (CFL: 96–98).

21. On recycling history as a modern and inventive form of nostalgia, see

Madeleine Yue Dong, *Republican Beijing: The City and Its Histories* (Berkeley: University of California Press, 2003).

22. Susan Stewart has observed that fascination with antiques and exotic objects amounts to a throwback to childhood and playthings and that this fascination is similar to the impulse for collecting things, which stems from a desire to master birth and death (*On Longing*, pp. 75–76). There is, however, a crucial difference between a collection and a single antique item. In a collection, the context of origins is destroyed and all times are made synchronous to the collector's. Stewart called it the replacement of origins by classification (151). An antique object, on the other hand, "presents itself as a myth of origins" (76). It embodies a nostalgia for origins and an obsession with authenticity.

23. Judith Zeitlin, "The Petrified Heart: Obsession in Chinese Literature, Art, and Medicine," *Late Imperial China* 12, no. 1 (June 1991): 1–26.

24. These are the *Xiangyan congshu* and *Shuofu*. There are many compilations by the title of *Shuofu* through the dynasties. This particular compilation was by Wang Wenru, a late-Qing man of letters from Wuxing, who claimed to use only rare or hand-copied manuscripts from reliable collections in Jiangsu and Zhejiang. Wang's "rules of compilation" *(liyan)* are dated 1915. Fang's treatises are entitled "Fangshi wuzhong" (Five treatises of Mr. Fang), *Shuofu* (Taipei: Xinxing shuju, 1963), pp. 1241–55. They are "Xianglian pinzao" (Aesthetics of the fragrant lotus), the treatise most often cited; "Jinyuan zazuan" (Miscellaneous sayings from Jinyuan); "Guanyue cha" (The moon-circulating wine cup); "Cailian chuan" (The lotus-picking boat); and "Xiangxie pu" (High-heeled shoe chessboard). This last contains instructions for a board game that uses shoe-shaped chess pieces; it is attributed to a Song dynasty author, with extensive annotations by Fang Xuan. *Xiangxie* (literally the shoe that echoes) refers to the sound that the high heels make as a beauty walks across a hallway. The first four treatises also appear in a later collectanea: Gao Jianhua, comp., *Hongxiu tianxiangshi congshu* (Shanghai: Shanghai qunxue she, 1936), 2: 108–53. Gao is the wife of Xu Xiaotian, a commentator of Fang's treatises (CFL II: 292–96).

25. Fang Xuan, "Jinyuan zazuan," in *Xiangyan congshu*, vol. 8, *juan* 1 [n.p.: Guoxue fulunshe, 1914], p. 2072. Jinyuan is one of Fang Xuan's names.

26. Fang, "Xianglian pinzao," *Xiangyan congshu*, pp. 2069–70.

27. Ibid., p. 2067. One hundred *guihua* trees were planted on the grounds of Pingshantang during its renovation in 1736 (Zhao Zhibi, *Pingshantang tuzhi* [Kyoto: Dōhōsha, 1981], 1.4b). I am grateful to Tobie Meyer-Fong for this information. A popular destination for literati touring in the Qing, the Pingshantang was not associated with prostitutes or women-viewing in the Qianlong period (Tobie Meyer-Fong, personal communication, July 1998). This rare mentioning of a real place in Fang Xuan's work yields no conclusive evidence about his dates or veracity, but suggests that he was a post-Qianlong writer. Fang's descriptions here of the gaze from the bottom up is imitative of Li Yu (see chap. 5).

28. *Xiangyan congshu* traced the origins of Fang's works to hand-copied manuscripts in the Xu family collection in Nanling, Anhui. The Nanling Xushi collec-

tion was associated with the connoisseurship of women. Its owner, Xu Naichang (1862–1936), published the monumental *Xiao tanluanshi huike guixiu ci,* an anthology of song-lyrics by one hundred women, in 1895–96, and a sequel, *Guixiu cicao,* in 1909. They are boxed together and published under the earlier title (n.p. [Nanling]: Xiao tanluanshi, 1895–1909).

29. Fang, "Jinyuan zazuan," *Xiangyan congshu,* p. 2086.

30. See commentaries to "Jinyuan zazuan" by Xu Xiaotian, CFL II: 292–96. For citations of Fang's treatises in fragments within the *Caifeilu,* see CFL: 131; CFL II: 230, 234, 291ff; CFXB: 8.

31. Zhou Ying, editor of a section entitled "Fengfei xiantan" (Random chats on radishes), stated that his editorial principle was to seek "confirmation from ancient texts" *(duizheng guben)* for every modern practice described (e.g., female massaging her own feet; CFL II: 185). This is clearly an unattainable goal but jibes with his and Yao's posture as mimetic literati. On the lack of interiority in discourses of sexuality in Ming fiction, see Kang Zhengguo, *Chongshen fengyuejian* (Taipei: Maitian chuban, 1996), 252–53 and *passim.*

32. One such account in CFL IV, by a Zhao Yixin, is unusual in that boyhood memories of playing with a neighbor woman's feet directly led into his adult world of the here-now as he sat writing, complete with the convenient foil that his wife and daughter were taking a nap. A footbound woman who lived across the courtyard was bathing when her aunt came to visit. The woman called over for Zhao to open the gate, and he saw that the aunt also had small feet. He, too aroused to keep writing, was quite willing to be seduced by the two. The provocative encounter in the here-now has to be tamed by Yao Lingxi's announcement that this is a posthumous work (305–7). The same strategy of claiming boyhood innocence in narrating a taboo subject was used by contemporary writer Yang Yang—son of a footbound woman—who took his readers straight to the boudoir and inner worlds of women in Liuyi village (*Xiaojiao wudao: Dian-nan yige xiangcun de chanzu gushi* [Hefei: Anhui wenyi chubanshe, 2001], pp. 1–5, 37).

33. The same narrator, again claiming to transmit the experience of Yu Aitong, elaborated on how fondling the golden lotus creates pleasure for both the male and female. This pleasure is as good as, if not better than, sexual intercourse (CFL IV: 48–49).

34. A Faithful of Lotus-ism—Lianjiao xinshi—harks back to *Qingshi,* a late Ming manifesto of the cult of *qing* in which Feng Menglong vowed to establish a Qingjiao (a religion or teaching of love). Yao Lingxi's evocation of the cult of *qing,* discussed above, rings true, but this imitation seems contrived. Even as he referred to Fang Xuan and Feng Menglong, Lianjiao xinshi gave explicit expression to both male and female sexual desires that would have been unspeakable in the traditional genres Fang adhered to. The connoisseur's love of feet is construed as an instinct arising from the inside and expressed in behavior. Yao Lingxi thus described the psychological process of modern connoisseurship: "Since we love the tiny foot, of course we adore concubines with tiny feet. When love becomes extreme, it propels all kinds of rebel-

lious acts, such as disobeying mother, abandoning wife, casting away sons. Hence a love inside the psyche *[xinli shang]* becomes expressed in behavior. Other behaviors are expressions of the sex drive *[xingyu shang]*, such as sodomy. . . . This is more disgusting than biting or smelling bound feet, yet there are people who do this" (CFL: 294). At least to Yao, love of feet and sex drive are distinct instincts.

35. On the trope of the femme fatale in Ming-Qing erotic novels, see Kang, *Chongshen fengyuejian,* pp. 57–81.

36. Li, *Yuemantang riji,* cited in Daqiao Shiyu, *Hu Xueyan waizhuan,* in *Wan-Qing xiaoshuo daxi* (Taipei: Guangya chuban, 1984), *tiyao,* p. 1.

37. A reader of *Caifeilu* recalled buying a lithographed copy of *Hu Xueyan* from a book stall only to be disappointed that it was so thin and lacking in explicit description of footbinding. Yao Lingxi described one 96-page version by Daqiao Shiyu, printed in stereotype by Duotian Tailang (Tada Taro) and distributed by a Riben Aishan she (Nippon Aizen sha), none of which are "real" Japanese names (CFL IV: 34). This is probably the version on which the 1984 retypeset is based.

38. Xu Ke related that wealthy merchants in Taigu, Shanxi, favored concubines who wore jade soles in the summer, which were cool to the touch (*Qingbai leichao* [Beijing: Zhonghua shuju, 1986], p. 6210).

39. Jean Baudrillard has placed antique and exotic objects in nonfunctional systems of objects. Marginalized, they are "warm" objects associated with childhood (*The System of Objects,* trans. James Benedict [London and New York: Verso, 1996], p. 146). The function of jade soles as an opium roller does not stem from any intrinsic nature of the material; any surface would do, hence its extravagant appeal. Indeed, an imitator, a former governor of Guangdong, reportedly used the bare heels of his Guangdong attendants to hold snuff (CFL: 301). In a slightly different version the official, a *zhongtong* in Guangdong, was said to use the heels of footbound women (CFL II: 233). A contributor to *Radishes* called into question both the physical possibility and aesthetic desirability of containing fragrance in an orifice usually associated with foulness even though a perfectly bound foot should have a heel that resembles the smooth and lustrous texture of a snuff dish (CFL II: 152).

40. Some argued that the practice of drinking wine from a shoe started in Song, as evinced by a poem by Wang Shenfu, but the practice became firmly associated with Yang Tieya (CFL: 180; cf. Su Fu, *Xianggui xiewa dianlüe* [Haining Zoushi shizu youlanshi manuscript edition, 1879], p. 37). Yang once drank from a giant lotus cup at a brothel party in Suzhou, but made no mention of drinking from a shoe in his poetry (*Yang Weizhen shiji* [Hangzhou: Zhejiang guji chubanshe, 1994], p. 377). In a series of poems emulating the "Xianglian" poems of Han Wo, Yang expressed his fondness for bound feet. The last couplet from "Swing," for example, reads: "A robust wind blows, lifting the gaze to the edge of space, / A pair of upside-down golden lotus reaching to the sky" (404).

41. Yang sojourned in Suzhou in 1344–49, often working as a music teacher (Su, *Xianggui xiewa,* p. 39). The disclaimer is in Tao Zhongyi, *Chuogeng lü,* cited in Su, *Xianggui xiewa,* p. 36. The Japanese scholar Aoki Masaru has found a story of a cer-

tain Tang Fuming drinking directly from a shoe in a Tang collection of jottings. The shoe was made of cloth and sealed in wax ("Shushō shudan," in *Aoki Masaru zenshū*, vol. 8 [Tokyo: Shunjū sha, 1984], pp. 85–86).

42. Shen Defu, *Wanli yehuo bian* (n.p.: Fuli shanfang, 1827), 23.28a; cf. Ni Zan, *Qingmige quanji*, in *Yuandai zhenben wenji huikan* (Taipei: Guoli zhongyan tushuguan, 1970), p. 483. Stories about Ni's obsession with cleanliness were etched in his funerary epitaphs, and many more circulated in the late Ming and early Qing. He was said to build his toilet on stilts and line the cesspool with goose feathers that would cover feces dropping (Ni, *Qingmige*, pp. 481–84). He had the rocks and trees in his garden scrubbed and his clothes changed scores of times daily. In the eyes of the Donglin patriots Gu Xiancheng and Gao Panlong, Ni's love of physical cleanliness is sign of his moral purity and love of political tranquility (634, 668). It is no accident that Xu Ke, proponent of natural feet, cited Shen's version of the Tieya story to emphasize the unseemly nature of lotus-loving ("Tianzu kaolue," in *Tiansuke congkan*, ed. Xu Ke [Shanghai: Shangwu yinshuguan, 1914], 13a).

43. Ji Yun, *Yuewei caotang biji;* cited in CFL: 331. Yao Lingxi recounted another tale: a gang of hoodlums was drinking when a boy walked by toying with a dainty shoe. They snatched it and proceeded to drink from it. A wrinkled granny entered the scene, cursing her grandson who stole her decades-old wedding slipper. The merrymakers were so revolted that they vomited (CFL: 332).

44. The Jingdezhen kiln in Jiangxi had been making these shoe-shaped wine cups since at least the late Ming period. For an underglaze blue specimen from the second quarter of the seventeenth century, see "Wine cup in the shape of a shoe," in Wu Tung, *Earth Transformed: Chinese Ceramics in the Museum of Fine Arts, Boston* (Boston: MFA Publications, 2001), p. 142. The words *xiaoxiao jinlian fengyibei* (tiny-tiny-golden-lotus-offering-one-cup) were inscribed on the insole. I thank Alex Tunstall for bringing this to my attention.

45. CFL: 7, 12–13. Lao Xuan's theory about the origins of footbinding is also woman-centered, but is more problematic: women's "natural" inclination is to beautify themselves to win over men's love. Hence women invented footbinding just as they invented tight-lacing, waved hair, high heels, and so on (CFL: 17). His rendition of female agency: woman is the fisher; man the fish; and adornment, the hook (CFL: 20). Hence the only true woman in this heterosexuality-as-biology model is one who courts man. Lao Xuan was a teacher of English, geography, and history in Beijing who also wrote columns for *Shibao, Tuhua shijie,* and *Beiyang huabao.* An unabridged version of Lao Xuan's composite essay "Nannü" is in his *Luanyu quanshu* (Beijing: Hualing chubanshe, 1996), pp. 1–137. The historian Yang Nianqun has found Lao Xuan's historicist insistence refreshing (" 'Guoduqi' lishi de lingyimian," *Dushu* 6 [2002]: 128–35).

46. Hu Yepin, "Xiao xiancheng zhong de liangge furen," *Dongfang zazhi* 26, no. 18 (Sept. 1929): 103. In emphasizing the difficulty if not the impossibility of letting feet out, this story reverses the prevailing trend established by Tang Yisuo's *Huang Xiuqiu.*

47. In yet another example of the supplemental relationship between *Radishes* and the anti-footbinding polemics, most of the female testimonies in the anthologies are replicas of the latter. In fact, Yao Lingxi placed them in a section called "Admonitions," or anti-footbinding literature (CFL: 231–62; CFL II: 39–68; CFL III: 13–23; not in CFL IV but see 126–43; not in CFXB).

48. In the 1934 *Caifeilu* anthology, the spectrum of female voice/authorship in the "Admonitions" section was presented in three ways: Madam Axiu's "Painful History" was written in the first person and published under her name; "The Self Narration of the Binding Process by Madam Jin Suqing" was presented as oral testimony by an unnamed scribe (CFL: 258–61); "The Self Narration of the Binding Process by Madam Lin Yanmei" was attributed to her younger brother, Lin Zhangliu, who was named as the scribe (261–62). In all cases, male intervention is undeniable. I am not interested in ascertaining which is the more "authentic" female voice. Taking as a given that they came to us marked as "female," I ask questions about what this femaleness meant to the readers at the time.

49. The third narrative, as told by Madam Lin Yanmei to her younger brother, defies this stereotype in its description of a completely pliant female body. She started binding at age four but her feet grew back to an unbent albeit very narrow shape, when she unbound at age nine. Madam Lin attributed her success to a secret-formula tonic known only to her dead mother. So reversible was her binding that she called the experience "irrelevant to my body" (CFL: 262).

50. The Repentant Scholar was also a collector. He once sent Yao Lingxi a soft sock-like slipper he found in an antique market in Beiping to inquire about its use. Yao asked an elder and confirmed that prostitutes gave such coarsely made slippers to clients as souvenirs of one-night stands (CFL II: 368–70).

51. Thomas Richards, "Archive and Utopia," *Representations* 37 (Winter 1992): 104–35; quote from p. 104.

4. FROM ANCIENT TEXTS TO CURRENT CUSTOMS

1. Although erotic paintings and pictures existed, their mode of enticement is similar to that of written discourses: indirection. R. H. Van Gulik observed that "representation of woman's uncovered feet is completely taboo" in erotic prints from the Ming (*Erotic Colour Prints of the Ming Period* [Tokyo: privately published, 1951], p. 170). Nineteenth-century prints are more explicit, mirroring the growing explicitness of the textual discourse. For an eighteenth-to-nineteenth-century album of erotic paintings see *Dreams of Spring: Erotic Art in China from the Bertholet Collection* (Amsterdam: Pepin Press, 1997). For the early-Qing painter Gu Jianlong (1606–ca. 1694) and his erotic albums, see the articles by James Cahill, "Where Did the Nymph Hang?" *Kaikodo Journal* 7 (1998): 8–16; and "The Emperor's Erotica," *Kaikodo Journal* 9 (1999): 24–43.

2. Zhang Bangji, *Mozhuang manlu*, 8.5a–b, in *Qinding siku quanshu*. The PRC writer Gao Hongxing deduced from internal reference that this book was completed after 1148 (*Chanzu shi* [Shanghai: Shanghai wenyi chubanshe, 1995], p. 12). Char-

lotte Furth has called attention to the correlation between the initial spread of foot-binding and the emergence of gynecology *(fuke)* as a specialized field in the Northern Song dynasty (960–1125). In its preoccupation with the reproductive functions of the female body, the rise of Song gynecology signified a heightened medical and social attention on maternity. The maternal body, or the body parts associated with gestation, became de-eroticized, leading to a "splitting of the body of desire from the body of reproduction." The arched foot became a "fetishist signifier of woman as desirable" exactly because "it was not identified with any part of the body associated with a reproductive function" (*A Flourishing Yin: Gender in China's Medical History, 960–1665* [Berkeley: University of California Press, 1999], p. 133; for the rise of Song *fuke,* see pp. 59–93). Coincidentally, in contrast to this *fuke* assumption that the foot is an asexual organ, recent studies in cognitive science have shown that on a brain surface sensory system map, the foot and toes are located next to the genitals (Eric R. Kandel, James H. Schwartz, and Thomas M. Jessell, *Principles of Neural Science,* 3rd ed. [New York, Elsevier Science Publishing Co., 1991], p. 372). I am grateful to Suzanne Cahill for bringing this book to my attention.

3. The writer Tao Zongyi (ca. 1316–ca. 1403), for example, wrote that: "Therefore, we know that the binding of feet *[zajiao]* did not start until the Five Dynasties period (907–960). Practitioners were few before the reigns of Xining (1068–77) and Yuanfeng (1078–85) [of the northern Song emperor Shenzong]. But in the recent years everybody has been imitating it, and those who do not are ashamed"(*Chuogenglu,* 10.16a-17a, in *Qinding Siku quanshu*). Modern analyses of material cultures and gender perceptions do suggest that footbinding as a social practice was likely to have begun in the tenth century. See my *Every Step a Lotus: Shoes for Bound Feet* (Berkeley: University of California Press, 2001), chap. 1. See also Gao Shiyu's nuanced account, which argues that footbinding arose as an aesthetic ideal among court dancers during the Five Dynasties period and became a regulatory measure restricting female behavior in the southern Song ("Chanzu zaiyi," *Shixue yuekan* 2 [1999]: 20–24, 111).

4. Zhang, *Mozhuang manlu,* 8.5a–b. Although the line on six inches of succulent flesh was often cited, the rest of Han Wo's poem is almost never mentioned in the origin discourse. It reads: "Glowing, glowing, six inches of succulent flesh, / Embroidered shoe in white silk, lined in red. / Not much of a romantic, the southern dynasty son of heaven, / Yet he prefers the red lotus to green leaves" (*Quan Tangshi* [Shanghai: Shanghai guji chubanshe, 1995], p. 1719). The title of the poem, "Jizi," originally referred to clogs, a ritual footwear in antiquity, but later became a generic term for shoes. In some versions "six" *(liu)* appears as "square" *(fang),* a word almost identical in shape. The genre of "fragrant toilette" heralded by Han Wo portrays the gestures, bodies, and dress of beautiful women in the boudoir. See Kang Zhengguo, *Fengsao yu yanqing* [Zhengzhou: Henan Renmin chubanshe, 1988], pp. 239–48. The scholar Gao Wenxian argued that the *Xianglian ji* was wrongly attributed to Han Wo and that its likely author was the Jin scholar He Ning (898–955) (*Han Wo* [Taipei: Xinwenfeng, 1984], pp. 63–81).

5. The only exception was the Ming scholar Shen Defu, who cited a painting "Embroidering Shoes" depicting Empress Changsun of the Tang and a portrait of the Tang Empress/Emperor Wu Zetian as proof that Tang women did not bind their feet *(Wanli yehuo bian* [n.p.: Fuli shanfang, 1827], 23.26a).

6. Che Ruoshui, *Jiaoqi ji,* 20a, in *Qinding Siku quanshu, zibu* 10, *zajia lie* 3.

7. Hu Yinglin identified the *Runan xianxianzhuan* reference. See his *Dianqian xinlu,* in *Shaoshi shanfang bicong* (Beijing: Zhonghua shuju, 1958), p. 151.

8. For the stories of Consort Yang and the femme fatale tradition in official histories, see Fan-Pen Chen, "Problems of Chinese Historiography as Seen in the Official Records on Yang Kuei-fei," *T'ang Studies* 8–9 (1990–91): 83–96.

9. Zhou Mi attributed the Yaoniang legend to *Daoshan xinwen,* a work that is no longer extant *(Haoranzhai yatan* [Shenyang: Liaoning jiaoyu chubanshe, 2000], p. 19). The Yaoniang story, again attributed to *Daoshan xinwen,* appeared in a Yuan scholar's notation book, *Chuogenglu,* preface dated 1366 (Tao Zongyi, *Chuogenglu,* 10.16a–17a). Both Hu Yinglin and Zhao Yi mentioned that the Yaoniang legend first appeared in Zhang Bangji's notation, but it is not in the authoritative *Qinding siku quanshu* edition of *Mozhuang manlu,* nor is it in the more recent compilation, *Congshu jicheng chubian.*

10. The possible Buddhist influence has prompted the Japanese scholar Furugaki Koichi to hypothesize that footbinding was an import from "the West," or Central Asia ("Chūgoku ni okeru josei no tensoku: toku ni jissō to Sodai no kigen ni tsuite," *Chūgoku kankei ronsetsu shiliao* 29, no. 1 [1987]: p. 49). For the popularity of Buddhism in Southern Tang court and society, see Zou Jingfeng, *Nan-Tang guoshi* (Nanjing: Nanjing daxue chubanshe, 2000), pp. 141–43, and *Nan-Tang lishi yu wenhua* (Chengdu: Sichuan daxue chubanshe, 2000), pp. 110–12. For Li Yu's accomplishments in music and dance and the cultural effervescence at his court, see *Nan-Tang guoshi,* pp. 199–205 and *Nan-Tang lishi,* pp. 98–109. The Southern Tang kingdom was also known for its innovative women's fashions. High chignons, "slender jackets," and skirts with form-fitting waists were in style (Zhou Xibao, *Zhongguo gudai fushi shi* [Taipei: Nantian shuju, 1992], pp. 256–57). The look resembles that of a dancing bodhisattva found in Tang Buddhist art (see fig. 10).

11. For Yang Shen's impressive corpus, the rites controversy, and his reputation, see L. Carrington Goodrich and Choaying Fang, eds., *Dictionary of Ming Biography, 1368–1644* (New York: Columbia University Press, 1976), pp. 1531–35. For a convenient two-volume compilation of Chinese articles on Yang's life, classical scholarship, and lyrical output, see Lin Qingzhang and Jia Shunxian, comp., *Yang Shen yanjiu ziliao huibian* (Taipei: Institute of Chinese Literature and Philosophy, Academia Sinica, 1992).

12. Goodrich and Fang, *Dictionary of Ming Biography,* p. 1532.

13. Yang Shen, "Gongzu," in *Tanyuan tihu,* in *Congshu jicheng chubian,* no. 334 (Changsha: Shangwu, 1939), p. 20 [*juan* 3]. One of the scholars Yang chided was Tao Zongyi.

14. Ibid. For a summary of the theory that footbinding originated in the Qin-

Han period, see Zhao Yi, "Gongzu," in *Gaiyu congkao* (Shanghai: Shangwu, 1957), p. 656.

15. Yang, *Danqian yulu,* 11.15b, and *Danqian zonglu,* 25.15b, both in *Qinding siku quanshu, zibu* 10, *zajia lei* 2. Yang refuted the Daji story without recounting it, which suggests that it was well-known. It can be found in a Ming-dynasty encyclopedia, Wang Sanpin, *Gujin shiwu kao* (Taipei: Shangwu, 1973), 6.28b.

16. Yang, *Sheng'an quanji,* juan 75, cited in Lin and Jia, *Yang Shen yanjiu ziliao,* p. 701. Song *daoxue* learning became the Ming imperial orthodoxy in 1414 with the compilation of the *Great Collection [of commentaries] for the Five Classics and Four Books.* Yang Shen's privileging of Han learning was a reaction against this Ming orthodoxy. For intellectual and institutional contexts of this development, see Benjamin Elman, *A Cultural History of Civil Examinations in Late Imperial China* (Berkeley: University of California Press, 2000), chap. 2. He has argued that the formation of Song *daoxue* orthodoxy is primarily the work of early Ming emperors.

17. Yang, *Sheng'an waiji, juan* 26, cited in Lin and Jia, *Yang Shen yanjiu ziliao,* p. 572.

18. Yang, *Sheng'an quanji, juan* 3, cited in Lin and Jia, *Yang Shen yanjiu ziliao,* pp. 808–9. See also pp. 912–32 for the importance of natural emotions in Yang's literary theory.

19. Yang, *Danqian zhailu,* 8.13a–b; *Danqian zonglu,* 17.9a–b, 18.22a; both in *Qinding siku quanshu, zibu* 10, *zajia lei* 2.

20. Yang Shen's attitude toward footbinding is unclear. Yang and his wife Huang E were renowned composers of a genre of amorous songs called *sanqu* (free songs). In Yang's extensive *sanqu* works, I found several erotically charged references to "arched shoes" *(gongxie).* See Xie Boyang, ed., *Quan-Ming sanqu* (Ji'nan: Qilu shushe, 1994), pp. 1408, 1417. It is hard to tell, however, if Yang was using a common poetic allusion or if he was expressing his own love for the arched foot.

21. Yang, *Han zashi mixin,* in *Xiangyan congshu, ji 3, juan 2,* pp. 655–56. The title is also rendered *Zashi mixin.* Since these words are ambiguous even in Chinese, I have opted to adopt an equally inscrutable English title, *Han Footles.* The obscure word *footles* does mean "trifles," which approximates *zashi.* My act of creative translation is a tribute to Yang Shen's playfulness. This work was widely anthologized in the Ming and Qing periods, despite early and virtually universal doubts about its authenticity. For its textual history, see Lin and Jia, *Yang Shen yanjiu ziliao,* pp. 443–44. It appears that Yang Shen did not try too hard to cover his tracks. This problem did not deter many subsequent writers, such as Yu Huai discussed below, from citing it as a Han text.

22. These measurements are supposed to be in Han feet and inches, but the length of a Han foot is controversial among the philologists (see below).

23. Yu Huai cited both Maiden Ying's eight-inch foot and Han Wo's poem about a six-inch foot to argue that "women's feet before the Tang were not bent into the shape of the new moon" ("Furen xiewa kao," in *Tanji congshu,* ed. Wang Zhuo and Zhang Chao, 31.2a; Fei Xihuang's rebuttal is on 31.3a). Another scholar who cited

the "eight-inch" statement as proof of absence of footbinding is Hu Yinglin's con-temporary, Xie Zhaozhe (Zaihang; 1567–1624), *Wenhai pisha* (Shanghai: Dada tushu gongyingshe, 1935), p. 63.

24. Yang, preface to *Danqian xulu*, cited in Lin and Jia, *Yang Shen yanjiu ziliao*, p. 628.

25. For Hu Yinglin's biography and works, see Goodrich and Fang, *Dictionary of Ming Biography*, pp. 645–647.

26. Benjamin Elman, *From Philosophy to Philology: Intellectual and Social Aspects of Change in Late Imperial China* (Cambridge, Mass.: Council of East Asia Studies, Harvard University, 1984).

27. One example is Hu Yinglin's friend Shen Defu (1578–1642), who accused Hu of inconsistency and faulted him for not being comprehensive enough in his investigation of ancient texts (*Wanli yehuo bian* 23.27a–b).

28. Cited in Hu Yinglin, *Danqian xinlu*, p. 145. Yang's original is in *Danqian yulu*, 11.15a–b.

29. A 100-*juan* collection of *Yuefu shiji* was compiled in the Song dynasty (*Ciyuan* [Hong Kong: Shangwu Yinshuguan, 1987], p. 881).

30. Hu, *Danqian xinlu*, pp. 145–46. Hu's use of the term *guojiao* for leg-binding is confusing, for it was also used to denote footbinding. Leg-binding is also known as *guotui, xingteng, tengyue*. A Ming encyclopedia lists *guojiao* as a synonym of *xingteng* and *xingchan*, suggesting that it was construed as leg-binding (Yu Tingbi, *Shiwu yiming jiaozhu* [Taiyuan: Shanxi guji chubanshe, 1993], p. 194). During the Zhou dynasty, leg-binding (called *bi; xiefu*) was a form of respectable clothing fashioned by juniors in audience with their seniors, such as officials in audience with their king. In providing support for the leg muscles, it enhanced running or jumping. In modern times only peasants or soldiers used them (Wang Yuqing, *Zhong-guo fuzhuang shigang* [Taipei: Zhonghua minzu yishu wenjiao jijinhui, 1994], p. 104.

31. Hu, *Danqian xinlu*, p. 165. Besides cattail shoes, the wooden clog is another kind of footwear that women gave up after the emergence of footbinding. For its history, which began as early as Confucius's times, see Zhou Xun and Gao Chun-ming, *Zhongguo zhuantong fushi xingzhishi* (Taipei: Nantian shuju, 1998), pp. 127–32. There is, however, conflicting information on differences between male and female footwear in antiquity. Although the *Zhouli* materials suggest that they were virtu-ally identical, the *Taiping yulan*, a tenth-century compilation based on earlier sources, says: "In the past shoes for females had round toes; shoes for males had square toes. The purpose is to distinguish the sexes" (*Taiping yulan* [Taipei: Dai-hua shuju, 1977], 698.4b–5a). Hu's reading is that in the past, women could freely imitate male footwear if they so chose. But in the age of bound feet, they could not wear square toes even if they had wanted to crossdress (147).

32. According to regulations in the *Rites of Zhou (Zhouli)*, *lü*-shoes are single-soled ritual footwear. They differ from *xie*-shoes, which have raised platform soles, probably for outdoor ceremonies. In later times, *lü* became the generic name for

shoes, as attested to by Hu's notations. His investigations into female shoes are in *Danqian xinlu,* pp. 149–52; on shoes in general, pp. 152–65. These references call the reader's attention to a cultural phenomenon that has a strange resonance with footbinding. In the 148 Tang and Song tales about *lü*-shoes, about one-tenth depict shoes or shoes and garments as synecdoche of the body-self. A recurring trope: empty coffin; no trace of the bodily remains; a lone pair of shoes. There is a long tradition, then, of viewing footwear and garments as synecdoche of self. Could this account for the fetishizing of female feet and the fixation on her footwear? Can we view the bound foot as a synecdoche for the female body-self?

33. For the dating, discovery, reception, and textual history of *Zhouli,* also known as *Zhouguan* and *Zhou guanli,* see the informative chapter "Chou li" by William Boltz, in Michael Loewe, ed., *Early Chinese Texts: A Biographical Guide* (n.p.: The Society for the Study of Early China and The Institute of East Asian Studies, University of California, Berkeley, 1993), pp. 24–32. Some believed that it was authored by the Duke of Zhou. Others suspected it was a forgery by the Han scholar Liu Xin (46 B.C.E.–23 C.E.), citing the fact that this work was not known before the Former Han. Modern scholarly consensus holds that it was a genuine pre-Han text, written in the classical Chinese of late Spring and Autumn and Warring States periods (ca. sixth to third century B.C.E.). For its influence on the administrative structures of subsequent dynasties, see Charles Hucker, *A Dictionary of Official Titles in Imperial China* (Stanford, Calif.: Stanford University Press, 1985), pp. 6–7.

34. Coincidentally the original "winter office" section was lost when the *Zhouli* first became known in the mid-second-century B.C.E. The *Kaogong ji* (Records of the scrutiny of crafts) was substituted in its place, hence its structural anomalies (Boltz, "Chou li," pp. 25–26).

35. Yang, *Danqian zhailu,* 11.2b; *Danqian zonglu,* 11.18b; Hu, *Danqian xinlu,* p. 144.

36. Yang, *Danqian zhailu,* 11.2b; *Danqian zonglu,* 11.18b; Hu, *Danqian xinlu,* p. 144.

37. Hu, *Danqian xinlu,* pp. 144–45. For the names, designs, and degree of formality of these shoes, see Wang Yuqing, *Zhongguo fuzhuang,* pp. 105–7; Zhou Xibao, *Zhongguo gudai fushi,* pp. 18, 58.

38. Hu, *Danqian xinlu,* pp. 144–45.

39. Hu gave several examples suggesting that even before the advent of footbinding, in an age when male and female footwear were identical in form and shape, embroidered patterns marked the footwear as female. Hence women's leg-binders were embroidered, as were shoes (ibid., pp. 146, 147, 150).

40. Ibid., pp. 146–47. The sex of the term for the child who appreciates small feet (lit., five-foot child, *wuchi tongzi)* is ambiguous.

41. Ibid., pp. 147–48. Among the literary works that contributed to footbinding's popularity after the Yuan dynasty is the late-Ming erotic novel *Jinpingmei,* discussed in chap. 6.

42. Ibid., p. 148.

43. Ibid., p. 147. Hu hypothesized that the silk socks *(luowa)* eulogized in Tang poetry may resemble these knee-high leggings.

44. Ibid., p. 146. If one interprets the "bamboo shoots" being measured and reduced in size as the foot, then Du Mu's poem can be construed as signaling the beginning of footbinding as social practice. Conversely, if one interprets them as toes, then the poem describes slender toes being packed in socks. They are thus indicative of a cultural preference for slender feet, but not the arching of the foot. Hu's lack of a clear-cut stance was faulted by Shen Defu as "waffling" (*Wanli yehuo bian,* 23.27a–b).

45. Hu, *Danqian xinlu,* p. 149. Hu did not elaborate on the connections between printing and footbinding beyond their chronological overlap. We may speculate that both are related to the breakdown of aristocratic society. Instead of heredity, new determinants of power and new markers of wealth and status are needed. The dissemination of knowledge afforded by printing enabled the scholar-official class to dominate the bureaucracy starting in the Song. Footbinding is their form of conspicuous consumption. The problem, of course, is that such speculations are easy to make and very difficult to prove.

46. Ibid., p. 149. By Hu's own admission, he was neither the first nor the only one to subscribe to the tenth-century theory. We may recall that it started with Zhang Bangji, and was the predominant view of authors of notations in the Yuan and Ming (p. 146).

47. Yu Huai, "Furen xiewa kao," in *Tanji congshu,* ed. Wang Zhuo and Zhang Chao, 31.2b–3a. The *Tanji congshu* was first published in 1695. In late-Ming writings, urban fashion is often referred to as "dressing the human prodigy" *(fuyao).* See Lin Liyue, "Yichang yu fengjiao: Wan-Ming de fushi fengshang yu 'fuyao' yilun," *Xinshixue* 10, no. 3 (1999): 111–57; and Wu Renshu, "Mingdai pingmin fushi de liuxin fengshang yu shidafu de fanying," *Xinshixue* 10, no. 3 (1999): 55–109.

48. Zhao Yi, "Gongzu," in *Gaiyu congkao,* p. 656. Alternative reading for the third sentence: The same is true for the Luomiao ("naked Miao") and Boyi ("barbarian Bo") peoples in Yunnan and Guizhou.

49. The Manchu rulers issued prohibition edicts in 1636, 1638, and 1664. I have argued that they had the opposite effect: in making footbinding an ethnic marker, the attempted ban led to a spread of the practice among Han women during the seventeenth and eighteenth centuries. See my "The Body as Attire: The Shifting Meanings of Footbinding in Seventeenth-Century China," *Journal of Women's History* 8, no. 4 (Winter 1997): 8–27. Susan Mann has suggested that "we can plausibly assume that" in the Qianlong reign "the desirability of footbinding and the spread of women's home handicrafts in peasant households were systematically linked." *Precious Records: Women in China's Long Eighteenth Century* (Stanford, Calif.: Stanford University Press, 1997), p. 168.

50. According to Bai Ting, "Huai, the sixth-generation grandson of the [Song Neo-Confucian philosopher] Cheng Yichuan [Yi, 1033–1107] lives in Chiyang. The women in this family have kept up their tradition of not binding their feet, nor do

they pierce their ears." The implication is that other families of their standing often did. Tao Zongyi, in turn, flatly stated that "footbinding only started in the Five Dynasties period." Cited in Zhao, "Gongzu," in *Gaiyu congkao,* p. 656.

51. The discourse of footbinding in a small body of vernacular plays and songs will be taken up in chap. 5. Unfortunately, it is beyond the scope of this book to consider the wealth of information on footbinding in Ming-Qing fiction, nor can it analyze the large body of Tang and Song poetry on the allure of small feet. For poetry as a conduit of footbinding's aura, see Wang Ping, *Aching for Beauty: Footbinding in China* (Minneapolis: University of Minnesota Press, 2000). On the large number of Song poems eulogizing small feet and dainty steps as well as an analysis of the terminologies used, see Tao Jinsheng, "Geji wuji yu jinlian," in *Tang-Song nüxing yu shehui,* ed. Deng Xiaonan (Shanghai: Shanghai cishu chubanshe, 2003), pp. 365–74.

52. Zhao Yi, "Jinfeng ranzhi," in *Gaiyu congkao,* pp. 656–57.

53. Zhao Yi, "Zanhua," in *Gaiyu congkao,* pp. 657–58.

54. One significant exception is that footbinding (*nürenzu,* women's feet) appears under the "body" category in the encyclopedia *Gezhi jingyuan* compiled by Chen Yuanlong ([Shanghai: Shanghai guji chubanshe, 1992], pp. 155–56).

55. Zhao Yi, "Tuowa dengxi," in *Gaiyu congkao,* pp. 652–53. The expressions "defilement" and "obscenity" are from the notation "Zhuxue," p. 654. Zhao observed that the leg-binders fashioned by envoys and dancers from Siam to the Qing imperium are "colorful and quite lovely" (654). So perhaps the leg-binders in Chinese antiquity were just that.

56. Zhao Yi, "Zhuxue," in *Gaiyu congkao,* pp. 653–54.

57. Zhao Yi, "Furen bai," in *Gaiyu congkao,* pp. 659–60; "Guren guizuo xianglei," pp. 660–61. Zhao did not describe how people sat on low platforms. Sarah Handler has suggested that they sat with legs tucked up instead of hanging over the edge ("The Chinese Bed," in *Chinese Furniture: Selected Articles from "Orientations," 1984–1994* [Hong Kong: Orientations Magazine Ltd., 1996], p. 5). There is a large secondary literature on the history of chairs in China; see the bibliography of my *Every Step a Lotus.* A recent syncretic discussion with a good bibliography is Ke Jiahao, "Yizi yu Fojiao liuchuan zhi guanxi," *Zhongyang yanjiuyuan lishiyuyan yanjiusuo jikan* 69, no. 4 (Dec. 1998): 727–63.

58. Handler, "Chinese Bed," pp. 5, 9.

59. For the emergence of the concept of gender distinctions in the Han, see Lin Weihong, "Chastity in Chinese Eyes: Nan-Nü Yu-Pieh," *Chinese Studies* 9, no. 2 (Dec. 1991): 13–40. See also Lisa Raphals, *Sharing the Light: Representations of Women and Virtue in Early China* (Albany: State University of New York Press, 1998).

60. See my "Footbinding as Female Inscription," in *Rethinking Confucianism: Past and Present in China, Japan, Korea, and Vietnam,* ed. Benjamin Elman, John Duncan, and Herman Ooms (Los Angeles: Asia Pacific Monograph Series in International Studies, UCLA, 2002). The explanation that footbinding safeguarded female chastity was certainly known to Chinese and European readers, but no se-

rious scholar seemed to have found it a plausible or sufficient explanation. In Chinese, the argument was advanced in *Langxuanji,* a purportedly Yuan text forged in the late Ming. See Yi Shizhen, *Langxuanji,* 2.19b–20a, in *Xuejin taoyuan,* ed. Zhang Haipeng (Yangzhou: Guangling guji keyinshe, n.d.).

61. Qian Yong, "Guozu," in *Lüyuan conghua* (Taipei: Guangwen shuju, 1969), 23.15a–b.

62. This is part of Li's argument that the classic description of gendered division of labor in Chinese society, "men plow, women weave," did not become a reality until the professionalization of male agricultural labor in the late-Ming. For this argument, see his "Cong 'fufu bingzuo' dao 'nangeng nüzhi,'" *Jingjishi yanjiu* 3 (1996): 99–107. For his estimates of female textile income, see " 'Nangeng nüzhi' yu 'funu banbiantian' jiaose de xingcheng," *Jingjishi yanjiu* 3 (1997): 10–22. The economic historians Song Lizhong and Fan Jinmin have suggested that Li confused domestic division of labor with social division of labor, resulting in a muddled definition of professionalization. See their review of Li's book, *Jiangnan de zaoqi gongyehua, 1550–1850,* in *Xinshixue* 12, no. 4 (Dec. 2001): 193–205.

63. Qian also speculated that the "sharp shoes" mentioned in *Shiji* referred to dancing slippers. "Dancing slippers are red in color, with design patterns and flat soles. The front is pointy and decorated with pearls, very similar to women's shoes today" (*Lüyuan conghua,*23.14b–15a). Reference to "mean people" is on 23.16a.

64. Ko, "Footbinding as Female Inscription."

65. The writer Yang Yang interviewed an eighty-seven-year-old widower in his native village of Liuyi about boudoir rituals. The man, Mr. Zhou, recounted five sexual plays involving the naked bound foot. One was "hanging," whereby the husband untied the binding cloth and used it to hang the wife's foot from the canopy of the bed (*Xiaojiao wudao: Dian-nan yige xiangcun de chanzu gushi* [Hefei: Anhui wenyi chubanshe, 2001], pp. 48–49). But the taboo against exposed feet did not vanish in the twentieth century. When Yang was a young boy, his aunt once let him watch her wash her feet. But she muttered while unwrapping the cloth, as if casting off a spell: "They should not be seen—they are stinky and poisonous!" (*xiu dudu de, buneng kan;* 37).

5. THE EROTICS OF PLACE

1. For descriptions of the Datong style of shoes and a photograph, see my *Every Step a Lotus: Shoes for Bound Feet* (Berkeley: University of California Press, 2001), p. 114.

2. CFL: 274–75. The second half of this passage, not translated here, suggests that "in the past" refers to a time before Yan Xishan's anti-footbinding campaigns, which the author deemed successful in diminishing the prestige of footbinding. Li Hong's account has spun textual imitations. One writer from the 1930s noted that women in Datong, Suiyuan, and Baotou placed benches in front of their boudoir instead of in fair grounds (CFL II: 309–10). A similar description to Li's of the grandstand can be found in a contemporary compilation, Lu Zhengwen, Qi Fengyi, and

Nie Yuanlong, eds., *Shanxi fengsu minqing* (Taiyuan: Shanxi sheng difangzhi bianhui weiyuanhui bangongshi, 1987), p. 269.

3. Su Fu, *Xianggui xiewa dianlue* (Haining Zoushi shizu youlanshi manuscript
edition, 1879), pp. 90–91. For an almost identical description attributed to a different source, see CFL: 273. For composite descriptions of feet contests in recent publications, see Yao Jushun, *Zhongguo chanzu fengsu* (Shenyang: Liaoning daxue
chubanshe, 1991), pp. 25–26; Lin Qiumin, "Yan Shishan yu Shanxi tianzu yundong,"
Guoshiguan guankan, fukan n.s. 18 (June 1995): 129; Zhang Zhong, *Xiaojiao yu bianzi*
(Taipei: Youshi wenhua shiye gongsi, 1995), pp. 61–62. No photographic documentation for feet contests can be found, although it may well have existed. Nor
can I locate references to their existence before the nineteenth century.

4. Nagao Ryūzō, *Shina minzoku shi* (Tokyo: Kokusho kankōkai, 1973), 2:
846–47. See also p. 461 for feet contests in Gansu. Nagao, who graduated from the
Tō-A dōbun shoin (East Asian Common Culture Academy) in Shanghai in 1906,
joined the Southern Manchurian Railway Company in 1932; he resigned in 1936,
but stayed in Manchuria to continue his ethnographic research under the auspices
of the Japanese Foreign Ministry and Mantetsu. He was said to have conducted the
interviews himself; several Chinese assistants then compiled the field notes into "research reports" *(chōsa hōkoku)*. Nagao compiled the book on the basis of such reports and his own "verification" *(kōshō),* in part from textual sources ("Shina min-
zokushi hihan ippan," in appendix, p. 5). Nagao also supplied the dates of the
gatherings but did not specify his source. They are: Datong, the fifteenth day of
the eighth month; Yongping, ten days before and after Qingming; Xuanhua, twice
yearly: ten days before and after Qingming as well as three days before and after
the fifteenth of the fifth month. For similar descriptions by Chinese writers, see
CFL: 272–74; CFL II: 242–43; CFL IV: 163–64. For scenes of feet contests in fiction,
see CFL II: 194–95, 244. In these accounts, the dates for feet contests in each locale vary considerably. For Datong, the following has been suggested: the thirteenth
of the fifth month (CFL: 341), the sixth of the sixth month (CFL II: 197, 201), the
fifteenth of the eighth month (CFL: 273). It is not clear if these occurred concur-
rently or in different decades.

5. The blame for misinformation is always cast on "nonlocals" or "outsiders."
See *Xuanhua xian xinzhi* (1922), in *Zhongguo difangzhi minsu jiliao huibian, Huabei
juan* (Beijing: Shumu wenxian chubanshe, 1989), p. 135. See also Lu Zhengwen et
al., eds., *Shanxi fengsu minqing,* p. 269. Some of the towns associated with feet
contests—Yongping, Zhangjiakou, Xuanhua, and Datong, for example—were situated along established trade routes that crisscrossed northern China. They, and
others, were later linked by the Beijing-Suiyuan railroad. It is tempting to hypothesize that the culture of feet contests had spread along trade routes. But equally
plausible is the simple fact that it was more likely for reports on customs along better traveled roads to surface. For northern trade routes, see Man Bun Kwan, *The
Salt Merchants of Tianjin: State-Making and Civil Society in Late Imperial China*
(Honolulu: University of Hawaii Press, 2001), pp. 21–26.

6. "Xijiao dahui," *Dainshizhai huabao,* no. 127 (1887), no page. See also descriptions based on this lithograph in CFL II: 245. Yang Yang interviewed a seventy-year-old woman, Mrs. Luo, née Wang, who took part in a feet-washing gathering in 1948 by a spring in front of Sanjiao si, about 2 kilometers from Liuyi village. No men were present (*Xiaojiao wudao: Dian-nan yige xiangcun de chanzu gushi* [Hefei: Anhui wenyi chubanshe, 2001], pp. 114–17). The women also remembered a more public feet contest in Tonghai held on the sixteenth day of the first month, but a renowned Optimus from the contest in 1925 had just passed away when Yang managed to locate her family. So there is no conclusive evidence for the latter (111–14).

7. Su Fu, *Xianggui xiewa dianlue,* p. 90; *Xuanhua xian xinzhi* (1922), p. 135. The word *liang* (to air) is often used as a synonym of *sai* (to air), as in "liangjiao hui." The word *jia* (armor) also means "examination status," which is yet another example of the conflation of footbinding with the examination discussed in chap. 3. On the origins of confusing "armor" for "feet," Yao Lingxi cited a source published in 1912 but attributed to a writer who flourished around 1765 (CFL II: 317–18). For another explanation of the confusion, see CFL II: 316. Yao rejected this origin myth, which he had earlier helped to transmit, by arguing that the sounds of *jiao* (feet) and *jia* (armor) are too divergent in northern dialects for the confusion to occur (CFL II: 317–18).

8. CFL IV: 165–66. See also CFL II: 245–46.

9. CFL II: 193–205. Included here are some graphic descriptions of Datong footbinding customs, which almost certainly were the source for similar episodes in Feng Jicai's novella *Three-Inch Golden Lotus.* For example, professional footbinders were also expert shoemakers. Among their specialties were "plum-sole shoes" *(meihua di)* with hollow heels, which left traces of fragrant powder in the shape of blossoms (CFL II: 196–97). Another ritual was the slitting of the belly of a lamb on a girl's initial binding day and inserting both feet into the belly. The warm blood was supposed to soften the bones. After seven bedridden days, the girl would remove the binding cloth and shed one layer of skin as white as the fat *(zhi)* of a sheep (199). Binding is thus construed as a rebirth for the girl.

10. CFL II: 315.

11. CFL II: 315–26.

12. On the building of the Ping-Sui railroad, see Ling Hongxun (H. H. Ling), *Zhongguo tielu zhi* (Taipei: Changliu banyuekan she, 1954), pp. 183–86. The cargo traffic was largely one-way, with hides, grain, crystal, and coal going eastward. Tea, paper, and other products for daily use were shipped westward, but in less significant amounts. Joshua Goldstein has analyzed the northwest development project that ensued from the Ping-Sui railroad as a form of "utopic modernity" ("Getting from Here to There on the Pingsui Railroad," unpublished seminar paper, University of California at San Diego, 1994). On the impact of railroads on indigenous societies, James Zheng Gao has argued that the initial benefits of employment creation were offset later by the creation of social hierarchies and uneven development (*Meeting*

Technology's Advance: Social Change in China and Zimbabwe in the Railway Age [Westport, Conn.: Greenwood Press, 1997]). For an assessment of the economic impact, see Ralph William Huenemann, *The Dragon and the Iron Horse: The Economics of Railroads in China, 1876–1937* (Cambridge, Mass.: Harvard University Press, 1984).

13. CFL II: 315–17. Yao provided no attribution for his historical narrative. He claimed that scenes of contests from the second stage were told to him by some "old men from the past" *(gulao)*, one of his favorite tropes.

14. In his book on the history of *Wunderkammer* (cabinets of curiosity), Lawrence Weschler has described wonder as involving a "leap in rhetoric." Before the triumph of positivist certainty in the mid-1700s, wonder was a form of learning, "an intermediate, highly particular state akin to a sort of suspension of the mind that marks the end of unknowing and the beginning of knowing" (*Mr. Wilson's Cabinet of Wonder* [New York: Vintage Books, 1996], pp. 42, 89–90).

15. See n. 48 below on the geographic parameters of "Northwest": Qin (Shaanxi), Jin (Shanxi), Yan (Hebei), and Zhao (northern Shanxi and southern Hebei). As this chapter seeks to demonstrate, however, the "Northwest" (or "the south" for that matter) was less a geographic place than a cultural imaginary.

16. One such story is Pu Songling, "Zengbu xinyun qu," in *Liaozhai liqu ji* (Beijing: Guoji wenhua chubangongsi, 1999), discussed below. Another example is Mao Qiling, *Wuzong waiji,* in *Xiangyan congshu* (Shanghai: Guoxue fulun she, 1914), vol. 6, *ji* 11 *juan* 2, pp. 3001–24. For the trope of an emperor's amorous journey that afforded the pleasure of substitution for the male reader, see Kang Zhengguo, *Chongshen fengyuejian* (Taipei: Maitian chuban, 1996), pp. 182–99.

17. Li Yu, "Shouzu," in *Xianqing ouji* (Shanghai: Shanghai guji chubanshe, 2000), p. 136; emphasis mine. For a more elegant but slightly less literal translation, see Patrick Hanan, *The Invention of Li Yu* (Cambridge, Mass.: Harvard University Press, 1988), p. 68. Hanan has pointed out that Li's claims notwithstanding, he had traveled only occasionally; his first trip was not taken until 1666, when he was already a best-selling author, and took him to Beijing, Shaanxi, and Gansu. In 1668 he went to Guangzhou; 1670, Fuzhou; 1672, Hanyang; 1673, Beijing (6–7). Li Yu used the same trope of an all-seeing narrator in his novel *The Carnal Prayer Mat,* trans. Patrick Hanan (Honolulu: University of Hawaii Press, 1990), in the character of the Knave, a thief. If not for his comprehensive knowledge, gained from hovering on rooftops at night, his friend Vesperus would not have known that his natural penis was too tiny for his outsized fantasies.

18. My translation of the titles of the eight sections roughly follows that of Hanan (*Invention,* pp. 28, 196). See chap. 8 of *Invention of Li Yu* for Hanan's structural analysis of the prose *(xiaopin)* of *Xianqing ouji* and its significance to Li's corpus and literary history. Hanan has also shown that Li "used the book . . . in his quest for patronage" (196). He dispatched copies of the book to his most powerful former patrons as soon as they came off the press in late 1671, followed by letters and a visit to the capital seeking further commissions (1–6). At the same time, Li in-

tended his book for a broad literate readership, explaining that *wenren* (literatus) means "any one who can read" (199).

19. The heads and subheads of the "Feminine Beauty" section are suggestive of Li's priorities in his connoisseurship of women *(Xianqing ouji, passim)*:

I. Natural endowment *(xuanzi)*
    A. Skin
    B. Eyebrows and eyes
    C. Hands and feet
    D. Glance, gesture, and air *(taidu)*

II. Embellishments
    A. Caring for face and hair
    B. Fragrance
    C. Facial make-up

III. Attire
    A. Hair ornaments
    B. Clothing
    C. Shoes and stockings
        Appended: "On shoes and stockings for women," by Yu Huai

IV. Training and skills
    A. Literature
    B. Musical instruments
    C. Song and dance

Li's advice on desirable gait in general and binding feet in particular appear in essays B and C of section I and C of section III.

20. Li Yu, *Xianqing ouji*, p. 138, see also p. 134. More advice on how to "size up" *(xiang)* potential concubines is on pp. 132–42.

21. Ibid., p. 136. Li Yu received Miss Qiao as a gift in 1666 and Miss Wang in 1667 (Hanan, *Invention*, p. 8). For Hanan's arguments about their influence on *Xianqing ouji*, see *Invention*, pp. 29, 67.

22. One interesting example of the latter is a bundle of essays in Chu Jiaxuan's *Jianhu ji*. I have discussed one of them in an earlier essay, "Footbinding as Female Inscription," in *Rethinking Confucianism: Past and Present in China, Japan, Korea, and Vietnam*, ed. Benjamin Elman, John Duncan, and Herman Ooms (Los Angeles: Asia Pacific Monograph Series in International Studies, UCLA, 2002).

23. Hanan, *Invention*, p. 1; for Li's personae and contributions to the *xiaopin*-essay, see pp. 45–58.

24. This same attitude of "footbinding is natural" is also discernible from the early-Qing anti-footbinding edicts, as I have argued in an earlier article, "The Body as Attire: The Shifting Meanings of Footbinding in Seventeenth-Century China," *Journal of Women's History* 8, no. 4 (Winter 1997): 8–27. Here my reading of Li Yu's love of footbinding differs from that of many modern critics. Chun-shu Chang and

Shelley Hsueh-lun Chang, for example, have discerned a contradiction between Li Yu's "traditional sexist views of women"—treating them as sex objects—and his more woman-friendly views as evinced by his condemnation of Miss Carry. "Li Yu let his obsession with the beauty of tiny feet dominate in his intellectual reasoning. This is a serious contradiction in Li Yu's character and intellect" (*Crisis and Transformation in Seventeenth-Century China: Society, Culture, and Modernity in Li Yü's World* [Ann Arbor: University of Michigan Press, 1992], p. 70). This is a contradiction only to us, who start with the premise that footbinding is deplorable. This modern liberationist premise was not widely shared in Li Yu's times.

25. Li Yu, *Xianqing ouji,* p. 136.

26. Ibid., p. 134.

27. Most representative of the latter is Zhang Dai's essay "The Thin Horses of Yangzhou." See my *Teachers of the Inner Chambers: Women and Culture in Seventeenth-Century China* (Stanford, Calif.: Stanford University Press, 1994), pp. 261–63, for a translation and discussion. The courtesan of Yangzhou is a trope in Li Yu's poems, novels, and plays. See Huang Qiang's analysis in *Li Yu yanjiu* (Hangzhou: Zhejiang guji chubanshe, 1996), pp. 282–86. Using previously ignored episodes from fiction, Wang Hongtai has made an original argument that the grooming of thin horses represented a form of commodification of the late-Ming literati's sensory experiences ("Liudong yu hudong: You Ming-Qing xian chengshi shenghuo de tejing tance gongzhong changyi de kaizhan," Ph.D. diss., National Taiwan University, 1998, pp. 427–31).

28. Li Yu, "Xiewa," in *Xianqing ouji,* pp. 160–62. At the end of this essay Li appended his friend Yu Huai's essay "Furen xiewabian," which discourses on the origins of footbinding. The last paragraph of Yu's essay, radically different in tone, contains a recommendation that contrasting colors between socks and shoes would accentuate the smallness of the feet, as would shoes that contrast in color with the floor (163). Here smallness, or the optical illusion thereof, recurred as an overriding concern despite Li Yu's warnings. This paragraph is absent from Yu's essay "Furen xiewakao," in the collectanea *Tanji congshu,* published in 1695, which is otherwise identical. I suspect that the paragraph was written by Li Yu. See Wang Zhuo and Zhang Chao, eds., *Tanji congshu,* 31.1a–4b. For Li Yu's views on fashion in general, see Huang Qiang's chapter "Li Yu yu fushi wenhua," in *Li Yu yanjiu,* pp. 147–62.

29. Feng Erkang has suggested that the purpose of Wang Jingqi's trip was to seek patronage from Hu Qiheng, a provincial administrative commissioner and a protégé of Nian Gengyao in Xi'an (*Yongzheng zhuan* [Beijing: Renmin chubanshe, 1985], p. 118). "Private advisor" is an imprecise rendition of *muyou* (tent-friend), one of the several classes of personnel hired by a high-ranking official using his private coffers: *xuli, muyou, mensheng, jianü.* The *xuli* acted as intermediaries between the official and the runners. One of the jobs of the *muyou* was to supervise the *xuli.* Miyazaki Ichisada has argued that the importance of *muyou* grew during the Yongzheng reign; the secret memorial system he instituted created a paper trail that required enhanced assistance from advisors with literary and practical skills ("Shindai

no shuri to bakuyū: toku ni Yōsei chō o chūshin toshite," chap. in Tōyōshi ken-kyūkai, ed., *Yōsei jidai no kenkyū* [Kyoto: Dōhōsha, 1986], pp. 215–42).

30. An older generation of scholars tended to follow the explanation of the eminent Qing historian Meng Sen (1868–1937) that Yongzheng had to dispose of Nian because Nian knew too much about his subjugation of his brother Yinti, Kangxi's favorite son. See Meng, "Qingchu sanda yian kaoshi," in *Xinshi congkan, wai yi zhong* (Changsha: Yuelu shushe, 1986), pp. 279–330; see especially his arguments on Nian on pp. 295, 312. Fang Chao-ying's entry on Nian [Nien Keng-yao] in Arthur W. Hummel, ed., *Eminent Chinese of the Ch'ing Period* (Washington, D.C.: U.S. Government Printing Office, 1943), pp. 587–90, followed this argument. See also his entry on Wang Jingqi [Wang Ching-ch'i], pp. 812–13. Recent scholars tend to eschew a single-cause explanation. Feng Erkang, for example, has argued that Nian's arrogance, corruption, and factionalism accounted for Yongzheng's gradual change of heart (*Yongzheng zhuan,* pp. 104–20). For a brief but vivid account of Yongzheng's rage at Wang Jingqi and Nian Gengyao, see Jonathan Spence, *Treason by the Book* (New York: Viking, 2001), pp. 30–33, 40, 51–52.

31. Wang Jingqi, *Dushutang xizheng suibi* (Hong Kong: Longmen shudian, 1967). This is a facsimile copy of the 1928 typeset edition published by the Zhanggu bu (Section for Historical Documents) of the Palace Museum, Beiping. Yongzheng's handwritten comments are reproduced on page 1a following the preface. Details of the confiscation of Nian Gengyao's papers at his residence in Hangzhou are in a memorial by the two investigating officers, Fu Min and E Minda, cited in the preface by Li Wei, 1a–b. The last emperor Xuantong (personal name Puyi) vacated the palace on Nov. 5, 1924; on Nov. 20 a Commission for the Custody of the Property of the Manchu House (Qingshi shanhou weiyuanhui), headed by Li Shizeng, was established, and inspection of the palace began. In their initial inventory report, *Gugong wupin diancha baogao,* 6 vols. (Beiping: Qingshi shanhou weiyuanhui, 1925–26), there is no entry with Wang's name or the book under its present title. But item no. 1047 from the "Maoqin dian, Shangshufang" list (vol. 1, book 4, p. 114) refers to "two volumes of books" logged as "kuangyu fuzhe" (wild and stupid to the extreme). Could this be the one? The Maoqin Hall (Maoqin dian) in which the locked box was discovered is a western chamber inside the inner palace behind the Qianqing gate; it was where Yongzheng read documents, summoned ministers, and stored part of his archives. One of the committee members was Zhuang Yan; see his memoirs, *Shantang qinghua* (Taipei: National Palace Museum, 1980) for a fascinating account of the inventory-taking process. For the formation of the Palace Museum, see Hermann Köster, "The Palace Museum of Peiping," *Monumenta Serica,* vol. 2 (1936–37): 167–90. I am grateful to Susan Naquin for this reference. See also James Cahill, "Two Palace Museums: An Informal Account of Their Formation and History (*Ching Yüan Chai so-shih* IV)," *Kaikodo Journal* (Spring 2001): 30–39.

32. The story of Wang Sizhong is in "Yulin tongzhi Wang Yuanshi," *Dushutang xizheng suibi,* pp. 40a–41a; that of Zhang Pengge is in "Suining renpin," pp. 41a–

43b. Yao Lingxi was so taken with this story that he quoted it in his *Siwuxie xiaoji* (n.p., Caihua shulin, 1974), pp. 191–92. For the successful bureaucratic career of Zhang, see *Eminent Chinese of the Ch'ing Period,* pp. 49–51. He was said to be an "ardent Confucianist" who persecuted Christians in 1691 while serving as governor of Zhejiang (271). Jonathan Spence has recounted the Zhang story as told by Wang Jingqi in *Treason by the Book,* pp. 32–33.

33. This is one of those statements that cannot be proved. I say "probably" in part because the tone of Wang's letter to Nian Gengyao with six appended poems (*Xizheng suibi,* pp. 20a–22b) is solicitous if not downright obsequious. This suggests that Wang had intended to send the missives to Nian when he wrote them.

34. The ten towns are: Pingding zhou, Shouyang, Yuci, Pingyao, Jiexiu, Huozhou, Hongdong, Quwo, Anyi, Puzhou (*Dushutang xizheng suibi,* pp. 19b–20a).

35. Wang, "Buguang xiaozhuan," in ibid., pp. 5b–8b.

36. Ibid., p. 6a. The Gushe Mountain is located west of Linfen county, Shanxi, which was near Houma, where Wang met Lightning Steps. The name also appeared in the *Shanhaijing,* and Qing scholars debated if it is the same as the one mentioned in *Zhuangzi.* See *Ciyuan* (Hong Kong: Shangwu yinshuguan, 1987), p. 403.

37. Ibid., p. 6b. The titles of the three songs: "Fengguang hao" (Beautiful scenery), "Wang moulang xin buzhi" (He hasn't written), and "Moulang boxing" (He is heartless).

38. Ibid., p. 7a.

39. Wang's father, Wang Bin, was selected an Erudite in a *boxue hongci* examination of 1679 and served subsequently in the Imperial Academy and the Ministry of Revenue. Jingqi's elder brother, Jianqi (b. 1670), won a *jinshi* degree in 1709 and served as a secretary at the Ministry of Rites (*Eminent Chinese,* pp. 812–13).

40. Wang, *Dushutang xizheng suibi,* pp. 7b–8a. Ironically, Wang's spiteful remarks about southern scholars could have come from the mouth of Yongzheng, who harbored a visceral disgust toward Jiangnan scholars, especially those from Zhejiang. After he executed Wang Jingqi, in 1726 Yongzheng created a new office, Guanfeng zhengsu shi, which Spence renders "Supervisor of Public Morality," for the Province of Zhejiang (*Treason by the Book,* p. 26). Later, in 1729, similar offices were instituted in three other troublesome southern provinces, Fujian, Hunan, and Guangdong. See Yokoyama Hiroo, "Kanfū seizokushi kao," chap. in Tōyōshi kenkyūkai, *Yōsei jidai no kenkyū,* pp. 782–800.

41. Wang, "Yu Hongshicun sannü ji," in *Dushutang xizheng suibi,* pp. 8b–14b.

42. Both the terminology and definition of "pictorial cosmology" are from Jonathan Hay, "Beyond Style in the Connoisseurship and Interpretation of Chinese Painting," unpublished paper, 2002, pp. 18–20. See also his *Shitao: Painting and Modernity in Early Qing China* (Cambridge: Cambridge University Press, 2001), pp. 277–81. Hay uses "pictorial cosmology" to refer to the ordering of a painting's surface, one that shares a structural homology with social cosmologies or hierarchies. I use the term here to denote the ordering of space in a written text.

43. Wang, "Yi tuzhong suojian," *Dushutang xizheng suibi,* pp. 19b–20a.

44. Ibid., p. 20a.

45. Ibid., pp. 15a–17a. Wang included a list of names and deeds of martial prowess of a score of the other Red Rock rouge bandits. He asked Chang: "Have you heard of any lewd behavior on their parts?" and the answer was, "Never. I heard that they made a pact with each other; whoever served two husbands would be punished by the rest. The men they keep at their disposal outside their rooms and do not allow them to share a table with them." The translation for "divine-shouldered bowman" is Spence's (*Treason by the Book,* p. 32).

46. Wang, "Furen wa," in *Dushutang xizheng suibi,* p. 52a.

47. Ibid., p. 16b.

48. Wang, "Furen chanzu," in ibid., pp. 51a–52a. Wang, following a common practice in Chinese, used names of four ancient kingdoms to denote the northwestern region: Qin (Shaanxi), Jin (Shanxi), Yan (Hebei), and Zhao (northern Shanxi and southern Hebei). Here I have simplified them to three modern provinces. Both this and the "Furen wa" entry that follows are dated the twenty-sixth of the fifth month.

49. The red satin and gold style is typical of wedding shoes in the north. For a photograph of several examples, see *Every Step a Lotus,* p. 53.

50. These *liqu* circulated only in hand-copied format before the twentieth century. My primary Chinese text is a recent compilation arranged by Pu Xianming, Songling's twelfth-generation grandson, who has been collecting hand-copied manuscripts of the liqu from the Zichuan area for decades. It is published as Pu Songling, *Liaozhai liqu ji.* For reference I have consulted an earlier compilation with eleven of the titles (billed as ten in the book, which lists "Molan qu" under "Fugui shenxian"): Liu Jieping, comp., *Qingchu guci liqu xuan* (Taipei: Zhengzhong shuju, 1968). Pu wrote most of the liqu when he was in his sixties and seventies (ca. 1699–1711). For a study of the probable dates of composition, see Zou Zongliang, "Qianyan," in Pu, *Liaozhai liqu ji,* pp. 5–9. The plots of seven of the liqu are adopted from *Liaozhai zhiyi* tales. For titles, see Zou, "Qianyan," p. 10. For a pioneer study of the tunes and structures of the fifteen liqu, see Fujita Yuken, "Ryōsai zōkyoku kō," *Geibun kenkyū* no. 18 (1964): 29–43. See also an analysis of one play, "Rang duzhou," by Zhou Yibai, *Zhongguo xiju shi* (Shanghai: Zhonghua shuju, 1953), 3: 491–93.

51. Pu Songling, *Liaozhai liqu ji,* p. 903. All of the songs in the play are set to the same tune, "shua haier," which has eight lines. Only seven are translated here; the first line reads: "Your Majesty, your humble servant reports:". Fujita Yuken has argued that among the fifteen liqu "Zengbu xingyun qu" most resembles a novel. The use of "shua haier," a tune in vogue at the time, and colloquialisms allowed Pu to highlight the humanness of the characters and the richness of their mundane life ("Ryōsai zōkyoku," pp. 41–42).

52. Pu, *Liaozhai liqu ji,* p. 964.

53. Ibid., pp. 936, 959. Following a trope, Fo Dongxin is said to be a native of Yangzhou, daughter of a military officer, who was sold to the brothel when orphaned at age eight (945).

54. Ibid., p. 936. For Fo Dongxin singing *Kunqu,* see p. 1019. Other examples of the expression "half-a-*zha*" are on pp. 455, 483, 487, 524.

55. Purple cotton cloth *(zihuabu)* is a light reddish brown fabric made from purple cotton. Although coarse, it was popular and commanded prices double the standard varieties. See Nishijima Sadao, "The Formation of the Early Chinese Cotton Industry," in *State and Society in China: Japanese Perspectives on Ming-Qing Social and Economic History,* ed. Linda Grove and Christian Daniels (Tokyo: University of Tokyo Press, 1984), p. 54.

56. Pu, *Liaozhai liqu ji,* pp. 954–55. The fine gradation of domestic women with bound feet is expressed or sustained by way of fabric, color, and design of their shoes in the novel *Hu Xueyan waizhuan* discussed in chap. 3. The fabric and design of male clothing also marks their status distinctions. See a graphic scene of Zhengde and Dragon Wang dueling while disrobing in the bathhouse on pp. 1004–5. Without revealing his dragon robe, Zhengde trumped Dragon in displaying an undergarment made of pearls.

57. Pu, *Liaozhai liqu ji,* p. 557.

58. Ibid., pp. 618, 620.

59. Ibid., p. 648.

60. Ibid., p. 642. Zhang's mortal wife, Madame Fang, is repeatedly signified by her handiwork. In a later scene, the virtuous wife sat up with her son into the night. While he studied, she did fine embroidery using as many as fifteen strands of silk floss (659).

61. Ibid., p. 930.

62. "Zhang Hongjian," in Pu Songling, *Liaozhai zhiyi* (Ji'nan: Qilu shushe, 1981), pp. 1789–1803; the term *liren* is on p. 1791. This is a facsimile reprint of the "Ershisi juan chaoben" (24-fascicle manuscript). For a comparison of this manuscript with two others, the earlier "Zhuxue zhai chaoben" and Pu's own manuscript, see the appendix to Liu Jieping, *Pu Liuxian Songling xiansheng nianpu* (Taipei: Zhonghua shuju, 1985), pp. 193–211. For a history of the publication and reception of *Liaozhai zhiyi* during the Qing dynasty, see Judith T. Zeitlin, *Historian of the Strange: Pu Songling and the Chinese Classical Tale* (Stanford, Calif.: Stanford University Press, 1993), pp. 16–42. He Manzi has compared Pu Songling's tales and seven subsequent liqu that were based on the same plots, including the Zhang Hongjian story. He concluded that Pu "in his old age was leaning more toward the common people" (*Pu Songling yu Liaozhai zhiyi* [Shanghai: Shanghai chuban gongsi, 1955], pp. 41–108; quote from p. 71).

63. Zeitlin, *Historian of the Strange,* p. 125; emphases in the original.

64. Both the Liaozhai tales and the vernacular plays depict footbinding as a sign of natural femininity and as part of the female toilette. There are two salient differences, however. The plays abound in ridicule of big or poorly bound feet (see below in the chapter), which is absent in the tales. The tales, in turn, include several allusions to the explicit eroticism of bound feet, which is absent in the plays. In a provocative tale, "Zhinü" (The weaving maid), a pair of bound feet was called *xiati,*

which usually means "genitals" (*Liaozhai zhiyi*, p. 1783). The bound feet were conflated with private parts akin to genitals, the exposure of which brought shame and embarrassment (1077). In the tale "Yanzhi" (Rouge), the erotic charge of feet was extended to embroidered slippers, which were called *xiewu* (lewd object) and were construed as a love token (2004).

65. "Shang Sanguan," in Pu, *Liaozhai zhiyi*, pp. 571–76; quote from p. 574. "Hansen qu," in Pu, *Liaozhai liqu*, pp. 271–343; quote from p. 295.

66. Ibid., p. 351. "Qinse le" was considered so erotic that it was missing from many of the earlier editions of *Liaozhai liqu*, such as Liu Jieping's edited volume cited above. A copy is preserved at Keiō University and was studied by Fujita Yuken. The version reprinted in *Liaozhai liqu ji* is based on this manuscript and another copy collected by a "Mr. Sheng Wai" (35–36). Judith Zeitlin has discussed a colophon by fellow *liqu*-writer Gao Heng (*jinshi* 1643) who defended its propriety (*Historian of the Strange*, p. 224 n.7). "Qinse le" was reprinted as an erotic ballad with a new preface and afterword under the title of "Guiyan qinsheng," attributed to a Gu Gaoyang Xishan Qiaozi. I have consulted two versions of the latter: *Zhongguo guyan xipin congkan,* vol. [ji] 1, book [ze] 3 (n.p., n.d.), pp. 1–38, which appears to be a facsimile of a typeset edition compiled by none other than Yao Lingxi, with the title "Weike zhenpin congchuan" in the margins; and "Guiyan qinsheng," in Inoue Kōbai, *Shina fūzoku* (Shanghai: Nihondō shoten, 1920–21), 1: 205–30. The text of the two versions is similar, but the latter includes marginal comments in the top margins. "Guiyan qinsheng" differs only slightly from "Qinse le." An advertisement of "recently published books" by Tianjin shuju appended to CFL II identifies the compiler of *Weike zhenpin congchuan* as Yao Lingxi. A friend of Yao Lingxi by the name of Ya Fei discerned that "Guiyan qinsheng" (Romance of the boudoir in Shaanxi sounds) is a misnomer because the ballad is full of Shandong dialect and customs. See CFJHL: 144.

67. Pu, *Liaozhai liqu ji*, pp. 914–15. In another play, a prostitute Lanfang sits side by side with a patron and flirts with him by "secretly kicking her gilded lilies" under her skirt (542), as if anticipating his fondling.

68. Ibid., pp. 348, 351–52.

69. Both the bride and groom in "Pleasures of Marriage" are said to be "zaguo" or "zagua" (350). For similar usage in other vernacular plays, see ibid., pp. 455, 906, 936, 997, 1028. "Zagua" can also refer to the renovation or fixing-up of a house (214). The bride's song on the morning after continues: "Suddenly remembering the wedding kerchief, / I look for it on and off the bed. / But look he is holding it in his hand, / When I try to snatch it he slips away with a smile." The "wedding kerchief" (*xijuan; xihong*) is a piece of silk stained with virginal blood. Here Pu Songling exploits the erotic potential of footbinding-as-toilette, using the bride's dishevelment as invitation to the reader to imagine her deflowering.

70. Ibid., pp. 55, 57. "Gufu qu" is based on a Liaozhai tale, "Shanhu." The same scene in the tale is brief: "Every morning she pays respect to [her mother-in-law] in brilliant make-up and attire *[jingzhuang]*." Upon being reprimanded as "pro-

moting licentiousness," she "destroys her decoration *[weizhuang]* before entering" (Pu, *Liaozhai zhiyi,* p. 2067). See Zeitlin, *Historian of the Strange,* pp. 127–31, for a discussion of this tale in the context of Pu Songling's treatment of the shrew, a stock figure in Ming-Qing literature.

71. Pu, *Liaozhai liqu ji,* p. 472. *Lie* carries a similar, but more violent, connotation in another play, "Fan yanyang." To punish a loan shark, a magistrate orders a "ripping" of his clothes, which promptly disintegrate into strips upon strips of fine silk *(basi duan).* Workers at the yamen (government office) vied to take them home to be restitched into purses for tobacco (192).

72. Unlike imperial silk, there was no standard width for a bolt of cotton. Ye Mengzhu, a keen observer of fashion in the early Qing wrote of three common kinds of everyday cotton fabrics: *biaobu, zhongji,* and *xiaobu.* The narrowest and shortest was *xiaobu,* handwoven on a narrow loom, which was over one foot wide and sixteen feet long. See Nakayama Mio, "Shindai zenki Kōnan no bukka dōkō," *Tōyōshi kenkyū* 37, no. 4 (March 1979): 88–90. See also Nishijima, "Formation of the Early Chinese Cotton Industry," pp. 53–54; and Zhou Xun and Gao Chunming, *Zhongguo yiguan fushi dacidian* (Shanghai: Shanghai cishu chubanshe, 1996), pp. 524–25. Extant samples of nineteenth- and twentieth-century binding cloth are generally 4–5 inches wide and several feet long. Some are torn from a larger piece of fabric, as described here. Others are woven on a very narrow loom and are stored rolled up like a roll of bandage. For a photograph of the latter, see my *Every Step a Lotus,* p. 55.

73. Pu, *Liaozhai liqu ji,* pp. 212–13. *Duan* is a measure for the length of a bolt of fabric, but its exact length varies with time and context. In its early textual appearance, in *Xiao erya* and *Zuozhuan,* it means 2 *zhang* (1 *zhang* is 10 *chi,* or feet). But in other usage *duan* may be 1.6, 5, 6, or 8 *zhang.* The absolute length of one *zhang* also varied with time. A *duan* is also often understood to refer specifically to a bolt of cotton fabric 6 *zhang* long; a bolt of silk fabric was called *pi,* which was 4 *zhang* long. But *pi* and *duan* came to be used interchangeably for all fabrics (Zhou Xun and Gao Chunming, *Zhongguo yiguan,* p. 28). See also *Ciyuan,* p. 1271, and the editor's annotation to the passage cited here, in *Liaozhai liqu ji,* p. 218 n. 11. Although *chitou* could refer to fabric of all fibers, from a later description we know that it refers to silk here. See also Zhou Xun and Gao Chunming, *Zhongguo yiguan,* pp. 28–29.

74. Pu, *Liaozhai liqu ji,* pp. 212–13. Elder Sister, a widow, had returned to her natal family to care for her ailing stepmother after her son married. Although her husband left her meager properties, her widow status might have prompted her to be more humble and resistant to excessive gifts than her mother.

75. Ibid., p. 213. Tenants or renters are called *kejiazi* (guest people) and their wives, *kejia laopozi* (guest granny) or *kejia xifuzi* (guest daughter-in-law) in Shandong dialect. The women helped with cooking or served as personal attendants (183, 208). Due to regional variations and year-by-year fluctuations, it is difficult to ascertain the purchasing power of 200 coppers *(qian).* For a discussion of this problem, see Nakayama, "Shindai zenki Kōnan no bukka."

76. In contrast, the exchange of betrothal gifts was a formal patriarch-to-patriarch affair. Not surprisingly, in material terms that was also a lopsided exchange between the Fan and the Qiu families. The former sent a pair of boots, a hat, a blue robe, an embroidered wall hanging, a goat, a jug of wine, forty trays of gifts, and sixteen bowls of cooked dishes. The Qius' return gift consisted of sixteen trays of gifts (Pu, *Liaozhai liqu ji,* pp. 207). The garments are all male bureaucratic attire.

77. Status anxiety in the late-Ming and early-Qing is a well-studied subject, and I will not present full references here. In general, social historians have tended to treat "status" as essentialized social grouping—literati, merchant, artisan, peasant, and so on. For bibliographic references see Timothy Brook, *Confusions of Pleasure: Commerce and Culture in Ming China* (Berkeley: University of California Press, 1998). Art historians have captured the fluidities of an environment in which the very definition of a status group was being constantly questioned and reformulated. See Hay, *Shitao,* especially pp. 26–56, 200–209, for the fluidity of the category of *shi* or literati as a social group and as a painting style. See also Craig Clunas, *Superfluous Things: Material Culture and Social Status in Early Modern China* (Urbana and Chicago: University of Illinois Press, 1991), and *Pictures and Visuality in Early Modern China* (Princeton: Princeton University Press, 1997).

78. The term "social skin" is Terence Turner's; see his "The Social Skin," in *Not Work Alone: A Cross-Cultural View of Activities Superfluous to Survival,* ed. Jeremy Cherfas and Roger Lewin (Beverly Hills: Sage Publications, 1980), pp. 112–40. Turner has also made an insightful observation that as a "symbolic medium" that plays a key role in constructing the individual as a social actor or cultural subject, bodily adornment is comparable to language (136–37). The concept of an individual as a socialized self shifts attention from the inside of one's body as the seat of "true self" to the outside. I owe my understanding of the full analytic power of "social skin" to Alfred Gell, *Wrapping in Images: Tattooing in Polynesia* (Oxford: Clarendon Press, 1996), especially pp. 23–28. On "status sense," see Kishimoto Mio, "Minshin jidai no mibun kankaku," in *Min-Shin jidaishi no kihon mondai,* ed. Mori Masao (Tokyo: Kyūko shoin, 1997), pp. 403–28. Rooted in a scholastic tradition of legal history, the Japanese term *mibun* is broader than "status" and encompasses social position or identity either by birth or ascribed.

79. These expressions appear, in order of discussion here, in Pu, *Liaozhai liqu ji,* pp. 519, 956, 953, 518, 404. See p. 456 for a related expression, "a pair of your shoes takes up two feet worth of silk." The gendered unevenness of posing in the vernacular plays is evinced by the disguised emperor Zhengde in "Song of Blissful Clouds." His shabby military attire in cotton surely caused him grief, but his faux pas were mostly verbal and behavioral. Ultimately, he always managed to bail himself out of a sticky situation by throwing a handful of gold or pearls at his adversaries. In contrast, the women taunted for having poorly bound feet had no recourse. Women either had perfect feet or ugly feet in these plays. The trope of laughing at big feet is common in three other eighteenth-century collections of popular songs: *Nichang xupu, Baixue yiyin,* and *Zhui baiqiu.* See Li Xiaoti's analysis in "Shiba shiji

Zhongguo shehui zhongde qingyu yu shenti: Lijiao shijie yiwai de jianianhuahui,"
Bulletin of the Institute of History and Philology, Academia Sinica 72, part 3 (2001):
570–73.

80. Pu, *Liaozhai liqu ji*, p. 557. Earlier in the play it was mentioned that the annual salary for the chef was eight *shi* of grain. The trope of a greedy cook who pil-
fered the master's pantry is a familiar one. The meaning of *sanling* (three-twill
damask) is unclear. One possibility is a twill damask fabric thrice-dyed into a deep
red. For thrice-dyeing *(sanran)*, see Zhou Xun and Gao Chunming, *Zhongguo
yiguan,* pp. 545–46; see also p. 438 (under "luodai") for a photograph of a sash for
skirts. For leg sashes, see Ke Jisheng [Ko Chi-sheng], *Sancun jinlian* (Taipei: Chanye
qingbao zazhishe, 1995), pp. 68–69. A pair of red silk leg sashes in the author's collection measures 1⅞ inches wide and 34½ inches long, plus 5-inch tassels on each end.

81. This song from Wuxi was collected in the early twentieth century by Gu Jiegang and his associates. I use a convenient recent reprint: *Wuge; Wuge xiaoshi* (Nanjing: Jiangsu guji, 1999), pp. 487–88. For a variation on the trope of a fashionable
pilgrim, see "Ci'er shan," in Huaguangsheng, ed., *Baixue yiyin,* in *Ming-Qing minge
shidiao ji* (Shanghai: Shanghai guji chubanshe, 1987), 2: 731–32. The compilation
of *Baixue yiyin* was finished by 1804, but the volume was not published until 1828
(Zhou Yibai, *Zhongguo xiju shi,* p. 493; Li Xiaoti, "Shiba shiji," p. 549).

82. Wu tunes are often thought of as tunes from Suzhou, but in fact circulated
in a larger area in the Yangzi delta in the provinces of Jiangsu and Zhejiang. Feng
Menglong began to collect Wu "mountain songs" around 1596. For an introduction, see the preface by Guan Dedong, in Feng Menglong, ed., *Shan'ge,* in *Ming-
Qing minge shidiao ji* (Shanghai: Shanghai guji chubanshe, 1987), 1: 247–67. See
also Ōki Yasushi's informative study, *Fū Bō Ryu 'Sanka' no kenkyū* (Tokyo: Keisō
shobo, 2003).

83. Feng Menglong, *Shan'ge,* pp. 418–24. I am grateful to Ōki Yasushi for bringing this play to my attention.

6. CINDERELLA'S DREAMS

1. The earliest extant socks for both sexes are from the Western Han period.
The shape and fabric of socks from subsequent dynasties may diverge, but the basic construction has not changed. For an illustrated history of socks, see Zhou Xun
and Gao Chunming, *Zhongguo lidai funü zhuangshi* (Shanghai: Xuelin chubanshe
and Hong Kong: Sanlian shudian, 1997), pp. 290–93. In contrast, socks from the
early twentieth century are three-dimensional and more form-fitting (see fig. 8).

2. The state and whereabouts of the woman's bodily remains are unknown. The
binding cloth is now flat and resembles the socks in shape. It is 21.5 cm (8.6 inches)
long from the tip to the heel area. Understandably, I was not allowed to unwrap
the bundle to examine its inner layers. Although the shoes and socks are typical,
the binding cloth is curious and raises a number of questions about its use. The
knot, for example, seems too bulky to fit under the narrow shoes. Is this style of
binding feet reserved for dressing a corpse? These rare artifacts deserve further re-

search. A chemical analysis of the composition and dating had yet to be performed when I visited the museum in June 2003. I thank Dr. Zhao Feng, vice director of the museum and a foremost authority of ancient textiles in China, for his hospitality and generous assistance.

3. I have discussed the problems of knowing others' pain and sympathy in an early article, "The Subject of Pain," now collected in *From the Late Ming to the Late Qing: Dynastic Decline and Cultural Innovation,* ed. David Wang and Wei Shang (Stanford, Calif.: Stanford University Press, forthcoming). For the poetry of the Ming gentrywoman Shen Yixiu (1590–1635) and her daughters on the subjects of body and feet, see my *Teachers of the Inner Chambers: Women and Culture in Seventeenth-Century China* (Stanford, Calif.: Stanford University Press, 1994), pp. 167–71. For the works of other women poets, see *Women Writers of Traditional China: An Anthology of Poetry and Criticism,* ed. Kang-i Sun Chang and Haun Saussy (Stanford, Calif.: Stanford University Press, 1999). Although often vivid and poignant in conveying female sentiments and everyday life, these poems are by and large silent on women's bodily sensations and subjective feelings of footbinding.

4. See a similar pair from a Yuan tomb excavated in Wuxi, Jiangsu, in Zhou and Gao, *Zhongguo lidai funü zhuangshi,* p. 305.

5. *Gongxie* is an ambiguous term; in itself it does not indicate the design or shape of the shoes. For an array of textual references to the term from the Five Dynasties to the Qing, see Zhou Xun and Gao Chunming, *Zhongguo yiguan fushi dacidian* (Shanghai: Shanghai cishu chubanshe, 1996), p. 299. Similarly, "*phoenix-head*" is a generic name. For the wide-ranging varieties of "*fengtou xie,*" see Zhou and Gao, p. 298.

6. Jiangxisheng wenwu gongzuodui, "Jiangxi Nancheng Ming Yixuanwang Zhu Yiyin fufu hezang mu," *Wenwu* 8 (1982): 20, 22. The length and width of the shoes are not given in the archaeological report, but are furnished by the costume historians Zhou Xun and Gao Chunming (*Zhongguo lidai funü zhuangshi,* p. 298). For evolution of high-heeled footwear, see also their *Zhongguo chuantong fuzhuang xingzhi shi* (Taipei: Nantian shuju, 1998), pp. 125–26. Focusing on the height of the platform soles, they have suggested that Madam Sun's shoes from the Jiangxi tomb belong to the emergent fad of high-heeled shoes in the late Ming. Focusing on the physiology of the foot and way of binding, I opt to classify them with the flat-soled footwear tradition from the Song and Yuan.

7. Yang Shen, *Han zashi mixin,* in *Xiangyan congshu* (Shanghai: Guoxue fulunshe, 1914), p. 652. The anecdote about "Quick-mounting" in Song Lizong's court is from *Songshi* (Dynastic history of the Song), *Wuxingzhi;* cited in Gao Shiyu, "Chanzu zaiyi," *Shixue yuekan* 2 (1999): 23; and Su Fu, *Xianggui xiewa dianlüe,* p. 45.

8. Fujiansheng bowuguan, ed., *Fuzhou Nan-Song Huang Sheng mu* (Beijing: Wenwu chubanshe, 1982), p. 19. See also Fujiansheng bowuguan, "Fuzhou shi beijiao Nan-Song mu qingli jianbao," *Wenwu* 7 (1977): 1–17. Quanzhou silk was exported to Persia and Southeast Asia. Huang Sheng's shoes were made of fancy gauze woven with three-ply warps; two pairs were edged with gold-printed plum motifs.

Her six pairs of shoes are 13.3–14 cm (5.3–5.6 inches) long and 4.5–5 cm (1.8–2 inches) wide. The plain silk socks are all lined, measuring 16.4 cm (6.6 inches) from toe to heel, with shafts 16 cm (6.4 inches) tall. For Huang Sheng's shoes, see also my *Every Step a Lotus: Shoes for Bound Feet* (Berkeley: University of California Press, 2001), pp. 21–22. A modern photograph of the bare feet of a Mrs. Wu Han shows her toes curling upward (Howard S. Levy, *Chinese Footbinding: The History of a Curious Erotic Custom* [Taipei: Nantian shuju, 1984], p. 256).

9. Jiangxisheng wenwu kaogu yanjiusuo and De'an xian bowuguan, "Jiangxi De'an Nan-Song Zhoushi mu qingli jianbao," *Wenwu* 9 (1990): 1–13. The shoes are 18–22 cm (7.2–8.8 inches) long and 5–6 cm (2–2.4 inches) wide. The socks are all made of golden-yellow gauze; three pairs are knee-high (40 cm or 16 inches from heel to top), two are medium-length (20.5 cm or 8.2 inches), and two are short (17 cm or 6.8 inches). The binding cloth is 200 cm (6 ft. 8 in.) long and 10 cm (4 inches) wide.

10. There are two differences in the footwear fashion of the two ladies. Although their binding cloths are equal in length, Madam Huang's are ribbon-like, only 0.9 cm (0.4 inches) wide, whereas Madam Zhou's are 10 cm (4 inches) wide, a tad wider than the usual modern ones. This could be due to Huang's younger age, as young girls did tend to use narrower binding cloths in the modern period. A second difference is that Huang was buried with two styles of decorated silk leg-binders (Fujiansheng bowuguan, "Fuzhou shi beijiao Nan-Song mu qingli jianbao," *Wenwu* 7 [1977]: 9). There is no counterpart in Madam Zhou's tomb.

11. Yu Huai, "Furen xiewakao," in *Tanji congshu,* ed. Wang Zhuo and Zhang Chao (copy in Naikaku bunko), 31.2b–3a.

12. Liu Tingji, *Zaiyuan zazhi,* in *Jindai Zhongguo shiliao congkan,* ed. Shen Yunlong (Taipei: Wenhai chubanshe, 1969), 4.21a. The description begins with naming three types of fashionable footwear: "Female footwear include *gongxie* [arched or bow-shaped shoes], embroidered shoes, and phoenix-head shoes." It is not clear from Chinese syntax if all three types of footwear or only *gongxie* had high heels. Liu also wrote that after women adopted high heels, they abandoned socks with soles in favor of socks without soles. This is not accurate. Textual and material evidence show little correlation between the soles of socks and the heels of shoes.

13. Yu Huai, *Banqiao zaji,* 3.7a, in *Xiangyan congshu* (Shanghai: Guoxue fulunshe, 1914), p. 3665. Both *gong* and *wan* were used to describe feet before the sixteenth century, but the use of each adjective alone does not automatically imply a curved arch. For a similar use of *gongwan* as Yu Huai, see Xie Zaihang, *Wenhai pisha* (Shanghai: Dada tushu gongyingshe, 1935; preface dated 1609), p. 63. Xie stated: "The ancients did not curve their arches, but it does not mean that they did not bind feet."

14. In the myths of Consort Pan and Yaoniang, the golden lotus was a prop for palace dancers and retains traces of its Buddhist origins. In Song poetry, it became a euphemism for desirable women's feet or footsteps. See "jinlian" entry, Ye Dabing and Qian Jinbo, *Zhongguo xielü wenhua cidian* (Shanghai: Shanghai sanlian, 2001), p. 25.

15. Ye Mengzhu, *Yueshibian, juan* 8, cited in ibid., pp. 24–25.

16. Tian Yiheng, *Liuqing rizha* (Shanghai: Shanghai guji chubanshe, 1985; facsimile of 1609 edition), 20.6a–b. Most intriguing is Tian's description of the fashionable footwear in Guangdong, a province on the far southern edge of the empire: "Nowadays women in Guangdong wear wooden clogs even for bright sunny days and broad daylight." In a bit of doggerel Tian made it clear that the feet of these women were bare and that they did not bind their feet. He wrote: "Not that they lack the support of a lotus, / But they detest the shrinking of [the foot into] the bud of a bamboo shoot" (*Liuqing rizha,* 20.7a–b).

17. Gao Jiangcun, *Tianlu shiyu,* cited in Su Fu, *Xianggui xiewa,* xia 12b [p. 68]. In the nineteenth century, each region had also developed distinct styles for embroidered slippers. See my *Every Step a Lotus,* chap. 4. There is insufficient material evidence to ascertain the beginnings of these regional diversities. Wang's and Gao's remarks suggest that a broad north-south difference was evident by the late seventeenth century.

18. *Xuehong xiaoji,* cited in Su Fu, *Xianggui xiewa,* shang 11a–b [pp. 23–24]. This description is not in the *Xiangyan congshu* version of *Xuehong xiaoji* (ca. 1787) and its sequel, both attributed to Zhuquan jushi, and is likely to have been added later. Complaints about the feet of Yangzhou prostitutes are particularly common. In *Fengyuemeng* (preface dated 1848), a courtesan novel set in Yangzhou, all the women wore wooden soles. One had feet over six inches long; her soles were extra-small but the vamps were roomy. Her shoes were forcibly strapped onto her feet by the shoelaces (Cao Wugang and Hanshang mengren, *Wan-Qing yanqing xiaoshuo congshu—Meilan jiahua; Fengyuemeng* [Nanchang: Baihuazhou wenyi chubanshe, 1993], pp. 221–24).

19. For an analysis of this dynamic in the field of the civil service exam, see Benjamin Elman, *A Cultural History of Civil Examinations in Late Imperial China* (Berkeley: University of California Press, 2000).

20. Xue Ji, *Xue Ji yian,* 8.296, in *Tushu jicheng yibu quanlu, xin jiaoben* (Taipei: Xinwenfeng chuban gongsi, n.d. [1979]). I thank Charlotte Furth for her help with information on Xue Ji.

21. *Jujia biyong shilei* was first compiled during the reign of Shizu (r. 1260–94) of the Yuan dynasty. I have compared the Ming Neifu edition in the Naikaku bunko, the microfilmed version of the Ming Silijian edition in the Fu Ssu-nien Library, and a Japanese edition issued in 1673. The recipes are identical. For the sake of convenience I cite the widely available Japanese edition (Kyoto: Chubun shuppansha, 1984 [facsimile of 1673 edition printed in Japan]). *Shilin guangji* is catalogued in today's libraries as a Yuan dynasty work, but it was first compiled before the fall of the Southern Song by the scholar Chen Yuanjing (fl. 1195–1264), about whom little is known. The Song work is no longer extant. For a history of the different editions, see the preface to Chen Yuanjing, comp., *Shilin guangji* (Kyoto: Chubun shuppansha, 1988), pp. 1–27. This is a rather poor facsimile of the almanac published in the Yuan Zhishun reign (1330–33). The recipes in the two other editions I consulted at the Naikaku bunko, a magnificent Yuan edition and a Ming printing using Yuan

blocks, are identical. The order of the sections diverges. In the two Yuan editions, the recipes are in the first *(houji)* of four sequels. In the Ming printing using Yuan blocks, they are in the last sequel *(waiji)*.

22. Chen Yuanjing, comp., *Shilin guangji,* Yuan edition, *houji,* 10.13b–14b. Copy in the Naikaku bunko. See also pp. 658–59 of the 1988 facsimile.

23. *Jujia biyong shilei, geng ji,* 64a–b.

24. Ibid., 64b; *Shilin guangji, houji,* 10.14a.

25. All four recipes from the *Jujia biyong* and *Shilin guangji* were reprinted in *Wanbao quanshu,* a popular late-Ming almanac. They have now been separated from "Guige shiyi" and placed under their own category, "Binding and swaddling" ("Chanzha lei"). See, for example, *Wanli quanbu wenlin miaojin wanbao quanshu* (Shulin [Jianyang, Fujian]: Anzheng tang, 1612), 34.21b–22b; copy in the Harvard-Yenching Library. For the myriad versions of the *Wanbao quanshu,* their classification schemes and contents, see Wu Huifang, *Wanbao quanshu: Ming-Qing shiqi de minjian shenghuo shilu* (Taipei: Guoli Zhengzhi daxue lishixi, 2001). An abridged version of the *Shilin guangji* tonic recipe is in Zhang Dai, *Yehang chuan* (Hangzhou: Zhejiang guji chubanshe, 1981), p. 673. New recipes were added to the repertoire. See Shi Chengjin (b. 1659), *Chuanjia bao* (Family treasures, pub. 1692–1739), *duonengji,* cited in CFL III: 153–54, and the two new recipes "Lianxiang shan" and "Xiao jinlian fang" in Su Fu, *Xianggui xiewa, xia,* 21a–22a [pp. 85–87]. The tradition lasted into the modern times, but the recipe in *Jujia yiji,* an 1850 almanac, is much simplified ([n.p., preface 1820–50], *sanxulu* [third sequel, preface 1850], 42a–b); copy in the Fu Ssu-nien Library. A handful of these traditional recipes appeared before new recipes for letting out feet in CFL III: 153–55.

26. I thank Dr. Michael Fuhr, director of the Karl Ernst Osthaus Museum in Hagen, Germany, for inviting me to participate in the "Museutopia" project. Working with him, Thomas W. Rieger, and Hope Wurmfeld taught me a great deal about the utopian implications of the concept of overcoming the body.

27. Zhao Jingshen, "Tan Ming Chenghua kanben 'shuochang cihua,'" *Wenwu* 11 (1972), reprinted in a promotional brochure appended to *Ming Chenghua shuochang cihua congkan* (Beijing: Wenwu chubanshe, 1979).

28. Anne E. McLaren has discerned a "hierarchy of reading practices" whereby those of women and other less-educated readers were denigrated (*Chinese Popular Culture and Ming Chantfables* [Leiden: Brill, 1998]; quote from p. 49). See also Zeng Yongyi, *Shuo xuwenxue* (Taipei: Lianjing, 1984), pp. 67–74.

29. "Xinke shuochang Bao Longtu duan Cao Guojiu gongan zhuan," 4a, in *Ming Chenghua shuochang cihua.*

30. Not only princesses and maids, but also people from all walks of life are introduced by way of what they wear. Fine examples are the patched clothing and lice-infected hairdo of a beggar woman in "Rencong renmu zhuan" (3a–3b) and the frivolous, up-to-the-minute fashionable outfits of a pair of ne'er-do-wells in "Duanwai wupan zhuan" (20a, in *Ming Chenghua shuochang cihua*).

31. "Xinbian shuochang quanxiang Shilang fuma zhuan," 2a–3b, in *Ming*

Chenghua shuochang cihua. "Shiyang jin" refers to a famous pattern of ten auspicious motifs, among them bamboo, lozenge, and tawny daylily, first found on brocades from the Shu kingdom in Sichuan during the Five Dynasties. The pattern remained popular in the Yuan and Ming dynasties. Shen Congwen, *Zhongguo gudai fushi yanjiu* (Taipei: Nantian, 1988), p. 364; Zhou Xibao, *Zhongguo gudai fushi shi* (Taipei: Nantian shuju 1998), p. 256.

32. The princess's toilette, with an emphasis on her fashion sense *(shixin)*, is in "Zhang Wengui zhuan," 7b–8a. The entertainer with bound feet appears in "Zhang Wengui zhuan," 14a; the master weaver's wife is in "Liu Dusai zhuan," 2b–3a, 3b–4a, 29b, in *Ming Chenghua shuochang cihua.*

33. Anne McLaren, "Crossing Gender Boundaries in China: Nüshu Narratives," *Intersections* (1998): 1–16; quote from p. 6.

34. In a fluid society, the dangers of downward mobility are real and keenly felt. Hu Shilan, an eighteenth-century gentrywoman who fell upon hard times in midlife, expressed this pathos eloquently in a poem. See my discussion of this poem in "Footbinding as Female Inscription," in *Rethinking Confucianism: Past and Present in China, Japan, Korea, and Vietnam,* ed. Benjamin Elman, John Duncan, and Herman Ooms (Los Angeles: Asia Pacific Monograph Series in International Studies, UCLA, 2002) and "The Sex of Footbinding," in *Good Sex: Women's Religious Wisdom,* ed. by Radhika Balakrishnan, Mary E. Hunt, and Patricia Beattie Jung (New Brunswick, N.J.: Rutgers University Press, 2001).

35. "Xiuru ji" was first written in the Chenghua and Hongzhi reigns. The present version was revised by Xu Lin (1462–1538). Xu Shuofang estimated the year of revision to be around 1493 or before ("Xu Lin nianpu," in *Xu Shuofang ji* [Hangzhou: Zhejiang guji chubanshe, 1993]); the expression "jiaoxiao xiegong . . . wo xingzou buguan" is cited in this study (5).

36. Xu Sanyou, ed., *Xinqie quanbu tianxia simin liyong bianguan Wuche bojin* (Fujian: Jianyun chai, 1597), 9.3a; copy in the Library of Congress. The other chant for the arrival of the bride also calls attention to her feet: "Bright red candles cast a bright red shadow, / The peacock displays its feathers, adding to the happiness. / Please bride, step off the palanquin with joy, / Gently moving your lotus steps to the reception hall" (9.3a).

37. Suzanne E. Cahill, "Discipline and Transformation: Body and Practice in the Lives of Daoist Holy Women of Tang China," in *Women and Confucian Cultures in Premodern China, Korea, and Japan,* ed. Dorothy Ko, JaHyun Kim Haboush, and Joan R. Piggott (Berkeley: University of California Press, 2003), pp. 251–78.

38. According to the official report published over three decades after the excavation, this pair (X16:3) was found in a box placed on the southern edge of Xiaojing's coffin. Also in the box were ten other pairs of high-heeled shoes that have badly decomposed, leaving only the heels. Thus this is the only complete pair of high-heeled shoes extant from the Ding mausoleum. Both Xiaojing and Empress Xiaoduan were buried with flat *fengtou* shoes on their feet. The former pair (J131) measured 10.8 cm (4.3 inches) long and the latter (D114), 13.5 cm (5.4 inches). See

Zhongguo shehuikexue yuan et al., *Dingling* (Beijing: Wenwu chubanshe, 1990), 1: 39, 121–22, 299, 325–26. For a color photograph of Xiaojing's high-heeled shoes, see Wang Yan, *Wanli dihou de yichu: Ming Dingling shizhi jijin* (Taipei: Dongda tushu gongsi, 1995), pp. 111–12. The album of photographic highlights of the mausoleum suggests that Xiaojing's high heels were found in her coffin; this is probably incorrect (Zhongguo shehuikexue yuan kaogu yanjiusuo, ed., *Dingling duoying* [Beijing: Wenwu chubanshe, 1989], p. 21).

39. All Ming palace ladies were recruited from commoner families in the vicinities of the capital. Lady Wang's son, Zhu Changlou, was designated heir apparent only in 1601. Wanli never favored Lady Wang after their fateful encounter and wanted to install the son of Lady Zheng, born 1586, against the wish of his Grand Secretary. See Ray Huang, *1587: A Year of No Significance* (New Haven: Yale University Press, 1981).

40. The *yuntou* shoes are numbered X17:11; the *fengtou* shoes, J78 (Zhongguo shehui kexueyuan, *Dingling*, 1: 121–22, 325–26). For a pair of flat phoenix-head shoes in the collection of Dr. Ke Jisheng, see his *Qianzai jinlian fenghua* (Taipei: Guoli lishi bowuguan, 2003), p. 23. He has dated it as fifteenth century.

41. Shang Wei, "The Making of the Everyday World: *Jin Ping Mei Cihua* and Encyclopedias for Daily Use," unpublished paper. For a summary of the plot and a discussion of authorship, editions, dating, and techniques, see David Roy's "Introduction" to the first installment of his magisterial translation of the novel, *The Plum in the Golden Vase or, Chin P'ing Mei,* vol. 1: *The Gathering,* trans. David Tod Roy (Princeton: Princeton University Press, 1993). Roy has suggested that the implied author was an adherent of the Confucian philosopher Xunzi (third century B.C.E.), who bemoaned the disorder of the world and attributed it to evilness in human nature. Paraphrasing J. Hillis Miller's discussion of Charles Dickens's *Bleak House,* Roy has concluded: "In writing the *Jinpingmei,* the author constructed a model in little of Chinese society in his time" (xxvii).

42. *Plum in the Golden Vase,* 1: 83. Unless otherwise noted, all translations of this novel are Roy's. I have, however, changed the Wade-Giles romanization that he used to Pinyin.

43. The competition between Jinlian and Huilian is most vividly conveyed in a scene of almost identical footwear in chapter 28. Looking for her lost shoe, Jinlian also found one of Huilian's, both of which Ximen had kept in his stationery box: "they were both embroidered shoes of scarlet silk, figured with flowers from each of the four seasons and the symbolic representations of the 'eight treasures,' with flat, white satin soles, green heel lifts, and blue hook and eye fastenings. Only the chain stitching of the two shoes was slightly different." Huilian's willful act of imitation was all the more threatening because her shoes were slightly smaller than Jinlian's. *The Plum in the Golden Vase or, Chin P'ing Mei,* vol. 2: *The Rivals,* trans. David Tod Roy (Princeton: Princeton University Press, 2001), p. 155.

44. *Plum,* 2: 53. According to the insightful analysis of Ding Naifei of the role played by the accoutrements of footbinding in the concealed sexual politics in Xi-

men's household, Huilian is both Jinlian's competitor and "narrative double" who relives Jinlian's life at a lower social stratum ("Qiuqian, jiaodai, hong shuixie," in *Xing/bei yanjiu duben,* ed. Zhang Xiaohong [Taipei: Maitian chuban, 1998], pp. 23–60).

45. Ida Pruitt, *A China Childhood* (San Francisco: Chinese Materials Center, Inc., 1978), p. 118. In chapter 23 of *Jinpingmei,* Song Huilian declined to braise a pig's head and trotters, using the excuse that she was "stitching shoe soles for the mistress" *(Plum,* 2: 44). Kitchen help was even lower in the hierarchy of labors than stitching soles.

46. *Plum,* 2: 166–69; the sleeping-shoe episode of the night before is on p. 163. Ding Naifei has suggested that Ximen's love of red shoes on Jinlian's feet was a substitute for his own desire to wear red shoes ("Qiuqian, jiaodai, hong shuixie," pp. 24–25).

47. In her analysis of the female fashion culture in *Jinpingmei,* Zhang Jinlan has reminded us that footwear was merely a part of the sartorial regime in Ximen's household, from hairstyle, headdress, jackets, and skirts, to footwear (*"Jinpingmei* nü-xing fushi wenhua yanjiu," master's thesis, Department of Chinese literature, National Cheng-chi University, Taipei, Taiwan, 2000). I thank Hsiung Ping-chen and Ms. Zhang for making this thesis available. Having tabulated all the footwear mentioned in the novel, Zhang has concluded that the shoes of "wives" were made of mostly satin or damask; high heels predominated, although flats were also used; only three of the maids, all Ximen's favorites, were said to have bound feet (81–83).

48. To ingratiate herself to Jinlian the morning after Huilian spent the night with Ximen in the garden grotto, Huilian offered to pick up Jinlian's sleeping shoes and binding cloth, presumably for the laundry maid *(Plum,* 2: 55). These two items thus appear to be similar to underwear: erotically charged, "dirty," and defiling. In the late Qing, sleeping shoes are virtually indistinguishable from socks. See the photograph in my *Every Step a Lotus,* p. 71; and in Beverley Jackson, *Splendid Slippers: A Thousand Years of an Erotic Tradition* (Berkeley, Calif.: Ten Speed Press, 1997), p. 48.

49. *Plum,* 2: 144. Ding Naifei ("Qiuqian, jiaodai, hong shuixie," pp. 49–50) has pointed out that the binding cloth was used to vastly different effect by Huilian, Jinlian's narrative double, who fastened them to the doorpost and hanged herself in chapter 26 *(Plum,* 2: 123). In the mid-Qing erotic novel *Lin Lanxiang,* there is a scene in Geng Lang's household in which his second wife Xianger stripped fifth wife Caiyun naked, "not leaving her even her footbindings." Like the grape arbor scene in *The Plum,* this scene also epitomizes the sexual abandon of the men and women in a degenerate household. See Keith McMahon, *Misers, Shrews, and Polygamists: Sexuality and Male-Female Relations in Eighteenth-Century Chinese Fiction* (Durham and London: Duke University Press, 1995), pp. 214–15.

50. Li Yu, *The Carnal Prayer Mat,* trans. Patrick Hanan (Honolulu: The University of Hawaii Press, 1990), p. 50.

51. Hu Yinglin, *Dianqian xinlu,* in *Shiaoshi shanfang bicong* (Beijing: Zhonghua shuju, 1958), p. 145.

52. Fan Lian, *Yunjian jumucao,* 2.2b (p. 2628), in *Biji xiaoshuo daguan, bian* 22, *ze* 5. Many writers, including Hu Yinglin (*Dianqian xinlu,* p. 165), commented on the fad of straw shoes *(puxie)* for men.

53. C. R. Boxer, ed., *South China in the Sixteenth Century* (London: The Hakluyt Society, 1953), p. 124. Gaspar da Cruz's work, *Tractado,* was printed in Evora in 1569–70 (lxii). For other anecdotes on the shoe market in China, see Wang Hongtai's rich study, "Liudong yu hudong: You Ming-Qing jian chengshi shenghuo de texing tance gongzhong changyi de kaizhan," Ph.D. diss., National Taiwan University, 1998, pp. 450–52. In arguing that "everyday tastes were dictated by the styles from the market" (452), Wang may have underestimated the resilience of domestic shoemaking and overstated the power of the market forces.

54. Yu Xiangdou, comp., *Santai wanyong zhengzong* (Jianyang, Fujian: Yushi Shuangfang tang, 1599), 21.19b–20a; copy in the Tōyō bunka kenkyūjo, University of Tokyo. "Shoes" were listed in a checklist of commodities, after "summer cotton cloth" and "bamboo and wooden boards." Also mentioned were the pros and cons of straw shoes *(caoxin xie)* from various villages.

55. Ibid.

56. Shen Fu, *Six Records of a Floating Life,* trans. Leonard Pratt and Chiang Su-hui (London and New York: Penguin Books, 1983), p. 44. Shen described the attire of prostitutes in Guangzhou: "Those with bound feet wore skirts, those without bound feet wore short stockings, butterfly shoes, and long trousers" (120).

57. Lin Sumen, *Hanjiang sanbaiyin* (Yangzhou: Jiangsu Guangling guji keyinshe, 1988), 6.2a–b. This collection was originally published in the Jiaqing reign (1796–1820), with a preface dated 1808. I thank Tobie Meyer-Fong for giving me a copy of this text. The jet butterfly motif is abstract, more like a bat or a cloud. Lin also mentioned that Yangzhou perfume stores made a sleeping shoe with a strong fragrance, possibly in powder form, sandwiched between the vamps and lining and also in the soles (6.3b–4a). Over a century later, Yao Lingxi reported that stores selling toiletry items and embroidered purses also sold sleeping shoes for several coppers; these were love tokens that prostitutes dispensed freely to their clients, often in sizes much smaller than their feet (CFJHL: 142–43). Perhaps the Yangzhou fragrant shoes were also so intended.

58. Zhang, a native of Taiyuan, Shanxi, moved to Jinzhou in 1730. He was Wang's neighbor before she married (*Neige xingke tiben,* bundle 150, Qianlong 3.3.27). The erotic charge attached to sleeping shoes was also evident in the south. In a case from Funing, Jiangsu, a casual laborer, also named Zhang, desired to marry a fellow villager named Zeng. Zhang showed a ring and a sleeping shoe to a matchmaker, claiming that these items were love tokens. When Zeng's parents refused the proposal because of Zhang's low social status, the matchmaker mentioned the shoe and ring. Zeng's mother, assuming that her daughter had indeed slept with Zhang, slapped and upbraided her. That night, the daughter committed suicide (*Neige xingke tiben,* "Marriage and illicit sex" *[hunyin jianqing]* category , #209–3, microfilm reel 1–33, Qianlong 8.6.17). I am extremely grateful to Matthew Sommer, who has taken the

trouble to share these episodes, the one in the following note, and a number of other cases involving shoes and feet through the years.

59. *Neige xingke tiben,* "Marriage and illicit sex" category, #208–2, microfilm reel 1–33, Qianlong 8.6.10.

60. Tongxi manshi, *Tingyu xiantan* (Shanghai: Shanghai guji chubanshe, 1983), p. 104. Pu was also skilled in carving wood and ivory. See also Huaipu jushi, *Liu Rushi shiji* (Beiping: Wenzi tongmengshe, 1930), 7a. Although leather was occasionally used for boots and for toe reinforcements, traditional Chinese shoes for men, women, and children were made of vegetable fiber. Children's tiger shoes, popular tourist souvenirs in China today, are remnants of the old domestic female shoe-making tradition. Flat-heeled shoes for bound feet from remote areas were still made of homespun cloth in the twentieth century. See *Every Step a Lotus,* pp. 118–19.

61. Li-Young Lee, whose mother was a granddaughter of Yuan Shikai, the late-Qing general and president of the Republic, recalled that in the family compound in Tianjin there was a building called the sewing room: "Lined with tables at which thirty women sit behind mounds of various fabrics of any color, the room whines and rings with the rapid pounding of several hand-operated sewing machines. Forbidden to wear against their bodies any piece of cloth cut or sewn by men, all the female members of the nine households have their clothes made by women in the sewing hall"(*The Winged Seed: A Remembrance* [New York: Simon and Schuster, 1995], p. 21). Although the strictures are excessive, it seems reasonable to expect that wealthy and large households in an earlier period would have hired sewing women to supply the needs of the family.

62. For wedding shoes and gift shoes for the in-laws, see *Every Step a Lotus,* pp. 69–72; CFJHL: 143–47.

63. Tian Yiheng, *Liuqing rizha,* 20.8a. Tian did not say if the entire vamp was made of gilded leather. In *Plum in the Golden Vase,* it is used only for edging or tip reinforcements. My analysis of the styles of footwear in Ximen's household benefits from the table compiled by Zhang Jinlan, in her "*Jinpingmei* nüxing fushi wenhua," pp. 81–83. In the Song, monochrome was so normative that soles made of different-colored fronts and backs (known as *Cuo daodi*) elicited special comment (Tian, *Liuqing,* 20.8b).

64. The reference to brush-painting is from CFJHL, diagram 11, between pp. 86 and 87. For a full translation of the captions to this series of diagrams, see fig. 22. For auspicious symbols on shoes, see *Every Step a Lotus,* pp. 105–9. For the history of auspicious symbols on Chinese objects and their proliferation in the Qing, see *Kisshō: Chūgoku bijitsu ni komerareta imi* (Tokyo: Tokyo National Museum, 1998).

65. CFJHL: 98. Information about vendors calling out and the filing tool is from a different report, CFJHL: 110–11.

66. CFJHL: 98. For photographs of a string of five wooden heels from Shandong and a set of ten from Shanxi, see Ke Jisheng, *Qianzai jinlian fenghua,* p. 110. For curvatures of the wooden soles and detailed instructions for carving them, see CFXB: 33.

67. The earliest extant paper shoe patterns were excavated from the tomb of Madam Zhou (1240–74) in De'an, Jiangxi. Among an array of garments, toiletry items, and sewing implements found were two patterns for the sole (length 20–24 cm, or 8–9.6 inches) and two for the uppers (length 19–22 cm, or 7.6–8.8 inches) of shoes. See Jiangxisheng wenwu kaogu yanjiusuo and De'an xian bowuguan, "Jiangxi De'an Nan-Song Zhoushi mu qingli jianbao," p. 12.

68. Tanmian daoren [Zhang Lüping], comp., *Kunde baojian* (n.p.: Yuxiutang, 1777), *juan* 8–9. Although not identical, the rectangular skirt panels look remarkably similar to the Qing-dynasty skirts in Western collections studied by Mary V. Hays. The patterns of flower, bird, landscape, and lucky symbols appear to be generic. See Hays, "Chinese Skirts of the Qing Dynasty," *The Bulletin of the Needle and Bobbin Club* 72, nos. 1 & 2 (1989): 4–41. I thank Terry Milhaupt for supplying me with this article.

69. *Kunde baojian*, "Zixu," 2b–3a. Chapters 1–2 consist of stories of woman exemplars from such classics as Liu Xiang's *Biographies of Women (Lienü zhuan)*. Chapter 3 continues with stories of retribution recycled from popular religious texts. The same set of thirteenth-century recipes for treating bound feet that we have seen above appears in chapter 4, on textile work and the toilette. Chapters 5–7 are cooking recipes. Although its contents are recycled except for the sewing patterns, *Precious Mirror* marks the beginning of an encyclopedic knowledge that was explicitly gendered female. Previous almanacs, even as they dispensed ministrations for troubled feet and other body- or home-management techniques, presented such information to a presumed male readership.

70. Entitled *Zengshan kunde baojian* (Precious mirror of feminine virtues, with additions and deletions), the copy is bound in two separate volumes and is signed "Kuimiutang zhuren xuancao" (selected and copied by the Master of the Ashamed-of-Mistakes Studio). I list this in the Works Cited under Tanmian daoren, although the name of the original editor does not appear on the copy. The first volume (the original chapter 8) is numbered chapter 4 and given a new title, "Nanpei chengshi" (Patterns for male ornaments); the second (the original chapter 9), is now chapter 5 under the title "Nügong chengshi" (Patterns for women's work). It is not clear what chapters 1–3 could have been. I thank Don J. Cohn for so generously sharing these modern volumes in his collection with me.

71. Huang Sheng's binding cloth was the only narrow, ribbon-like specimen that we know of (Fujiansheng bowuguan, "Fuzhou shi beijiao," p. 9). The choice of silk recalls the legendary description of Yaoniang's binding cloth, which was said to be made of silk *(bo)*. The pair of binding cloths of Madam Xiong (1482–1537), whose tomb was found in De'an, Jiangxi province, is made of plain-woven cotton. Each cloth is 216 cm (86.4 inches) long and 21 cm (8.4 inches) wide. Xiong appears to be the wife of a low-ranking official. See De'anxian bowuguan, "Jiangxi De'an Mingdai Xiongshimu qingli jianbao," *Wenwu* 10 (1994):34. The use of cotton might have become customary by the sixteenth century. Among the confiscated household goods of former grand secretary Yan Song (1480–1565) were 85 pairs of cot-

ton binding cloths (assessed at 2.55 ounces of silver for the lot). Also included were "female boots of various colors" (70 pairs; 10.5 ounces); "female shoes: (1,700 pairs; 54 ounces); "embroidered leggings and socks" (20 pairs; 2 ounces). *Tianshui bingshan lu, Congshu jicheng chubian,* vol. 1502 (Shanghai: Shangwu yinshuguan, 1937), pp. 302–3.

72. See p. 251, n. 63. For photographs of one such loom from Taiwan and rolls of binding cloth in plain, red, and indigo cotton, see Ke Jisheng, *Qianzai jinlian,* pp. 106–7.

73. Sunü, "Gaozubu shi bin gongyong," CFJHL: 95–96. There was also an abbreviated five-layered regimen. Yang Yang's description of the binding routine in Tonghai, Yunnan, is almost identical to this passage (*Xiaojiao wudao,* pp. 38–39); in all likelihood Yang had copied his information from *Caifeilu.*

74. Footbinding ended in Tonghai in the 1950s, the last area in China to effectively outlaw the practice. The remoteness of this area on the Yunnan plateau seems to account for this belatedness. In 1933, local authorities in Tonghai established a Tianzu weiyuanhui (Natural feet committee) and dispatched male foot inspectors to the villages. Local son Yang Yang has suggested that Liuyi village, which is the closest to the county seat, was ironically the most successful in the cat-and-mouse game of defeating the inspectors because those villagers were best-informed about the timing of the visits (*Xiajiao wudao,* p. 71). One example of the recent tourism literature is Li Xu and Huang Yanhong, "Xiaojiao nüren cun," *China Tourism* 208 (Oct. 1997): 40–51. In 1997, over three hundred women with once-bound feet, about a third of them over sixty, still lived in Liuyi village. The golden-lotus snooker team and dancing troupe garnered one page in the official album that the local authorities produced to promote tourism. See Zhonggong Zhongyang xianwei xuanzhuanbu and Tonghai xian wenxue yishujie lianhehui, ed., *Tonghai: Xiujia nan Dian* (Tonghai, Yunnan: Zhonggong Tonghai xian wei and Tonghai xian renmin zhenfu, n.d. [1999]), p. 37.

75. Yang, *Xiaojiao wudao,* p. 6.

76. Interview with Ma Qiaofen, June 30, 2003. See also Yang, *Xiaojiao wudao,* pp. 206–7.

77. The cloth, "Hexi tubu," was named after Hexi, a market town near Tonghai. It was woven from imported machine-spun yarn which became available in southern Yunnan in the late 1880s, and especially after the building of the Tonkin-Kunming Railway in 1895–99. Laurel Bossen has argued that the continued viability of weaving as a livelihood in areas more accessible by trade routes saved women from having to work in the fields and allowed them to continue footbinding. Hence the irony that footbinding ended earlier in the more remote and less commercialized areas (*Chinese Women and Rural Development,* chap. 3, especially pp. 70–78). Although plausible, this argument is difficult to prove. See also Yang, *Xiaojiao wudao,* p. 7.

ailian qiaosheng	愛蓮僑生
Bai Lewen	柏樂文
Bai Ting	白挺
bancha	半叉
ban chanjiao	半纏腳
banchi bu de guojiao	半尺布的裹腳
banghe	棒喝
banlan jiao	半欄腳
ban lanzi jiao	半攬子腳
banwa	半襪
bi	偪
bu	堡
Bu chanzu hui	不纏足會
Bu guozu hui	不裹足會
Cai Aihua	蔡愛花
Caifeng caifei/ wuyi xiati	采葑采菲,無以下體
changyou qi shen	娼優其身
chanjiao	纏腳
chanzu	纏足
che mudi	車木底
Chen Jitong	陳濟同

chenshe	陳設
chi	尺
chi luoluo	赤裸裸
chitou	尺頭
chuai chuantou	揣船頭
chuang	床
cun	寸
dajiao	大腳
dai yi guiren xiangqie	代一貴人相妾
dangzhi zi fengren	當職之縫人
Deng Changyao	鄧長耀
dengtan	登壇
diban chan xie	底板沈些
dili	地理
dingnan	丁男
dingnü	丁女
duan	端
etoujiao	鵝頭腳
Fameng xuetang	發蒙學堂
fangzu	放足
fangzu jinian hui	放足紀念會
fanrao	反繞
fantou jiao	翻頭腳
Fei Xihuang	費錫璜
fengjian	封建
Fengren	風人
fengsu shi	風俗史
fengtou	鳳頭
fenli	分利
fugong	婦工
fuke	婦科
fushi guanren	服侍官人
fuyang zhijian, yicheng chenji	俯仰之間,已成陳跡
fuyao	服妖
gaifang tianzu	改放天足
gaodeng xiaoxue	高等小學
gaodi	高底
gaodi xunlü	高底荀履
gaoxie	高屐

gongshi	公事
gongwan	弓彎
gongwan xianxiao	弓彎纖小
gongxian	弓纖
gongxian zhuang	弓纖狀
gongxiao	弓小
gongxie	弓鞋
gongxing	弓形
gongzu	弓足
guancheng	管城
guangfu guti	光復故體
guangfu guwu	光復故物
guanren	官人
guige shiyi	閨閣事宜
guojiao	裹腳
guolairen	過來人
guozu	裹足
huafang	畫房
Huajian ji	花間集
huaji tuti	滑稽突梯
huajuishi	花蕊石
huang huashiling	黃花士令
huazhuang jiangyan	化妝講演
hudie lü	蝴蝶履
huizhu	會主
Hu Yanxian	胡燕賢
jia	甲
jianzhe zhifu	賤者之服
jiaotong	交通
jiaoxiao xiegong xingbuwen	腳小鞋弓行不穩
jiaoxiao xiejian nanxingzou	腳小鞋尖難行走
"Jie chanzu lun"	戒纏足論
jiefang	解放
jiepi	潔癖
jieyou suoju	皆有所據
jinguo yilao	巾幗遺老
jinlian	金蓮
jinlian juechang, wenji qiwu	金蓮絕唱,聞雞起舞
jishi	記實
jiyuan	紀元
jizi	屐子

kanjian 看見
kanwan 看翫
kaozheng 考證
koushi daizi 扣絲帶子
kuai shangma 快上馬
kunxie 坤鞋

lei 累
lianban 蓮瓣
liang (ounce) 兩
liang (to air) 晾
liangjia guixiu 良家閨秀
li gaodi 裏高底
lilü 利屜
Liucun fuyuan guangzhizhi 六寸膚圓光緻緻
Liuyi village 六一村
lujiaocai 鹿角菜
luowa 羅襪
lü 履
lüren 履人

Ma Qiaofen 馬喬芬
mianhua taozi 棉花套子
minsu xue 民俗學
mudi 木底

neijia zhilü 內家之履
nei sifu 內司服
niang laole, you buxiang mai yangzi 娘老了,又不想賣樣子
Ni Mu'ou 倪慕歐
Ni Yuanzhen (Zan) 倪元鎮(瓚)
nügong 女紅
nüzhuang 女妝
nüzi ziqiang 女子自強

pi 癖
pingquan pingdeng 平權平等
pojia 婆家
pudu zhongsheng 普渡眾生
Pu Jifen 濮紀芬
Pu Zhongqian 濮仲謙

qian 錢

qiangwu gushi	羌無故實
queyou mingju	确有明據
qunzhong	群眾
renyao	人妖
ruan xiewa	軟鞋襪
Runan xianxian zhuan	汝南先賢傳
sai (to air under the sun)	曬
sai (to compete)	賽
saijiao hui	賽脚會
sanling	三綾
shangdeng renjia	上等人家
shen	身
shengji yuhong gao	肌玉紅膏
shenli	神力
shenshou	身受
shexiang chuanling ao	射香川綾襖
sheyue	社約
shidafu	士大夫
shinü	侍女
shishu	私塾
shizu zhi nü	世族之女
shoushu weiru jinzhong	收束微如禁中
shuanggou	雙鈎
"Shuang xingchan"	雙行纏
shunrao	順繞
shuzu xianzhi	束足纖之
suanteng	酸痛
subai	肅拜
sui	歲
suoshi	瑣事
suzu	素足
suzu nü	素足女
Tang Yisuo	湯頤瑣
taowa	套襪
tengchen	痛陳
tianbu	天步
Tianfeng bao	天風報
tianguan	天官
tianran zhi zu	天然之足
tianwen	天文

tianxing zhi ziqiang	天行之自強
tianzu	天足
Tianzu hui	天足會
tianzu sixiang	天足思想
tongqun	同群
tongzhi	同志
wai	歪
waike	外科
wanzhuan rugong	彎轉如弓
weizhi bokao	未之博考
wenming sixiang	文明思想
wo nu shen	我奴身
wujiao	無交
xian	纖
xiang	相
Xiangjiang shuilang qun	湘江水浪裙
Xianglian ji	香奩集
xiangxie	響屧
xianxiao	纖小
xianzu	跣足
xiao wailagu	小歪辣骨
xiaoxian	消閒
Xiao Xiuxiang	蕭秀香
xiaozu hui	小足會
xichuan shiyang jin	西川十樣錦
xiefu	邪幅
xiegong jiaoxiao bunanxing	鞋弓腳小步難行
xijiao dahui	洗腳大會
xiku	膝褲
xingchan	行纏
xingteng	行滕
xinxue	新學
Xiuqiu (elegant autumn)	秀秋
Xiuqiu (embroidering Earth)	繡球
xiuzhuang	繡莊
xizu	洗足
xuanjiang yuan	宣講員
Xu Ke	徐珂
xunya	荀芽
yanshuo	演説

yaoji	妖姬
yaojing	妖精
yibo raojiao	以帛繞脚
yi butiao lanzhu	以布條攔住
yicheng pianduan	已成片段
yilao	遺老
yi yanjian wei zhun	以眼見為準
yong	用
youjiao	有交
you kuaikuai zoushi liao	有塊塊就是了
youxi	遊戲
yuexian powa	約纖迫襪
yuntou	雲頭
za	扎
zagua	扎挂
zaguo	扎裹
zajiao	扎脚,札脚
zaoxie	皂鞋
zazu	札足
zha	凸
zhangjue teng	脹撅痛
zhanglao	長老
Zhanyuan jingyu	湛淵靜語
zhen	真
zhending	枕頂
zheng	正
zhengti	政體
Zhou Ying	鄒英
zi shu	自述
zuxin	足心
zuzhi gongxiao	足之弓小

WORKS CITED

Adams, Sandra May. "Nineteenth Century Representations of Footbinding to the English Reading Public." Ph.D. diss., University of Macau, 1993.

Al-Akl, F. M. "Bound Feet in China." *American Journal of Surgery* n.s. 18, no. 3 (Dec. 1932): 545–50.

Aoki, Masaru 青木正兒. "Shushō shudan" 酒觴趣談 (Stories about wine cups). In *Aoki Masaru zenshū* 青木正兒全集 (Complete works of Masaru Aoki), vol. 8, pp. 77–87. Tokyo: Shunjū sha, 1984.

Bao Tao, Jialin [Chia-lin Pao Tao]. "The Anti-Footbinding Movement in Late Ch'ing China: Indigenous Development and Western Influence." *Research on Women in Modern Chinese History* 2 (June 1994): 141–73.

Baudrillard, Jean. *The System of Objects.* Translated by James Benedict. London and New York: Verso, 1996.

The Book of Songs. Translated by Arthur Waley; edited with additional translations by Joseph R. Allen. New York: Grove Press, 1996.

Bossen, Laurel. *Chinese Women and Rural Development: Sixty Years of Change in Lu Village, Yunnan.* Lanham, Md.: Rowman & Littlefield, Inc., 2002.

Boxer, C. R., ed. *South China in the Sixteenth Century.* London: The Hakluyt Society, 1953.

Broadwin, Julie. "Walking Contradictions: Chinese Women Unbound at the Turn of the Century." *The Journal of Historical Sociology* 10, no. 4 (Dec. 1997): 418–43.

Brook, Timothy. *The Confusions of Pleasure: Commerce and Culture in Ming China.* Berkeley: University of California Press, 1998.

Buck, Pearl. *East Wind; West Wind.* London: Methuen and Co., Ltd., 1934.

Cahill, James. "The Emperor's Erotica (*Ching Yüan Chai so-shih* II)." *Kaikodo Journal* 11 (Spring 1999): 24–43.

———. "Two Palace Museums: An Informal Account of Their Formation and History (*Ching Yüan Chai so-shih* IV)." *Kaikodo Journal* 19 (Spring 2001): 30–39.

———. "Where Did the Nymph Hang? (*Ching Yüan Chai so-shih* I)" *Kaikodo Journal* 7 (Spring 1998): 8–16.

Cahill, Suzanne E. "Discipline and Transformation: Body and Practice in the Lives of Daoist Holy Women of Tang China." In *Women and Confucian Cultures in Premodern China, Korea, and Japan,* edited by Dorothy Ko, JaHyun Kim Haboush, and Joan R. Piggott, pp. 251–78. Berkeley: University of California Press, 2003.

Cao, Wugang 曹梧岡 and Hanshang mengren 邗上蒙人. *Wan-Qing yanqing xiaoshuo congshu—Meilan jiahua; Fengyuemeng* 晚清艷情小説叢書-梅蘭佳話; 風月夢 (Collectanea of late-Qing novels: The plum and orchid romance and dreams of wind and moon). Nanchang: Baihuazhou wenyi chubanshe, 1993.

Chang, Chun-shu, and Shelley Hsueh-lun Chang. *Crisis and Transformation in Seventeenth-Century China: Society, Culture, and Modernity in Li Yü's World.* Ann Arbor: University of Michigan Press, 1992.

Chau, Virginia Chiu-tin. "The Anti-Footbinding Movement in China, 1850–1912." Master's thesis, Columbia University, 1966.

Che, Ruoshui 車若水. *Jiaoqi ji* 脚氣集 (Collection compiled during recovery from beriberi). In *Qinding siku quanshu* 欽定四庫全書 *zibu* 10, *zajia lei* 3.

Chen, Fan-Pen. "Problems of Chinese Historiography as Seen in the Official Records on Yang Kuei-fei." *T'ang Studies* 8–9 (1990–91): 83–96.

Chen, Yuanjing 陳元靚, comp. *Shilin guangji* 士林廣記 (Comprehensive compendium in the forest of affairs). Kyoto: Chubun shuppansha, 1988. Facsimile of Yuan Zhishun (1330–33) edition.

———, comp. *Shilin guangji* (Comprehensive compendium in the forest of affairs). Yuan edition. Copy in the Naikaku bunko.

Chen, Yuanlong 陳元龍, comp. *Gezhi jingyuan* 格致鏡原 (Mirror origins of the investigation of things and the extension of knowledge). Shanghai: Shanghai guji chubanshe, 1992.

Chow, Rey. *Woman and Chinese Modernity: The Politics of Reading between West and East.* Minneapolis: University of Minnesota Press, 1991.

Clunas, Craig. *Pictures and Visuality in Early Modern China.* Princeton: Princeton University Press, 1997.

———. *Superfluous Things: Material Culture and Social Status in Early Modern China.* Urbana and Chicago: University of Illinois Press, 1991.

Cohen, Paul A. *Between Tradition and Modernity: Wang T'ao and Reform in Late Ch'ing China.* Cambridge, Mass.: Harvard University Press, 1987.

Dai, Qing 戴晴 and Luo Ke 洛恪. *Chanzu nüzi: Dangdai Zhongguo nüxing wenti* 纏足女子-當代中國女性問題 (The woman with bound feet: women's problems in contemporary China). Hong Kong: Mingbao chubanshe, 1996.

Daly, Mary. *Gyn/Ecology: The Metaethics of Radical Feminism.* Boston: Beacon Press, 1978.

Daqiao shiyu 大橋式羽. *Hu Xueyan waizhuan* 胡雪巖外傳 (The unofficial biography of Hu Xueyan). In *Wan-Qing xiaoshuo daxi* 晚清小説大系 (Series on late-Qing fiction). Taipei: Guangya chuban, 1984.

Davin, Delia. *Woman-Work: Women and the Party in Revolutionary China.* Oxford and New York: Oxford University Press, 1978.

De'anxian bowuguan 德安縣博物館. "Jiangxi De'an Mingdai Xiongshimu qingli jianbao" 江西德安明代熊氏墓清理簡報 (Preliminary report on the excavation of the tomb of Madam Xiong from the Ming dynasty in De'an county, Jiangxi province). *Wenwu* 10 (1994): 32–36.

Ding, Naifei 丁乃非. "Qiuqian, jiaodai, hong shuixie" 鞦韆, 脚帶, 紅睡鞋 (The swing, binding cloth, and red sleeping slippers). In *Xing/bei yanjiu duben* 性／別研究讀本 (A reader in the study of sex/gender differences), edited by Zhang Xiaohong 張小虹. Taipei: Maitian chuban, 1998.

Dong, Madeleine Yue. *Republican Beijing: The City and Its Histories.* Berkeley: University of California Press, 2003.

Dooling, Amy D., and Kristina M. Torgeson, eds. *Writing Women in Modern China: An Anthology of Women's Literature from the Early Twentieth Century.* New York: Columbia University Press, 1998.

Drucker, Alison. "The Influence of Western Women on the Anti-Footbinding Movement, 1840–1911." In *Women in China: Current Directions in Historical Scholarship,* edited by Richard W. Guisso and Stanley Johannesen, pp. 179–99. Youngstown, N.Y.: Philo Press, 1991.

Duara, Prasenjit. *Rescuing History from the Nation: Questioning Narratives of Modern China.* Chicago and London: University of Chicago Press, 1995.

Dworkin, Andrea. *Woman Hating.* New York: Plume, 1974.

Elman, Benjamin. *A Cultural History of Civil Examinations in Late Imperial China.* Berkeley: University of California Press, 2000.

———. *From Philosophy to Philology: Intellectual and Social Aspects of Change in Late Imperial China.* Cambridge, Mass.: Council of East Asia Studies, Harvard University, 1984.

Evans, Harriet. "The Language of Liberation: Gender and *Jiefang* in Early Chinese Communist Party Discourse." *Intersections: Gender, History, and Culture in the Asian Context,* inaugural issue (Sept. 1998): 1–20 (http://www.sshe.murdoch.edu.au/hum/as/intersections).

Fan, Hong. *Footbinding, Feminism, and Freedom: The Liberation of Women's Bodies in Modern China.* London: Frank Cass, 1997.

Fan, Lian 范濂. *Yunjian jumucao* 雲間據目鈔 (Jottings on things witnessed in Songjiang), 2.2b (p. 2628), in *Biji xiaoshuo daguan* 筆記小説大觀, *bian* 22, *ze* 5.

Fang, H. S. Y., and F. Y. K. Yu. "Foot Binding in Chinese Women." *Canadian Journal of Surgery* 3 (April 1960): 195–202.

Fang, Xuan 方絢. "Cailian chuan" 采蓮船 (The lotus-picking boat). *Xiangyan congshu* 香艷叢書, vol. 8 *juan* 1. N.p.: Guoxue fulunshe, 1914.

———. "Fangshi wuzhong" 方氏五種 (Five treatises of Mr. Fang), in *Shuofu* 説郛, comp. Wang Wenru 王文濡, pp. 1241–55. Taipei: Xinxing shuju, 1963.

———. "Guanyue cha" 貫月查 (The moon-circulating wine cup). *Xiangyan congshu*, vol. 8 *juan* 1. N.p.: Guoxue fulunshe, 1914.

———. "Jinyuan zazuan" 鏡園雜纂 (Miscellaneous sayings from Jinyuan). *Xiangyan congshu*, vol. 8 *juan* 1. N.p.: Guoxue fulunshe, 1914.

———. "Jinyuan zazuan," "Xianglian pinzao," "Guanyue cha," and "Cailian chuan." In *Hongxiu tianxiangshi congshu* 紅袖添香室叢書 (Collectanea from the red-sleeve-fragrance-enhanced studio), comp. Gao Jianhua 高劍華, vol. 2, pp. 108–53. Shanghai: Shanghai qunxueshe, 1936.

———. "Xianglian pinzao" 香蓮品藻 (Aesthetics of the fragrant lotus). *Xiangyan congshu*, vol. 8 *juan* 1. N.p.: Guoxue fulunshe, 1914.

Feng, Erkang 馮爾康. *Yongzheng zhuan* 雍正傳 (A biography of Emperor Yongzheng). Beijing: Renmin chubanshe, 1985.

Feng, Menglong 馮夢龍, ed. *Shan'ge* 山歌 (Mountain songs). In *Ming-Qing minge shidiao ji* 明清民歌時調集 (A collection of folk songs and popular tunes from the Ming-Qing period), vol. 1, pp. 245–444. Shanghai: Shanghai guji chubanshe, 1987.

Freud, Sigmund. "Fetishism." In *Sexuality and the Psychology of Love,* edited and with an introduction by Philip Rieff, pp. 214–19. New York: Collier Books, 1963.

Fujiansheng bowuguan 福建省博物館. "Fuzhou shi beijiao Nan-Song mu qingli jianbao" 福州市北郊南宋墓清理簡報 (A brief excavation report of a Southern-Song tomb in the northern suburb of Fuzhou city). *Wenwu* 文物 7 (1977): 1–17.

———, ed. *Fuzhou Nan-Song Huang Sheng mu* 福州南宋黃昇墓 (The Southern Song tomb of Huang Sheng). Beijing: Wenwu chubanshe, 1982.

Fujita, Yuken 藤田祐賢. "Ryōsai zōkyoku kō" 聊齋俗曲考 (The fifteen popular plays of Liaozhai). *Geibun kenkyū* 藝文研究 no. 18 (1964): 29–43.

Furth, Charlotte. *A Flourishing Yin: Gender in China's Medical History, 960–1665.* Berkeley: University of California Press, 1999.

———. *Ting Wen-chiang: Science and China's New Culture.* Cambridge, Mass.: Harvard University Press, 1970.

Furugaki, Koichi 古垣光一. "Chūgoku ni okeru josei no tensoku: toku ni jissō to Sodai no kigen ni tsuite" 中国における女性の纏足—特に実相と宋代の起源について (Female footbinding in China: A study of its realities and origins in the Song dynasty). *Chūgoku kankei ronsetsu shiliao* 中國關係論説資料 29, no. 1 (1987): 44–53.

Gao, Hongxing 高洪興. *Chanzu shi* 纏足史 (A history of footbinding). Shanghai: Shanghai wenyi chubanshe, 1995.

Gao, James Zheng. *Meeting Technology's Advance: Social Change in China and Zimbabwe in the Railway Age.* Westport, Conn.: Greenwood Press, 1997.

Gao, Shiyu 高世瑜. "Chanzu zaiyi" 纏足再議 (A revisionist thesis on footbinding). *Shixue yuekan* 史學月刊 2 (1999): 20–24, 111.

Gao, Wenxian 高文顯. *Han Wo* 韓偓. Taipei: Xinwenfeng, 1984.

Gates, Hill. *China's Motor: A Thousand Years of Petty Capitalism.* Ithaca: Cornell University Press, 1996.

———. "Footbinding and Homespinning in Sichuan: Capitalism's Ambiguous Gifts to Petty Capitalism." In *Constructing China: The Interaction of Culture and Economics,* edited by Kenneth G. Lieberthal, Shuen-fu Lin, and Ernest P. Young, pp. 177–194. Ann Arbor: University of Michigan Press, 1997.

Gell, Alfred. *Wrapping in Images: Tattooing in Polynesia.* Oxford: Clarendon Press, 1996.

Goldstein, Joshua. "Getting from Here to There on the Pingsui Railroad." Unpublished seminar paper, University of California at San Diego, 1994.

Gu Gaoyang Xishan Qiaozi 古高陽西山樵子. "Guiyan qinsheng" 閨艷秦聲 (Boudoir pleasures in Shaanxi tunes). In Inoue Kōbai 井上紅梅, *Shina fūzoku* 支那風俗 (Chinese customs), vol. 1, book 3, pp. 1–38. Shanghai: Nihondō shoten, 1920–21.

———. "Guiyan qinsheng." *Zhongguo guyan xipin congkan* 中國古艷稀品叢刊 (Collectanea of rare books from the Chinese erotica), vol. [ji] 1, book [ze] 3, pp. 1–38. N.p., n.d.; copy in the Fu Ssu-nien Library, Academia Sinica.

Gu, Hongming [Ku Hung-ming] 辜鴻銘. *Gu Hongming wenji* 辜鴻銘文集 (Collected works of Gu Hongming), 2 vols. Haikou: Hianan chubanshe, 1996.

———. *Zhongguoren de jingshen* 中國人的精神 (Spirit of the Chinese people). Translated from English by Huang Xingtao 黃興濤 and Song Xiaoqing 宋小慶. Haikou: Hainan chubanshe, 1996.

Gu, Jiegang 顧頡剛 et al., eds. *Wuge; Wuge xiaoshi* 吳歌; 吳歌小史 (Wu songs; A short history of Wu songs). Nanjing: Jiangsu guji, 1999.

Gugong wupin diancha baogao 故宮物品點查報告 (An inventory of objects in the former Qing palace). Beiping: Qingshi shanhou weiyuanhui, 1925–26.

Gujintan bianji weiyuanhui 古今談編輯委員會, ed. *Gujin mingren zhuanji* 古今名人傳記 (Biographies of notables from the past and present). Taipei: Gujintan zazhishe, 1972.

Hanan, Patrick. *The Invention of Li Yu.* Cambridge, Mass.: Harvard University Press, 1988.

Handler, Sarah. "The Chinese Bed." In *Chinese Furniture: Selected Articles from "Orientations," 1984–1994.* Hong Kong: Orientations Magazine Ltd., 1996.

Hay, Jonathan. *Shitao: Painting and Modernity in Early Qing China.* Cambridge: Cambridge University Press, 2001.

Hays, Mary V. "Chinese Skirts of the Qing Dynasty." *The Bulletin of the Needle and Bobbin Club* 72, nos. 1 & 2 (1989): 4–41.

He, Manzi 何滿子. *Pu Songling yu Liaozhai zhiyi* 蒲松齡與聊齋誌異 (Pu Songling and *Liaozhai zhiyi*). Shanghai: Shanghai chuban gongsi, 1955.

Hershatter, Gail. "The Subaltern Talks Back: Reflections on Subaltern Theory and Chinese History." *positions: east asia cultures critique* 1, no. 1 (Spring 1993): 103–30.

Hong, Minlin 洪敏麟. "Chanjiao yu Taiwan de tianranzu yundong" 纏腳與台灣

的天然足運動 (Footbinding and the natural feet movement in Taiwan). *Taiwan wenxian* 台灣文獻 27, no. 3 (Sept. 1976): 143–57.

Hong, Renqing 洪認清. "Minguo shiqi de quanjin chanzu yundong" 民国时期的劝禁缠足运动 (The anti-footbinding movement in the Republican period). *Minguo chunqiu* 民国春秋 6 (1996): 18–19.

Honig, Emily. *Sisters and Strangers: Women in the Shanghai Cotton Mills, 1919–1949.* Stanford, Calif.: Stanford University Press, 1986.

Hu, Yepin 胡也頻. "Xiao xiancheng zhong de liangge furen" 小縣城中的兩個婦人 (Two women in a small county town). *Dongfang zazhi* 東方雜誌 26, no. 18 (Sept. 1929): 101–6.

Hu, Ying. "Re-Configuring Nei/Wai: Writing the Woman Traveler in the Late Qing." *Late Imperial China* 18, no. 1 (June 1997): 72–99.

———. *Tales of Translation: Composing the New Woman in China, 1899–1918.* Stanford, Calif.: Stanford University Press, 2000.

Hu, Yinglin 胡應麟. *Danqian xinlu* 丹鉛新錄 (The revised scarlet and lead scrolls). In *Shaoshi shanfang bicong* 少室山房筆叢. Beijing: Zhonghua shuju, 1958.

Huaguangsheng 華廣生, ed. *Baixue yiyin* 白雪遺音 (Residual tunes on white snow). In *Ming-Qing minge shidiao ji* 明清民歌時調集 (A collection of folk songs and current tunes from the Ming and Qing periods), vol. 2, pp. 453–907. Shanghai: Shanghai guji chubanshe, 1987.

Huaipu jushi 懷圃居士. *Liu Rushi shiji* 柳如是事蹟 (The life and deeds of Liu Rushi). Beiping: Wenzi tongmengshe, 1930.

Huang, Qiang 黃強. *Li Yu yanjiu* 李漁研究 (A study of Li Yu). Hangzhou: Zhejiang guji chubanshe, 1996.

Huang, Ray. *1587: A Year of No Significance.* New Haven: Yale University Press, 1981.

Huang, Xintao 黃興濤. *Xianhua Gu Hongming* 閒話辜鴻銘 (Random talks on Gu Hongming). Haikou: Hainan chubanshe, 1997.

Huang, Yufu 黃育馥. *Jingju, qiao he Zhongguo de xingbei guanxi, 1902–1937* 京劇,蹺和中國的性別關係 (Peking opera, stilts, and gender relations in China, 1902–1937). Beijing: Sanlian shudian, 1998.

Hucker, Charles O. *A Dictionary of Official Titles in Imperial China.* Stanford, Calif.: Stanford University Press, 1985.

Huenemann, Ralph William. *The Dragon and the Iron Horse: The Economics of Railroads in China, 1876–1937.* Cambridge, Mass.: Harvard University Press, 1984.

Hummel, Arthur W., ed. *Eminent Chinese of the Ch'ing Period.* Washington, D.C.: United States Government Printing Office, 1943.

Jackson, Beverley. *Splendid Slippers: A Thousand Years of an Erotic Tradition.* Berkeley, Calif.: Ten Speed Press, 1997.

Jia, Shen 賈伸. *Zhonghua funü chanzu kao* 中華婦女纏足考 (A survey of footbinding of Chinese women). Beijing: Xiangshan ciyouyuan, 1925.

Jiangxisheng wenwu gongzuodui 江西省文物工作隊. "Jiangxi Nancheng Ming Yixuanwang Zhu Yiyin fufu hezang mu" 江西南城明益宣王朱翊鈏夫婦合

葬墓 (The tomb of Zhu Yiyun, Prince Yixuan, in Nancheng, Jiangxi). *Wenwu* 8 (1982): 16–28.

Jiangxisheng wenwu kaogu yanjiusuo 江西省文物考古研究所 and De'an xian bowuguan 德安縣博物館. "Jiangxi De'an Nan-Song Zhoushi mu qingli jianbao" 江西德安南宋周氏墓清理簡報 (A brief excavation report of the Southern-Song tomb of Madam Zhou in De'an, Jiangxi province). *Wenwu* 9 (1990): 1–13.

Jin, Qihua 金啓華, trans. *Shijing quanyi* 詩經全譯 (The *Book of Songs,* with a complete vernacular translation). Jiangsu: Jiangsu guji chubanshe, 1996.

Jujia biyong shilei 居家必用事類 (Essentials of domestic living). Kyoto: Chūbun shuppansha, 1984. Facsimile of 1673 edition printed in Japan.

Jujia biyong shilei. Ming Silijian edition in the Fu Ssu-nien Library.

Jujia biyong shilei. Ming Neifu edition in the Naikaku bunko.

Jujia yiji 居家宜忌 (Do's and don'ts at home). N.p., preface 1820–50. Copy in the Fu Ssu-nien Library.

"Kai tensoku setsu" 戒纏足説 (Quit binding feet). *Taiwan kanshū kiji* 台灣慣習記事 2, no. 11 (1902): 43–49 [887–93].

Kandel, Eric R., James H. Schwartz, and Thomas M. Jessell. *Principles of Neural Science.* 3rd ed. New York: Elsevier Science Publishing Co., Inc., 1991.

Kang, Laixin 康來新. *Wan-Qing xiaoshuo lilun yanjiu* 晚清小説理論研究 (A study of theories about fiction in the late Qing). Taipei: Da'an chubanshe, 1986.

Kang, Zhengguo 康正果. *Chongshen fengyuejian* 重審風月鑑 (Re-examining the mirror of wind and moon). Taipei: Maitian chuban, 1996.

———. *Fengsao yu yanqing* 風騷與艷情 (The feminine in Chinese literature). Zhengzhou: Henan Renmin chubanshe, 1988.

Karl, Rebecca E. *Staging the World: Chinese Nationalism at the Turn of the Twentieth Century.* Durham and London: Duke University Press, 2002.

Karl, Rebecca E., and Peter Zarrow, eds. *Rethinking the 1898 Reform Period: Political and Cultural Change in Late Qing China.* Cambridge, Mass.: Harvard University Asia Center, 2002.

Ke, Jiahao [John Kieschnick] 柯嘉豪. "Yizi yu Fojiao liuchuan zhi guanxi" 椅子與佛教流傳之關係 (The relationship between chairs and the transmission of Buddhism). *Zhongyang yanjiuyuan lishiyuyan yanjiusuo jikan* 69, no. 4 (Dec. 1998): 727–63.

Ke, Jisheng [Ko Chi-sheng] 柯基生. *Qianzai jinlian fenghua* 千載金蓮風華 (A thousand years of bound feet). Taipei: Guoli lishi bowuguan, 2003.

———. *Sancun jinlian* 三寸金蓮 (Three-inch golden lotus). Taipei: Chanye qingbao zazhishe, 1995.

Kikuchi, Takaharu 菊池貴晴. "Futensoku undō ni tsuite" 不纏足運動について (On the anti-footbinding movement). *Rekishi kyōiku* 歴史教育 5, no. 12 (1957): 31–39.

Kishimoto, Mio 岸本美緒. "Min-shin jidai no mibun kankaku" 明清時代の身分感覚 ("Status sense" in the late-Ming–early-Qing period). In *Min-Shin jidaishi no kihon mondai* 明清時代史の基本問題 (Foundational problems in Ming-Qing history), edited by Mori Masao 森正夫, pp. 403–28. Tokyo: Kyūko shoin, 1997.

Kisshō: Chūgoku bijitsu ni komerareta imi 吉祥—中国美術にこめられた意味 (Jixiang: Auspicious motifs in Chinese art). Tokyo: Tokyo National Museum, 1998.

Ko, Dorothy. "The Body as Attire: The Shifting Meanings of Footbinding in Seventeenth-Century China." *Journal of Women's History* 8, no. 4 (Winter 1997): 8–27.

———. "Bondage in Time: Footbinding and Fashion Theory." *Fashion Theory: The Journal of Dress, Body, & Culture* 1, no. 1 (March 1997): 3–28.

———. "The Emperor and His Women: Three Views of Footbinding, Ethnicity, and Empire." In *Life in the Imperial Court of Qing Dynasty China, Proceedings of the Denver Museum of Natural History,* series 3, no. 15, edited by Chuimei Ho and Cheri Jones. Denver: Denver Museum of Natural History Press, 1998.

———. *Every Step a Lotus: Shoes for Bound Feet.* Berkeley: University of California Press, 2001.

———. "Footbinding as Female Inscription." In *Rethinking Confucianism: Past and Present in China, Japan, Korea, and Vietnam,* edited by Benjamin Elman, John Duncan, and Herman Ooms, pp. 147–77. Los Angeles: Asia Pacific Monograph Series in International Studies, University of California, Los Angeles, 2002.

———. "The Sex of Footbinding." In *Good Sex: Women's Religious Wisdom,* edited by Radhika Balakrishnan, Mary E. Hunt, and Patricia Beattie Jung, pp. 140–57. New Brunswick, N.J.: Rutgers University Press, 2001.

———. "The Subject of Pain." In *From the Late Ming to the Late Qing: Dynastic Decline and Cultural Innovation,* edited by David Wang and Wei Shang. Stanford, Calif.: Stanford University Press, forthcoming.

———. *Teachers of the Inner Chambers: Women and Culture in Seventeenth-Century China.* Stanford, Calif.: Stanford University Press, 1994.

Köster, Hermann. "The Palace Museum of Peiping." *Monumenta Serica,* vol. 2 (1936–37): 167–90.

Kristeva, Julia. *About Chinese Women.* Translated by Anita Barrows. New York and London: Marion Boyars, 1991.

Kwan, Man Bun. *The Salt Merchants of Tianjin: State-Making and Civil Society in Late Imperial China.* Honolulu: University of Hawaii Press, 2001.

Kwok, D. W. Y. *Scientism in Chinese Thought,* 1900–1950. New Haven: Yale University Press, 1962.

Lao Xuan 老宣 [Xuan Yongguang 宣永光]. *Luanyu quanshu* 亂語全書 (Complete book of crazy words). Beijing: Hualing chubanshe, 1996.

Lee, Li-Young. *The Winged Seed: A Remembrance.* New York: Simon & Schuster, 1995.

Levy, Howard S. *Chinese Footbinding: The History of a Curious Erotic Custom.* Taipei: Nantian shuju, 1984.

Li, Bozhong 李伯重. "Cong 'fufu bingzuo' dao 'nangeng nüzhi'" 從"夫婦並作"到 "男耕女織" (From "husband-and-wife working side-by-side in the fields" to "men plow, women weave"). *Jingjishi yanjiu* 经济史研究 3 (1996): 99–107.

———. "'Nangeng nüzhi' yu 'funü banbiantian' jiaose de xingcheng" "男耕女织" 与"妇女半边天"角色的形成(From "men plow, women weave" to the formation of the role of "women shouldering half the sky"). *Jingjishi yanjiu* 经济史研究 3 (1997): 10–22.

Li, Xiaoti [Li Hsiao-t'i] 李孝悌. "Shiba shiji Zhongguo shehui zhongde qingyu yu shenti: Lijiao shijie yiwai de jianianhuahui" 十八世紀中國社會中的情欲與身體一禮教世界以外的嘉年華會 (Desire and body in eighteenth-century Chinese society: a carnival beyond "civil" society). *Bulletin of the Institute of History and Philology, Academia Sinica* 72, part 3 (2001): 543–95.

Li, Xu 李旭 and Huang Yanhong 黃焱紅. "Xiaojiao nüren cun" 小腳女人村 (Village of tiny-footed women). *China Tourism* 208 (Oct. 1997): 40–51.

Li, Youning 李又寧 and Zhang Yufa 張玉法 [Li Yu-ning and Chang Yü-fa], eds. *Jindai Zhongguo nüquan yundong shiliao* 近代中國女權運動史料(Documents on the feminist movement in modern China, 1842–1911). Taipei: Zhuanji wenxue chubanshe, 1975.

Li, Yu. *The Carnal Prayer Mat.* Translated by Patrick Hanan. Honolulu: The University of Hawaii Press, 1990.

——— 李漁. *Xianqing ouji* 閒情偶寄 (Casual expressions of idle feeling). Shanghai: Shanghai guji chubanshe, 2000.

Liang, Jinghe 梁景和. *Jindai Zhongguo lousu wenhua shanbian yanjiu* 近代中國陋俗文化嬗變研究 (A study of the evolution of the culture of undesirable customs in modern China). Beijing: Shoudu shifan daxue chubanshe, 1998.

Lin, Liyue [Lin Li-yueh] 林麗月. "Yichang yu fengjiao: Wan-Ming de fushi fengshang yu 'fuyao' yilun" 衣裳與風教-晚明的服飾風尚與"服妖"議論(Clothing and morality: Fashion trends and the discourse on "dressing the human prodigy" in the late-Ming period). *Xinshixue* 10, no. 3 (1999): 111–57.

Lin, Qingzhang 林慶彰 and Jia Shunxian 賈順先, comps. *Yang Shen yanjiu ziliao huibian* 楊慎研究資料彙編 (Resource materials on the study of Yang Shen). Taipei: Institute of Chinese Literature and Philosophy, Academia Sinica, 1992.

Lin, Qiumin 林秋敏. "Jindai Zhongguo de Buchanzu yundong (1895–1937)" 近代中國的不纏足運動 (The anti-footbinding movement in modern China). Master's thesis, Guoli Zhengzhi daxue, 1990.

———. "Qingmo de Tianzu hui, 1895–1906" 清末的天足會 (The Natural Feet Society in the Late Qing period). *Guoshiguan guankan* 國史館館刊, *fukan* [n.s.] 16 (1994): 115–24.

———. "Yan Xishan yu Shanxi de tianzu yundong" 閻錫山與山西的天足運動 (Yan Xishan and the Natural feet movement in Shanxi). *Guoshiguan guankan, fukan* [n.s.] 18 (June 1995): 129–44.

Lin, Sumen 林蘇門. *Hanjiang sanbaiyin* 邗江三百吟 (Three hundred verses from Yangzhou). Yangzhou: Jiangsu Guangling guji keyinshe, 1988 [preface dated 1808].

Lin, Weihong [Lin Wei-hung] 林維紅. "Chastity in Chinese Eyes: Nan-nü Yu-Pieh." *Chinese Studies* 9, no. 2 (Dec. 1991): 13–40.

———. "Qingji de funü buchanzu yundong (1894–1911)" 清季的婦女不纏足

運動 (The anti-footbinding movement of late-Qing women). *Guoli Taiwan daxue lishi xuexi xuebao* 國立台灣大學歷史學系學報 16 (1991): 139–80.

Ling, Hongxun [H. H. Ling] 凌鴻勳. *Zhongguo tielu zhi* 中國鐵路誌 (A comprehensive survey of railway development in China). Taipei: Changliu banyuekan she, 1954.

Little, Mrs. Archibald [Alicia]. *The Land of the Blue Gown.* London: T. Fisher Unwin, 1902.

Liu, Jieping 劉階平. *Pu Liuxian Songling xiansheng nianpu* 蒲留仙松齡先生年譜 (A chronological biography of Mr. Pu Songling). Taipei: Zhonghua shuju, 1985.

———, comp. *Qingchu guci liqu xuan* 清初鼓詞俚曲選 (A selection of ballads from the early Qing). Taipei: Zhengzhong shuju, 1968.

Liu, Lydia H. "The Desire for the Sovereign and the Logic of Reciprocity in the Family of Nations." *Diacritics* 29, no. 4 (1999): 150–77.

———. "The Female Body and Nationalist Discourse." In *Scattered Hegemonies: Postmodernity and Transnational Feminist Practices,* edited by Inderpal Grewal and Caren Kaplan, pp. 37–62. Minneapolis: University of Minnesota Press, 1994.

Liu, Tingji 劉廷璣. *Zaiyuan zazhi* 在園雜誌 (Miscellaneous notes from Zai manor). Series 38, no. 379 of *Jindai Zhongguo shiliao congkan* 近代中國史料叢刊 (Collectanea of historical documents from modern China). Edited by Shen Yunlong 沈雲龍. Taipei: Wenhai chubanshe, 1969.

Lo, Hui-min. "Ku Hung-ming: Homecoming [Part 1]." *East Asian History* 6 (1993): 163–82.

———. "Ku Hung-ming: Homecoming, Part 2." *East Asian History* 9 (1995): 67–96.

———. "Ku Hung-ming: Schooling." *Papers on Far Eastern History* 37–38 (1988): 45–64.

Loewe, Michael, ed. *Early Chinese Texts: A Bibliographical Guide.* [Berkeley]: The Society for the Study of Early China and The Institute of East Asian Studies, University of California, Berkeley, 1993.

Lü, Meiyi 呂美頤. "The Second Wave of the Movement for Unbound Feet." *Women of China* (April 1989): 44–45, 26.

———. "Small Steps Forward: Efforts Against Foot-Binding." *Women of China* (Feb. 1989): 42–44.

———. "The Unbound Feet Movement in the Reform of 1898." *Women of China* (March 1989): 51–53.

Lü, Meiyi, and Zheng Yongfu 鄭永福. *Zhongguo funü yundong (1840–1921)* 中國婦女運動 (The women's movement in China, 1840–1921). Henan Renmin chubanshe, 1990.

Lu, Zhengwen 路成文, Qi Fengyi 祁鳳義, and Nie Yuanlong 聶元龍, eds. *Shanxi fengsu minqing* 山西風俗民情 (Folkways and customs in Shanxi). Taiyuan: Shanxi sheng difangzhi bianhui weiyuanhui bangongshi, 1987.

MacGowan, John. *Beside the Bamboo.* London: London Missionary Society, 1914.

———. *How England Saved China.* London: T. Fisher Unwin, 1913.

————. *The Imperial History of China.* Shanghai: American Presbyterian Mission Press, 1906.

————. *Men and Manners of Modern China.* London: T. Fisher Unwin, 1912.

Mann, Susan. *Precious Records: Women in China's Long Eighteenth Century.* Stanford, Calif.: Stanford University Press, 1997.

Mao, Qiling 毛奇齡. *Wuzong waiji* 武宗外紀 (An unofficial history of the Ming emperor Wuzong). In *Xiangyan congshu* (Collectanea of the fragrant and the beautiful), 6: 3001–24. Shanghai: Guoxue fulun she, 1914.

Matignon, Dr. J.-J. *Superstition, crime, et misére en Chine: souvenirs de biologie sociale.* Lyon: A. Storck & Cie, 1899.

Maxwell, J. Preston. "On the Evils of Chinese Foot-Binding." *The China Medical Journal* 30, no. 6 (Nov. 1916): 393–96.

McLaren, Anne E. *Chinese Popular Culture and Ming Chantefables.* Leiden: Brill, 1998.

————. "Crossing Gender Boundaries in China: Nüshu Narratives." *Intersections* (1998): 1–16. (http://www.sshe.murdoch.edu.au/hum/as/intersections)

McMahon, Keith. *Misers, Shrews, and Polygamists: Sexuality and Male-Female Relations in Eighteenth-Century Chinese Fiction.* Durham and London: Duke University Press, 1995.

Meng, Sen 孟森. *Xinshi congkan, wai yi zhong* 心史叢刊, 外一種 (Collection of essays by Meng Sen). Changsha: Yuelu shushe, 1986.

Ming Chenghua shuochang cihua congkan 明成化説唱詞話叢刊 (A collection of chantefables from the Chenghua reign of the Ming dynasty). Beijing: Wenwu chubanshe, 1979.

Mitchell, Timothy. *Colonising Egypt.* Berkeley: University of California Press, 1991.

Morris, Andrew. *Marrow of the Nation: A History of Sport and Physical Culture in Republican China.* Berkeley: University of California Press, 2004.

Nagao, Ryūzō 永尾龍造. *Shina minzoku shi* 史那民俗志 (Ethnography of Chinese folk customs), vol. 2. Tokyo: Kokusho kankōkai, 1973.

Nakayama [Kishimoto], Mio 中山美緒. "Shindai zenki Kōnan no bukka dōkō" 清代前期江南の物価動向 (The secular trend of commodity prices in Jiangnan in the first half of the Qing period). *Tōyōshi kenkyū* 東洋史研究 37, no. 4 (March 1979): 77–106.

Neige xingke tiben 內閣刑科題本 (Grand Secretariat memorials on criminal matters). At the First Historical Archives, Beijing.

Ni, Zan 倪瓚. *Qingmige quanji* 清閟閣全集 (Complete collection from the Serene-Shelter Pavilion). In *Yuandai zhenben wenji huikan.* Taipei: Guoli zhongyan tushuguan, 1970.

Nishijima, Sadao. "The Formation of the Early Chinese Cotton Industry." In *State and Society in China: Japanese Perspectives on Ming-Qing Social and Economic History,* edited by Linda Grove and Christian Daniels. Tokyo: University of Tokyo Press, 1984.

Okamoto, Ryuzō 岡本隆三. *Tensoku monogatari* 纏足物語 (The story of footbinding). Tokyo: Tōhō shoten, 1986; first published 1963.

Ōki, Yasushi 大木康. *Fū Bō Ryu "Sanka" no kenkyu* 馮夢龍《山歌》の研究 (A study of Feng Menglong's "Mountain Songs"). Tokyo: Keisoo shobo, 2003.

Ono, Kazuko 小野和子. "*Kyōkaen no sekkai: Shincho kosho gakusha no ūdopia zō*"「鏡花縁」の世界—清朝考証学者のユートピア像 (The world of *Jinghuayuan*: a portrait of utopia of Qing evidential scholars). *Shisō* 思想 721 (July 1984): 40–55.

The Plum in the Golden Vase or, Chin P'ing Mei. Vol. 1: *The Gathering*. Translated by David Tod Roy. Princeton: Princeton University Press, 1993.

The Plum in the Golden Vase or, Chin P'ing Mei. Vol. 2: *The Rivals*. Translated by David Tod Roy. Princeton: Princeton University Press, 2001.

Pruitt, Ida. *A China Childhood*. San Francisco: Chinese Materials Center, Inc., 1978.

———. *A Daughter of Han: The Autobiography of a Chinese Working Woman*. Stanford, Calif.: Stanford University Press, 1967.

Pu, Songling 蒲松齡. *Liaozhai liqu ji* 聊齋俚曲集 (Song ballads from Liaozhai). Beijing: Guoji wenhua chuban gongsi, 1999.

———. *Liaozhai zhiyi* 聊齋誌異 (Records of the strange from Liaozhai). Ji'nan: Qilu shushe, 1981.

Qian, Nanxiu. "Revitalizing the Xianyuan (Worthy Ladies) Tradition: Women in the 1898 Reforms." *Modern China* 29, no. 4 (Oct. 2003): 399–454.

Qian, Yong 錢泳. *Lüyuan conghua* 履園叢話 (Collected words from Lüyuan). Taipei: Guangwen shuju, 1969.

Qiu, Weixuan 邱煒菱. *Shuyuan zhuitan jielü* 菽園贅談節錄 (Excerpts from random talk from the Bean Garden). *Xiangyan congshu*, vol. 8, *juan* 3. N.p.: Guoxue fulun she, 1914.

Quan Tangshi 全唐詩 (Complete Tang poetry). Shanghai: Shanghai guji chubanshe, 1995.

Raphals, Lisa. *Sharing the Light: Representations of Women and Virtue in Early China*. Albany: State University of New York Press, 1998.

Richards, Thomas. "Archive and Utopia." *Representations* 37 (Winter 1992): 104–35.

Sakamoto, Hiroko 坂元ひろ子. "Ashi no deisukōsu: tensoku; tensoku; kokuchi" 足のディスコース—纏足・天足・国恥 (The discourse of feet: Natural feet; bound feet; national shame). *Shisō* 思想 907 (Jan. 2000): 145–61.

Sang, Rou 桑柔. *Gu Hongming de youmo* 辜鴻銘的幽默 (The humor of Gu Hongming). Taipei: Jingmei chubanshe, 1985.

Scott, Joan Wallach. *Only Paradoxes to Offer: French Feminists and the Rights of Man*. Cambridge, Mass.: Harvard University Press, 1996.

Shang, Wei. "The Making of the Everyday World: *Jin Ping Mei Cihua* and Encyclopedias for Daily Use." Unpublished paper, 2002.

Shanghai Zhongguo Tianzu hui 上海中國天足會. *Tianzu huibao* 天足會報 no. 1 (Summer 1907). Copy in the Shanghai Municipal Library.

Shanxi cunzheng chu 山西村政處, comp. *Shanxi cunzheng huibian* 山西村政彙編 (Collected documents on village-based governance). n.p. [Taiyuan?]: Shanxi cunzhengchu, 1928.

Shen, Congwen 沈從文. *Zhongguo gudai fushi yanjiu* 中國古代服飾史 (A study of costumes in traditional China). Taipei: Nantian, 1988.

Shen, Defu 沈德符. *Wanli yehuo bian* 萬曆野獲編 (Unofficial gleanings from the Wanli era). N.p.: Fuli shanfang, 1827.

Shen, Fu. *Six Records of a Floating Life.* Translated by Leonard Pratt and Chiang Su-hui. London and New York: Penguin Books, 1983.

Shi, Meng 時萌. *Wan-Qing xiaoshuo* 晚清小説 (Late Qing fiction). Shanghai: Shanghai guji chubanshe, 1989.

Shuwu 舒蕪, ed. *Nüxing de faxian: Zhitong funülun leichao* 女性的發現—知堂婦女論類鈔 (The discovery of the female sex: A classified collection of Zhou Zuoren's writings on women). Beijing: Wenhua yishu chubanshe, 1990.

Song, Lizhong 宋立中 and Fan Jinmin 范金民. "Review of Li Bozhong, *Jiangnan de zaoqi gongyehua, 1550–1850*" 評李伯重, <<江南的早期工業化(1550-1850)>>. *Xinshixue* 新史學 12, no. 4 (Dec. 2001): 193–205.

Spence, Jonathan. *Treason by the Book.* New York: Viking, 2001.

Stewart, Susan. *On Longing: Narratives of the Miniature, the Gigantic, the Souvenir, the Collection.* Durham and London: Duke University Press, 1993.

Su, Bai 宿白. *Baisha Song mu* 白沙宋墓 (The Baisha Song tomb). Beijing: Wenwu chubanshe, 1957.

Su, Fu 穌馥. *Xianggui xiewa dianlüe* 香閨鞋襪典略 (Allusions to stockings and shoes in the fragrant chamber). Haining Zoushi shizu youlanshi manuscript edition, 1879. Copy in the Rare Book Room, National Central Library, Taipei, Taiwan.

Taiping yulan 太平御覽 (Encyclopedia for imperial perusal, compiled in the Taiping xingguo reign [976–984]). Taipei: Daihua shuju, 1977.

Takashima, Kō 高嶋航. "Kyōkai to shinja no aida de: Josei senkyōshi ni yoru tensoku kaihō no kokorumi" 教会と信者の間で女性宣教試による纏足解放の試み (Between the Church and the convents: Attempts of female missionaries to unbind feet). In *Chūgoku kindaika no dōtai kōzō* 中国近代化の動態構造 (The dynamic structures of Chinese modernity), ed. Mori Tokihiko, pp. 273–309. Kyoto: Kyōtō daigaku jinbun kagaku kenkyūjo, 2004.

[Tang], Yisuo 湯頤瑣. *Huang Xiuqiu* 黃繡球. In *Wan-Qing xiaoshuo daxi* 晚清小説大系 (Series in Late-Qing fiction), vol. 15. Taipei: Guangya shuju, 1984.

———. "Xu Zhongke xiansheng 'Tiansuke yuwantu' xu" 徐仲可先生 " 天蘇閣娛晚圖序 " (Preface to "Pictures for self-entertainment in old age in my Tiansu Pavilion" by Mr. Xu Zhongke [Xu Ke]). Appendix to Xu Ke, "Chunfeiguan ci" 純飛館詞 (Song lyrics from the Chunfei Mansion), 22b–24a. In *Tiansuke congkan* 天蘇閣叢刊 (Collectanea from the Tiansu Pavilion), edited by Xu Ke. Shanghai: Shangwu yinshuguan, 1914.

Tanmian daoren 醉眠道人 [Zhang Lüping 張履平], comp. *Kunde baojian* 坤德寶鑑 (Precious mirror of feminine virtues). N.p.: Yuxiutang, 1777. Copy in the Harvard-Yenching Library.

———. *Zengshan kunde baojian* 增刪坤德寶鑑 (Precious mirror of feminine virtues, with additions and deletions). Signed "Kuimiutang zhuren xuancao" 愧繆

堂主人選鈔 (selected and copied by the Master of the Ashamed-of-Mistakes Studio). Nineteenth–twentieth-century hand-copied edition. Collection of Don J. Cohn.

Tao, Anhua 陶安化 [Baopi 報癖]. "Xiaozu juan" 小足捐 (Excising small feet). *Yueyue xiaoshuo* 月月小説 1, no. 6 (Feb. 1907): 177–86.

Tao, Jinsheng 陶晉生. "Geji wuji yu jinlian" 歌姬舞妓與金蓮 (Singing girls, dancing girls, and the golden lotus). In *Tang-Song nüxing yu shehui* 唐宋女性與社會 (Women and society in the Tang and Song dynasties), edited by Deng Xiaonan 鄧小南. Shanghai: Shanghai cishu chubanshe, 2003.

Tao, Zongyi 陶宗儀. *Chuogenglu* 輟耕錄 (Notations from resting the plough). Preface dated 1366. In *Qinding siku quanshu* 欽定四庫全書, *zibu* 12, *xiaoshuojia lei* 1.

Tarumoto, Teruo 樽本照雄. *Shinmatsu shōsetsu kandan* 清末小説閑談 (Studies in late-Qing fiction). Kyoto: Hōritsu bunkasha, 1983.

Thiriez, Régine. "Photography and Portraiture in Nineteenth-Century China." *East Asian History* 17/18 (1999): 77–102.

Tianshui bingshan lu 天水冰山錄 (Heavenly waters melting the iceberg). Vol. 1502 of *Congshu jicheng chubian* 叢書集成初編. Shanghai: Shangwu yinshuguan, 1937

Tian Yiheng 田藝蘅. *Liuqing rizha* 留青日札 (Daily notations saved on green bamboo). Shanghai: Shanghai guji chubanshe, 1985; facsimile of 1609 edition.

Tongxi manshi 桐曲謾士. *Tingyu xiantan* 聽雨閒談 (Idle chats when listening to the rain). Shanghai: Shanghai guji chubanshe, 1983.

Tōyōshi kenkyūkai 東洋史研究會, ed. *Yōsei jidai no kenkyū* 雍正時代の研究 (A study of the Yongzheng period). Kyoto: Dōhōsha, 1986.

Turner, Christena L. "Locating Footbinding: Variations across Class and Space in Nineteenth and Early Twentieth Century China." *The Journal of Historical Sociology* 10, no. 4 (Dec. 1997): 444–79.

Turner, Terence. "The Social Skin." In *Not Work Alone: A Cross-Cultural View of Activities Superfluous to Survival,* edited by Jeremy Cherfas and Roger Lewin, pp. 112–40. Beverly Hills: Sage Publications, 1980.

Van Gulik, R. H. *Erotic Colour Prints of the Ming Period.* Tokyo: Privately published, 1951.

Veblen, Thorstein. *The Theory of the Leisure Class.* New York: Penguin Books, 1994.

Veith, Ilza. "The History of Medicine Dolls and Foot-binding in China." *Clio Medica* 14, no. 3/4 (1980): 255–67.

Wang, David Der-wei. *Fin-de-Siècle Splendor: Repressed Modernities of Late Qing Fiction, 1849–1911.* Stanford, Calif.: Stanford University Press, 1997.

Wang, Dongfang 王冬芳. *Maixiang xiandai: jianbian yu fangzu* 邁向現代—剪辮與放足 (March to modernity: Braid-cutting and foot-liberating). Shenyang: Liaohai chubanshe, 1997.

Wang, Hongtai 王鴻泰. "Liudong yu hudong: You Ming-Qing jian chengshi shenghuo de texing tance gongzhong changyi de kaizhan." 流動與互動—由明清間城市生活的特性探測公眾領域的開展 (Motion and interaction: tracing the development of a public field as gleaned from characteristics of city life in the Ming-Qing period). Ph.D. diss., National Taiwan University, 1998.

Wang, Jiaju 王家駒. "Lu'an diqu hunsang zhidu zai Xinhai geming qianhou di bian04ge" 潞安地區婚喪制度在辛亥革命前後的變革(Changes in the institutions of marriage and funerals in the Lu'an area before and after the 1911 Revolution). In *Shanxi wenshi zhiliao* 山西文史資料, vol. 7, pp. 104–24. Taiyuan: Wenshi zhiliao yanjiu weiyuanhui, 1984 [first published 1963].

Wang, Jingqi 汪景祺. *Dushutang xizheng suibi* 讀書堂西征隨筆 (Notes from my westward journey from the Dushu Studio). Hong Kong: Longmen shudian, 1967.

Wang, Ping. *Aching for Beauty: Footbinding in China.* Minneapolis: University of Minnesota Press, 2000.

Wang, Sanpin 王三聘. *Gujin shiwu kao* 古今事物考 (Things from past and present). Taipei: Shangwu, 1973.

Wang, Shucun 王樹村. *Zhongguo minjian nianhuashi tulu* 中國民間年畫史圖錄 (A pictorial history of vernacular new year prints in China). Shanghai: Renmin meishu chubanshe, 1991.

Wang, Shu-Hwai et al., eds. *International Union List of Chinese Journals Relating to Women.* Taipei: Institute of Modern History, Academia Sinica, 1995.

Wang, Yan 王岩. *Wanli dihou de yichu: Ming Dingling shizhi jijin* 萬歷帝后的衣櫥—明定陵絲織集錦 (The wardrobe of emperor Wanli and his empresses). Taipei: Dongda tushu gongsi, 1995.

Wang, Yuqing 王宇清. *Zhongguo fuzhuang shigang* 中國服裝史綱 (An outline history of Chinese costumes). Taipei: Zhonghua minzu yishu wenjiao jijinhui, 1994.

Wang, Zheng. *Women in the Chinese Enlightenment: Oral and Textual Histories.* Berkeley: University of California Press, 1999.

Wang, Zhuo 王 and Zhang Chao 張潮, eds. *Tanji congshu* 檀几叢書 (Collectanea from the low sandalwood table). Preface dated 1695. Copy in the Naikaku bunko.

Wang, Zijin 王子今. *Bozu diguo: Zhongguo chuantong jiaotong xingtai yanjiu* 跛足帝國—中國傳統交通形態研究 (The crippled empire: a study of traditional modes of transportation in China). Lanzhou: Dunhuang wenyi chubanshe, 1996.

Wanli Quanbu wenlin miaojin wanbao quanshu 萬曆全補文林玅錦萬寶全書 (A complete guide to myriad treasures). Shulin [Jianyang, Fujian]: Anzheng tang, 1612. Copy in the Harvard-Yenching Library.

Weschler, Lawrence. *Mr. Wilson's Cabinet of Wonder.* New York: Vintage Books, 1996.

Wu, Guoqing 伍國慶, comp. *Wentan guaijie Gu Hongming* 文壇怪杰辜鴻銘 (Gu Hongming, a maverick of the literary world). Changsha: Yuelu shushe, 1988.

Wu, Huifang 吳慧芳. *Wanbao quanshu: Ming-Qing shiqi de minjian shenghuo shilu* 萬寶全書：明清時期的民間生活實錄 (A complete guide to myriad treasures: Documents of vernacular lives in the Ming-Qing period). Taipei: Guoli Zhengzhi daxue lishixi, 2001.

Wu, Renshu [Wu Jen-shu] 巫仁恕. "Mingdai pingmin fushi de liuxing fengshang yu shidafu de fanying" 明代平民服飾的流行風尚與士大夫的反應 (The fashion trends of Ming commoners and the reactions of the scholar-officials). *Xinshixue* 新史學 10, no. 3 (1999): 55–109.

Wu, Tung. *Earth Transformed: Chinese Ceramics in the Museum of Fine Arts, Boston.* Boston: MFA Publications, 2001.

Xiao, Yun 笑雲. "Tianzu shuo" 天足說 (On natural feet). *Xiaoshuo congbao* 小說 叢報 3, no. 8 (1917): 2–3.

"Xiaojiao beige huasheng xiuzhifu" 小腳悲歌畫上休止符 (The sad song of small feet has come to a full stop). *Xinmin wanbao* 新民晚報, Nov. 22, 1999.

Xie, Boyang 謝伯陽, ed. *Quan-Ming sanqu* 全明散曲 (Sanqu songs from the Ming dynasty). Ji'nan: Qilu shushe, 1994.

Xie, Zaihang 謝在杭 [Zhaozhe 肇淛]. *Wenhai pisha* 文海披沙 (Panning for gold in the ocean of words). Shanghai: Dada tushu gongyingshe, 1935 [preface dated 1609].

Xu, Ke 徐珂. *Qingbai leichao* 清稗類鈔 (A classified collection of anecdotes on the Qing dynasty). Beijing: Zhonghua shuju, 1986.

———. "Tianzu kaolüe" 天足考略 (A survey of natural feet). In Xu Ke, ed. *Tiansuke congkan.*

———. "Zhizu yu" 知足語 (Words of knowing feet). In Xu Ke, *Tiansuke biji shisanzhong* 天蘇閣筆記十三種 (Thirteen notation books from the Tiansu Pavilion), vol. 2, pp. 141–71. Hong Kong: Zhongshan tushu gongsi, 1973.

———, ed. *Tiansuke congkan* 天蘇閣叢刊 (Collectanea from the Tiansu Pavilion). Shanghai: Shangwu yinshuguan, 1914.

Xu, Sanyou 徐三友, ed. *Xinqie quanbu tianxia simin liyong bianguan Wuche bojin* 新鍥全補天下四民利用便觀五車拔錦 (Five carriages of winning books for the convenient perusal of the four classes of people, revised and newly carved). Fujian: Jianyun chai, 1597. Copy in the Library of Congress.

Xu, Shuofang 徐朔方. "Xu Lin nianpu" 徐霖年譜 (A chronological biography of Xu Lin). In *Xu Shuofang ji* 徐朔方集 (Collected essays by Xu Shuofang). Hangzhou: Zhejiang guji chubanshe, 1993.

Xue, Ji 薛己. *Xue Ji yian* 薛己醫案 (Medical cases of Dr. Xue Ji). In *Tushu jicheng yibu quanlu, xin jiaoben* 圖書集成醫部全錄新校本 (A complete section on medicine from the collectanea *Tushu jicheng*, new collated edition). Taipei: Xinwenfeng chuban gongsi, n.d. [1979].

Xue, Shaohui 薛紹徽. "Fu Shen nüshi shu" 覆沈女士書. In *Daiyunlou wenji* 黛 韻樓文集, *juan xia*, 20b–21a; in Xue, *Daiyunlou yiji* 黛韻樓遺集. Fujian: Chenshi jiakanben, 1914.

Yan, Xishan 閻錫山. *Renmin xuzhi* 人民須知 (What the people should know). N.p., 1919. Collection of Dr. Ko Chi-sheng.

———, comp. *Shanxi Liuzheng sanshi huibian* 山西六政三事彙編 (Collected documents from the "Six policies, three matters" campaign, Shanxi province). N.p. [Taiyuan]: Shanxi cunzhengchu, 1929.

————, comp. *Zhi-Jin zhengwu quanshu chubian* 治晉政務全書初編 (The complete book of Shanxi governance). Taipei: Yanzhai, n.d. [1960].

Yang, Nianqun. 杨念群 "Cong kexue huayu dao guojia kongzhi: Dui nüzi chanzu you 'mei' bian 'chou' de duoyuan fenxi" 从科学话语到国家控制—对女子缠足由'美'变'丑'的多元分析 (From the discourse of science to control by the state: A multifarious analysis of the historical process whereby the bound foot changed from being "beautiful" to being "ugly"). *Beijing dang'an shiliao* 北京档案史料 4 (2001): 237–96.

————. "'Guoduqi' lishi de lingyinmian" 过渡期历史的另一面 (The other face of the history of the "transitional period"). *Dushu* 读书 6: (2002): 128–35.

Yang, Shen 楊慎. *Danqian xulu* 丹鉛續錄 (Sequel to the scarlet and lead scrolls). In *Qinding siku quanshu, zibu* 10, *zajia lei* 2.

————. *Danqian yulu* 丹鉛餘錄 (The scarlet and lead scrolls). In *Qinding siku quanshu, zibu* 10, *zajia lei* 2.

————. *Danqian zhailu* 丹鉛摘錄 (Selections from the scarlet and lead scrolls). First published 1547. In *Qinding siku quanshu, zibu* 10, *zajia lei* 2.

————. *Danqian zonglu* 丹鉛總錄 (The scarlet and lead scrolls, summary edition). In *Qinding siku quanshu, zibu* 10, *zajia lei* 2.

————. *Han zashi mixin* 漢雜事秘辛 (Han footles). In *Xiangyan congshu, ji* 3, *juan* 2. Shanghai: Guoxue fulunshe, 1914.

————. *Tanyuan tihu* 譚苑醍醐 (Purified ghee). Prefaced 1542. In *Congshu jicheng chubian*, no. 334. Changsha: Shangwu, 1939.

[Yang, Weizhen 楊維楨]. *Yang Weizhen shiji* 楊維楨詩集 (Collected poetry of Yang Weizhen). Hangzhou: Zhejiang guji chubanshe, 1994.

Yang, Xingmei 杨兴梅. "Nanjing guomin zhengfu jinzhi funü chanzu de nuli yu chengxiao" 南京國民政府禁止婦女纏足的努力與成效 (The efforts and effectiveness of the Nanjing regime in forbidding women from binding their feet). *Lishi yanjiu* 歷史研究 no. 3 (1998): 113–29.

Yang, Xingmei and Luo Zhitian 罗志田. "Jindai Zhongguoren dui nüxing xiaojiaomei de fouding" 近代中國人对女性小脚美的否定 (The denial of the beauty of small feet by the modern Chinese people). Paper presented at the Symposium on the History of Health and Beauty, Institute of History and Philology, Academia Sinica, Taipei, Taiwan, June 11–12, 1999.

Yang, Yang 楊楊. *Xiaojiao wudao: Dian-nan yige xiangcun de chanzu gushi* 小脚舞蹈—滇南一個鄉村的纏足故事 (Dancing on little feet: Stories of footbinding from a village in southern Yunnan). Hefei: Anhui wenyi chubanshe, 2001.

Yao, Jushun 姚居順. *Zhongguo chanzu fengsu* 中國纏足風俗 (Customs of binding feet in China). Shenyang: Liaoning daxue chubanshe, 1991.

Yao, Lingxi 姚靈犀. *Siwuxie xiaoji* 思無邪小記 (Minor notes from the Think-no-evil studio). N.p., Caihua shulin, 1974; reprint of Tianjin shuju edition, 1941.

————, comp. *Caifei jinghualu, shang juan* 采菲精華錄,上卷. Tianjin: Tianjin shuju, 1941.

———. *Caifeilu [chubian]* 采菲錄(初編). Tianjin: Shidai gongsi, 1934.

———. *Caifeilu sanbian* 采菲錄三編. Tianjin: Tianjin shuju, 1936.

———. *Caifeilu sibian* 采菲錄四編. Tianjin: Tianjin shuju, 1938.

———. *Caifeilu xubian* 采菲錄續編. Tianjin: Shidai gongsi, 1936.

———. *Caifei xinbian* 采菲新編. Tianjin: Tianjin shuju, 1941.

Ye, Dabing 葉大兵 and Qian Jinbo 錢金波. *Zhongguo xielü wenhua cidian* 中國鞋履文化辭典 (A dictionary of footwear culture in China). Shanghai: Shanghai sanlian, 2001.

Yi, Shizhen 伊世珍. *Langxuan ji* 瑯環記 (Records from the immortal grottos). In *Xuejin taoyuan* 學津討原 (Seeking the source of the stream of knowledge). Edited by Zhang Haipeng 張海鵬. Yangzhou: Guangling guji keyinshe, n.d.

Yu, Huai 余懷. *Banqiao zaji* 板橋雜記 (Miscellaneous records from the wooden bridge). In *Xiangyan congshu, ji* 13, *juan* 3. Shanghai: Guoxue fulunshe, 1914.

———. "Furen xiewa kao" 婦人鞋襪考 (An examination of women's shoes and socks). In *Tanji congshu* (Collectanea from the sandalwood table). Edited by Wang Zhuo and Zhang Chao. Preface dated 1695. Copy in the Naikaku bunko.

Yu, Tingbi 余庭璧. *Shiwu yiming jiaozhu* 事物異名校注 (Names and synonyms, annotated edition). Taiyuan: Shanxi guji chubanshe, 1993.

Yu, Xiangdou 余象斗, comp. *Santai wanyong zhengzong* 三台萬用正宗 (The authentic Santai encyclopedia of ten thousand uses). Jianyang, Fujian: Yushi Shuangfang tang, 1599. Copy in the Tōyō bunka kenkyūjo, University of Tokyo.

Zeitlin, Judith T. *Historian of the Strange: Pu Songling and the Chinese Classical Tale.* Stanford: Stanford University Press, 1993.

———. "The Petrified Heart: Obsession in Chinese Literature, Art, and Medicine." *Late Imperial China* 12, no. 1 (June 1991): 1–26.

Zeng, Yongyi 曾永義. *Shuo xuwenxue* 説俗文學 (On popular literature). Taipei: Lianjing, 1984.

Zengbu yizhi zazi quanshu 增補易知雜字全書 (Comprehensive guide to words and phrases, amended and expanded). Ming edition. Copy in the Niida bunko, Tōyō bunka kenkyūjo, University of Tokyo.

Zhang, Bangji 張邦基. *Mozhuang manlu* 墨莊漫錄 (Random notes from the Ink Manor). In *Congshu jicheng chubian* 叢書集成初編, no. 2864–66. Changsha: Shangwu, 1939.

———. *Mozhuang manlu*. In *Qinding siku quanshu* 欽定四庫全書, *zibu* 10, *zajia lei* 5.

Zhang, Dai 張岱, comp. *Yehang chuan* 夜航船 (A guide to safe sailing at night). Hangzhou: Zhejiang guji chubanshe, 1981.

Zhang, Daoyi 張道一, ed. *Lao xiqu nianhua* 老戲曲年畫 (Old New Year prints with drama scenes). Shanghai: Shanghai huabao chubanshe, 1999.

Zhang, Hongsheng 張宏生, ed. *Ming-Qing wenxue yu xingbie yanjiu* 明清文學與性別研究 (Ming-Qing literature and gender studies). Nanjing: Jiangsu guji chubanshe, 2002.

Zhang, Jinlan 張金蘭. "*Jinpingmei* nüxing fushi wenhua yanjiu" <<金瓶梅>> 女

性服飾文化研究 (A study of the culture of female fashion in the *Plum in the Golden Vase*). Master's thesis, Department of Chinese literature, National Chengchi University, Taipei, Taiwan, 2000.

Zhang, Nan 張 枬 and Wang Renzhi 王 忍 之, eds. *Xinhai geming qian shinian jian shilun xuanji* 辛亥革命前十年間時論選集 (Selections of current opinions from the decade preceding the 1911 revolution). Beijing: Sanlian shudian, 1978.

Zhang, Xiushu 張秀熟. "Qingmo minjian ertong duwu" 清末民間兒童讀物 (Primers for children in the late Qing). In *Sichuan wenshi ziliao xuanji* 四川文史資料選輯, 20: 180–90. Chengdu: Sichuan renmin chubanshe, 1979.

Zhang, Xudong. *Chinese Modernism in the Era of Reforms: Cultural Fever, Avant-Garde Fiction, and the New Chinese Cinema.* Durham and London: Duke University Press, 1997.

Zhang, Zhong 張 仲. *Xiaojiao yu bianzi* 小腳與辮子 (Small feet and the queue). Taipei: Youshi wenhua shiye gongsi, 1995.

Zhao, Feng 趙丰, ed. *Fangzhipin kaogu xinfaxian* 紡織品考古新發現 (Recent excavations of textiles in China). Hong Kong: ISAT/Costume Squad Ltd., 2002.

Zhao, Yi 趙翼. *Gaiyu congkao* 陔餘叢考 (Miscellaneous investigations during retirement). Shanghai: Shangwu, 1957; first published 1790.

Zhao, Zhibi 趙之壁. *Pingshan tang tuzhi* 平山堂圖志 (A pictorial gazetteer of Pingshan Hall). Kyoto: Dōhōsha, 1981; first published 1765.

Zhonggong Zhongyang xianwei xuanzhuanbu 中共中央縣委宣傳部 and Tonghai xian wenxue yishujie lianhehui 通海縣文學藝術界聯合會, ed. *Tonghai: Xiujia nan Dian* 通海—秀甲南滇 (Tonghai, the most elegant place in southern Yunnan). Tonghai, Yunnan: Zhonggong Tonghai xian wei and Tonghai xian renmin zhengfu, n.d. [1999].

Zhongguo shehuikexueyuan kaogu yanjiusuo 中國社會科學院考古研究所, ed. *Dingling duoying* 定陵掇英 (Highlights from the Ding Mausoleum). Beijing: Wenwu chubanshe, 1989.

Zhongguo shehuikexueyuan kaogu yanjiusuo, Dingling bowuguan 定陵博物館, and Beijingshi wenwu gongzuodui 北京市文物工作隊. *Dingling* 定陵 (The imperial tomb of the Ming dynasty, Dingling). 2 vols. Beijing: Wenwu chubanshe, 1990.

Zhongguo Tianzu hui 中國天足會. *Tianzu hui nianbao* 天足會年報 (Annual report of the Natural Feet Society). Shanghai: Meihua shuju, 1908. Copy in the Shanghai Municipal Library.

Zhou, Mi 周密. *Haoranzhai yatan* 浩然齋雅談 (Elegant words from the Haoran studio). Shenyang: Liaoning jiaoyu chubanshe, 2000.

Zhou, Songyao 周頌堯. *Chanzu* 纏足 (Footbinding). N.p.: n.d. [preface 1929]. Collection of Dr. Chi-sheng Ko.

Zhou, Xibao 周錫保. *Zhongguo gudai fushi shi* 中國古代服飾史 (A history of attire in traditional China). Taipei: Nantian shuju, 1992.

Zhou, Xun 周汛 and Gao Chunming 高春明. *Zhongguo lidai funü zhuangshi* 中國歷代婦女妝飾 (Women's attire from the imperial dynasties). Shanghai: Xuelin chubanshe and Hong Kong: Sanlian shudian, 1997.

————. *Zhongguo chuantong fuzhuang xingzhi shi* 中國傳統服飾形制史 (A typological history of traditional costumes in China). Taipei: Nantian shuju, 1998.

————. *Zhongguo yiguan fushi dacidian* 中國衣冠服飾大辭典 (A dictionary of cap and gown: dress and ornamentation in China). Shanghai: Shanghai cishu chubanshe, 1996.

Zhou, Yibai 周貽白. *Zhongguo xiju shi* 中國戲曲史 (A history of Chinese drama). 3 vols. Shanghai: Zhonghua shuju, 1953.

Zhu, Chuanyu 朱傳譽, comp. *Gu Hongming zhuanji zhiliao* 辜鴻銘傳記資料 (Sources in the biography of Gu Hongming). Vols. 1–2. Taipei: Tianyi chubanshe, 1979 [vol. 3, not cited in text, 1981].

Zhuang, Yan 莊嚴. *Shantang qinghua* 山堂清話 (Tranquil words from the Mountain pavilion). Taipei: National Palace Museum, 1980.

Zito, Angela. *Of Body and Brush: Grand Sacrifice as Text / Performance in Eighteenth-Century China.* Chicago: University of Chicago Press, 1997.

Zou, Jingfeng 鄒勁風. *Nan-Tang guoshi* 南唐國史 (A history of the Southern Tang kingdom). Nanjing: Nanjing daxue chubanshe, 2000.

————. *Nan-Tang lishi yu wenhua* 南唐歷史與文化 (The history and culture of the Southern Tang kingdom). Chengdu: Sichuan daxue chubanshe, 2000.

Amoy, 14, 36, 235n10
"analytic distance," 4–5
anti-footbinding legislation: as "gigantic
history," 12; Manchu, 132, 251n61,
266n49; of Sun Yat-sen, 234n3; of
Yan Xishan, 53–55, 248n30; in Yunnan,
292n74. *See also* feet inspection
anti-footbinding movement: and bias
in scholarship, 4, 67; and binding style,
195, 221; bureaucratization of, 65–66;
Chinese and Western, 18, 237–38n22;
of 1895–98, 17, 18, 237n19, 244–45n6;
facilitated binding of feet, 66, 81; literature of, 255n20, 260n47; and philological origins discourse, 142; power
inequalities in, 61, 67–68; program of,
41, 141; photography and, 42, 245n11;
rhetoric of, 27–28, 30–31, 96, 113; societies founded by women, 246n15; songs
of, 81; success of, 67–68. See also *fangzu*
movement; Tianzu hui; Yan Xishan
antique collecting, 81, 87, 256n22, 260n50.
See also connoisseurship
arch-shaped foot, 112, 125, 143, 170, 190,
221. *See also* curved arches; shoes,
arched-soled
archives, 112, 122, 133

armor, 151, 270n7
astronomy, 25, 26
Axiu, Madam, 100–101, 102, 260n48

Bai, Mrs., 20, 22, 23
Bai Ting, *Quiet Words from Deep Water,*
133, 266n50
bamboo shoots, 129, 266n44
Baoan she (Peace-Keeping Association),
50
bare feet, 41–42, 143, 212, 245n8, 268n65,
288n49
"bare-legs-tiny-feet" pageant, 64
Baudrillard, Jean, 258n39
Beiping Women's Normal College, 27
big feet, 183, 280n79
biji (notation books), 111. *See also* origin
discourses
binding cloths: from burials, 188, 281n2,
283n10, 291n71; collection of, under
Deng Changyao, 64, 66, 251n64;
exhibition of, 65; manipulation of,
and changes in fashion, 48, 221–23;
price of, 291–92n71; referred to in
Yuefu song, 124; size of, 279n72; Suzhou
ladies' instructions for eliminating, 48;
as symbol of footbinding, 64, 251n63;

DESIGNER: NOLA BURGER
TEXT: 10.75/13.75 ADOBE GARAMOND
DISPLAY: INTERSTATE
COMPOSITOR: INTEGRATED COMPOSITION SYSTEMS
PRINTER AND BINDER: THOMSON-SHORE, INC.